by
Kawahara

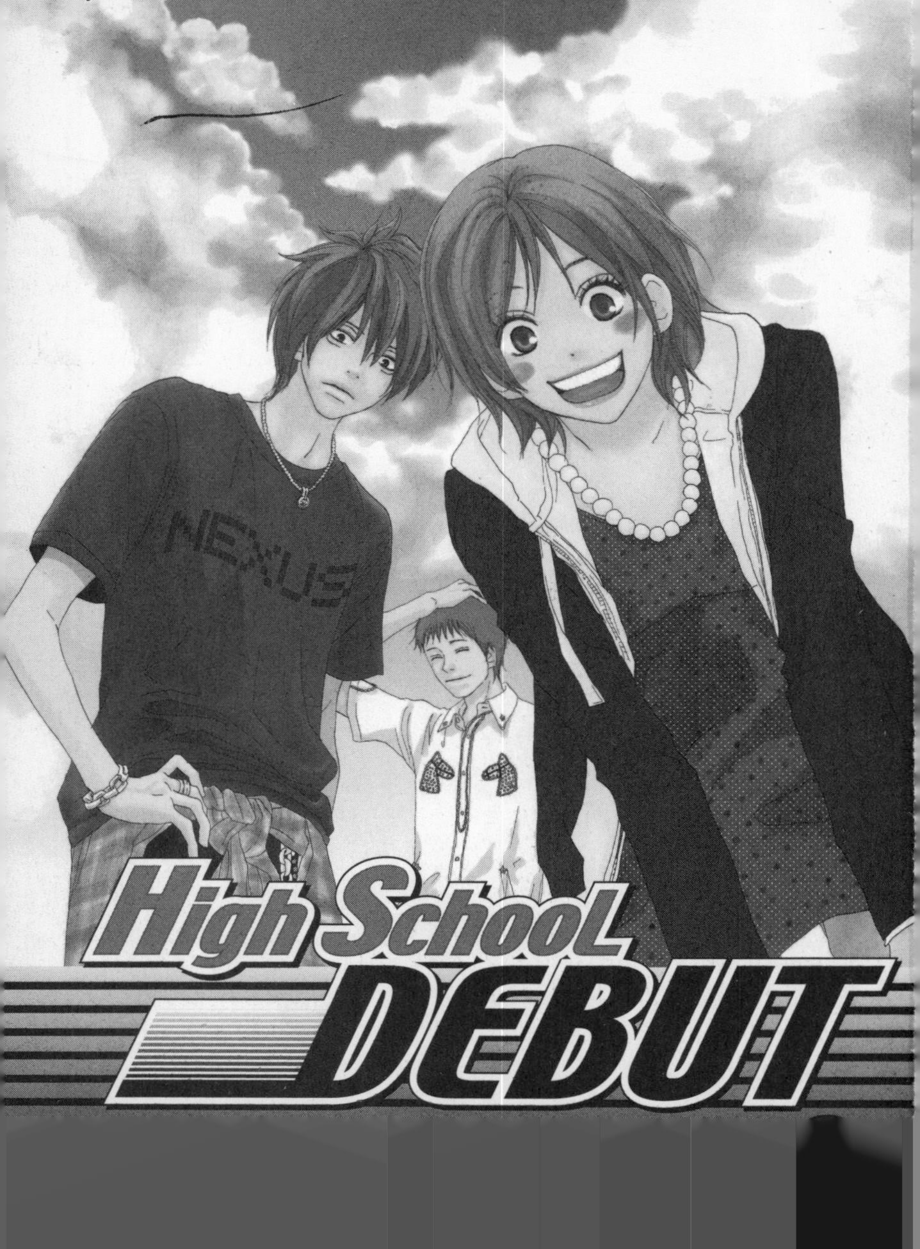
NEXUS

High School DEBUT

High School DEBUT

★★ Contents

Story Thus Far...

High school student Haruna used to spend all her time playing softball in junior high, but now she wants to give her all to finding true love instead! While her "love coach" Yoh is training her on how to be popular with guys, the two of them start dating.

At the beginning of the new school year, Yoh attracts a lot of attention from the freshman girls. Yoh holds Haruna's hand at school so that everyone knows that they're an item. However, Shinji, one of the freshman boys who wants to be like Yoh, kisses Haruna! Haruna feels guilty and freaks out! To make her feel better, Yoh kisses Shinji (?!)...

Then, on Haruna's 17th birthday, Haruna has an amazing day with Yoh. She's so happy that she can't stop herself from crying...♥

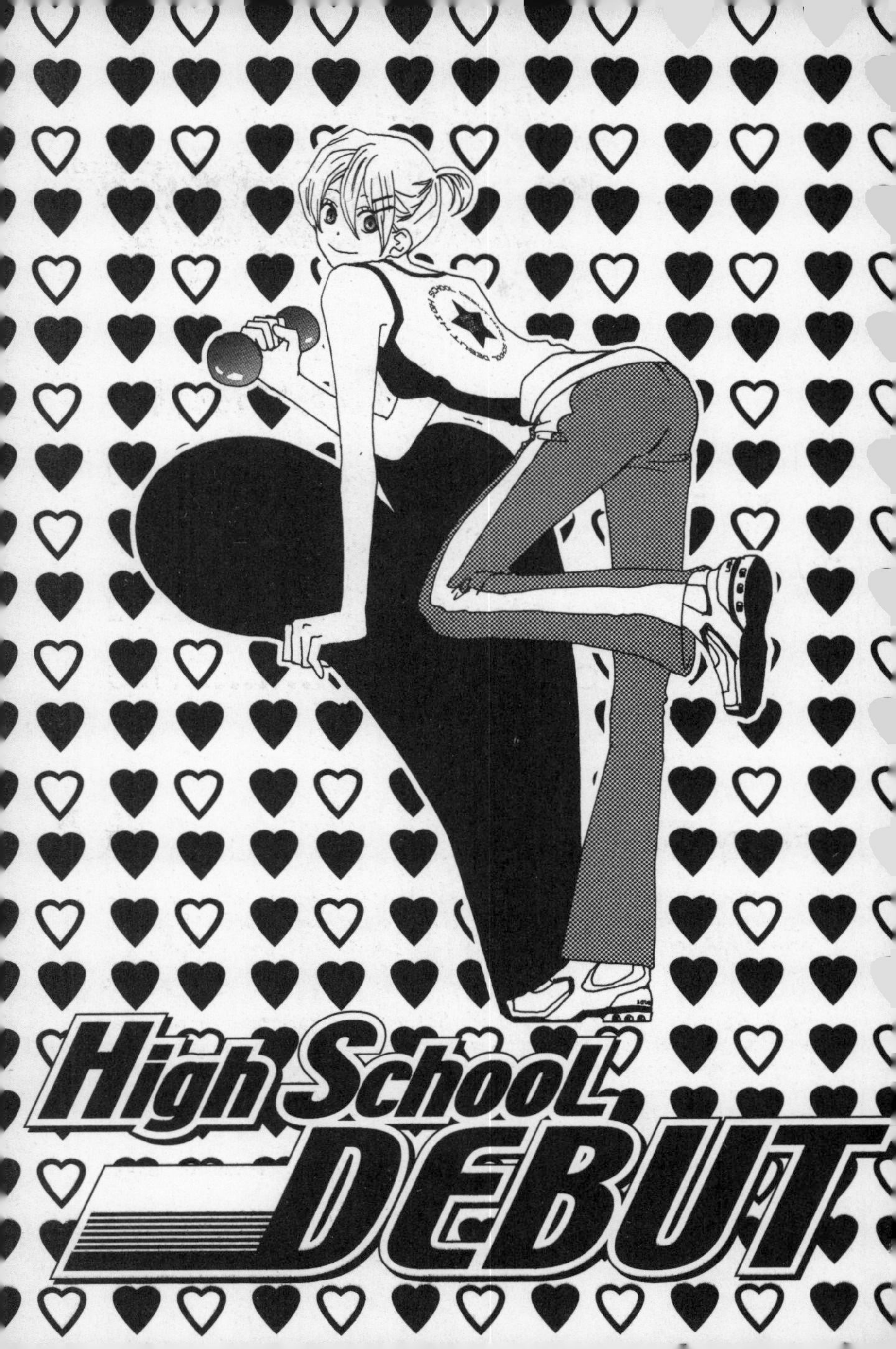
High School
DEBUT

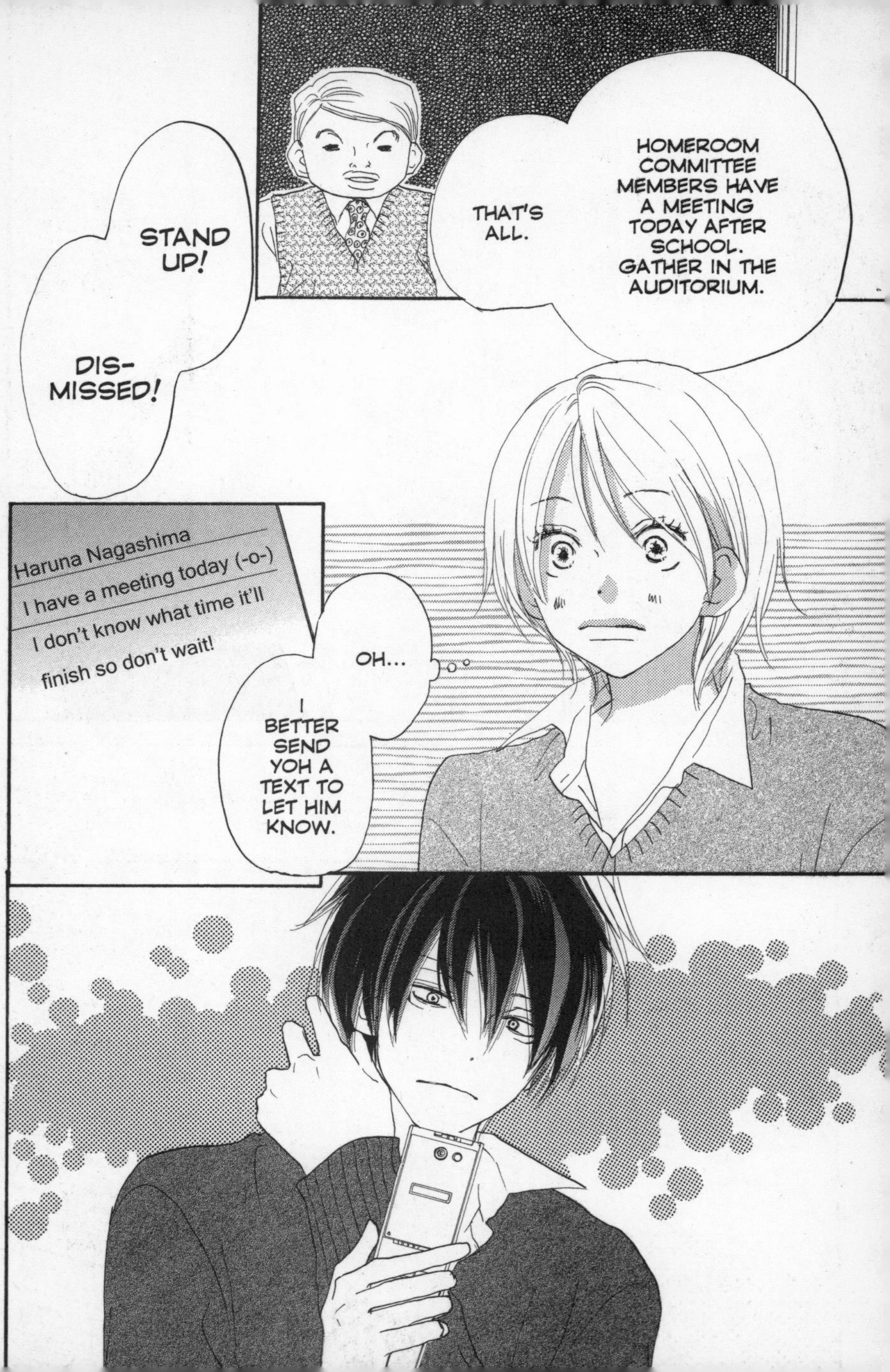
HOMEROOM COMMITTEE MEMBERS HAVE A MEETING TODAY AFTER SCHOOL. GATHER IN THE AUDITORIUM.
THAT'S ALL.
STAND UP!
DIS-MISSED!
OH...
I BETTER SEND YOH A TEXT TO LET HIM KNOW.
Haruna Nagashima
I have a meeting today (-o-)
I don't know what time it'll
finish so don't wait!

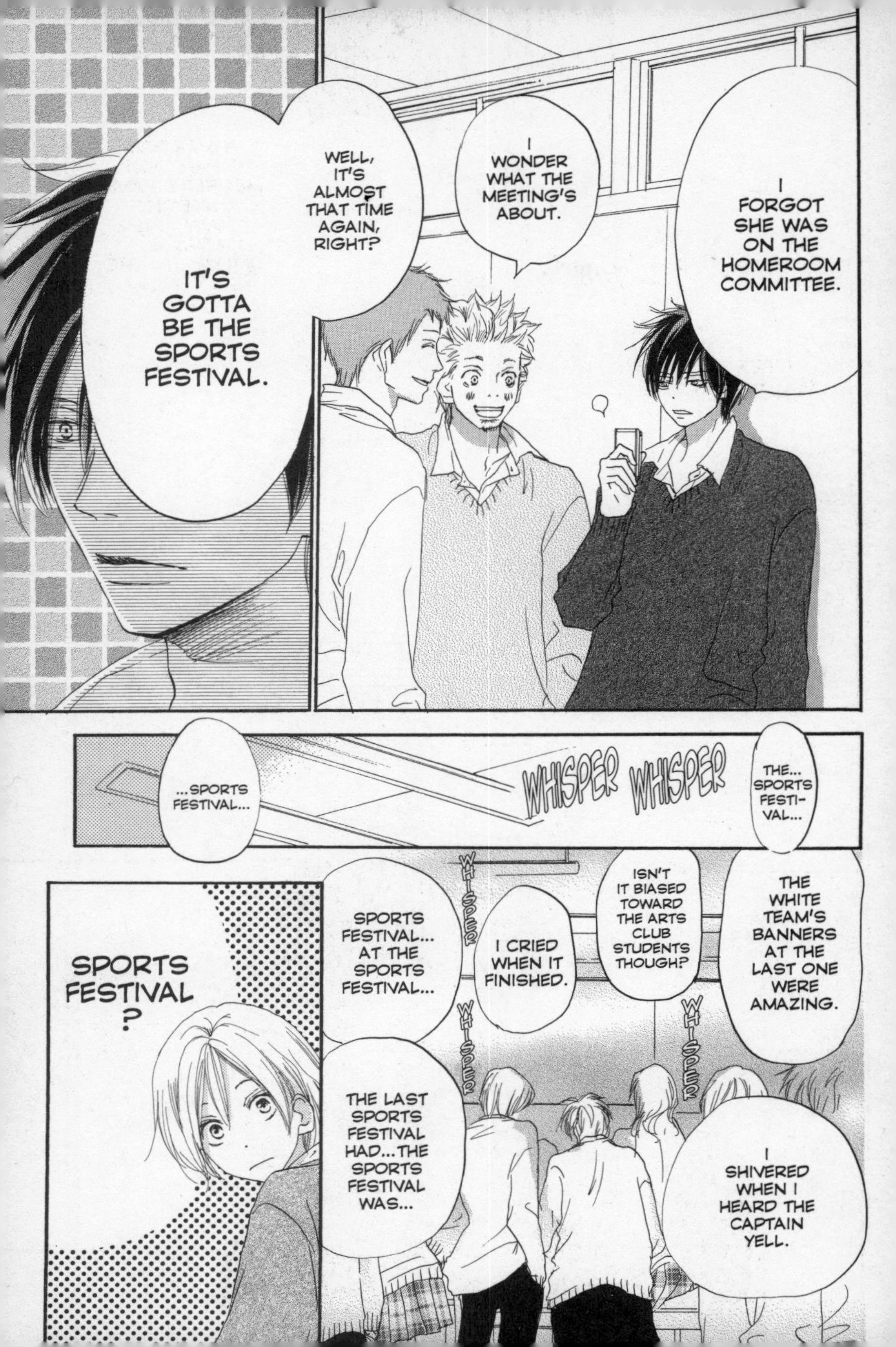
I FORGOT SHE WAS ON THE HOMEROOM COMMITTEE.
I WONDER WHAT THE MEETING'S ABOUT.
WELL, IT'S ALMOST THAT TIME AGAIN, RIGHT?
IT'S GOTTA BE THE SPORTS FESTIVAL.
THE... SPORTS FESTI- VAL...
WHISPER WHISPER
...SPORTS FESTIVAL...
THE WHITE TEAM'S BANNERS AT THE LAST ONE WERE AMAZING.
ISN'T IT BIASED TOWARD THE ARTS CLUB STUDENTS THOUGH?
WHISPER
I CRIED WHEN IT FINISHED.
WHISPER
SPORTS FESTIVAL... AT THE SPORTS FESTIVAL...
WHISPER
I SHIVERED WHEN I HEARD THE CAPTAIN YELL.
THE LAST SPORTS FESTIVAL HAD... THE SPORTS FESTIVAL WAS...
SPORTS FESTIVAL ?

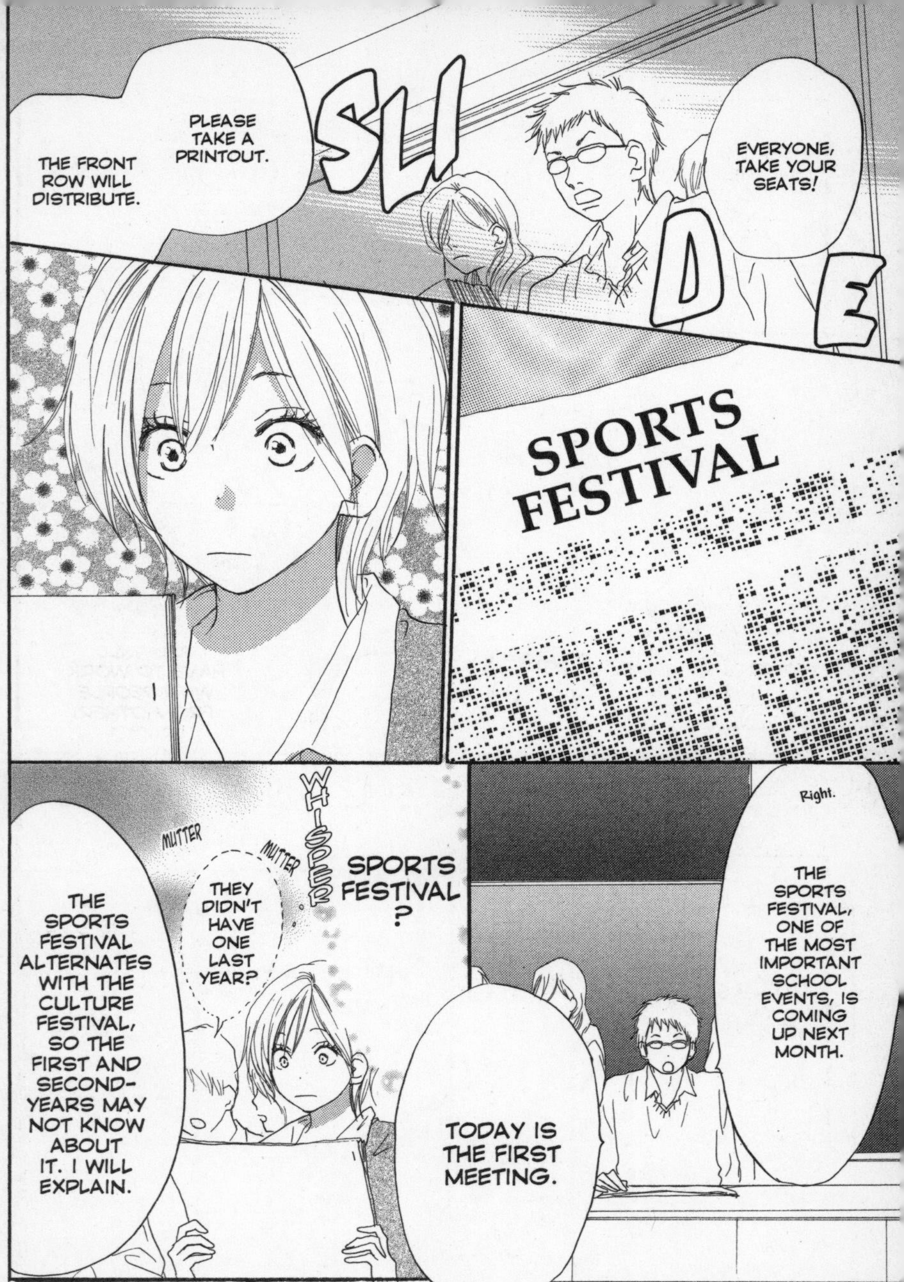
EVERYONE, TAKE YOUR SEATS!
SLIDE
PLEASE TAKE A PRINTOUT.
THE FRONT ROW WILL DISTRIBUTE.
SPORTS FESTIVAL
Right.
THE SPORTS FESTIVAL, ONE OF THE MOST IMPORTANT SCHOOL EVENTS, IS COMING UP NEXT MONTH.
TODAY IS THE FIRST MEETING.
SPORTS FESTIVAL?
WHISPER
MUTTER
THEY DIDN'T HAVE ONE LAST YEAR?
MUTTER
THE SPORTS FESTIVAL ALTERNATES WITH THE CULTURE FESTIVAL, SO THE FIRST AND SECOND-YEARS MAY NOT KNOW ABOUT IT. I WILL EXPLAIN.

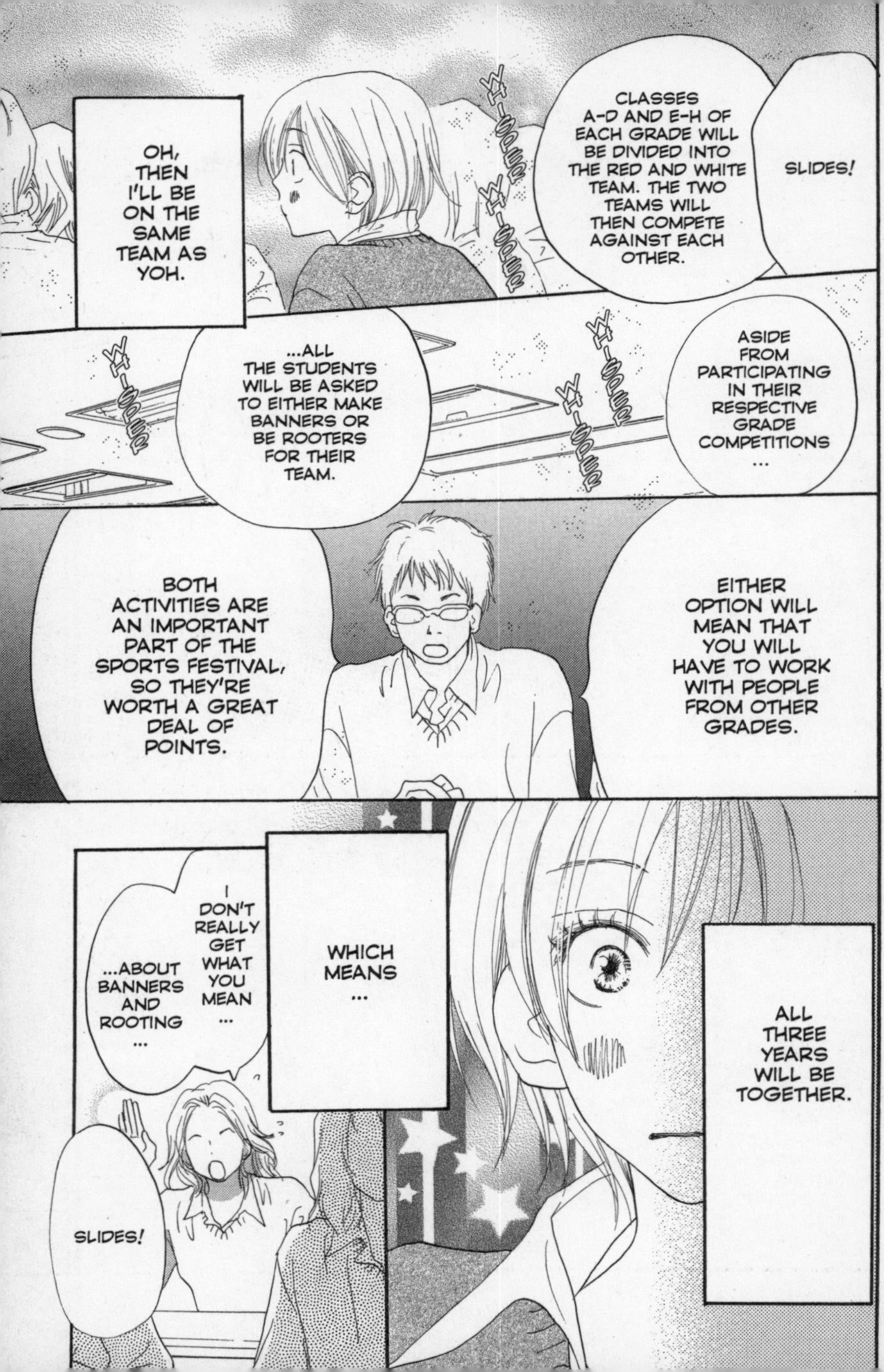
SLIDES!
CLASSES A-D AND E-H OF EACH GRADE WILL BE DIVIDED INTO THE RED AND WHITE TEAM. THE TWO TEAMS WILL THEN COMPETE AGAINST EACH OTHER.
OH, THEN I'LL BE ON THE SAME TEAM AS YOH.
ASIDE FROM PARTICIPATING IN THEIR RESPECTIVE GRADE COMPETITIONS ...
...ALL THE STUDENTS WILL BE ASKED TO EITHER MAKE BANNERS OR BE ROOTERS FOR THEIR TEAM.
EITHER OPTION WILL MEAN THAT YOU WILL HAVE TO WORK WITH PEOPLE FROM OTHER GRADES.
BOTH ACTIVITIES ARE AN IMPORTANT PART OF THE SPORTS FESTIVAL, SO THEY'RE WORTH A GREAT DEAL OF POINTS.
ALL THREE YEARS WILL BE TOGETHER.
WHICH MEANS ...
I DON'T REALLY GET WHAT YOU MEAN ...
...ABOUT BANNERS AND ROOTING ...
SLIDES!

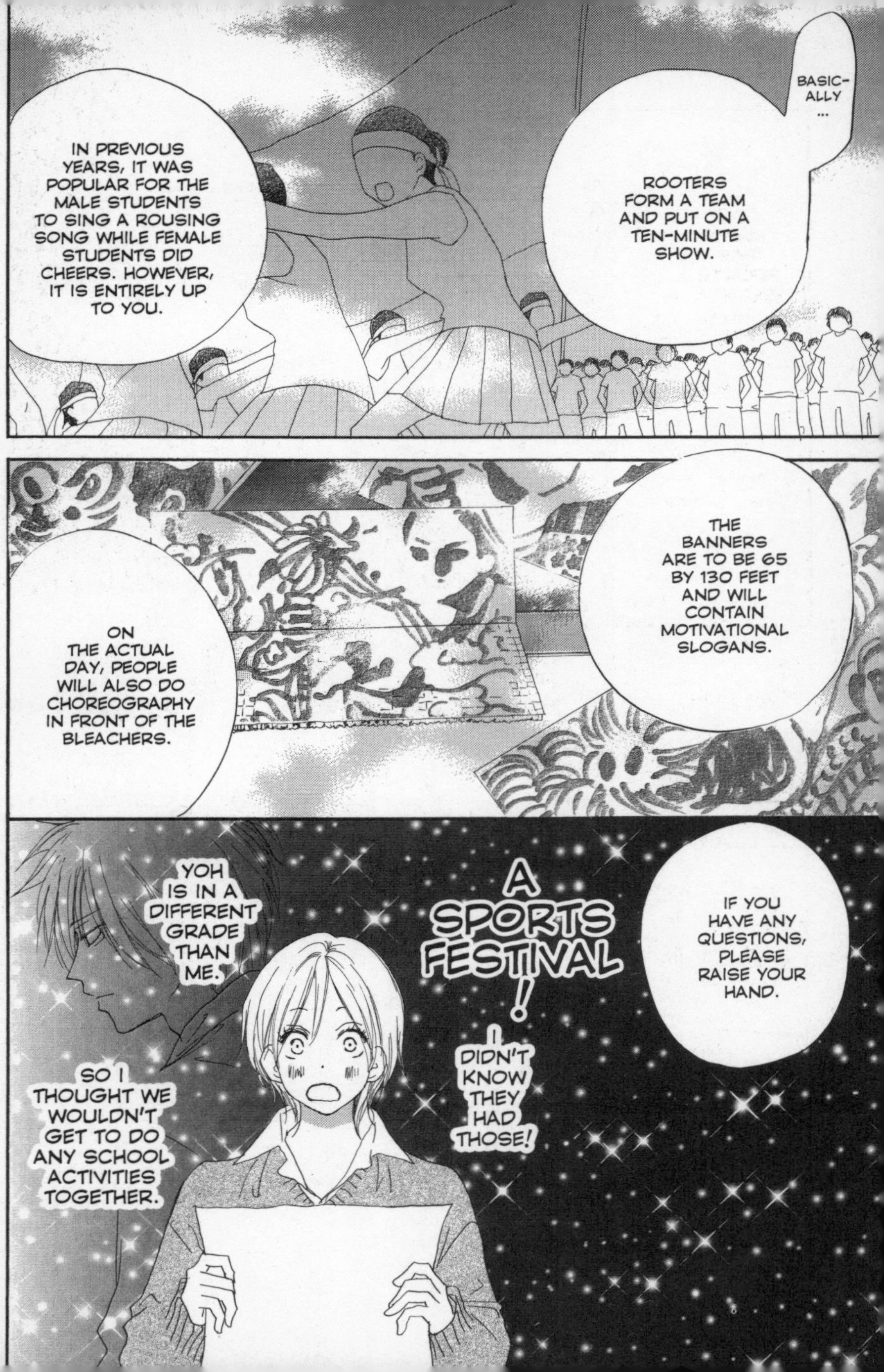
BASIC-ALLY ...
ROOTERS FORM A TEAM AND PUT ON A TEN-MINUTE SHOW.
IN PREVIOUS YEARS, IT WAS POPULAR FOR THE MALE STUDENTS TO SING A ROUSING SONG WHILE FEMALE STUDENTS DID CHEERS. HOWEVER, IT IS ENTIRELY UP TO YOU.
THE BANNERS ARE TO BE 65 BY 130 FEET AND WILL CONTAIN MOTIVATIONAL SLOGANS.
ON THE ACTUAL DAY, PEOPLE WILL ALSO DO CHOREOGRAPHY IN FRONT OF THE BLEACHERS.
IF YOU HAVE ANY QUESTIONS, PLEASE RAISE YOUR HAND.
A SPORTS FESTIVAL!
I DIDN'T KNOW THEY HAD THOSE!
YOH IS IN A DIFFERENT GRADE THAN ME.
SO I THOUGHT WE WOULDN'T GET TO DO ANY SCHOOL ACTIVITIES TOGETHER.

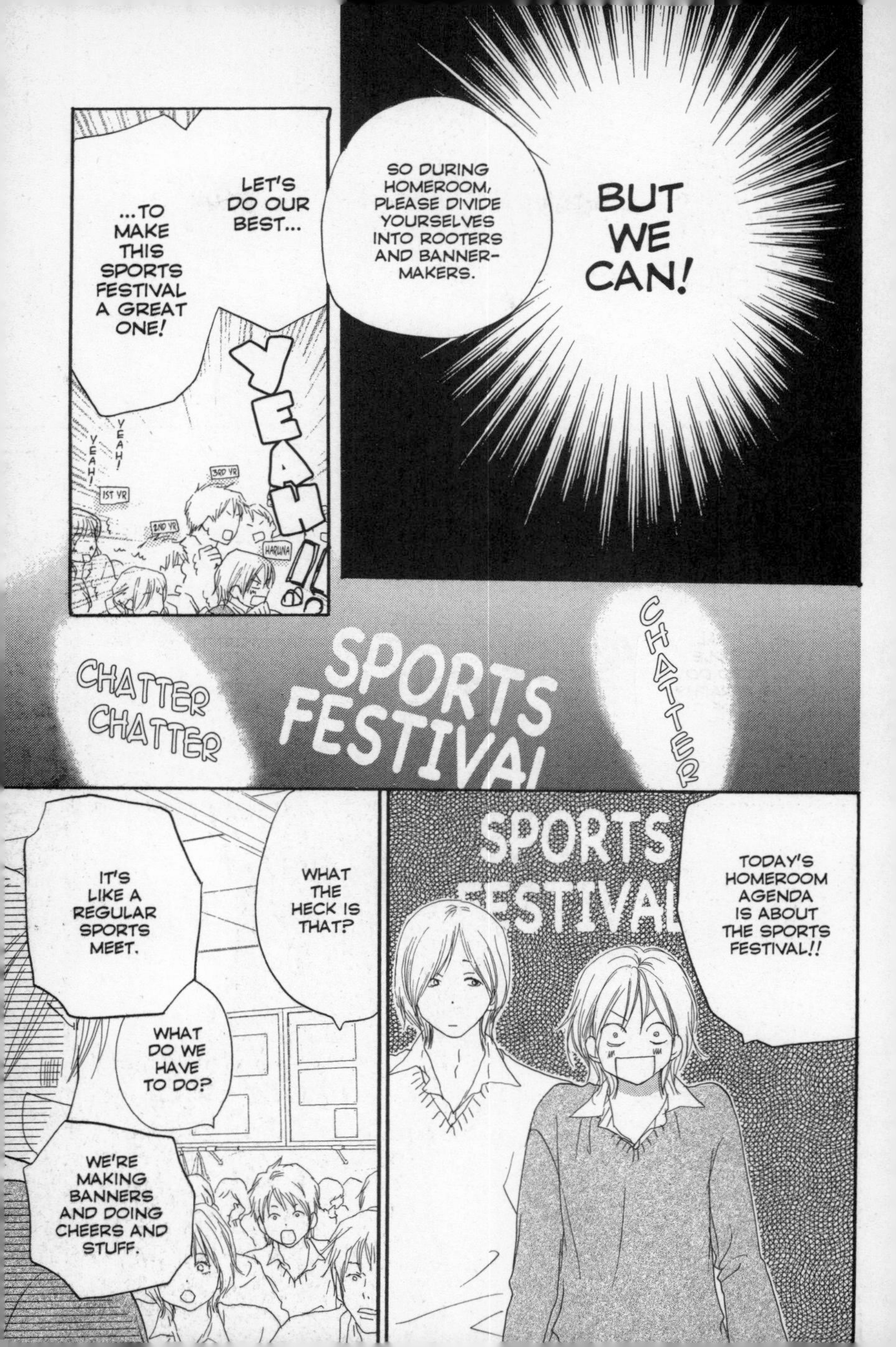
BUT WE CAN!
SO DURING HOMEROOM, PLEASE DIVIDE YOURSELVES INTO ROOTERS AND BANNER-MAKERS.
LET'S DO OUR BEST...
...TO MAKE THIS SPORTS FESTIVAL A GREAT ONE!
YEAH!!
YEAH!
YEAH!
3RD YR
1ST YR
2ND YR
HARUNA
CHATTER
SPORTS FESTIVAL
CHATTER CHATTER
TODAY'S HOMEROOM AGENDA IS ABOUT THE SPORTS FESTIVAL!!
SPORTS FESTIVAL
WHAT THE HECK IS THAT?
IT'S LIKE A REGULAR SPORTS MEET.
WHAT DO WE HAVE TO DO?
WE'RE MAKING BANNERS AND DOING CHEERS AND STUFF.

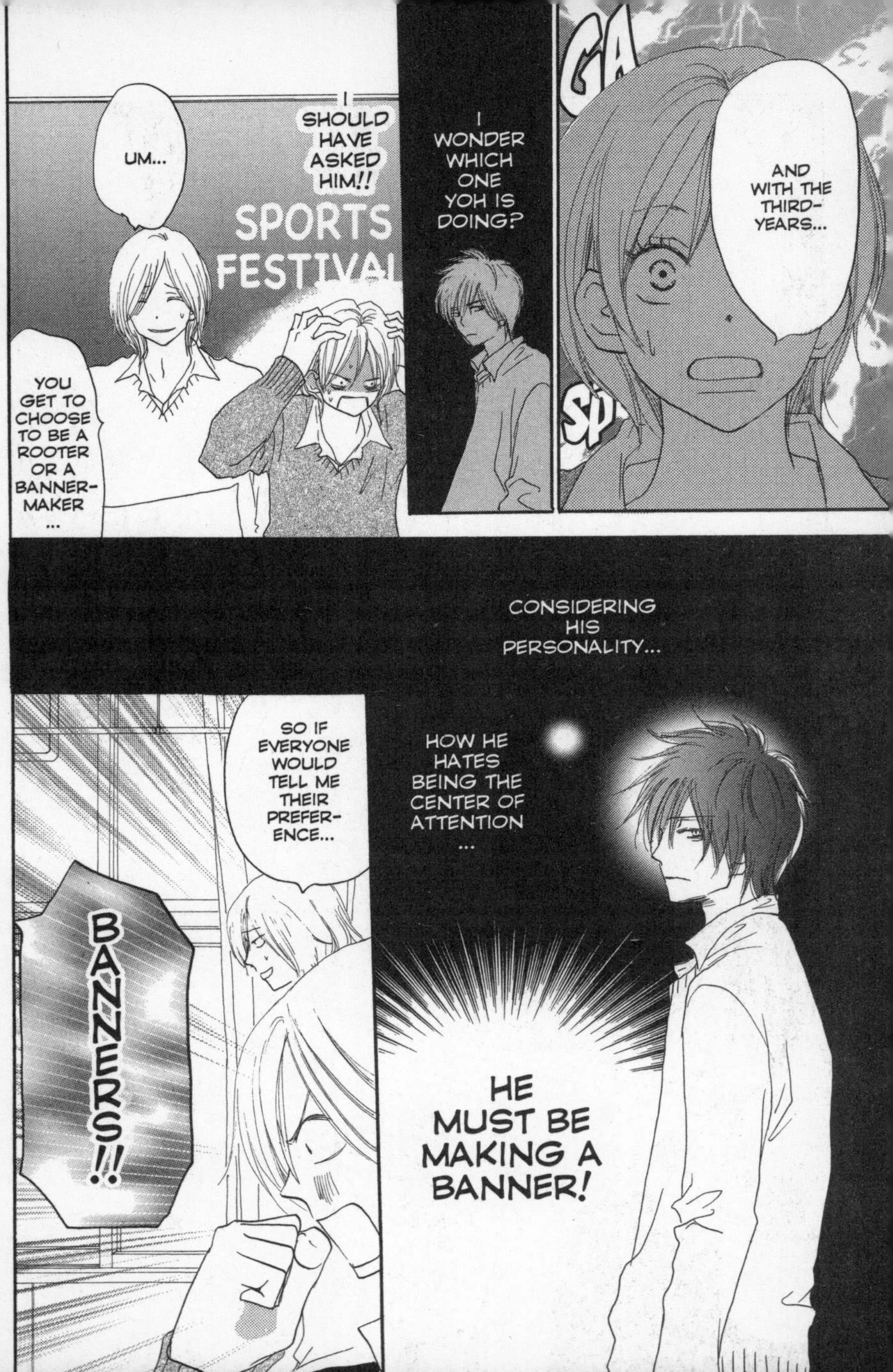

GA
AND WITH THE THIRD-YEARS...
SP
I WONDER WHICH ONE YOH IS DOING?
I SHOULD HAVE ASKED HIM!!
UM...
SPORTS FESTIVAL
YOU GET TO CHOOSE TO BE A ROOTER OR A BANNER-MAKER ...
CONSIDERING HIS PERSONALITY...
HOW HE HATES BEING THE CENTER OF ATTENTION ...
HE MUST BE MAKING A BANNER!
SO IF EVERYONE WOULD TELL ME THEIR PREFER-ENCE...
BANNERS!!

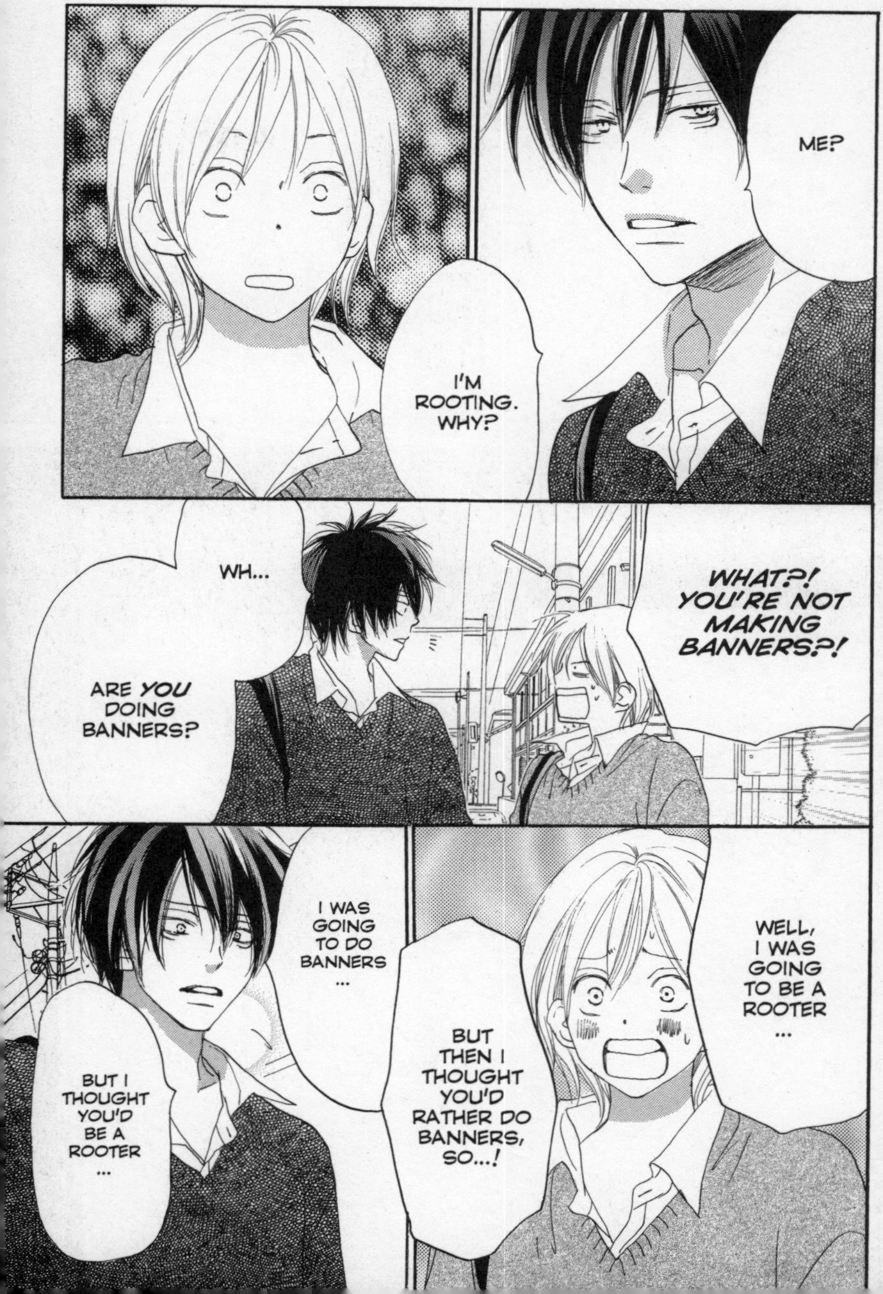
ME?
I'M ROOTING. WHY?
WHAT?! YOU'RE NOT MAKING BANNERS?!
WH...
ARE *YOU* DOING BANNERS?
WELL, I WAS GOING TO BE A ROOTER ...
BUT THEN I THOUGHT YOU'D RATHER DO BANNERS, SO...!
I WAS GOING TO DO BANNERS ...
BUT I THOUGHT YOU'D BE A ROOTER ...

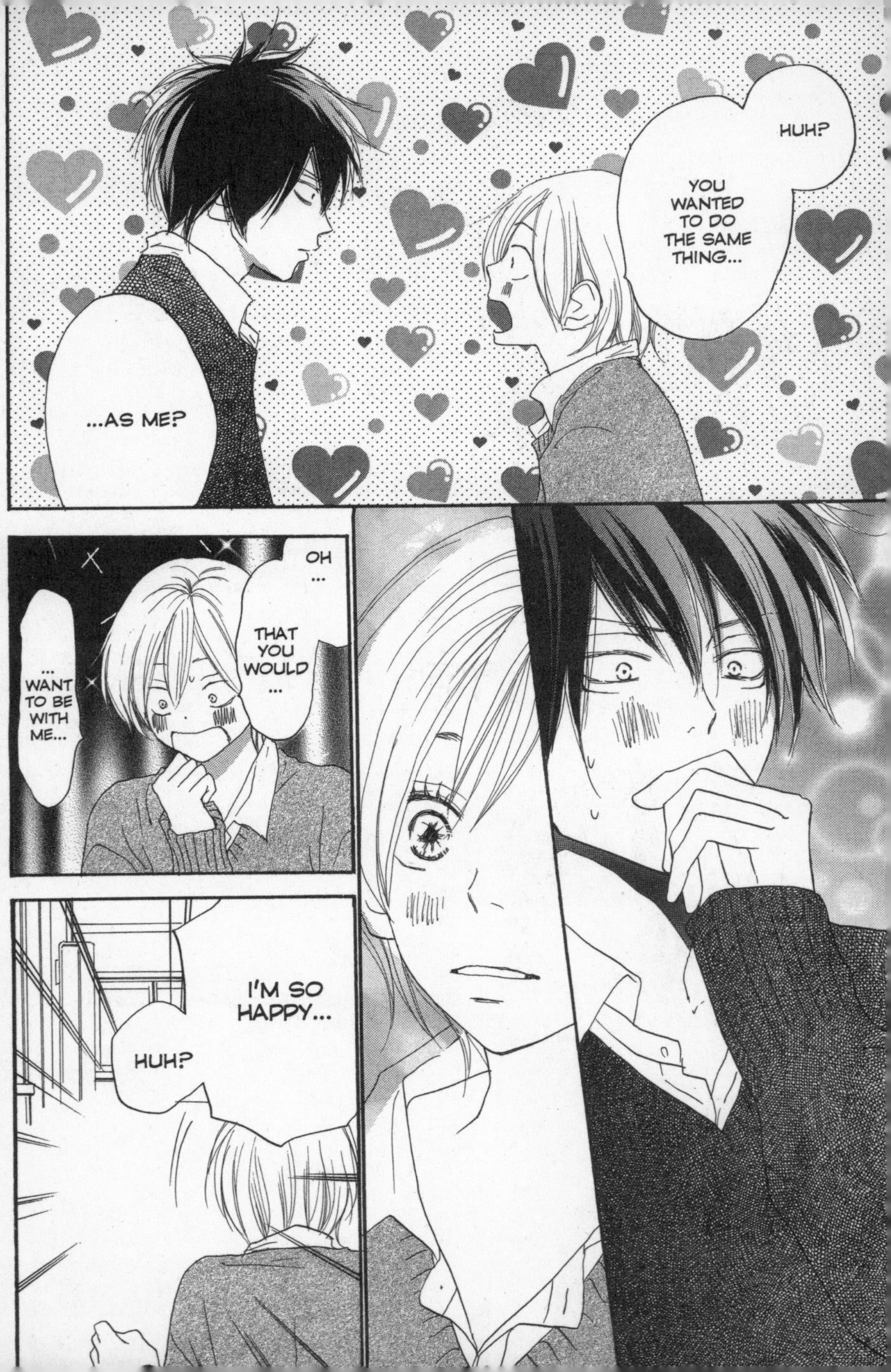
HUH?
YOU WANTED TO DO THE SAME THING...
...AS ME?
OH ...
THAT YOU WOULD ...
... WANT TO BE WITH ME...
I'M SO HAPPY...
HUH?

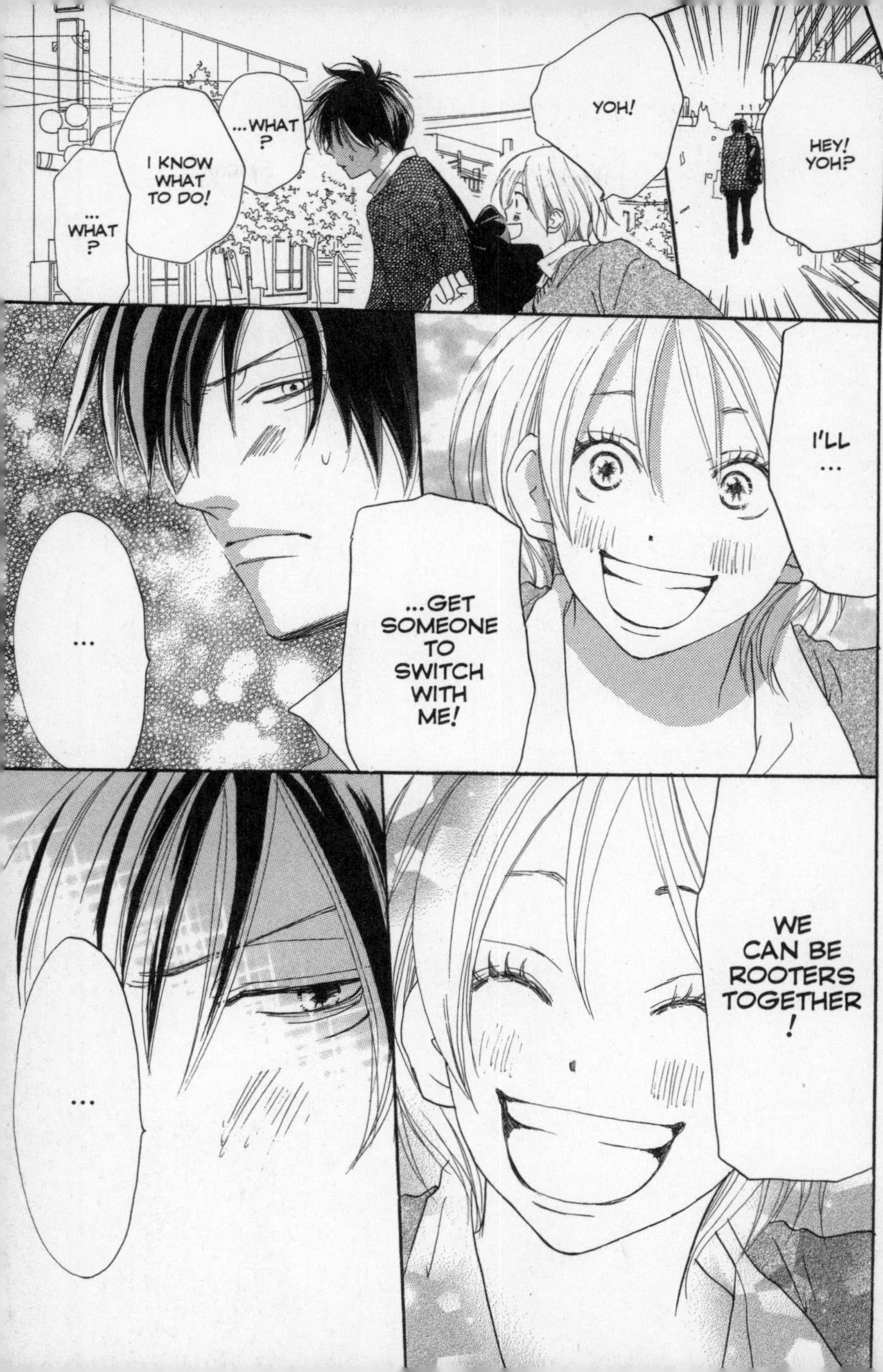
HEY! YOH?
YOH!
...WHAT?
I KNOW WHAT TO DO!
... WHAT?
I'LL ...
...GET SOMEONE TO SWITCH WITH ME!
...
WE CAN BE ROOTERS TOGETHER!
...

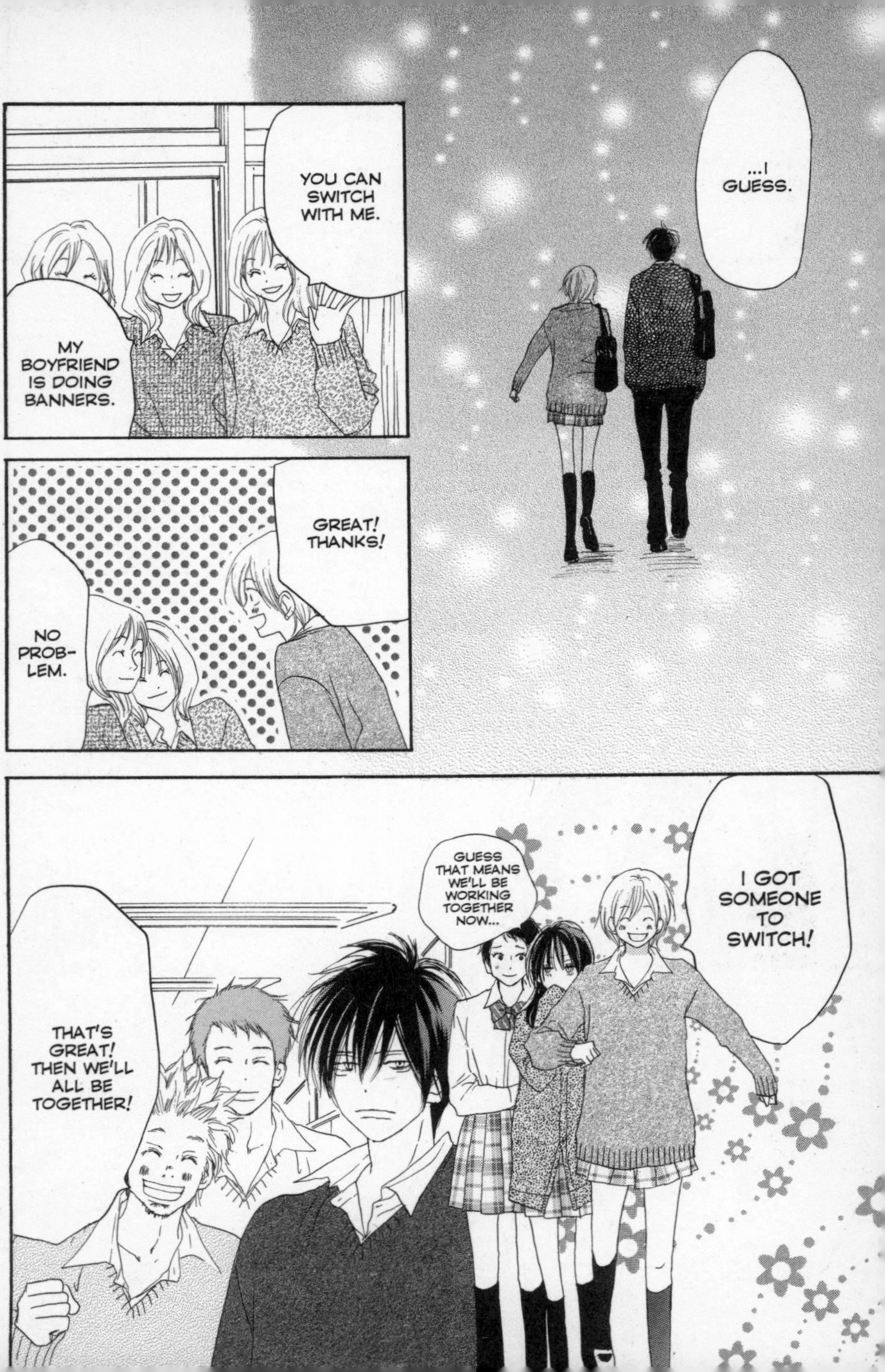
...I GUESS.
YOU CAN SWITCH WITH ME.
MY BOYFRIEND IS DOING BANNERS.
GREAT! THANKS!
NO PROB-LEM.
I GOT SOMEONE TO SWITCH!
GUESS THAT MEANS WE'LL BE WORKING TOGETHER NOW...
THAT'S GREAT! THEN WE'LL ALL BE TOGETHER!

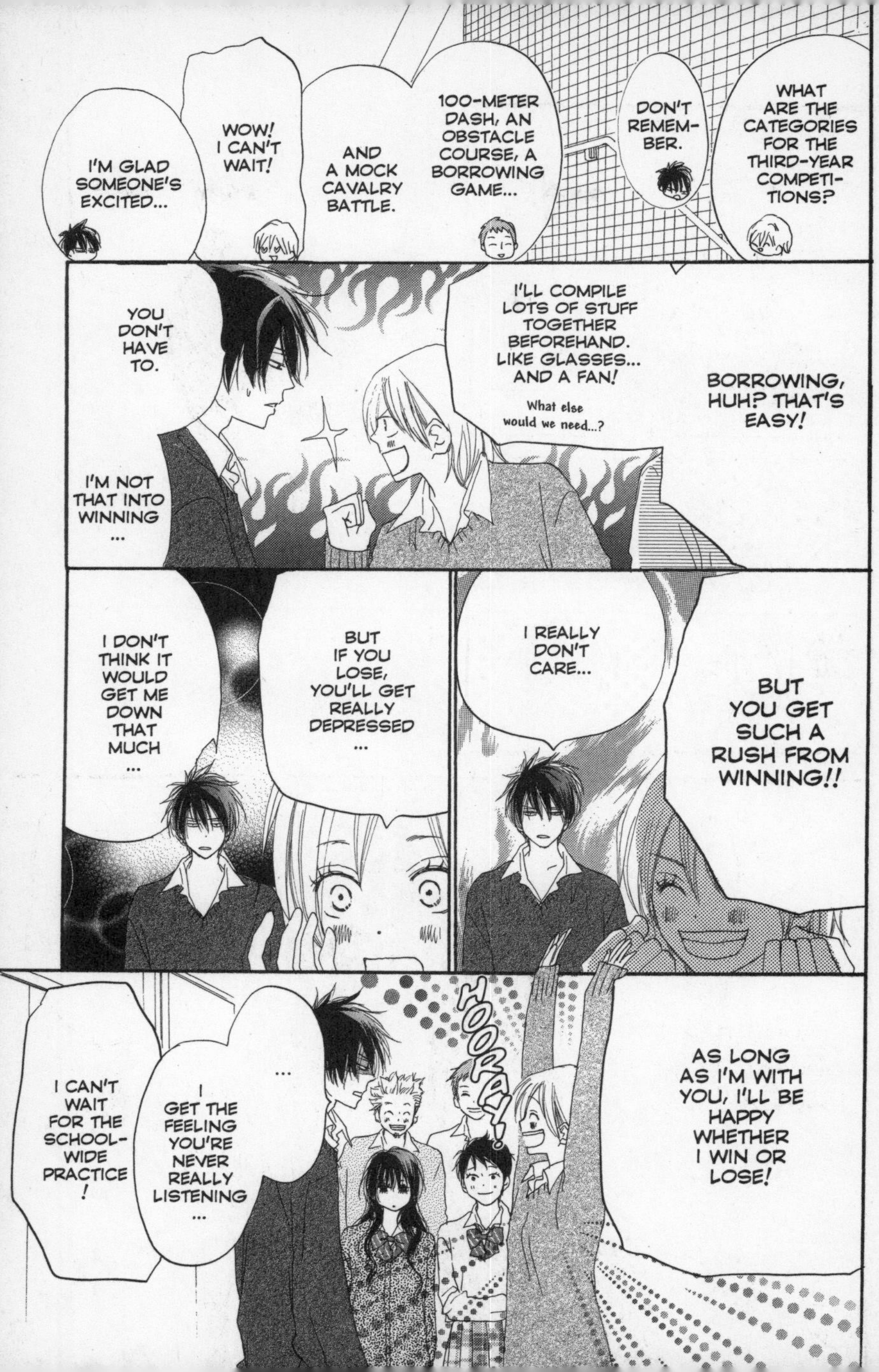
WHAT ARE THE CATEGORIES FOR THE THIRD-YEAR COMPETITIONS?
DON'T REMEMBER.
100-METER DASH, AN OBSTACLE COURSE, A BORROWING GAME...
AND A MOCK CAVALRY BATTLE.
WOW! I CAN'T WAIT!
I'M GLAD SOMEONE'S EXCITED...
BORROWING, HUH? THAT'S EASY!
I'LL COMPILE LOTS OF STUFF TOGETHER BEFOREHAND. LIKE GLASSES... AND A FAN!
What else would we need...?
YOU DON'T HAVE TO.
I'M NOT THAT INTO WINNING...
BUT YOU GET SUCH A RUSH FROM WINNING!!
I REALLY DON'T CARE...
BUT IF YOU LOSE, YOU'LL GET REALLY DEPRESSED...
I DON'T THINK IT WOULD GET ME DOWN THAT MUCH...
AS LONG AS I'M WITH YOU, I'LL BE HAPPY WHETHER I WIN OR LOSE!
HOORAY!
...
I GET THE FEELING YOU'RE NEVER REALLY LISTENING...
I CAN'T WAIT FOR THE SCHOOL-WIDE PRACTICE!

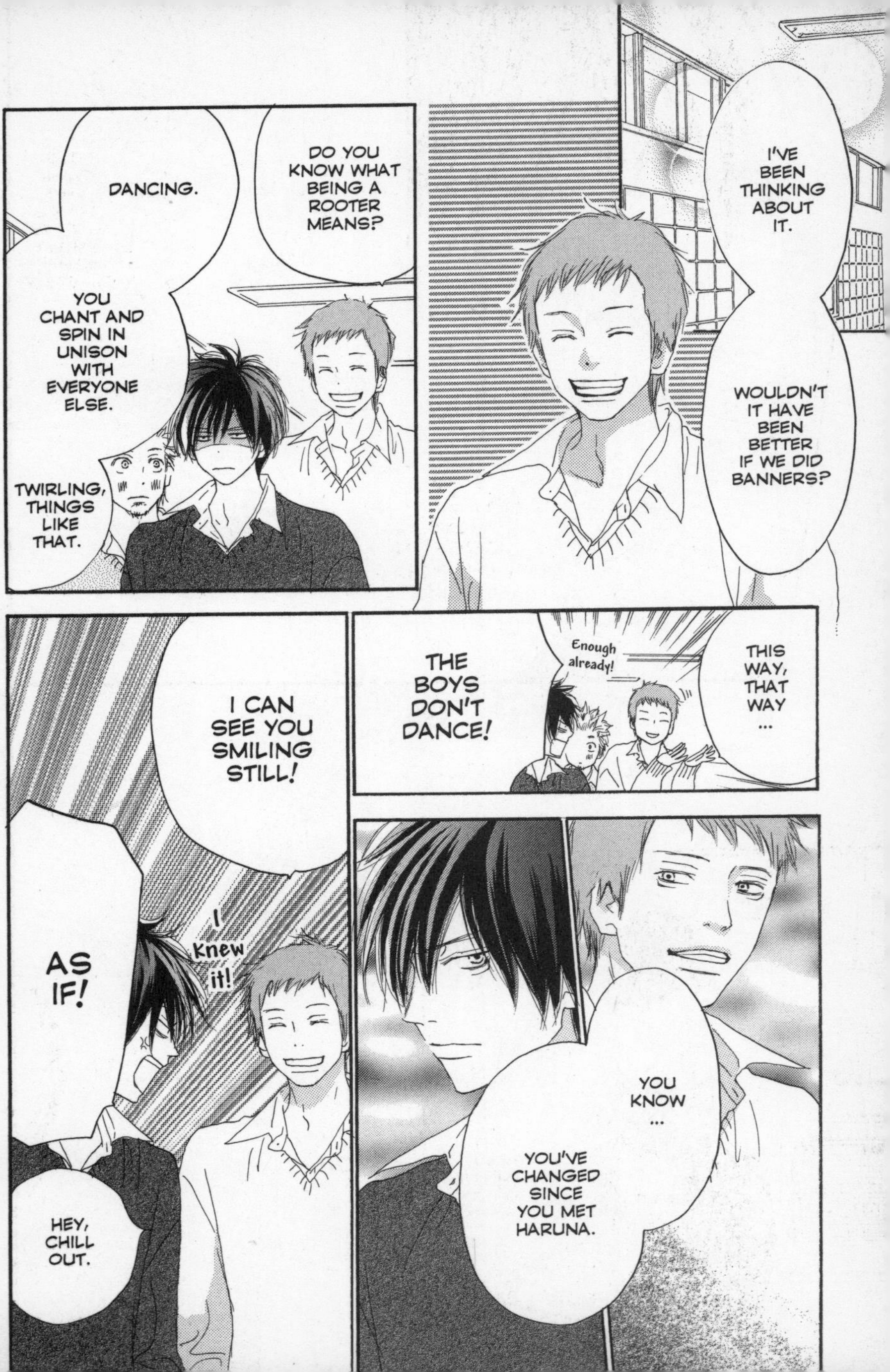
I'VE BEEN THINKING ABOUT IT.
WOULDN'T IT HAVE BEEN BETTER IF WE DID BANNERS?
DO YOU KNOW WHAT BEING A ROOTER MEANS?
DANCING.
YOU CHANT AND SPIN IN UNISON WITH EVERYONE ELSE.
TWIRLING, THINGS LIKE THAT.
THIS WAY, THAT WAY ...
Enough already!
THE BOYS DON'T DANCE!
YOU KNOW ...
YOU'VE CHANGED SINCE YOU MET HARUNA.
I CAN SEE YOU SMILING STILL!
I knew it!
AS IF!
HEY, CHILL OUT.

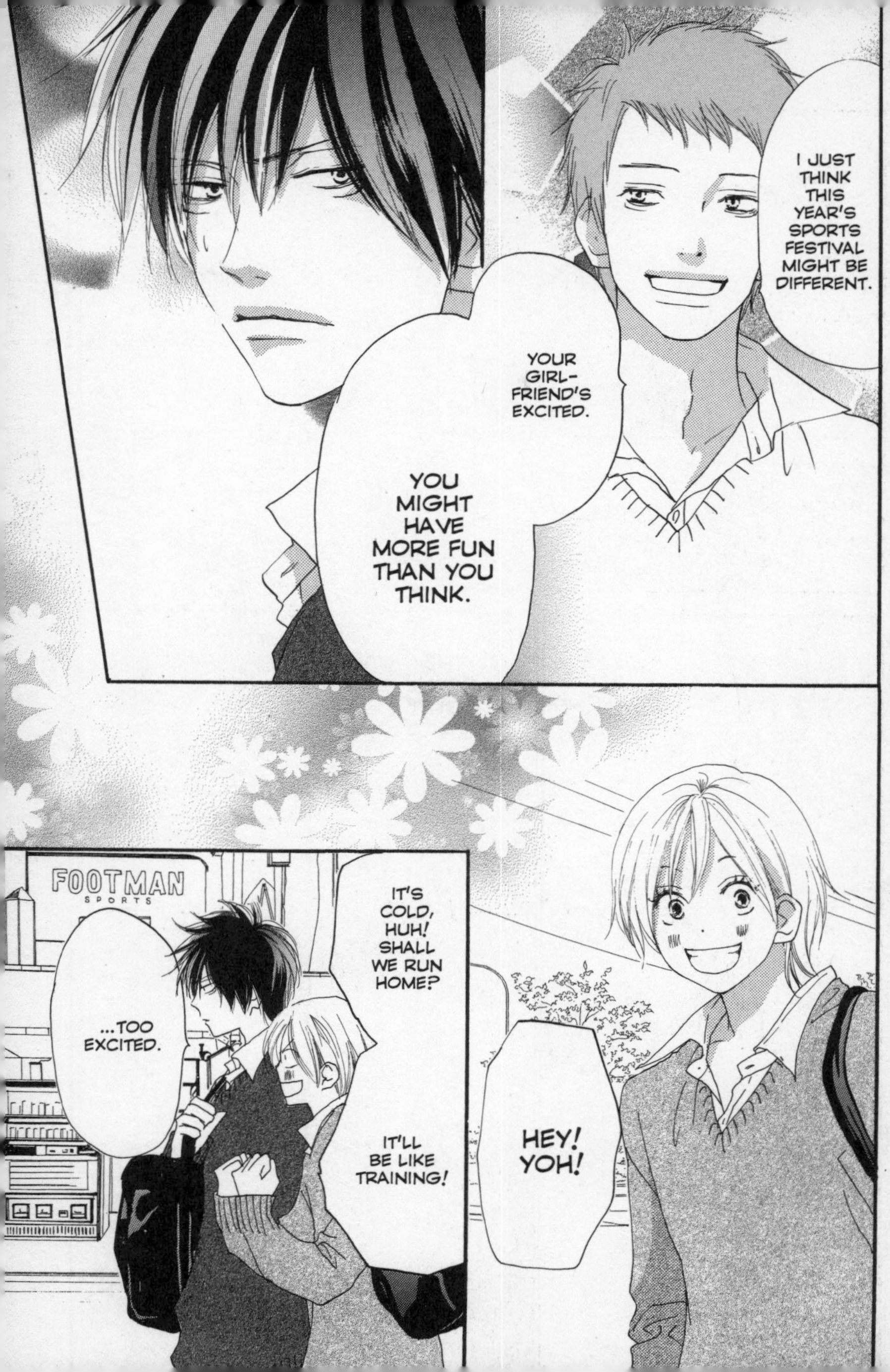
I JUST THINK THIS YEAR'S SPORTS FESTIVAL MIGHT BE DIFFERENT.
YOUR GIRL-FRIEND'S EXCITED.
YOU MIGHT HAVE MORE FUN THAN YOU THINK.
HEY! YOH!
FOOTMAN SPORTS
IT'S COLD, HUH! SHALL WE RUN HOME?
IT'LL BE LIKE TRAINING!
...TOO EXCITED.

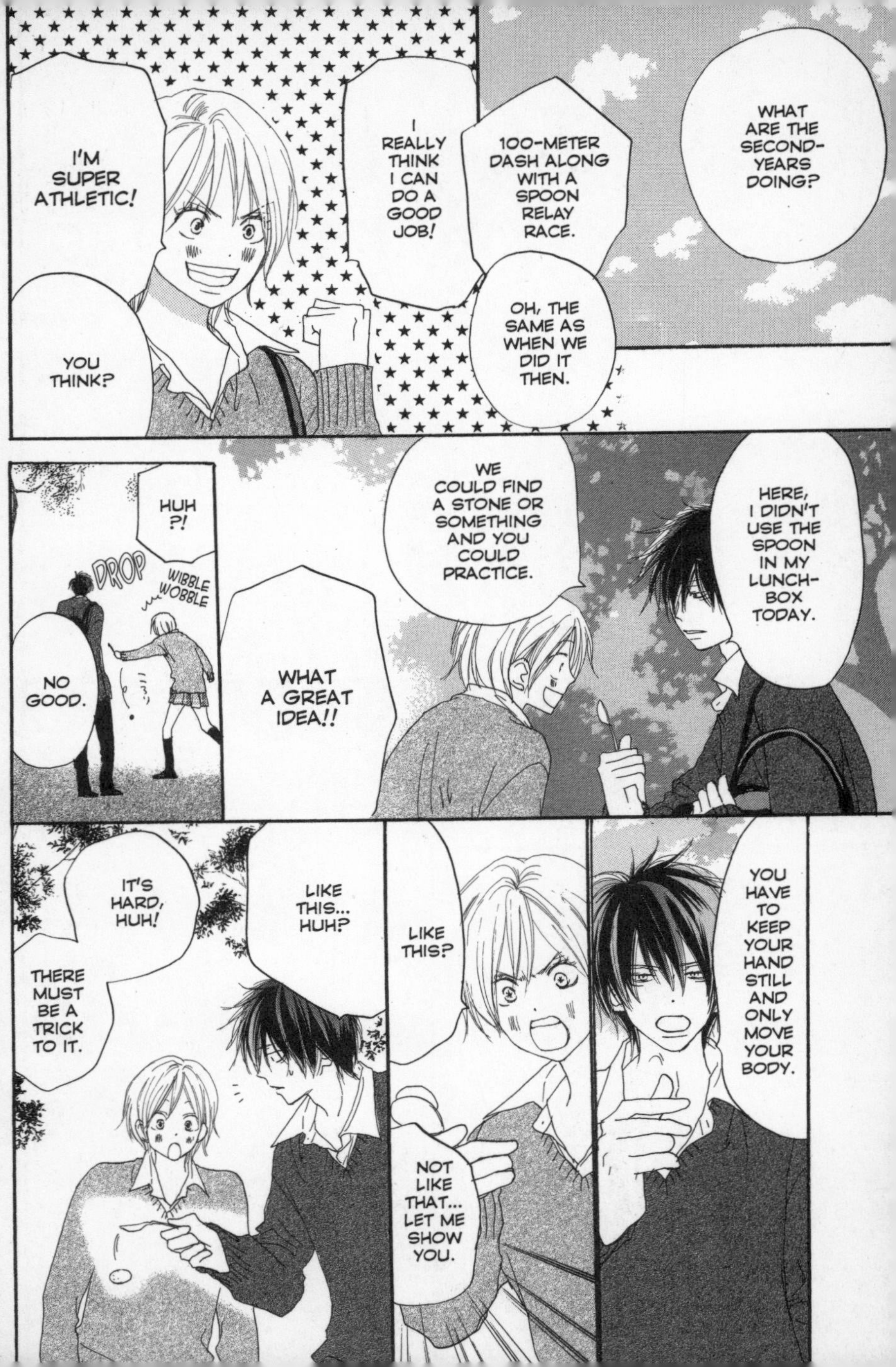
WHAT ARE THE SECOND-YEARS DOING?
100-METER DASH ALONG WITH A SPOON RELAY RACE.
OH, THE SAME AS WHEN WE DID IT THEN.
I REALLY THINK I CAN DO A GOOD JOB!
I'M SUPER ATHLETIC!
YOU THINK?
HERE, I DIDN'T USE THE SPOON IN MY LUNCH-BOX TODAY.
WE COULD FIND A STONE OR SOMETHING AND YOU COULD PRACTICE.
WHAT A GREAT IDEA!!
HUH ?!
DROP
WIBBLE WOBBLE
NO GOOD.
YOU HAVE TO KEEP YOUR HAND STILL AND ONLY MOVE YOUR BODY.
LIKE THIS?
NOT LIKE THAT... LET ME SHOW YOU.
LIKE THIS... HUH?
IT'S HARD, HUH!
THERE MUST BE A TRICK TO IT.

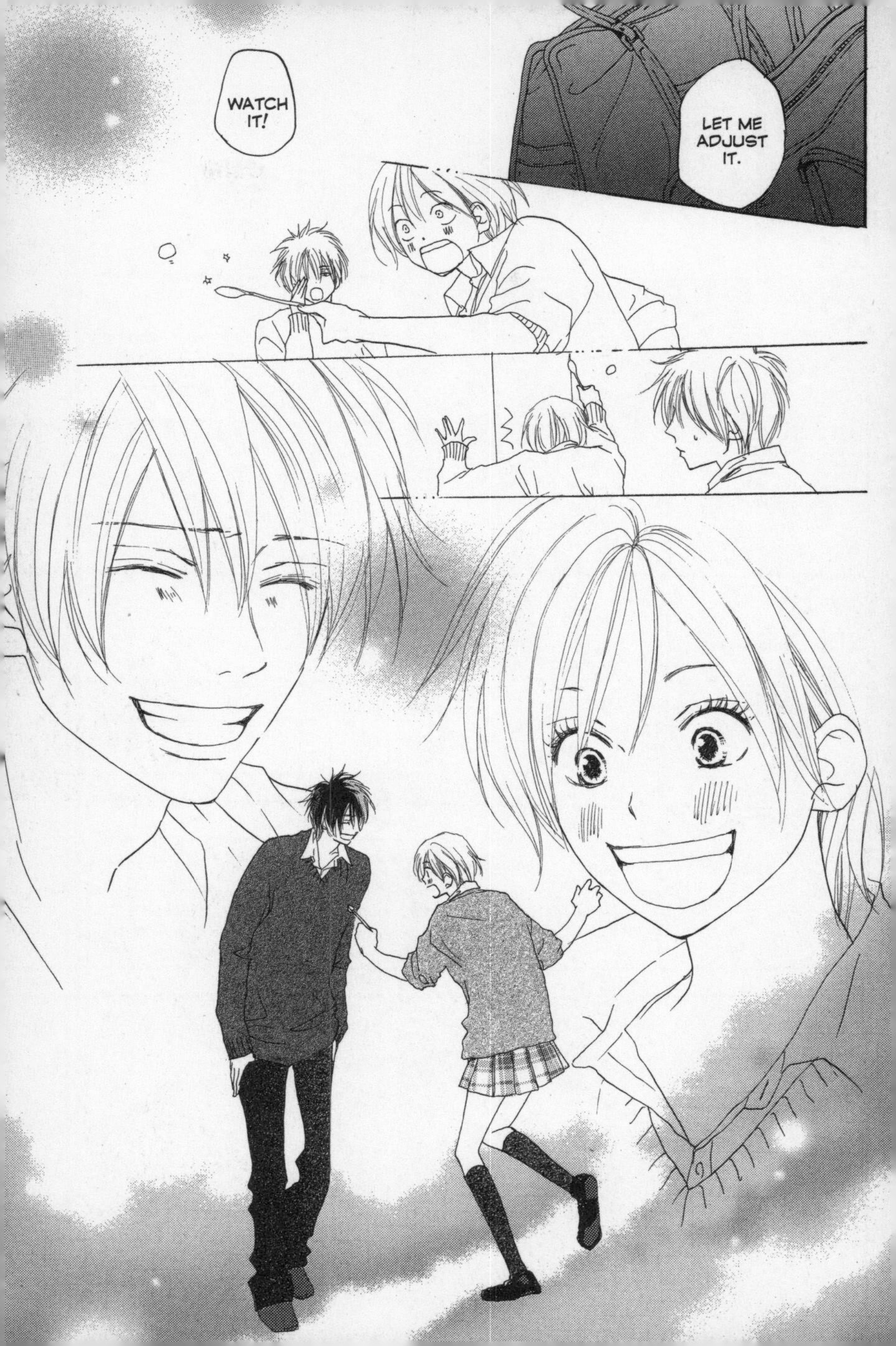
LET ME ADJUST IT.
WATCH IT!

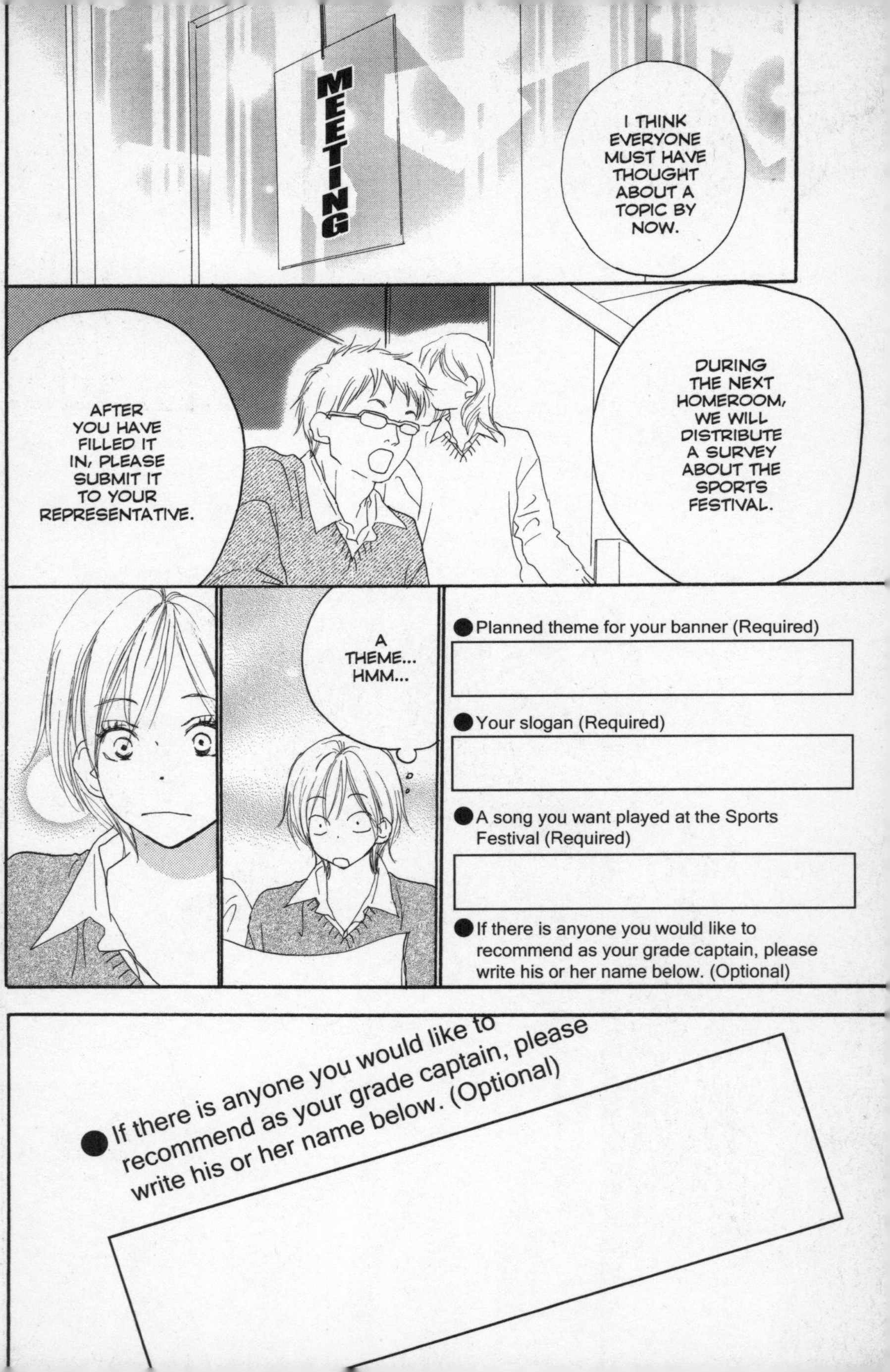
MEETING
I THINK EVERYONE MUST HAVE THOUGHT ABOUT A TOPIC BY NOW.
DURING THE NEXT HOMEROOM, WE WILL DISTRIBUTE A SURVEY ABOUT THE SPORTS FESTIVAL.
AFTER YOU HAVE FILLED IT IN, PLEASE SUBMIT IT TO YOUR REPRESENTATIVE.
● Planned theme for your banner (Required)
● Your slogan (Required)
● A song you want played at the Sports Festival (Required)
● If there is anyone you would like to recommend as your grade captain, please write his or her name below. (Optional)
A THEME... HMM...
● If there is anyone you would like to recommend as your grade captain, please write his or her name below. (Optional)

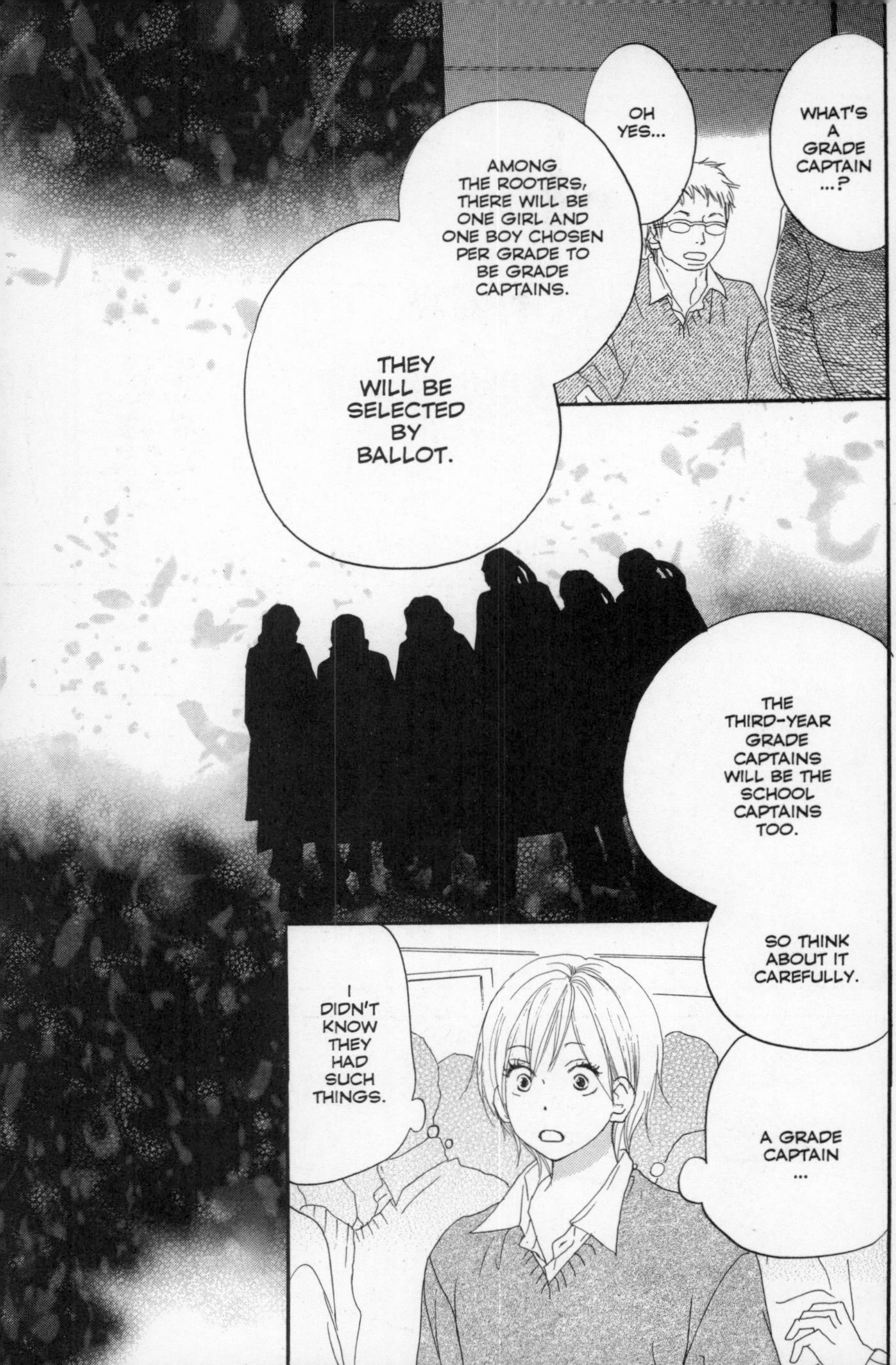
WHAT'S A GRADE CAPTAIN ...?
OH YES...
AMONG THE ROOTERS, THERE WILL BE ONE GIRL AND ONE BOY CHOSEN PER GRADE TO BE GRADE CAPTAINS.
THEY WILL BE SELECTED BY BALLOT.
THE THIRD-YEAR GRADE CAPTAINS WILL BE THE SCHOOL CAPTAINS TOO.
SO THINK ABOUT IT CAREFULLY.
A GRADE CAPTAIN ...
I DIDN'T KNOW THEY HAD SUCH THINGS.

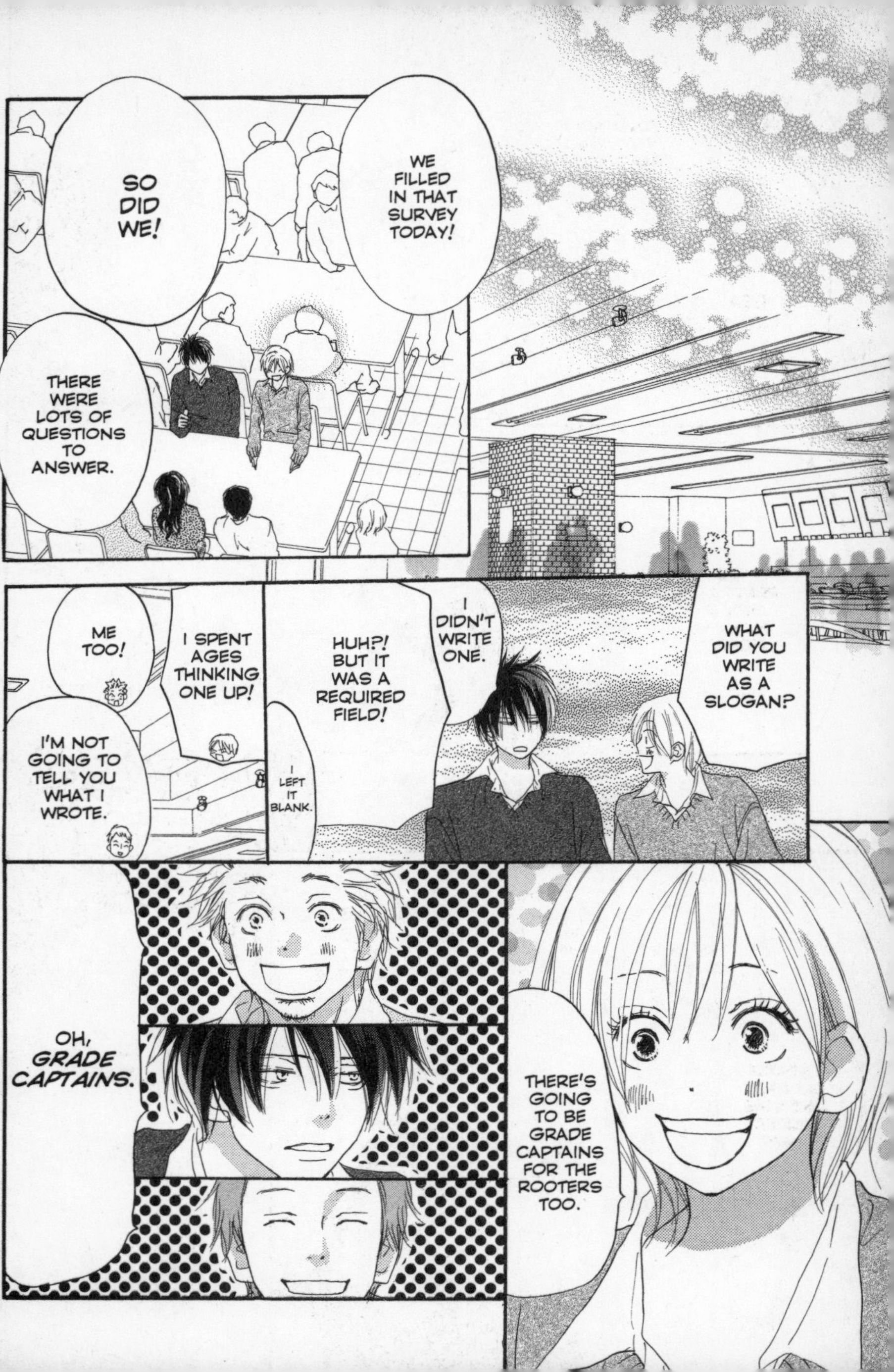
WE FILLED IN THAT SURVEY TODAY!
SO DID WE!
THERE WERE LOTS OF QUESTIONS TO ANSWER.
WHAT DID YOU WRITE AS A SLOGAN?
I DIDN'T WRITE ONE.
HUH?! BUT IT WAS A REQUIRED FIELD!
I LEFT IT BLANK.
I SPENT AGES THINKING ONE UP!
ME TOO!
I'M NOT GOING TO TELL YOU WHAT I WROTE.
THERE'S GOING TO BE GRADE CAPTAINS FOR THE ROOTERS TOO.
OH, GRADE CAPTAINS.

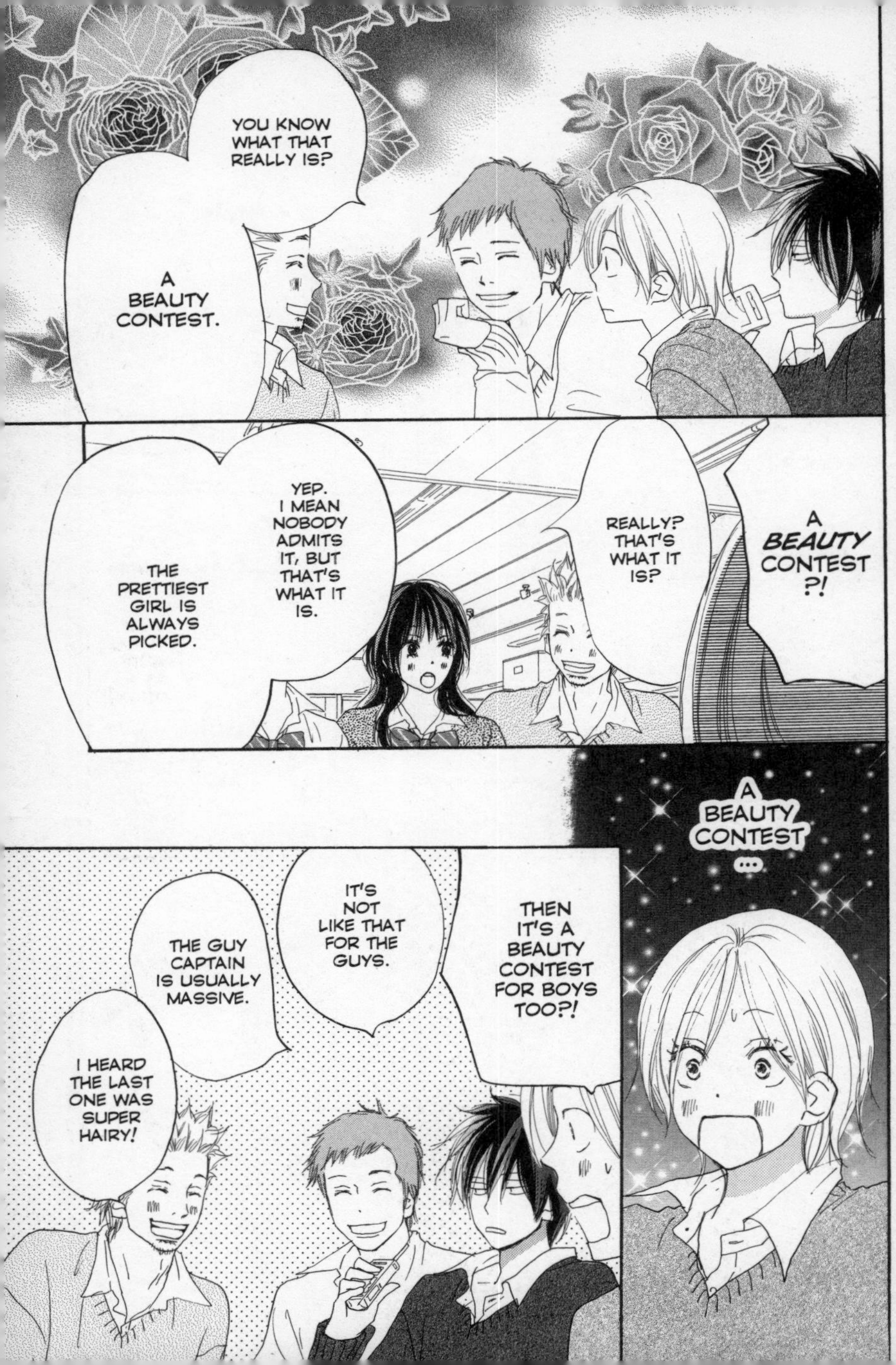
YOU KNOW WHAT THAT REALLY IS?
A BEAUTY CONTEST.
A *BEAUTY* CONTEST?!
REALLY? THAT'S WHAT IT IS?
YEP. I MEAN NOBODY ADMITS IT, BUT THAT'S WHAT IT IS.
THE PRETTIEST GIRL IS ALWAYS PICKED.
A BEAUTY CONTEST...
THEN IT'S A BEAUTY CONTEST FOR BOYS TOO?!
IT'S NOT LIKE THAT FOR THE GUYS.
THE GUY CAPTAIN IS USUALLY MASSIVE.
I HEARD THE LAST ONE WAS SUPER HAIRY!

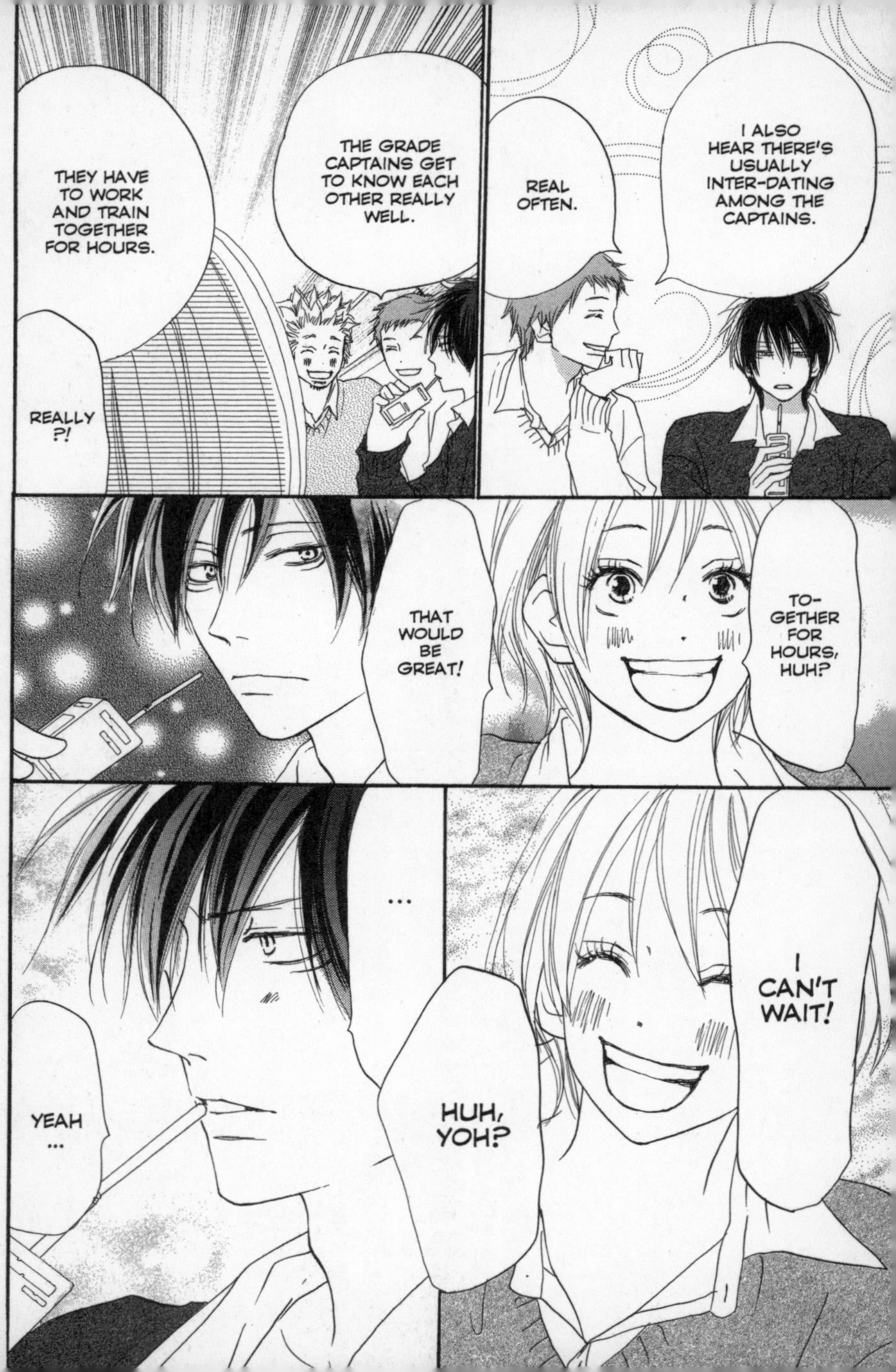
I ALSO HEAR THERE'S USUALLY INTER-DATING AMONG THE CAPTAINS.
REAL OFTEN.
THE GRADE CAPTAINS GET TO KNOW EACH OTHER REALLY WELL.
THEY HAVE TO WORK AND TRAIN TOGETHER FOR HOURS.
REALLY ?!
TO-GETHER FOR HOURS, HUH?
THAT WOULD BE GREAT!
I CAN'T WAIT!
HUH, YOH?
...
YEAH ...

SCHOOL-WIDE PRACTICE
SPORTS
FESTIVAL
ROOTERS: SPORTS FIELD
BANNERS: GYM

BZZ

CHATTER

OH, THERE HE IS!

YOH ...

WHERE'S YOH?

25

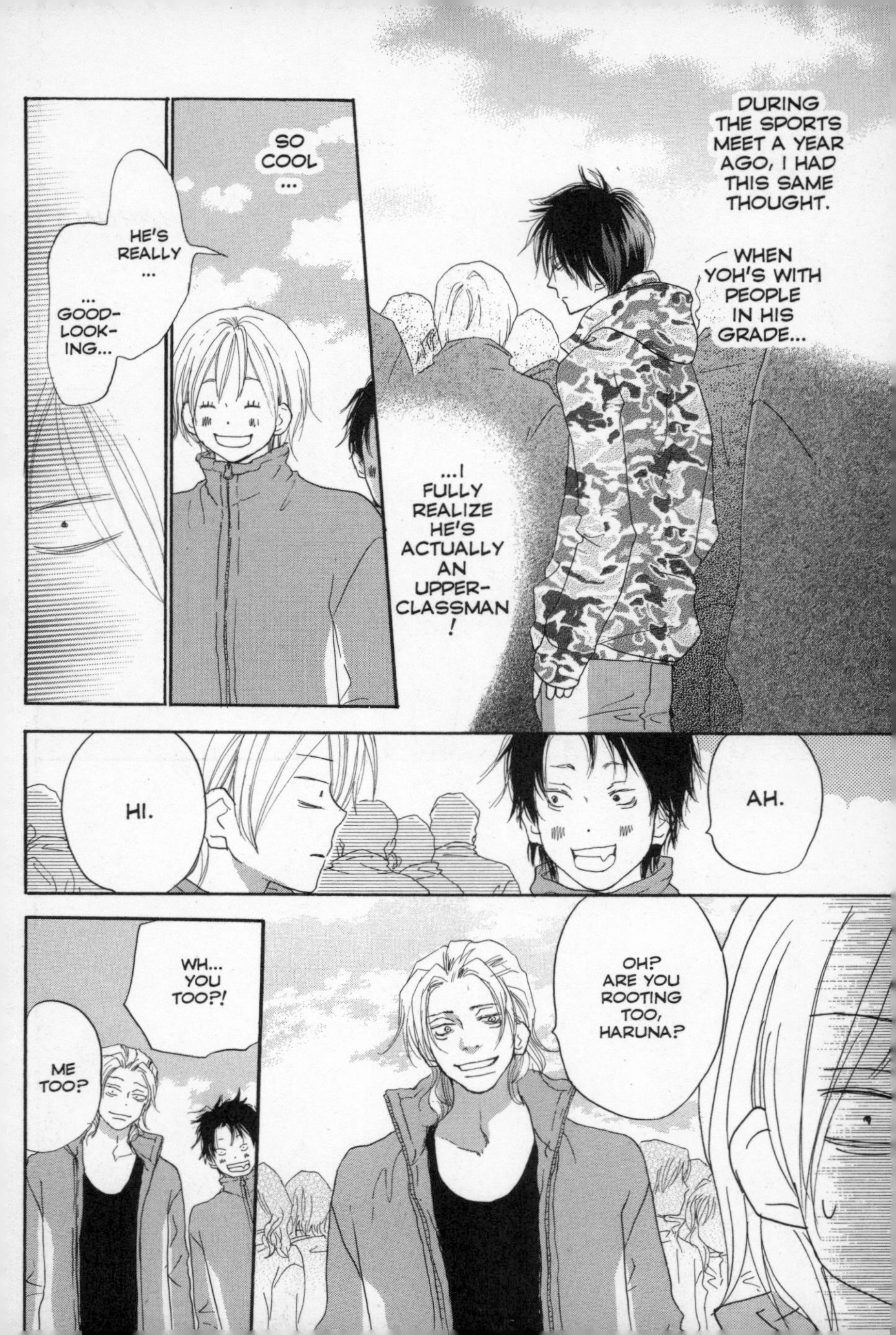
DURING THE SPORTS MEET A YEAR AGO, I HAD THIS SAME THOUGHT.
WHEN YOH'S WITH PEOPLE IN HIS GRADE...
...I FULLY REALIZE HE'S ACTUALLY AN UPPER-CLASSMAN!
SO COOL ...
HE'S REALLY ...
... GOOD-LOOKING...
AH.
HI.
OH? ARE YOU ROOTING TOO, HARUNA?
WH... YOU TOO?!
ME TOO?

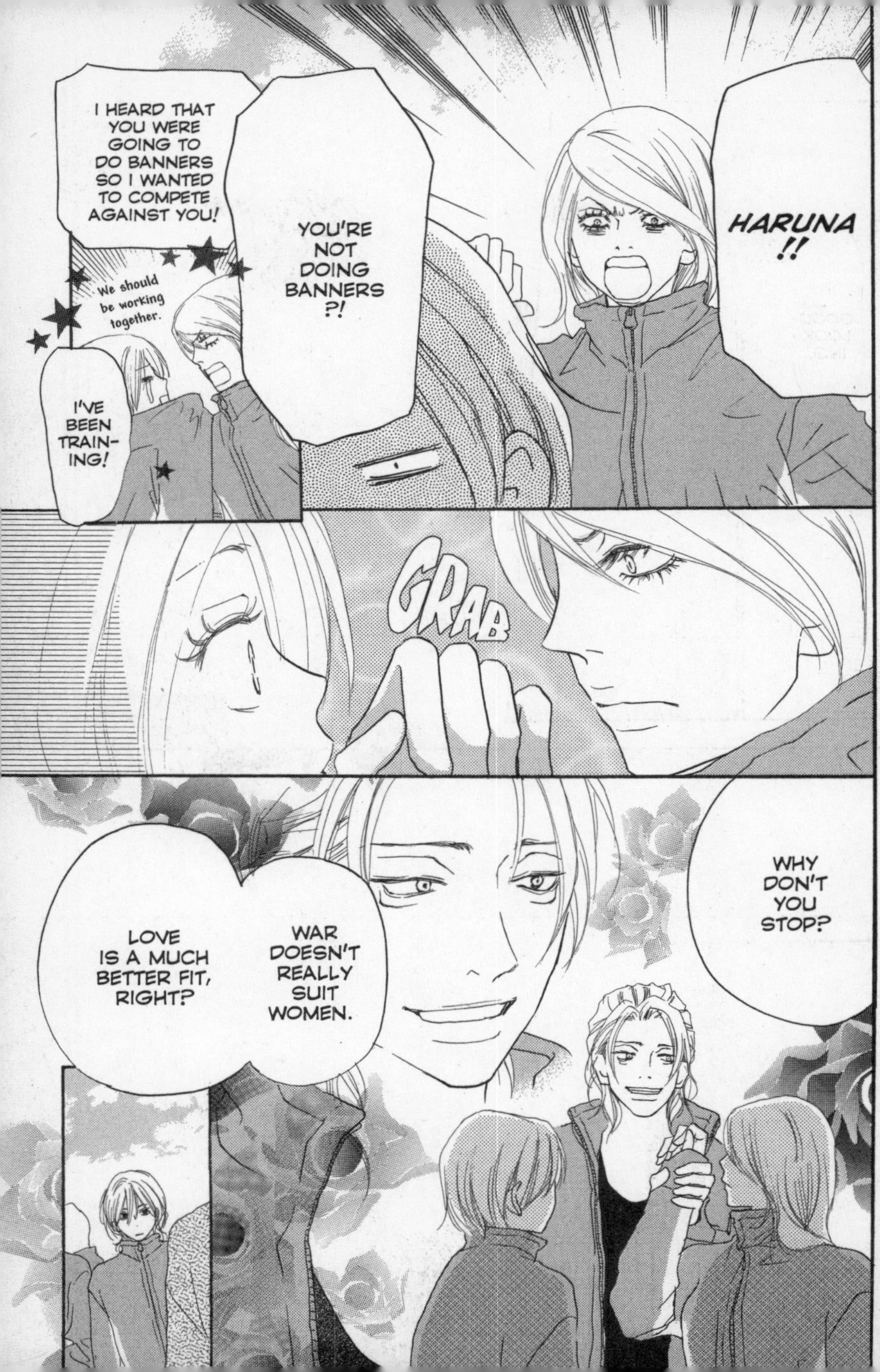
HARUNA!!
YOU'RE NOT DOING BANNERS?!
I HEARD THAT YOU WERE GOING TO DO BANNERS SO I WANTED TO COMPETE AGAINST YOU!
We should be working together.
I'VE BEEN TRAIN-ING!
GRAB
WHY DON'T YOU STOP?
WAR DOESN'T REALLY SUIT WOMEN.
LOVE IS A MUCH BETTER FIT, RIGHT?

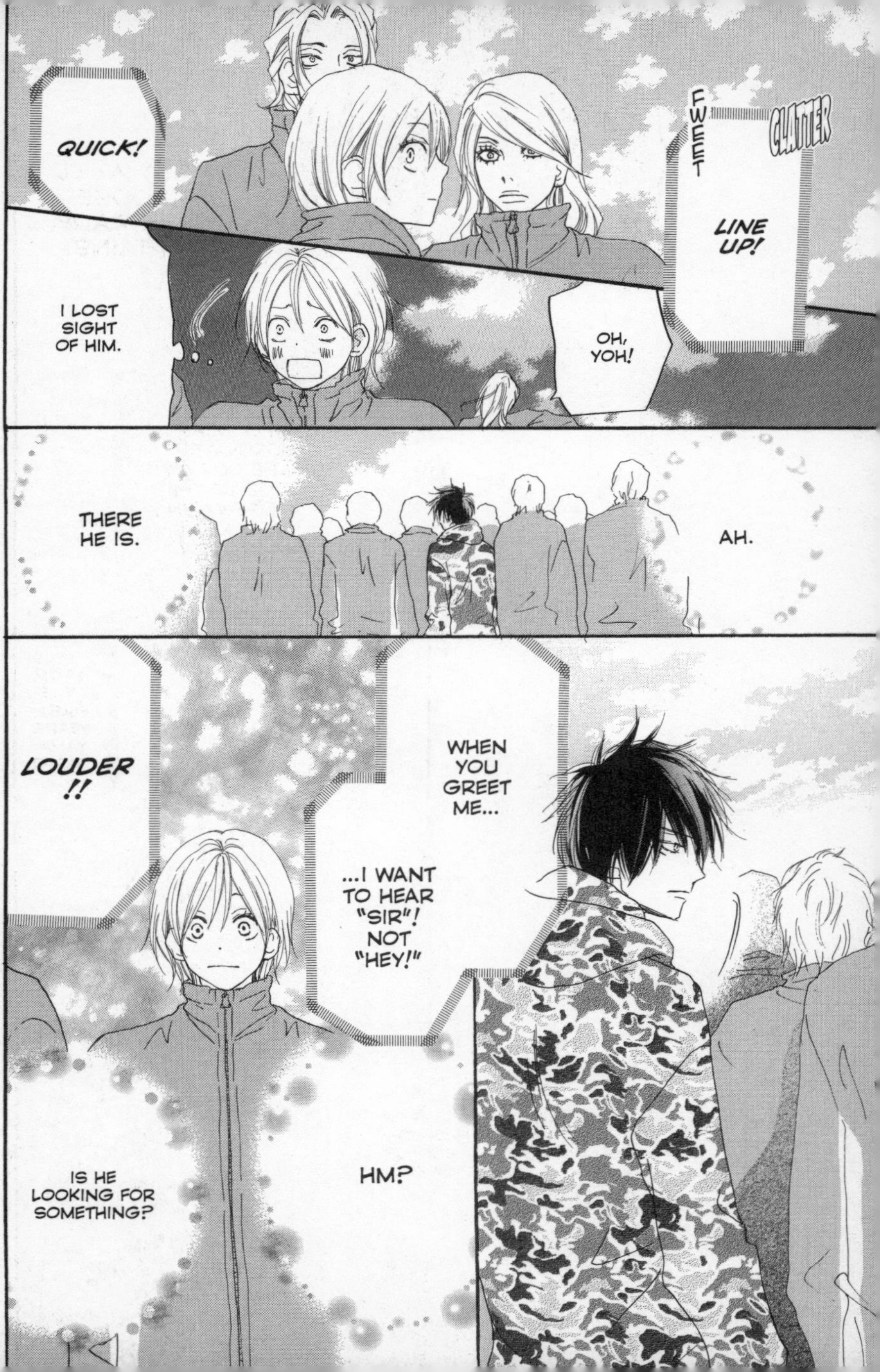
CLATTER
FWEET
LINE UP!
QUICK!
OH, YOH!
I LOST SIGHT OF HIM.
AH.
THERE HE IS.
WHEN YOU GREET ME...
...I WANT TO HEAR "SIR"! NOT "HEY!"
LOUDER!!
HM?
IS HE LOOKING FOR SOMETHING?

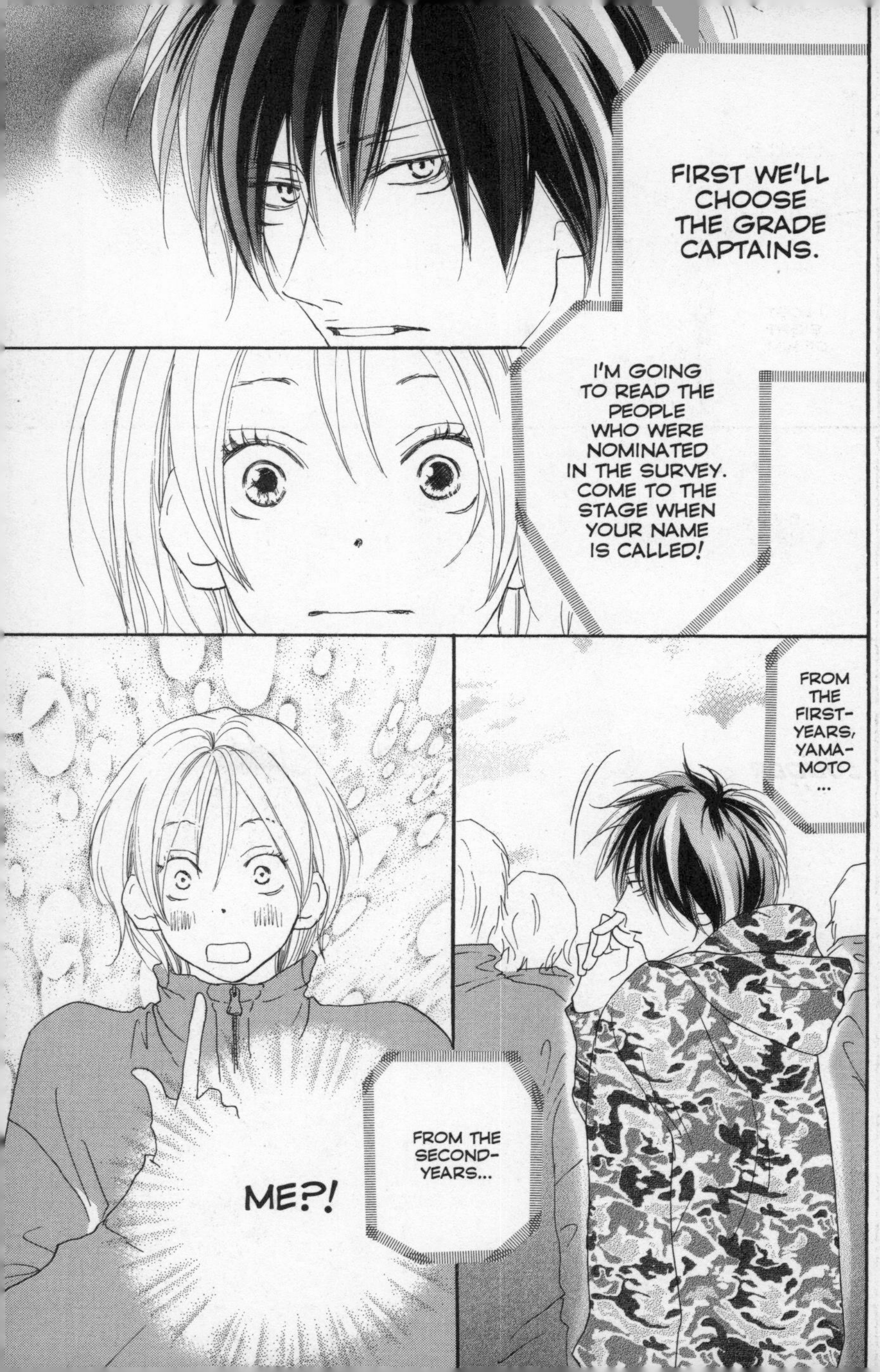
FIRST WE'LL CHOOSE THE GRADE CAPTAINS.
I'M GOING TO READ THE PEOPLE WHO WERE NOMINATED IN THE SURVEY. COME TO THE STAGE WHEN YOUR NAME IS CALLED!
FROM THE FIRST-YEARS, YAMA-MOTO...
FROM THE SECOND-YEARS...
ME?!

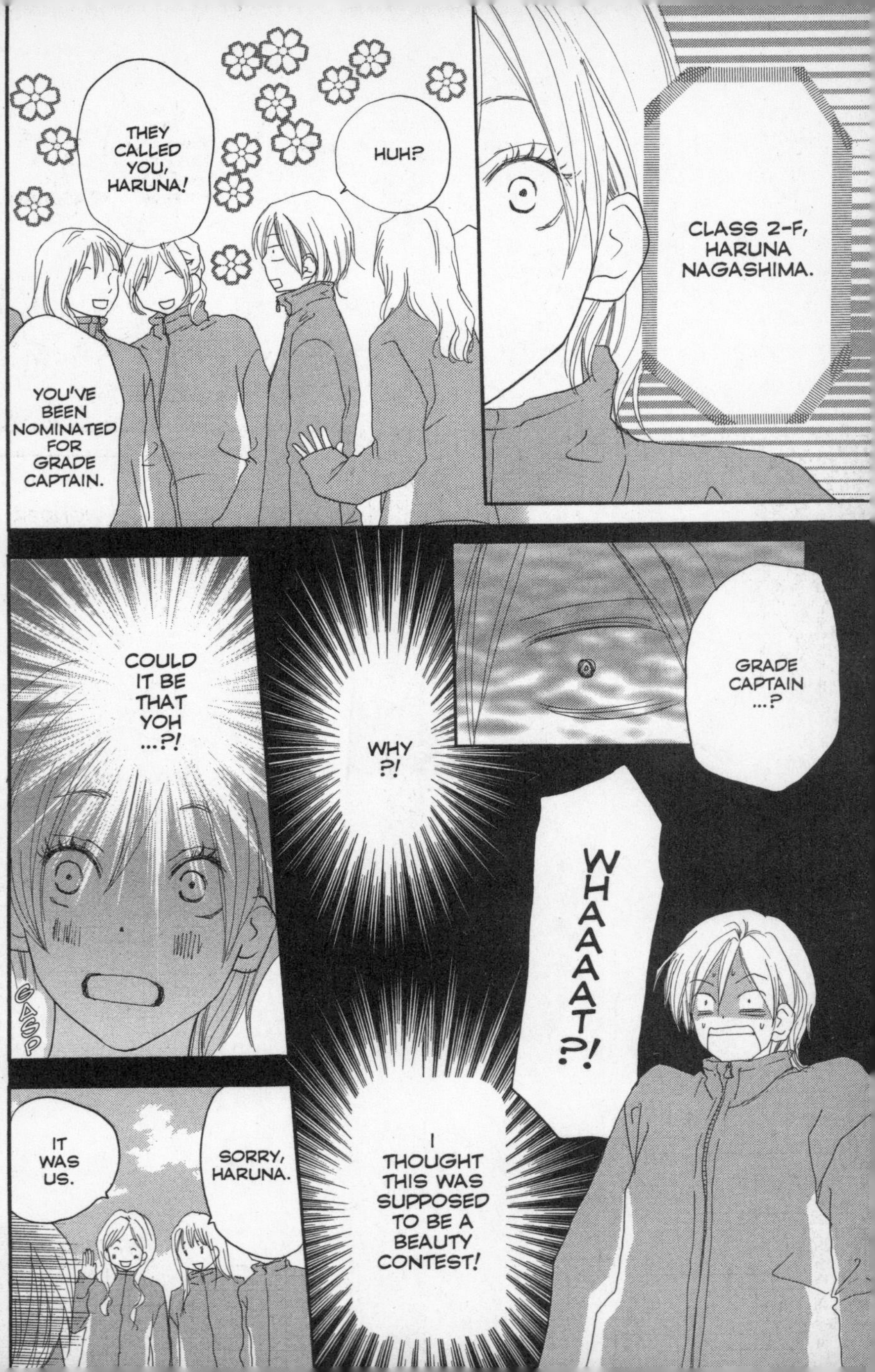
CLASS 2-F, HARUNA NAGASHIMA.
THEY CALLED YOU, HARUNA!
HUH?
YOU'VE BEEN NOMINATED FOR GRADE CAPTAIN.
GRADE CAPTAIN ...?
WHAAAAT?!
WHY ?!
COULD IT BE THAT YOH ...?!
GASP
I THOUGHT THIS WAS SUPPOSED TO BE A BEAUTY CONTEST!
SORRY, HARUNA.
IT WAS US.

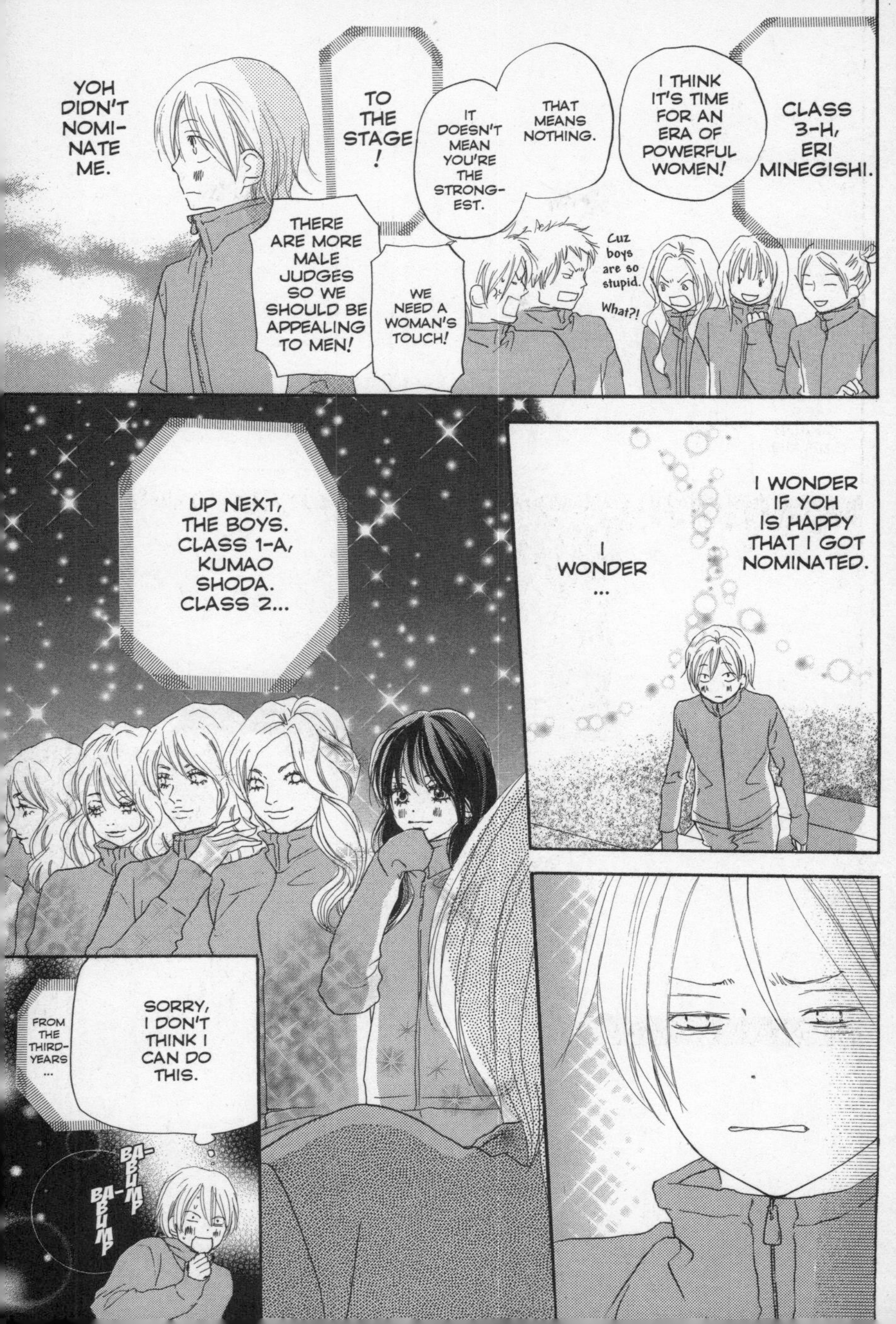
CLASS 3-H, ERI MINEGISHI.
I THINK IT'S TIME FOR AN ERA OF POWERFUL WOMEN!
Cuz boys are so stupid.
What?!
THAT MEANS NOTHING.
IT DOESN'T MEAN YOU'RE THE STRONG-EST.
WE NEED A WOMAN'S TOUCH!
TO THE STAGE!
THERE ARE MORE MALE JUDGES SO WE SHOULD BE APPEALING TO MEN!
YOH DIDN'T NOMI-NATE ME.
I WONDER IF YOH IS HAPPY THAT I GOT NOMINATED.
I WONDER ...
UP NEXT, THE BOYS. CLASS 1-A, KUMAO SHODA. CLASS 2...
FROM THE THIRD-YEARS ...
SORRY, I DON'T THINK I CAN DO THIS.
BA-BUMP
BA-BUMP

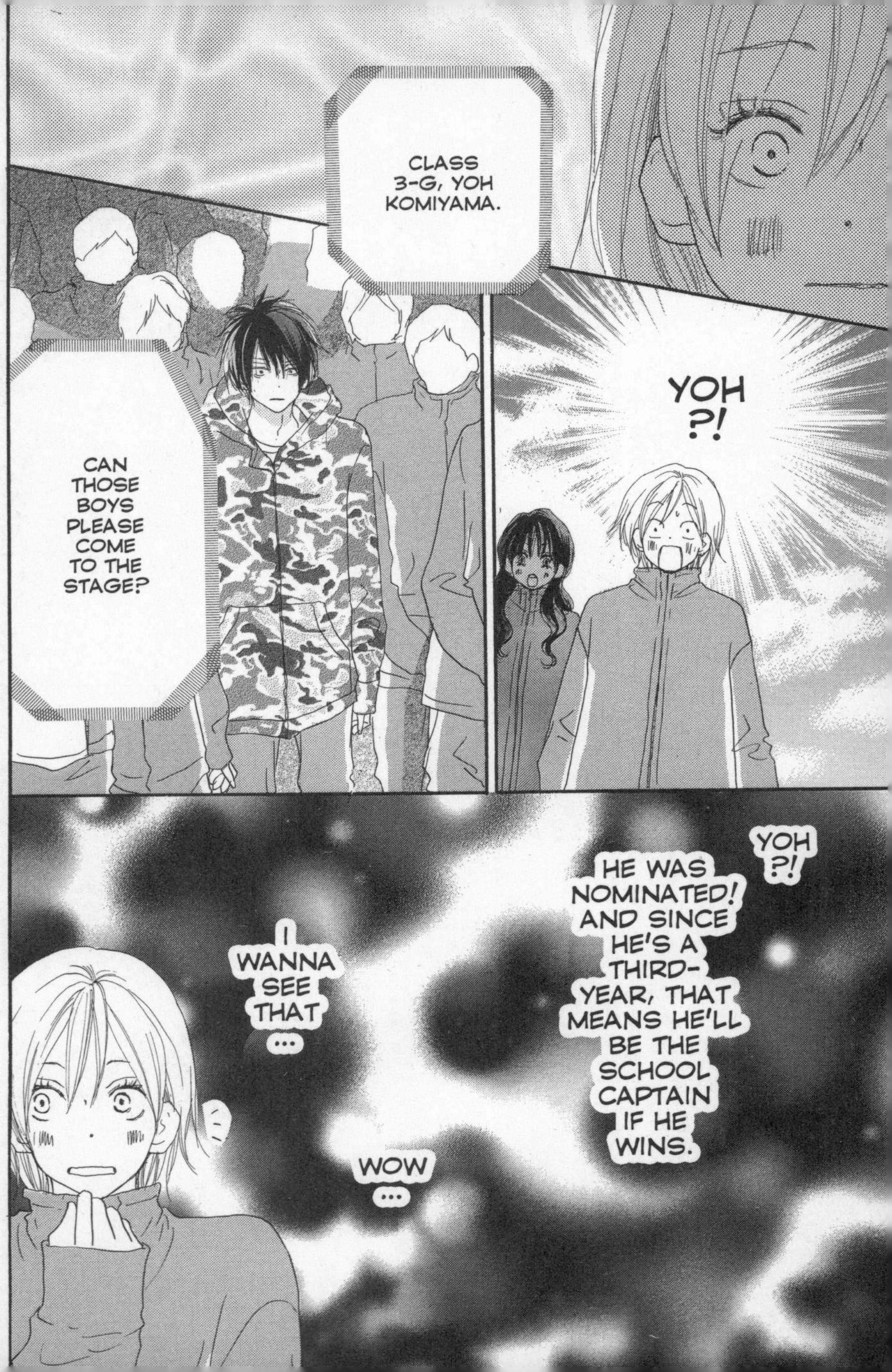
CLASS 3-G, YOH KOMIYAMA.
YOH ?!
CAN THOSE BOYS PLEASE COME TO THE STAGE?
YOH ?!
HE WAS NOMINATED! AND SINCE HE'S A THIRD-YEAR, THAT MEANS HE'LL BE THE SCHOOL CAPTAIN IF HE WINS.
I WANNA SEE THAT ...
WOW ...

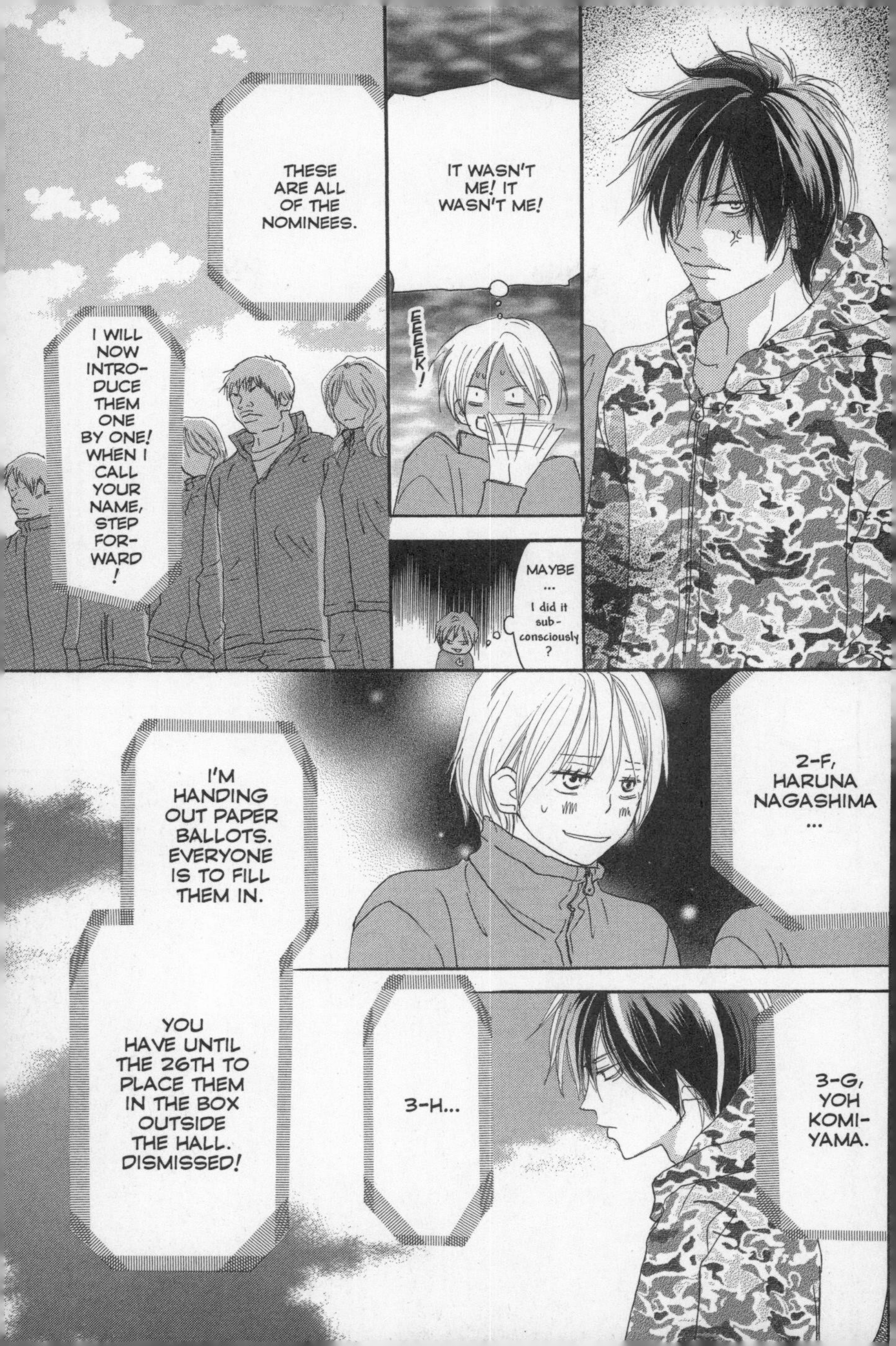
IT WASN'T ME! IT WASN'T ME!
EEEEK!
MAYBE ... I did it sub-consciously?
THESE ARE ALL OF THE NOMINEES.
I WILL NOW INTRO-DUCE THEM ONE BY ONE! WHEN I CALL YOUR NAME, STEP FOR-WARD!
2-F, HARUNA NAGASHIMA ...
3-G, YOH KOMI-YAMA.
3-H...
I'M HANDING OUT PAPER BALLOTS. EVERYONE IS TO FILL THEM IN.
YOU HAVE UNTIL THE 26TH TO PLACE THEM IN THE BOX OUTSIDE THE HALL. DISMISSED!

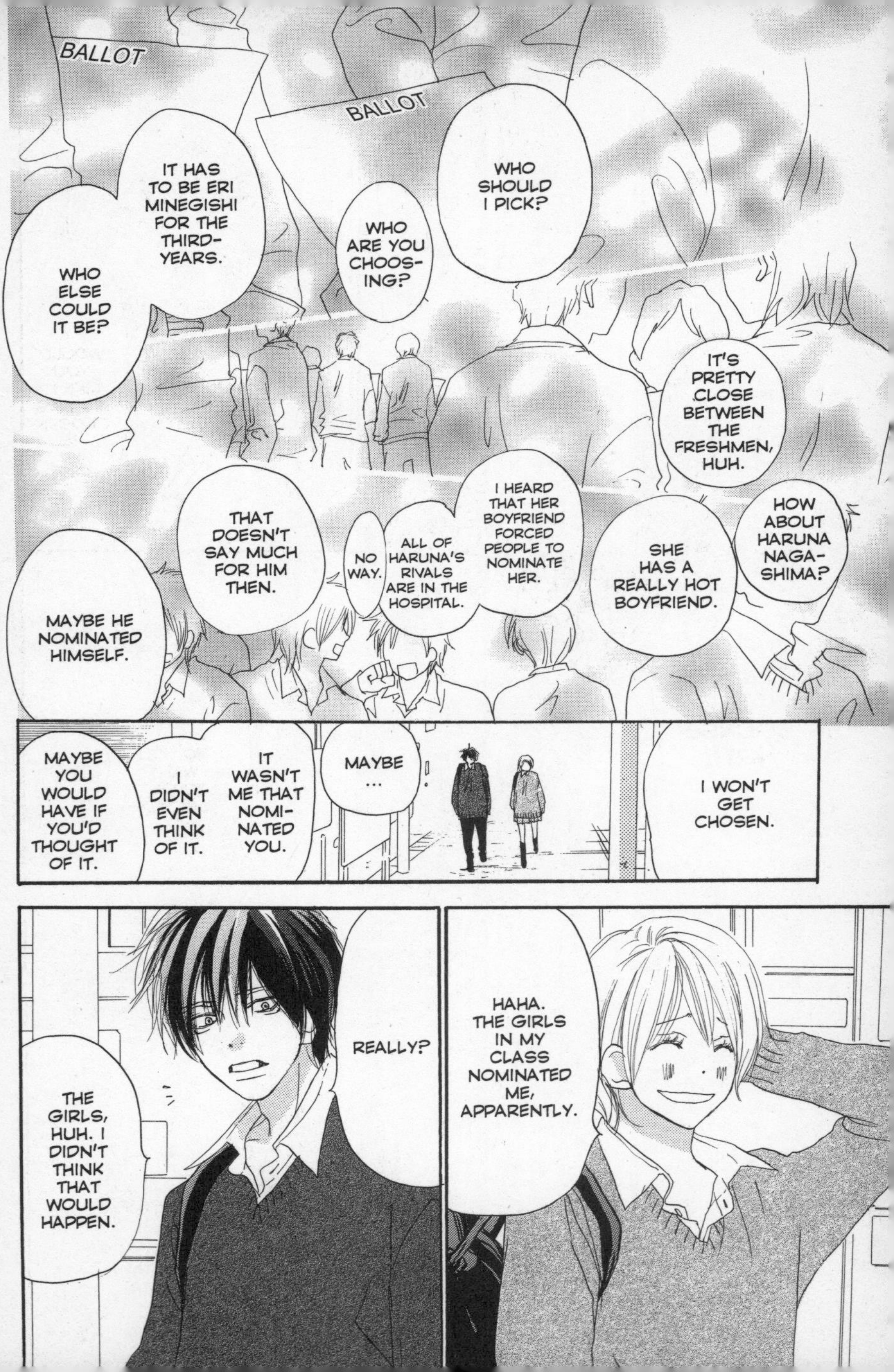
BALLOT
BALLOT
WHO SHOULD I PICK?
WHO ARE YOU CHOOSING?
IT HAS TO BE ERI MINEGISHI FOR THE THIRD-YEARS.
WHO ELSE COULD IT BE?
IT'S PRETTY CLOSE BETWEEN THE FRESHMEN, HUH.
HOW ABOUT HARUNA NAGASHIMA?
SHE HAS A REALLY HOT BOYFRIEND.
I HEARD THAT HER BOYFRIEND FORCED PEOPLE TO NOMINATE HER.
ALL OF HARUNA'S RIVALS ARE IN THE HOSPITAL.
NO WAY.
THAT DOESN'T SAY MUCH FOR HIM THEN.
MAYBE HE NOMINATED HIMSELF.
I WON'T GET CHOSEN.
MAYBE...
IT WASN'T ME THAT NOMINATED YOU.
I DIDN'T EVEN THINK OF IT.
MAYBE YOU WOULD HAVE IF YOU'D THOUGHT OF IT.
HAHA. THE GIRLS IN MY CLASS NOMINATED ME, APPARENTLY.
REALLY?
THE GIRLS, HUH. I DIDN'T THINK THAT WOULD HAPPEN.

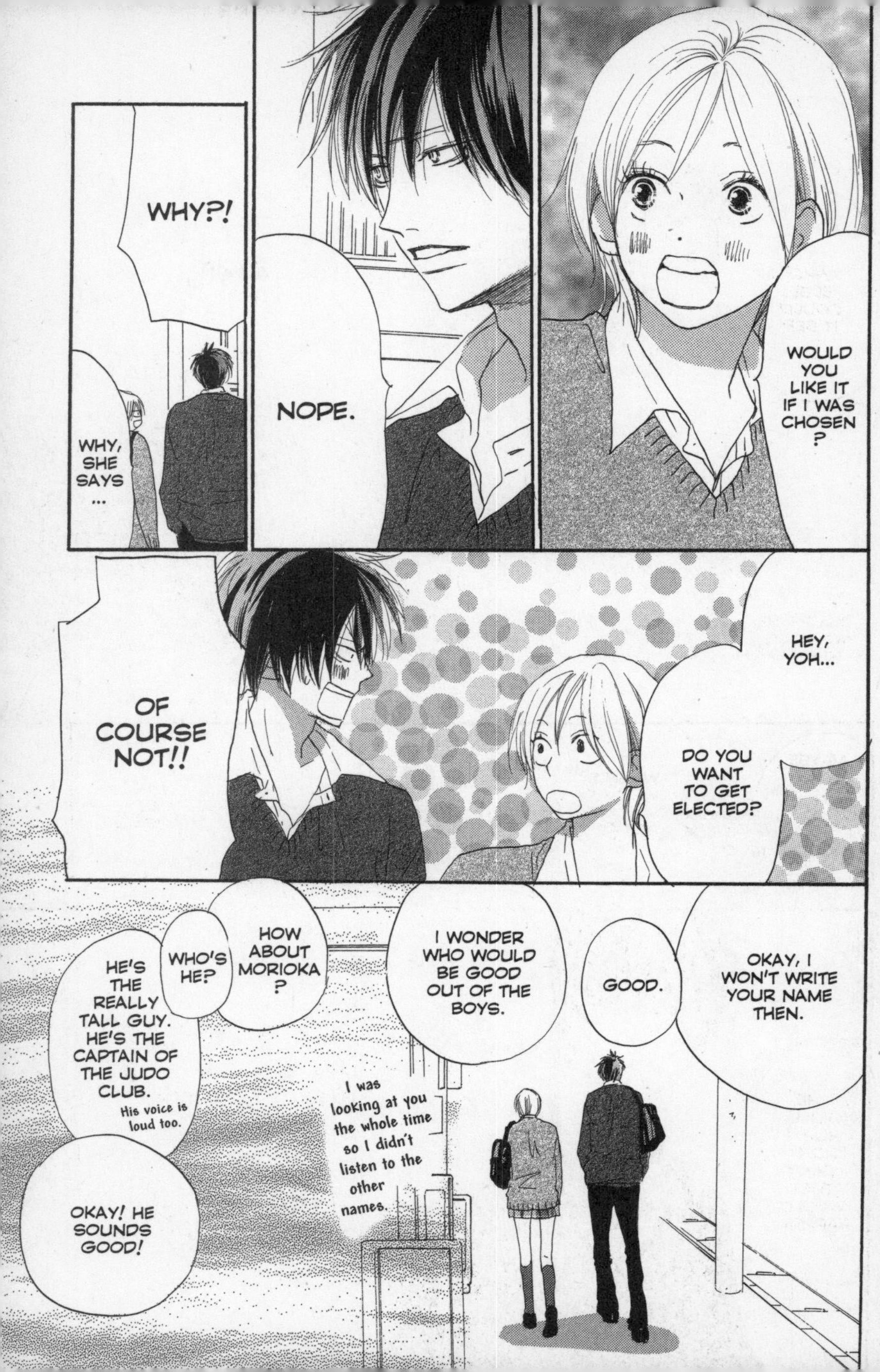
WOULD YOU LIKE IT IF I WAS CHOSEN?
NOPE.
WHY?!
WHY, SHE SAYS ...
HEY, YOH...
DO YOU WANT TO GET ELECTED?
OF COURSE NOT!!
OKAY, I WON'T WRITE YOUR NAME THEN.
GOOD.
I WONDER WHO WOULD BE GOOD OUT OF THE BOYS.
HOW ABOUT MORIOKA?
WHO'S HE?
HE'S THE REALLY TALL GUY. HE'S THE CAPTAIN OF THE JUDO CLUB.
His voice is loud too.
I was looking at you the whole time so I didn't listen to the other names.
OKAY! HE SOUNDS GOOD!

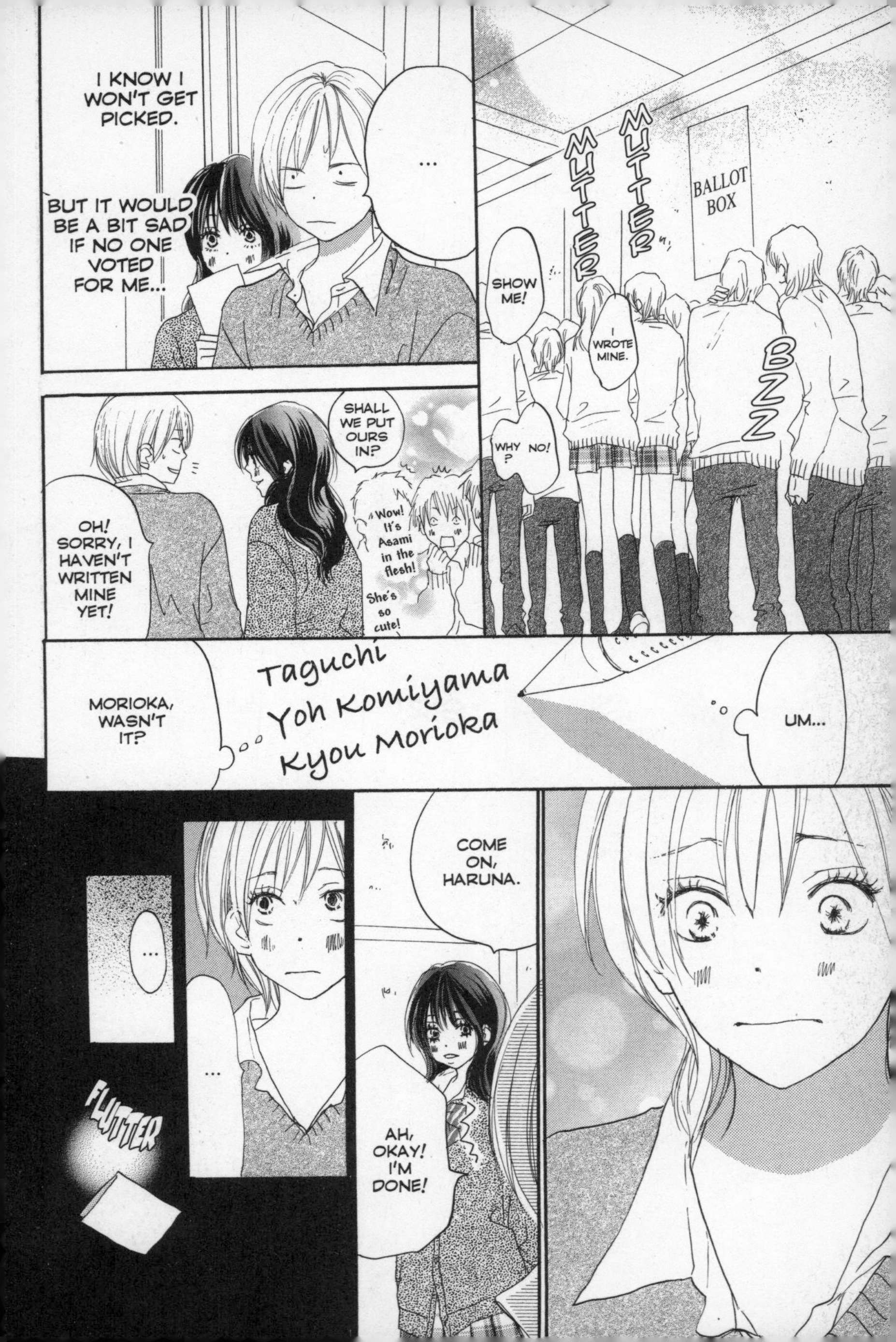
BALLOT BOX
MUTTER
MUTTER
SHOW ME!
I WROTE MINE.
BZZ
NO!
WHY?
...
I KNOW I WON'T GET PICKED.
BUT IT WOULD BE A BIT SAD IF NO ONE VOTED FOR ME...
SHALL WE PUT OURS IN?
Wow! It's Asami in the flesh!
She's so cute!
OH! SORRY, I HAVEN'T WRITTEN MINE YET!
UM...
Taguchi
Yoh Komiyama
Kyou Morioka
MORIOKA, WASN'T IT?
COME ON, HARUNA.
AH, OKAY! I'M DONE!
...
...
FLUTTER

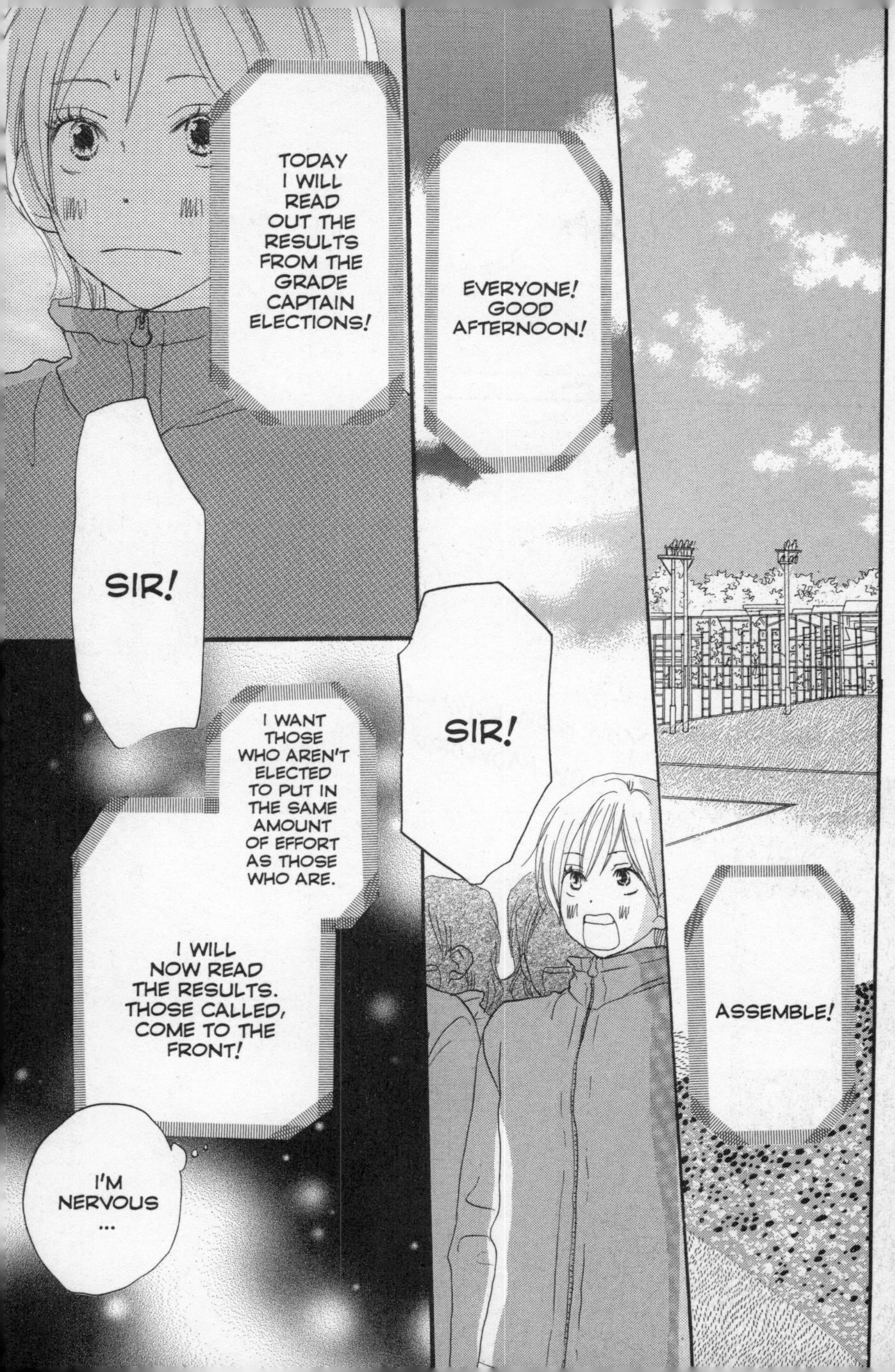
ASSEMBLE!
EVERYONE! GOOD AFTERNOON!
SIR!
TODAY I WILL READ OUT THE RESULTS FROM THE GRADE CAPTAIN ELECTIONS!
SIR!
I WANT THOSE WHO AREN'T ELECTED TO PUT IN THE SAME AMOUNT OF EFFORT AS THOSE WHO ARE.
I WILL NOW READ THE RESULTS. THOSE CALLED, COME TO THE FRONT!
I'M NERVOUS ...

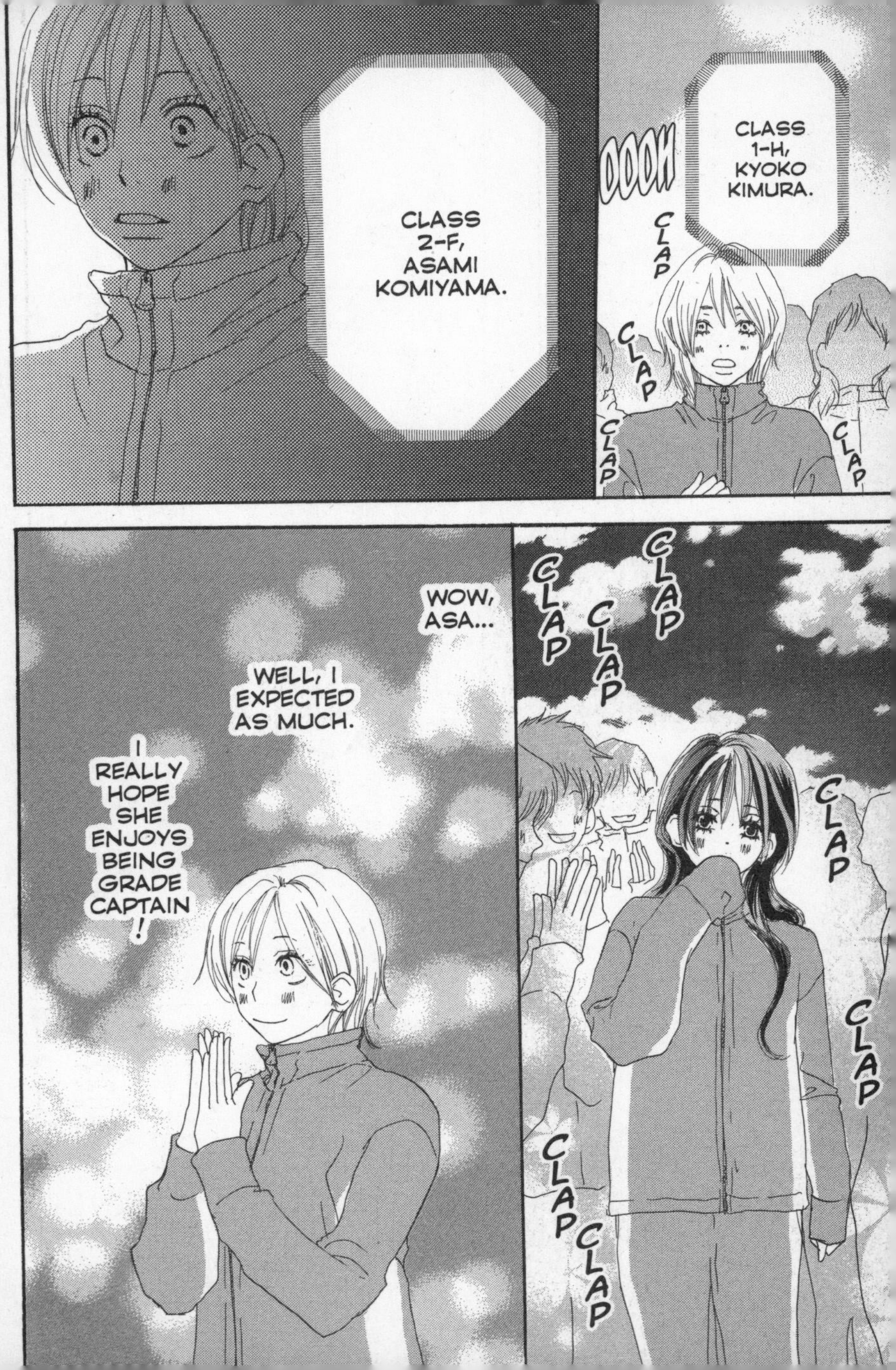
CLASS 1-H, KYOKO KIMURA.
OOOH
CLAP
CLAP
CLAP
CLAP
CLAP
CLASS 2-F, ASAMI KOMIYAMA.
CLAP
CLAP
CLAP
CLAP
CLAP
CLAP
CLAP
WOW, ASA...
WELL, I EXPECTED AS MUCH.
I REALLY HOPE SHE ENJOYS BEING GRADE CAPTAIN!

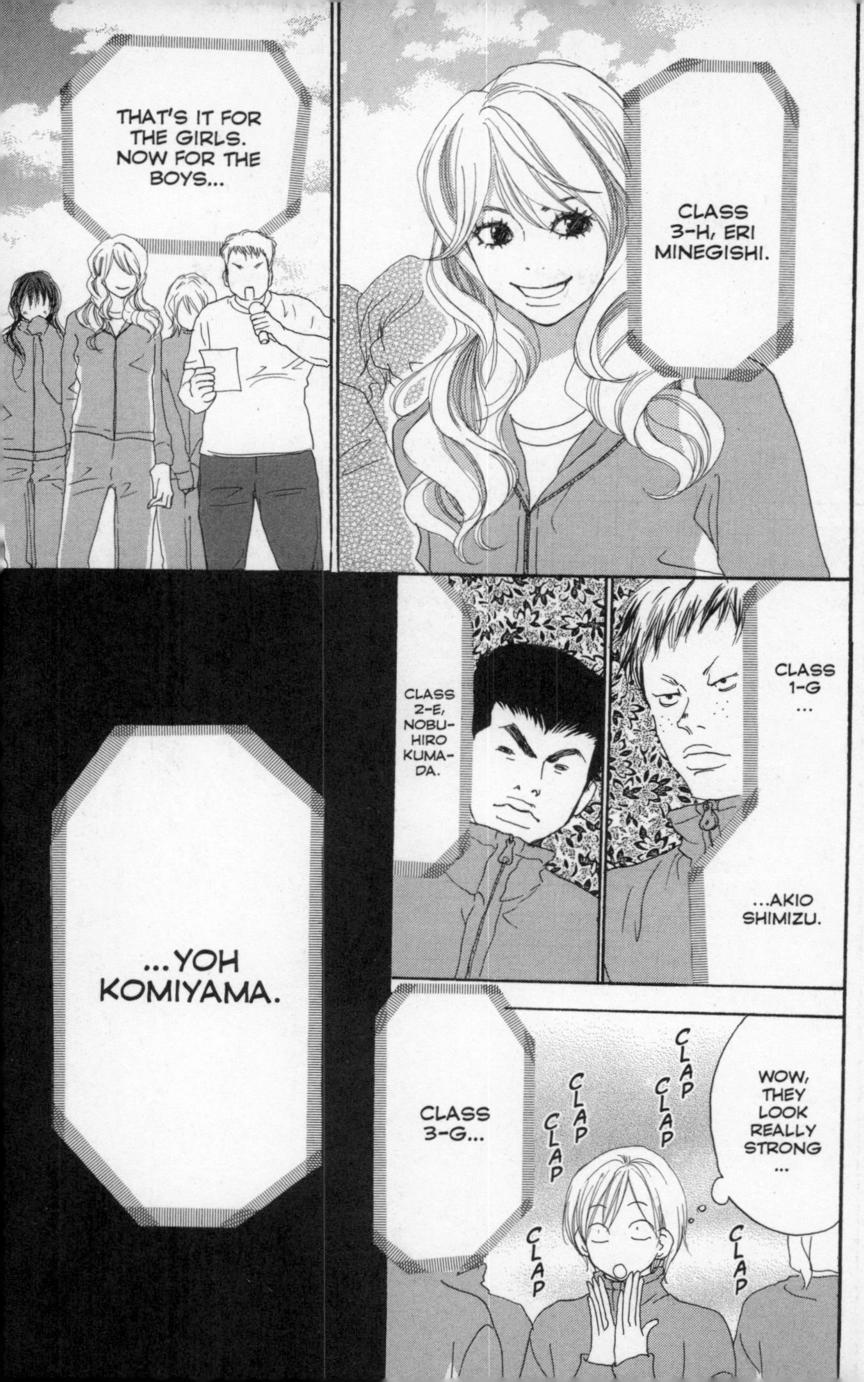
CLASS 3-H, ERI MINEGISHI.
THAT'S IT FOR THE GIRLS. NOW FOR THE BOYS...
CLASS 1-G ...
...AKIO SHIMIZU.
CLASS 2-E, NOBUHIRO KUMADA.
WOW, THEY LOOK REALLY STRONG ...
CLAP CLAP
CLAP CLAP
CLAP
CLAP
CLASS 3-G...
...YOH KOMIYAMA.

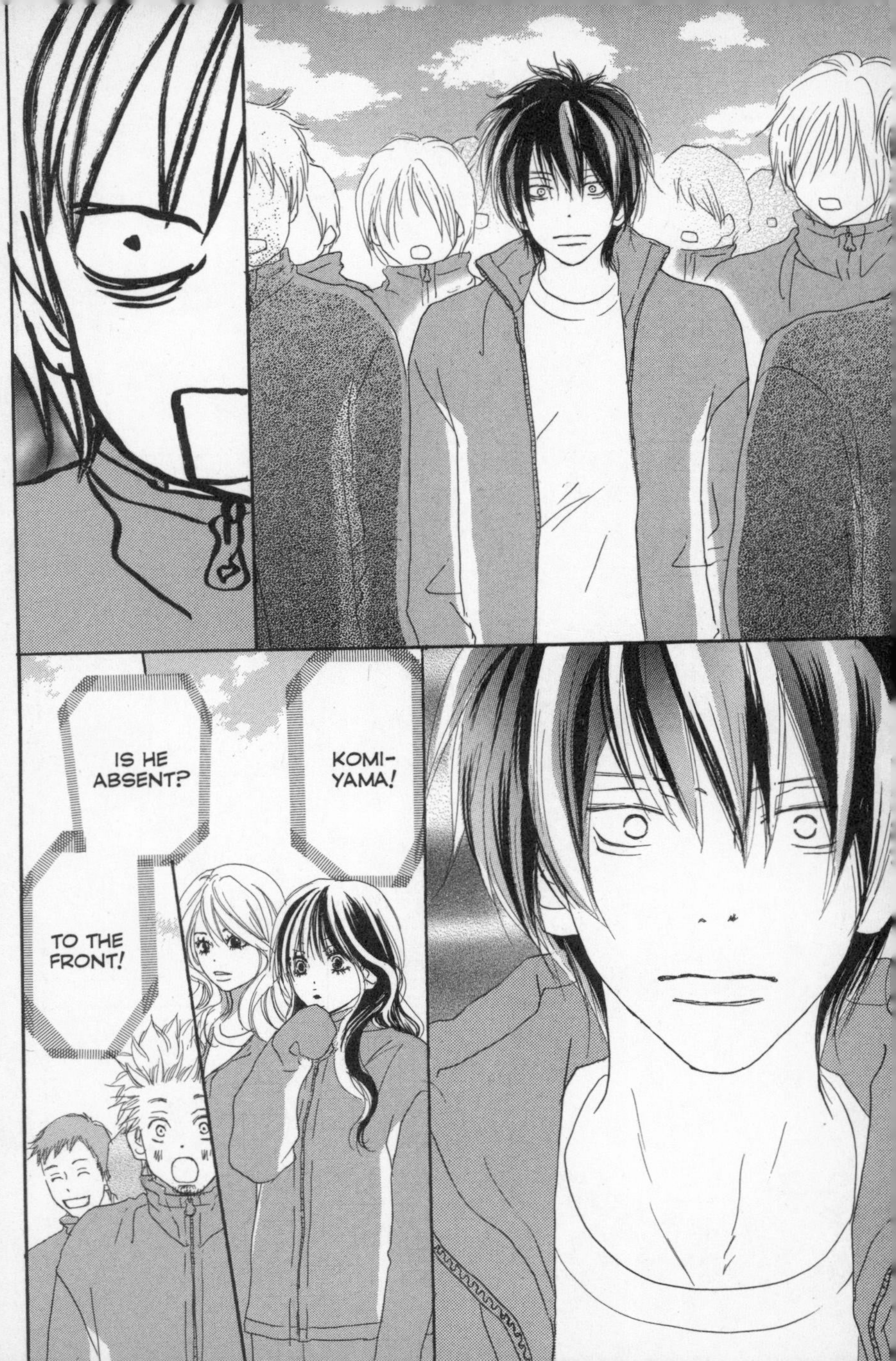
KOMI-
YAMA!
IS HE
ABSENT?
TO THE
FRONT!

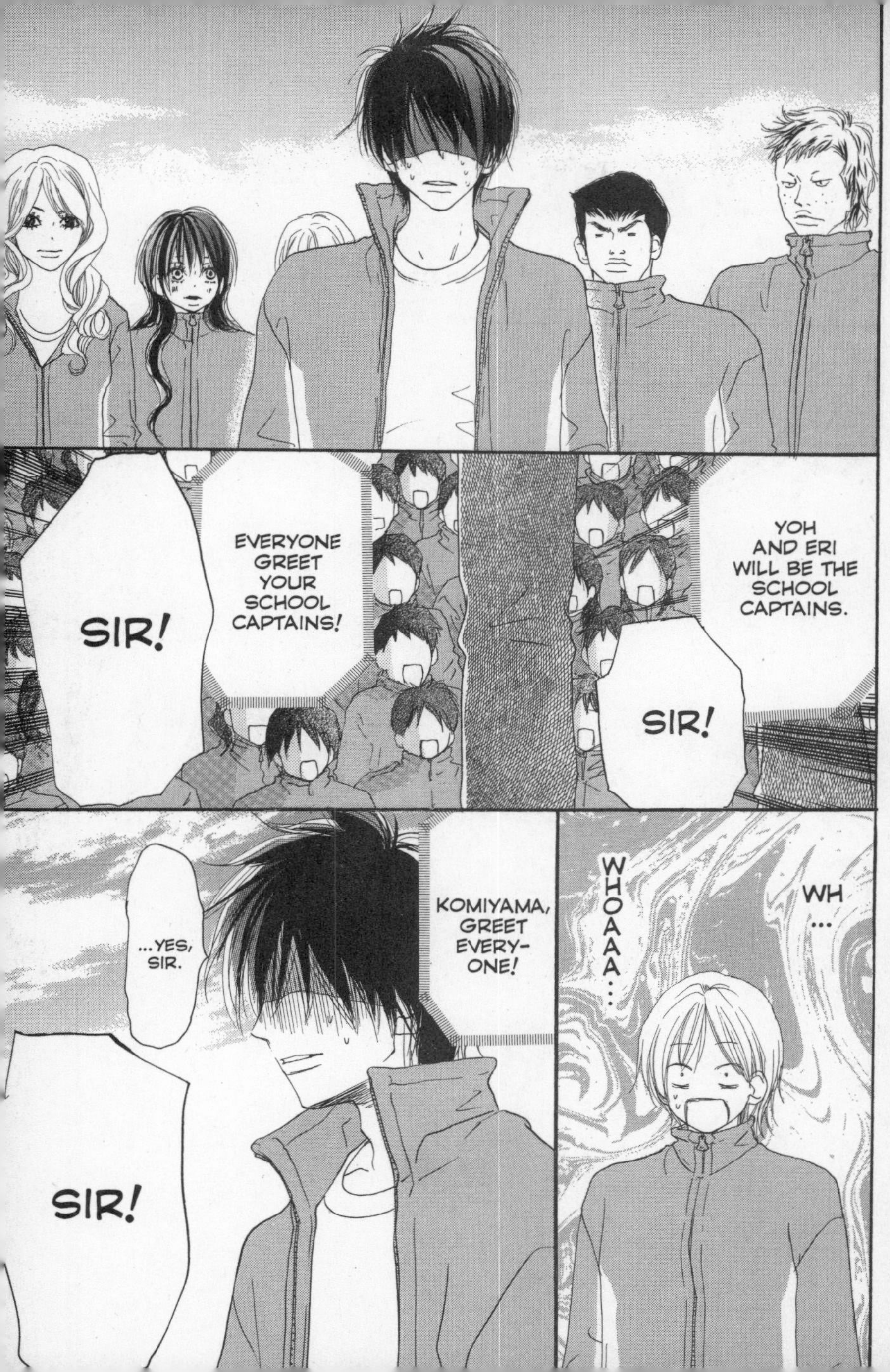
YOH AND ERI WILL BE THE SCHOOL CAPTAINS.
SIR!
EVERYONE GREET YOUR SCHOOL CAPTAINS!
SIR!
WH...
WHOAAA...
KOMIYAMA, GREET EVERY-ONE!
...YES, SIR.
SIR!

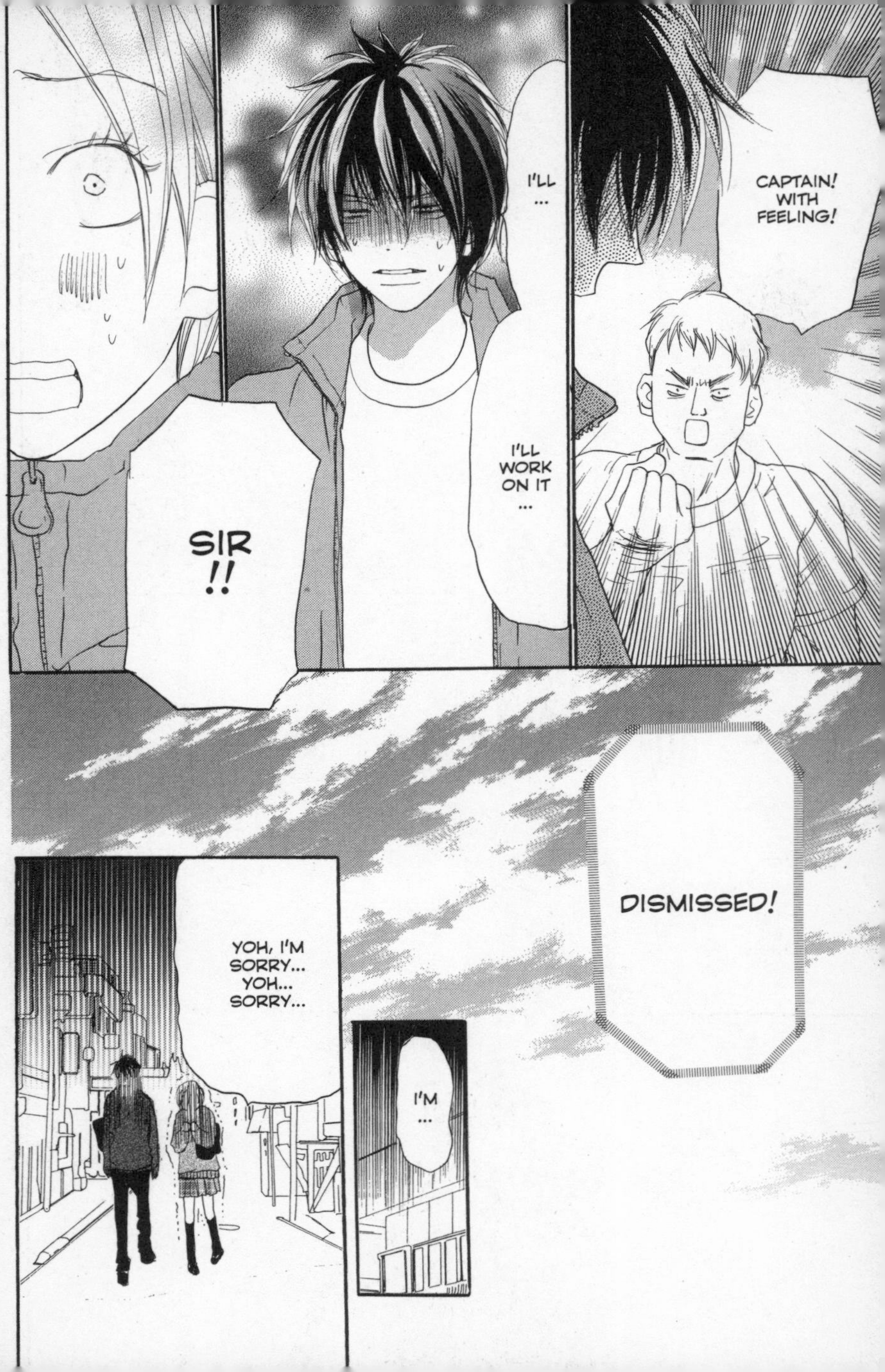
CAPTAIN! WITH FEELING!
I'LL ...
I'LL WORK ON IT ...
SIR !!
DISMISSED!
I'M ...
YOH, I'M SORRY... YOH... SORRY...

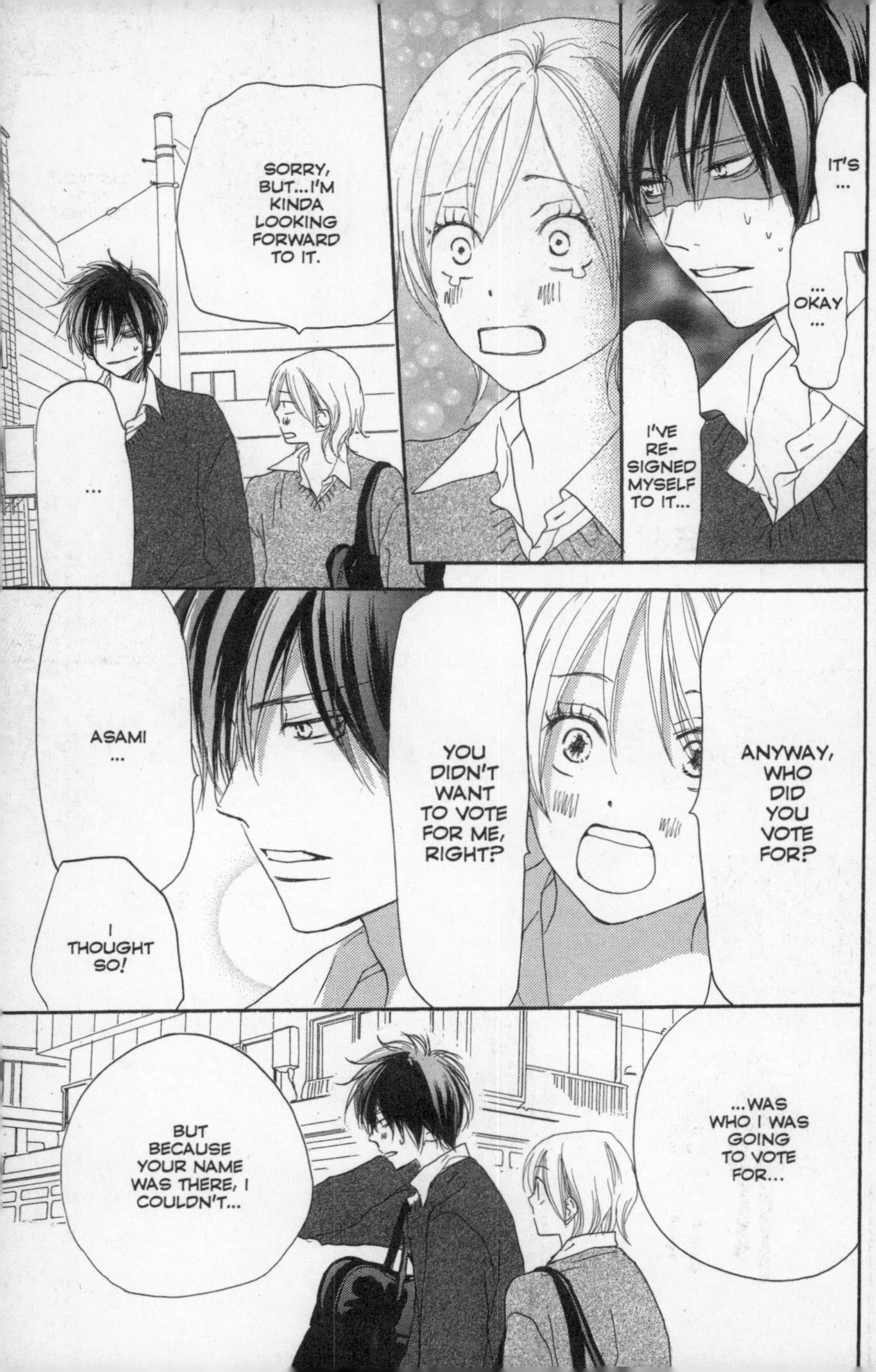
IT'S ...
... OKAY ...
I'VE RE-SIGNED MYSELF TO IT...
SORRY, BUT...I'M KINDA LOOKING FORWARD TO IT.
...
ANYWAY, WHO DID YOU VOTE FOR?
YOU DIDN'T WANT TO VOTE FOR ME, RIGHT?
ASAMI ...
I THOUGHT SO!
...WAS WHO I WAS GOING TO VOTE FOR...
BUT BECAUSE YOUR NAME WAS THERE, I COULDN'T...

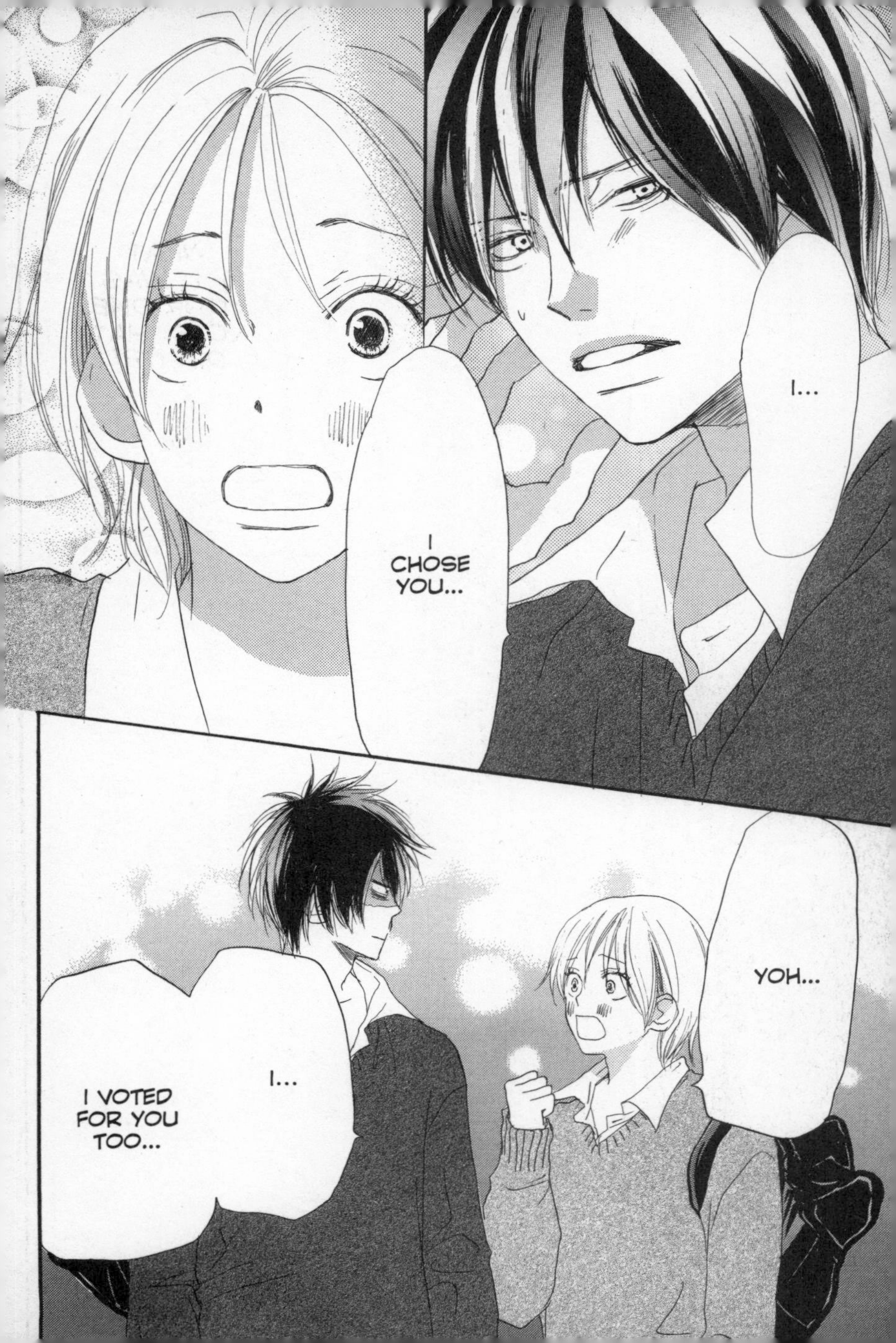
I...
I CHOSE YOU...
YOH...
I...
I VOTED FOR YOU TOO...

WHAT IF IT WAS YOUR ONE VOTE THAT DID IT?!
I'M SORRY! I COULDN'T *NOT* CHOOSE YOU!
SPORT FESTIVA 45 DAYS LEFT

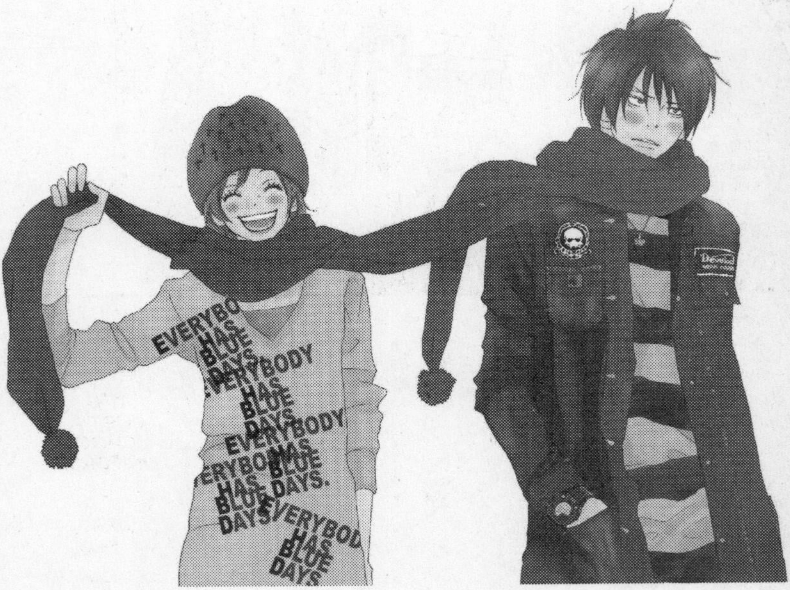
EVERYBODY HAS BLUE DAYS.

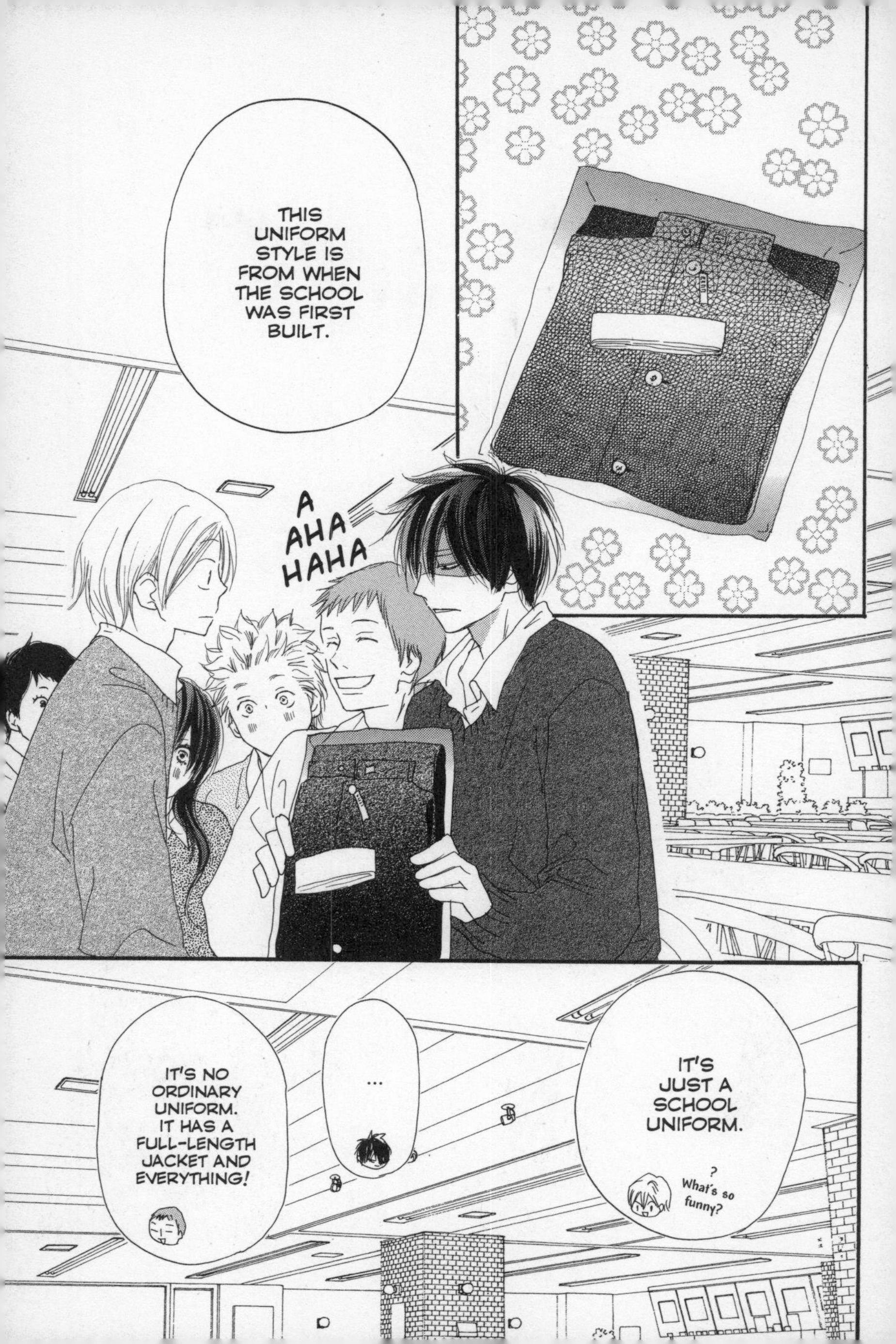
THIS UNIFORM STYLE IS FROM WHEN THE SCHOOL WAS FIRST BUILT.
A AHA HAHA
IT'S JUST A SCHOOL UNIFORM.
? What's so funny?
...
IT'S NO ORDINARY UNIFORM. IT HAS A FULL-LENGTH JACKET AND EVERYTHING!

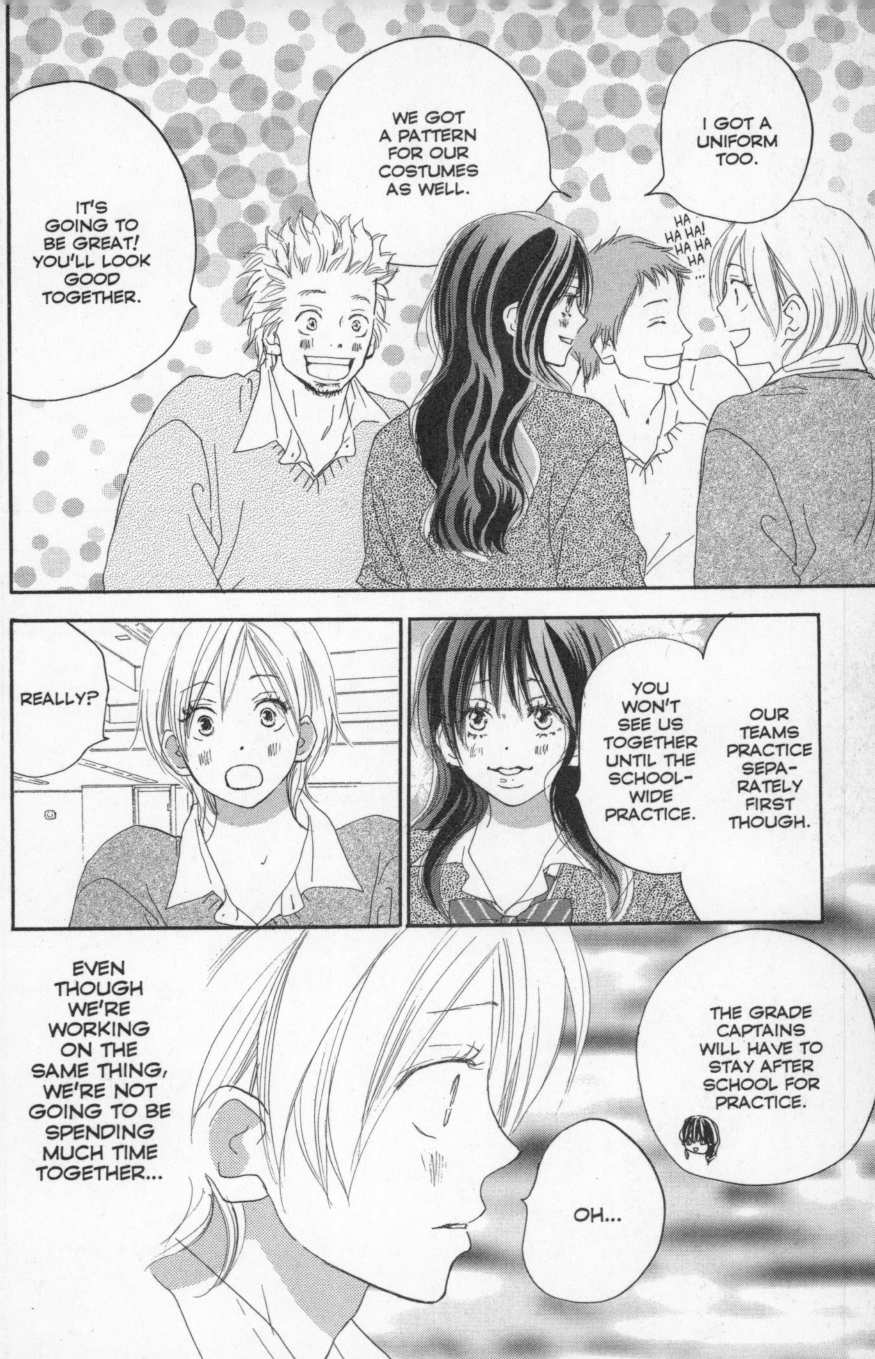
I GOT A UNIFORM TOO.
HA HA HA! HA HA HA ...
WE GOT A PATTERN FOR OUR COSTUMES AS WELL.
IT'S GOING TO BE GREAT! YOU'LL LOOK GOOD TOGETHER.
YOU WON'T SEE US TOGETHER UNTIL THE SCHOOL-WIDE PRACTICE.
OUR TEAMS PRACTICE SEPARATELY FIRST THOUGH.
REALLY?
THE GRADE CAPTAINS WILL HAVE TO STAY AFTER SCHOOL FOR PRACTICE.
OH...
EVEN THOUGH WE'RE WORKING ON THE SAME THING, WE'RE NOT GOING TO BE SPENDING MUCH TIME TOGETHER...

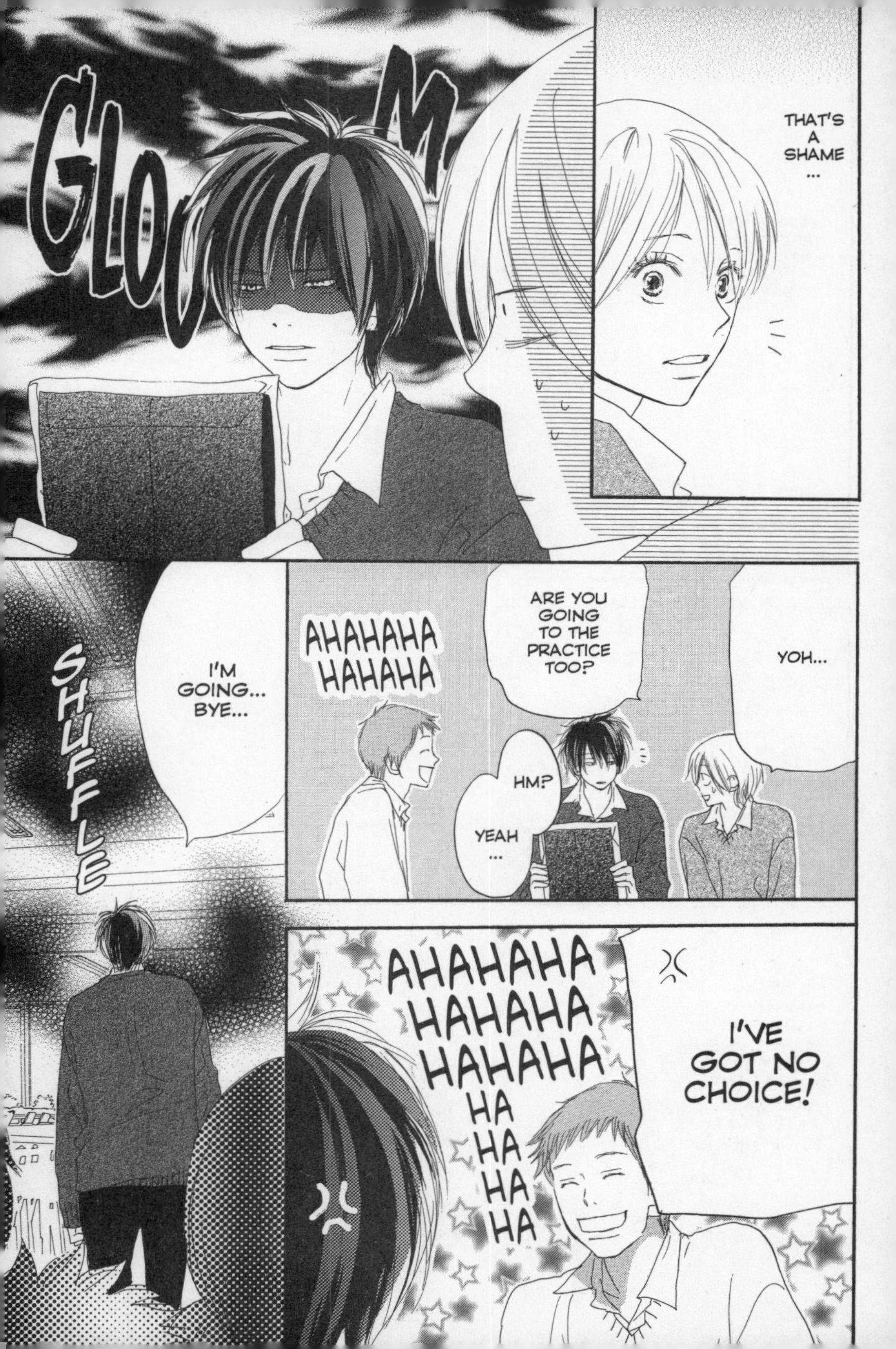
THAT'S A SHAME ...
GLOOM
YOH...
ARE YOU GOING TO THE PRACTICE TOO?
AHAHAHA HAHAHA
HM?
YEAH ...
I'VE GOT NO CHOICE!
AHAHAHA HAHAHA HAHAHA HA HA HA HA
I'M GOING... BYE...
SHUFFLE

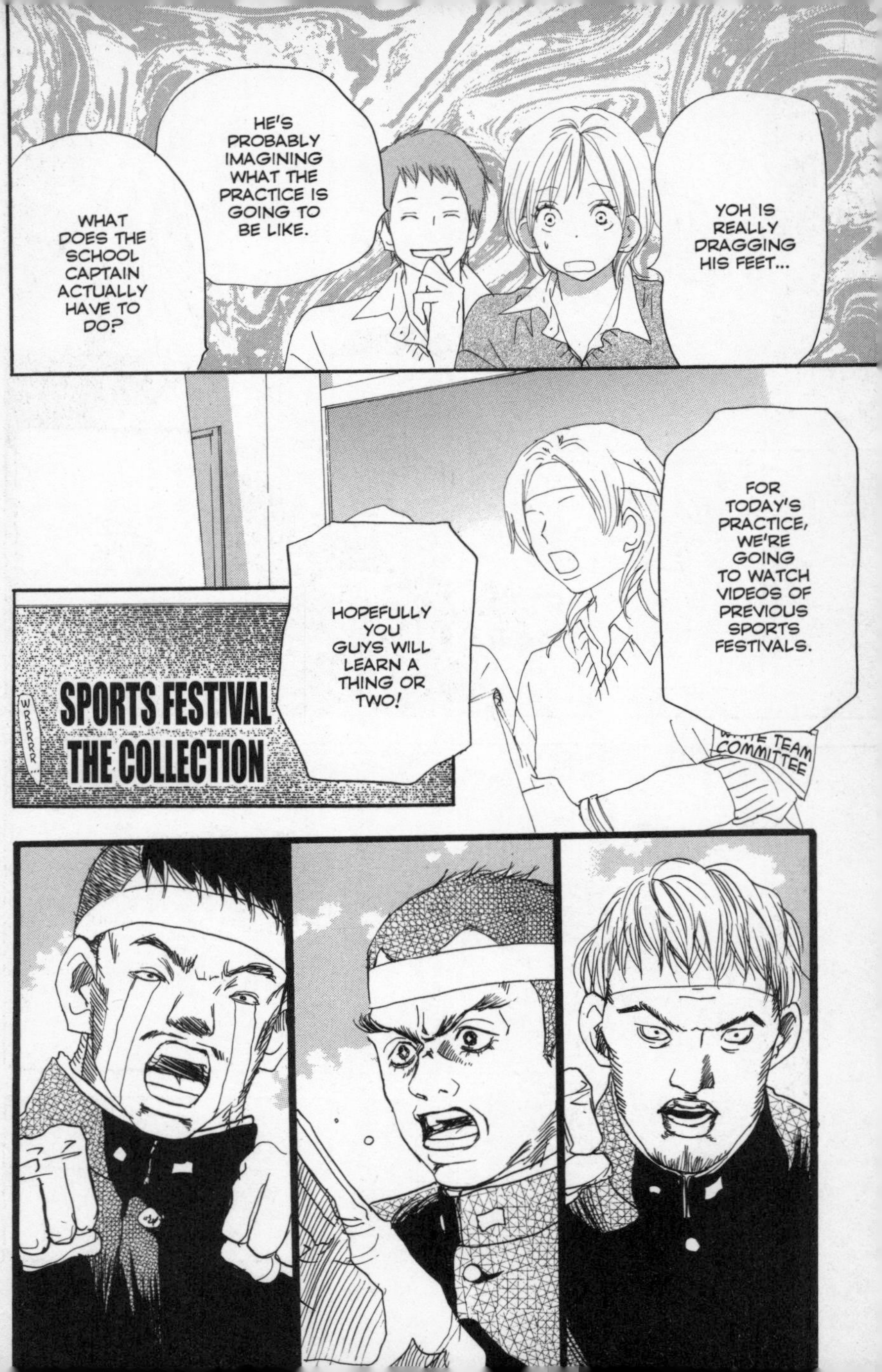
YOH IS REALLY DRAGGING HIS FEET...
HE'S PROBABLY IMAGINING WHAT THE PRACTICE IS GOING TO BE LIKE.
WHAT DOES THE SCHOOL CAPTAIN ACTUALLY HAVE TO DO?
FOR TODAY'S PRACTICE, WE'RE GOING TO WATCH VIDEOS OF PREVIOUS SPORTS FESTIVALS.
TEAM COMMITTEE
HOPEFULLY YOU GUYS WILL LEARN A THING OR TWO!
SPORTS FESTIVAL THE COLLECTION
WRRRR...

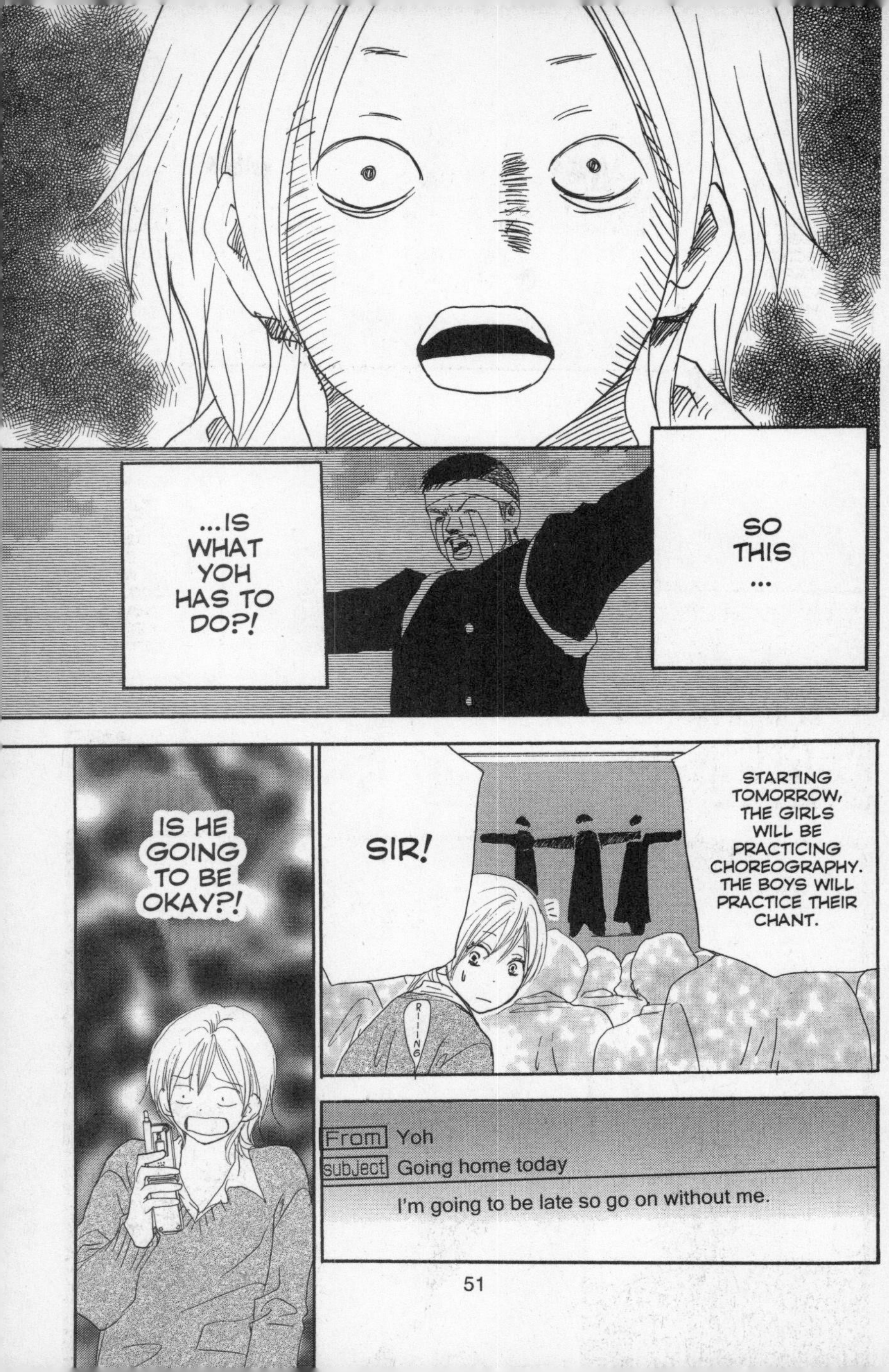
SO THIS ...
...IS WHAT YOH HAS TO DO?!
STARTING TOMORROW, THE GIRLS WILL BE PRACTICING CHOREOGRAPHY. THE BOYS WILL PRACTICE THEIR CHANT.
SIR!
RIIING
From Yoh
subject Going home today
I'm going to be late so go on without me.
IS HE GOING TO BE OKAY?!

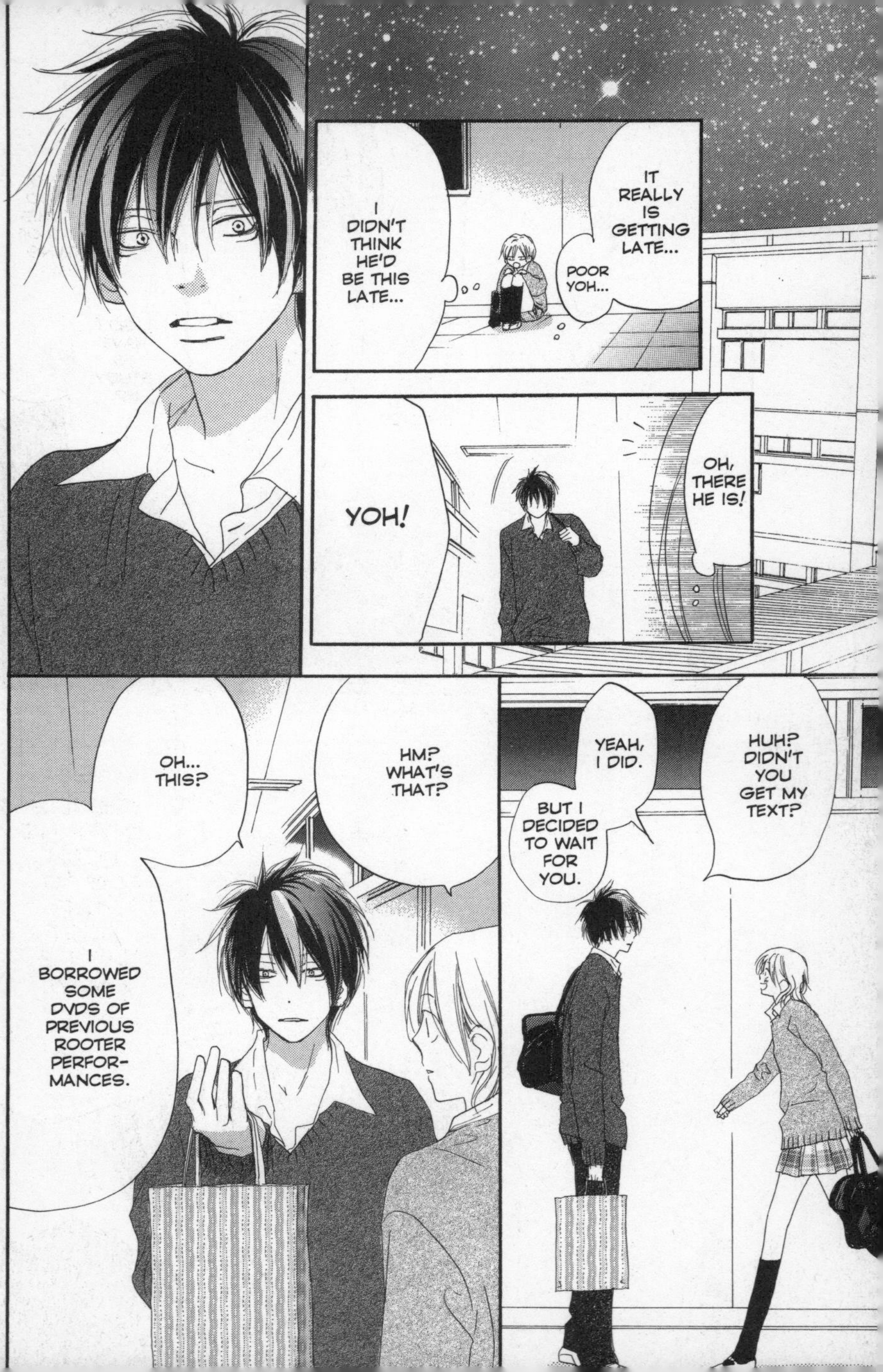
IT REALLY IS GETTING LATE...
POOR YOH...
I DIDN'T THINK HE'D BE THIS LATE...
OH, THERE HE IS!
YOH!
HUH? DIDN'T YOU GET MY TEXT?
YEAH, I DID.
BUT I DECIDED TO WAIT FOR YOU.
HM? WHAT'S THAT?
OH... THIS?
I BORROWED SOME DVDS OF PREVIOUS ROOTER PERFORMANCES.

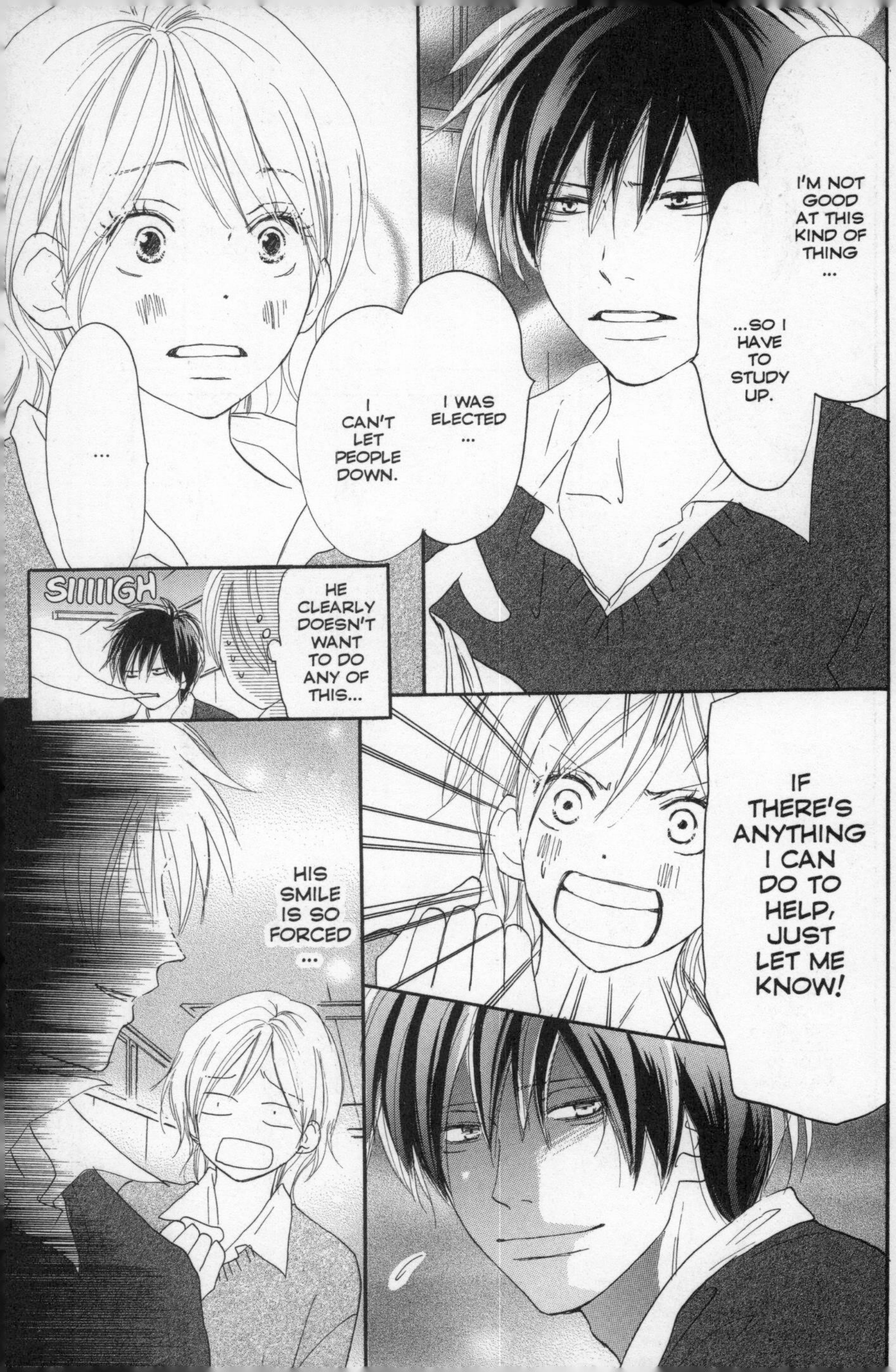
I'M NOT GOOD AT THIS KIND OF THING ...
...SO I HAVE TO STUDY UP.
I WAS ELECTED ...
I CAN'T LET PEOPLE DOWN.
...
SIIIIGH
HE CLEARLY DOESN'T WANT TO DO ANY OF THIS...
IF THERE'S ANYTHING I CAN DO TO HELP, JUST LET ME KNOW!
HIS SMILE IS SO FORCED ...

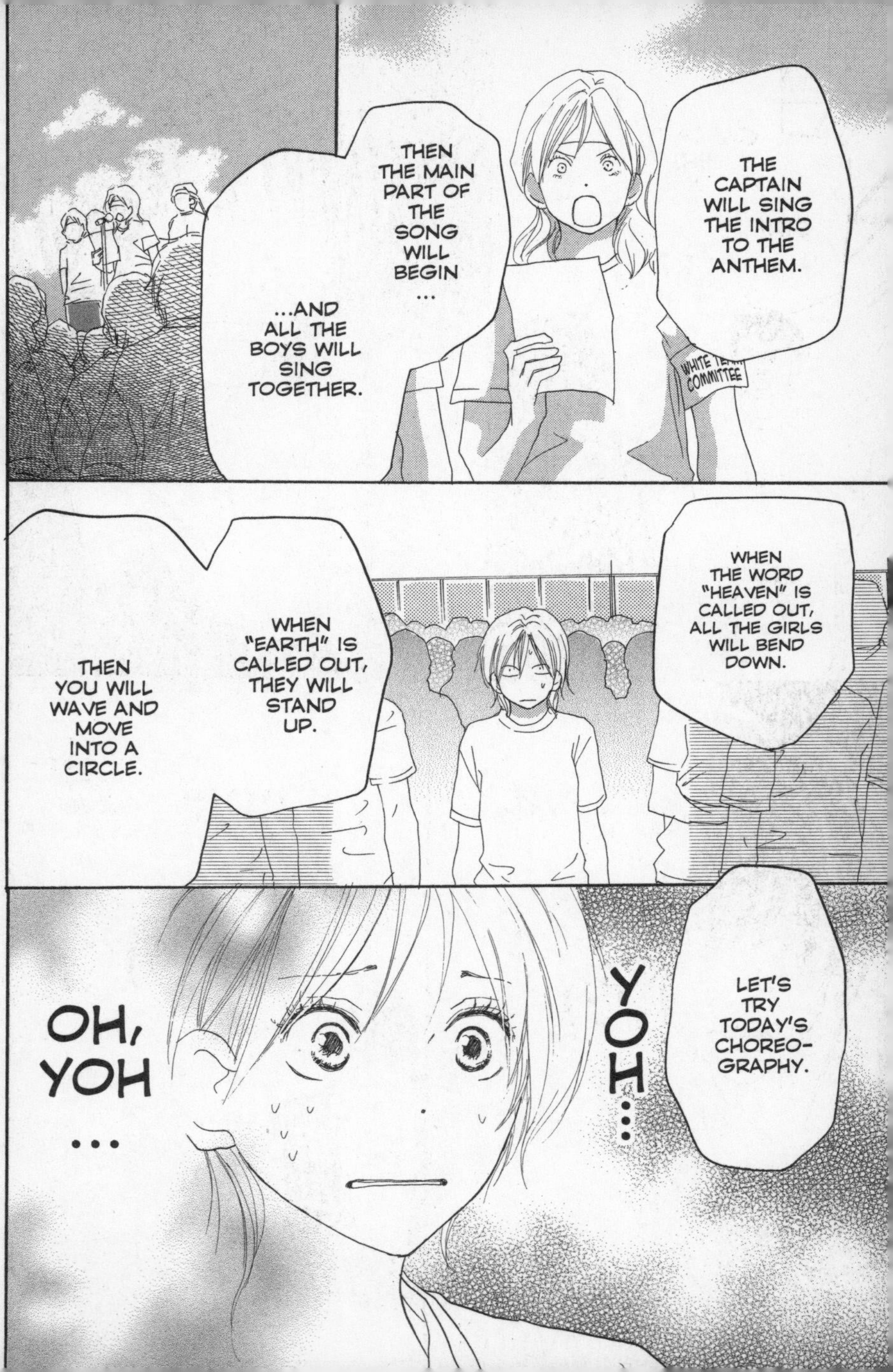
THE CAPTAIN WILL SING THE INTRO TO THE ANTHEM.
THEN THE MAIN PART OF THE SONG WILL BEGIN...
...AND ALL THE BOYS WILL SING TOGETHER.
WHEN THE WORD "HEAVEN" IS CALLED OUT, ALL THE GIRLS WILL BEND DOWN.
WHEN "EARTH" IS CALLED OUT, THEY WILL STAND UP.
THEN YOU WILL WAVE AND MOVE INTO A CIRCLE.
LET'S TRY TODAY'S CHOREOGRAPHY.
YOH...
OH, YOH...

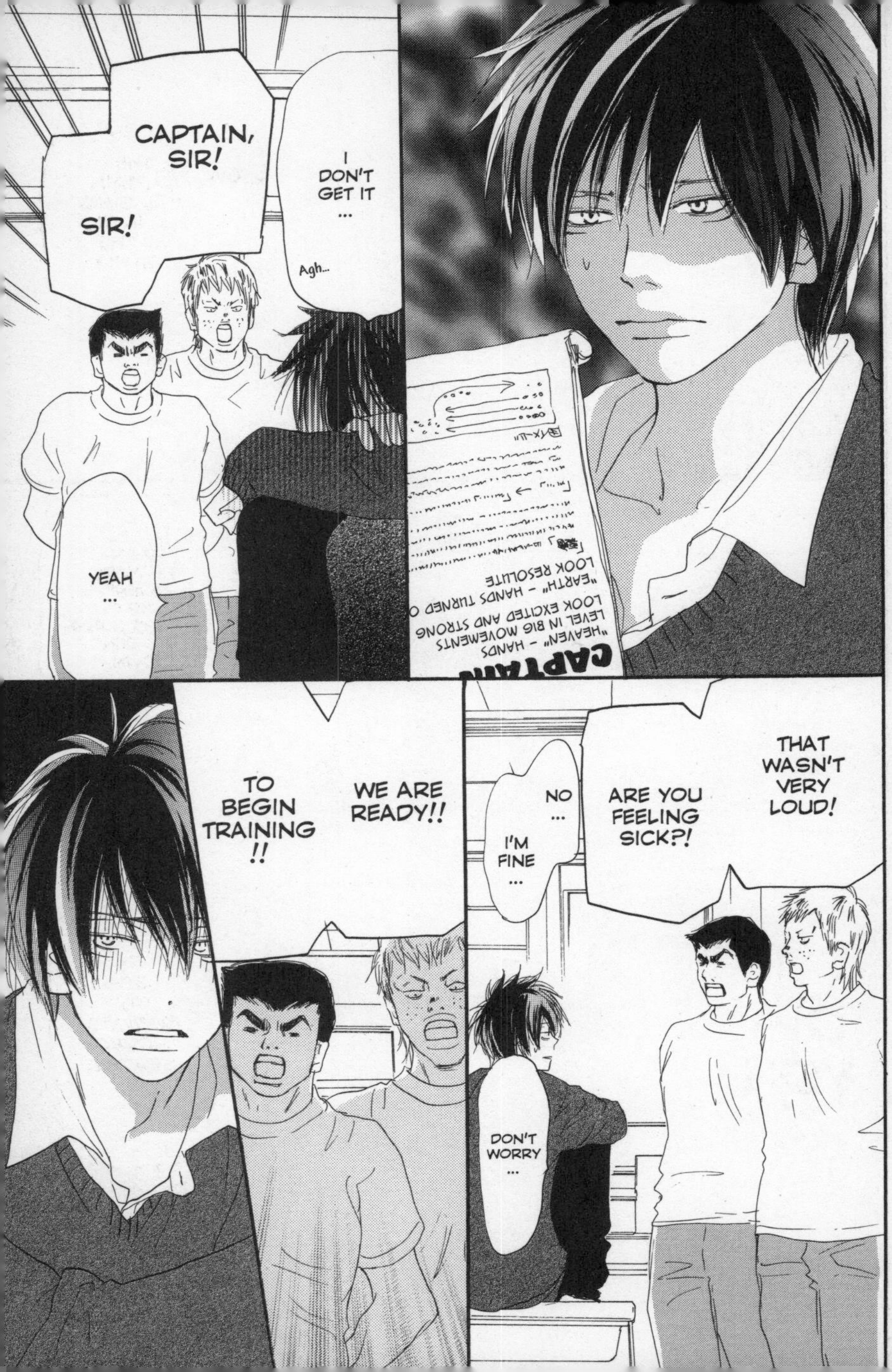
CAPTAIN
"HEAVEN" - HANDS LEVEL IN BIG MOVEMENTS LOOK EXCITED AND STRONG
"EARTH" - HANDS TURNED O
LOOK RESOLUTE
I DON'T GET IT ...
Agh...
CAPTAIN, SIR!
SIR!
YEAH ...
THAT WASN'T VERY LOUD!
ARE YOU FEELING SICK?!
NO ...
I'M FINE ...
DON'T WORRY ...
WE ARE READY!!
TO BEGIN TRAINING !!

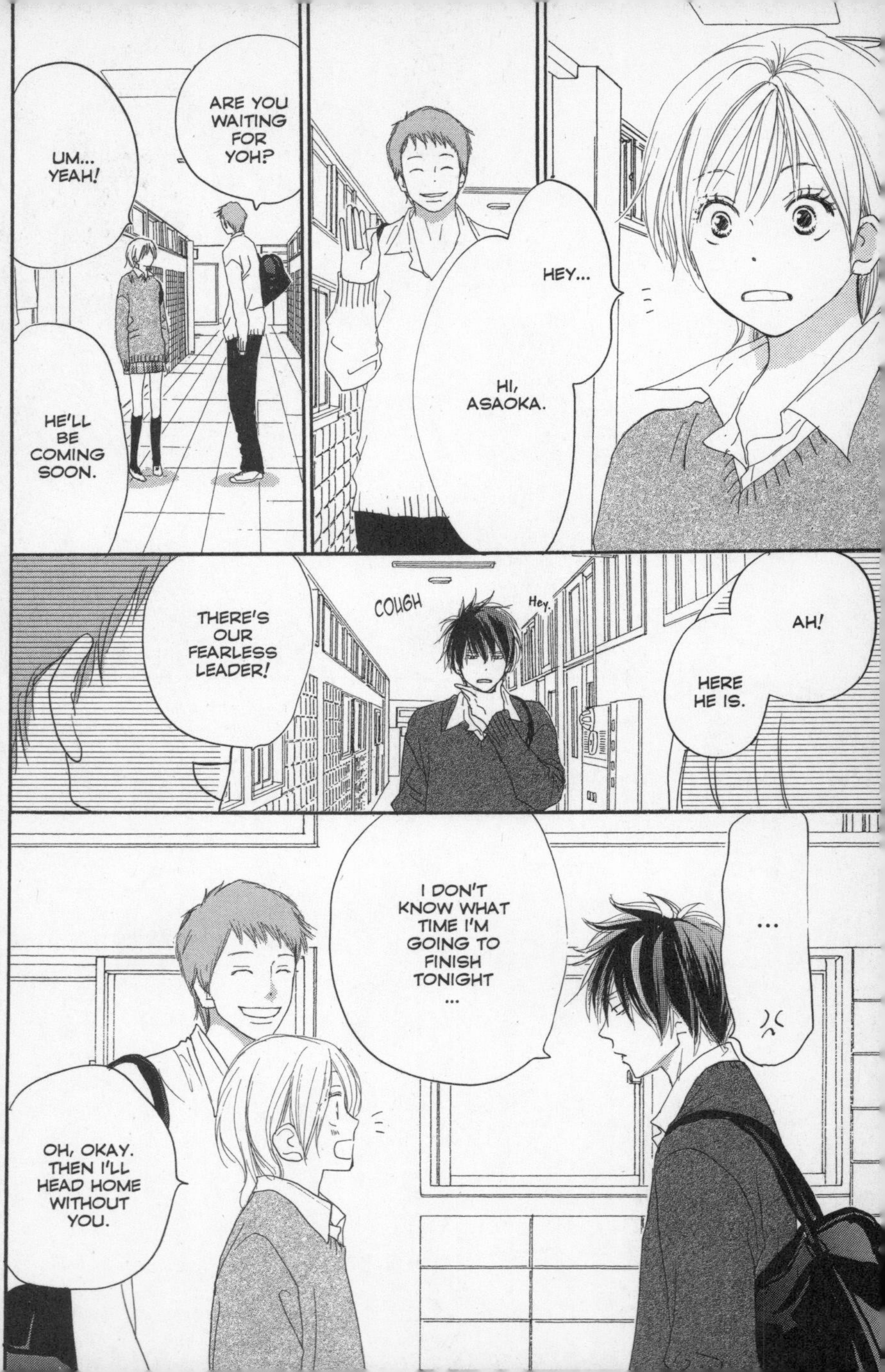
HEY...
HI, ASAOKA.
ARE YOU WAITING FOR YOH?
UM... YEAH!
HE'LL BE COMING SOON.
AH!
HERE HE IS.
Hey.
COUGH
THERE'S OUR FEARLESS LEADER!
...
I DON'T KNOW WHAT TIME I'M GOING TO FINISH TONIGHT ...
OH, OKAY. THEN I'LL HEAD HOME WITHOUT YOU.

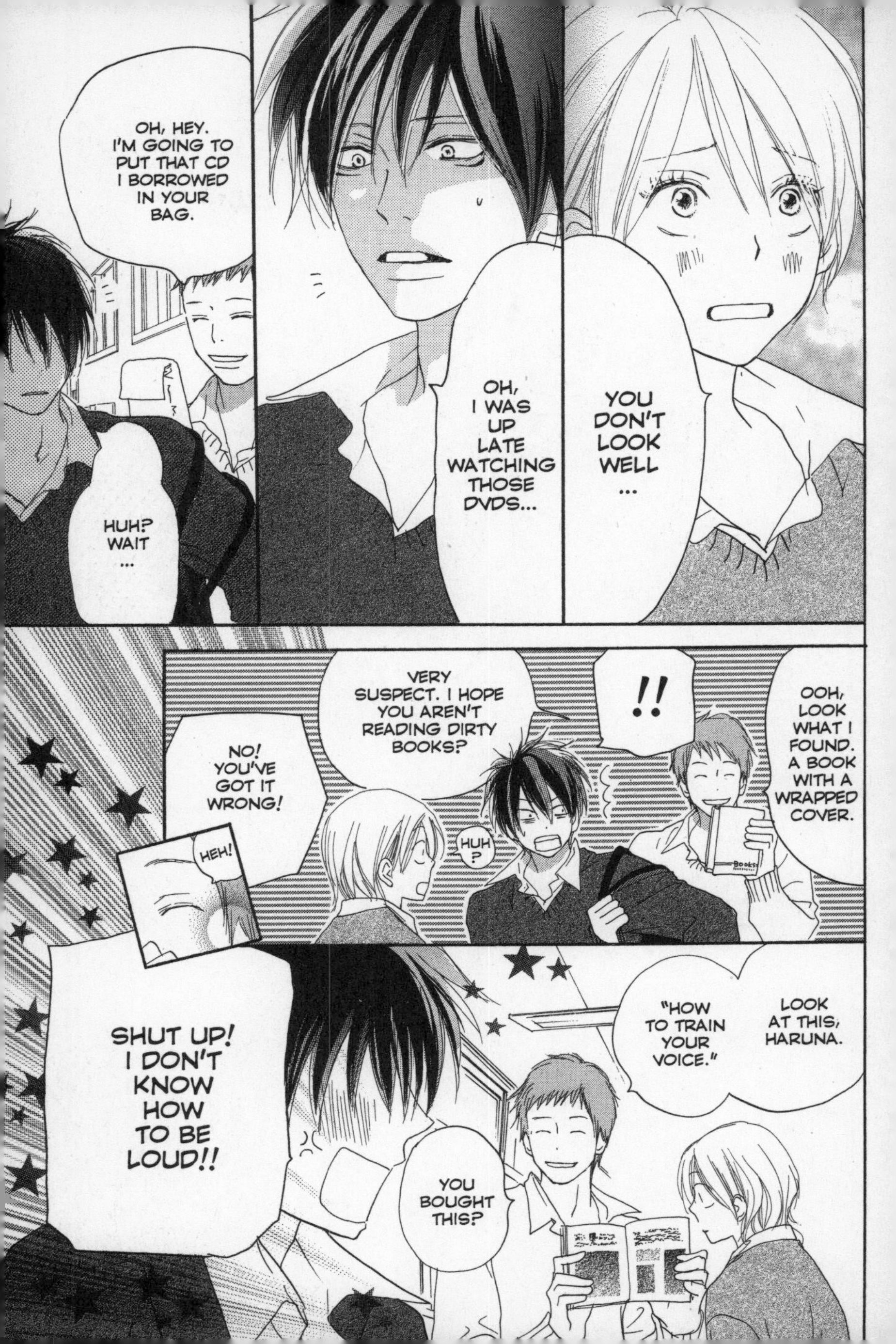
YOU DON'T LOOK WELL...
OH, I WAS UP LATE WATCHING THOSE DVDS...
OH, HEY. I'M GOING TO PUT THAT CD I BORROWED IN YOUR BAG.
HUH? WAIT...
OOH, LOOK WHAT I FOUND. A BOOK WITH A WRAPPED COVER.
!!
VERY SUSPECT. I HOPE YOU AREN'T READING DIRTY BOOKS?
HUH?
NO! YOU'VE GOT IT WRONG!
HEH!
LOOK AT THIS, HARUNA.
"HOW TO TRAIN YOUR VOICE."
YOU BOUGHT THIS?
SHUT UP! I DON'T KNOW HOW TO BE LOUD!!

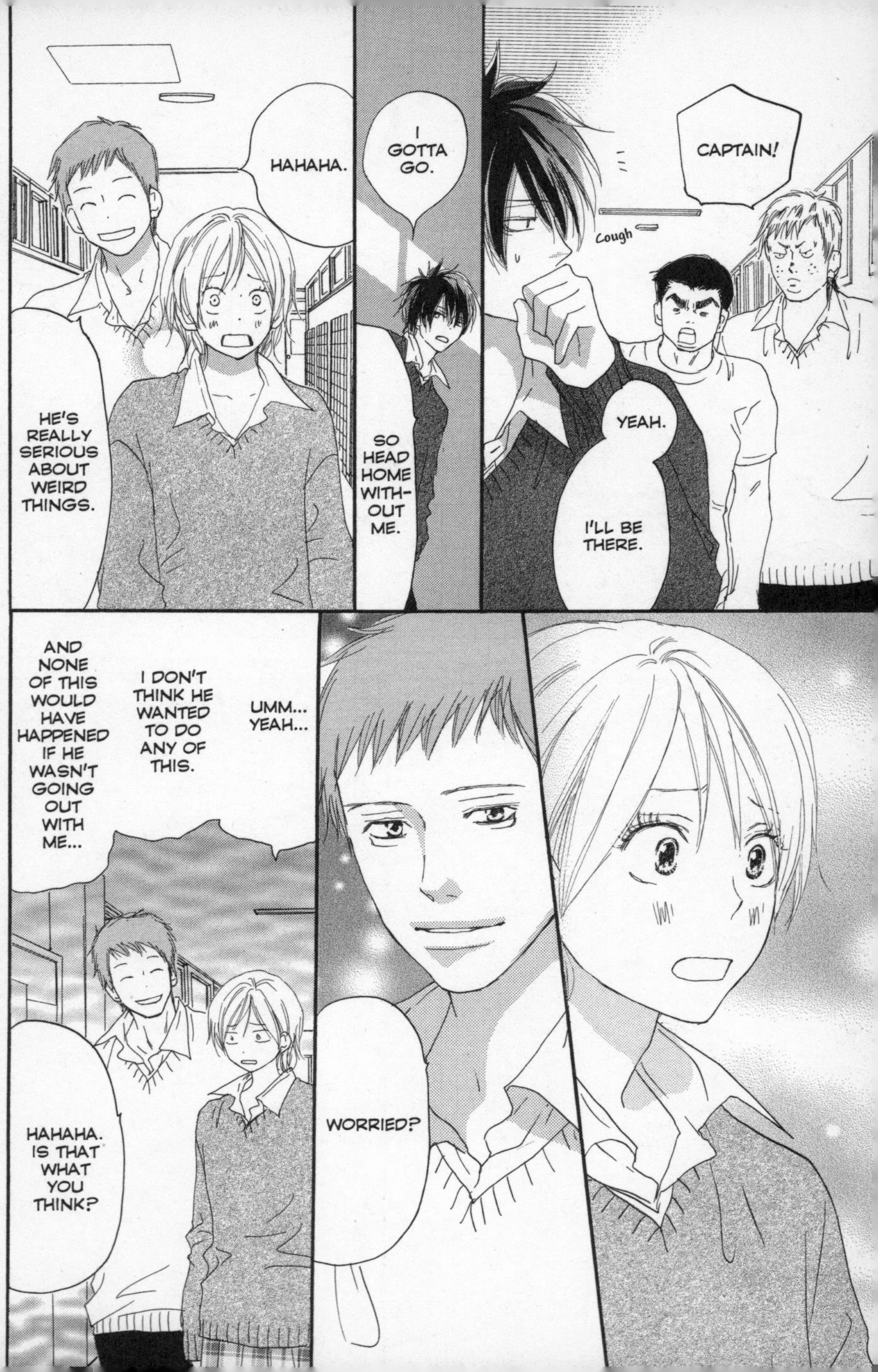
CAPTAIN!
Cough
YEAH.
I'LL BE THERE.
I GOTTA GO.
SO HEAD HOME WITHOUT ME.
HAHAHA.
HE'S REALLY SERIOUS ABOUT WEIRD THINGS.
WORRIED?
UMM... YEAH...
I DON'T THINK HE WANTED TO DO ANY OF THIS.
AND NONE OF THIS WOULD HAVE HAPPENED IF HE WASN'T GOING OUT WITH ME...
HAHAHA. IS THAT WHAT YOU THINK?

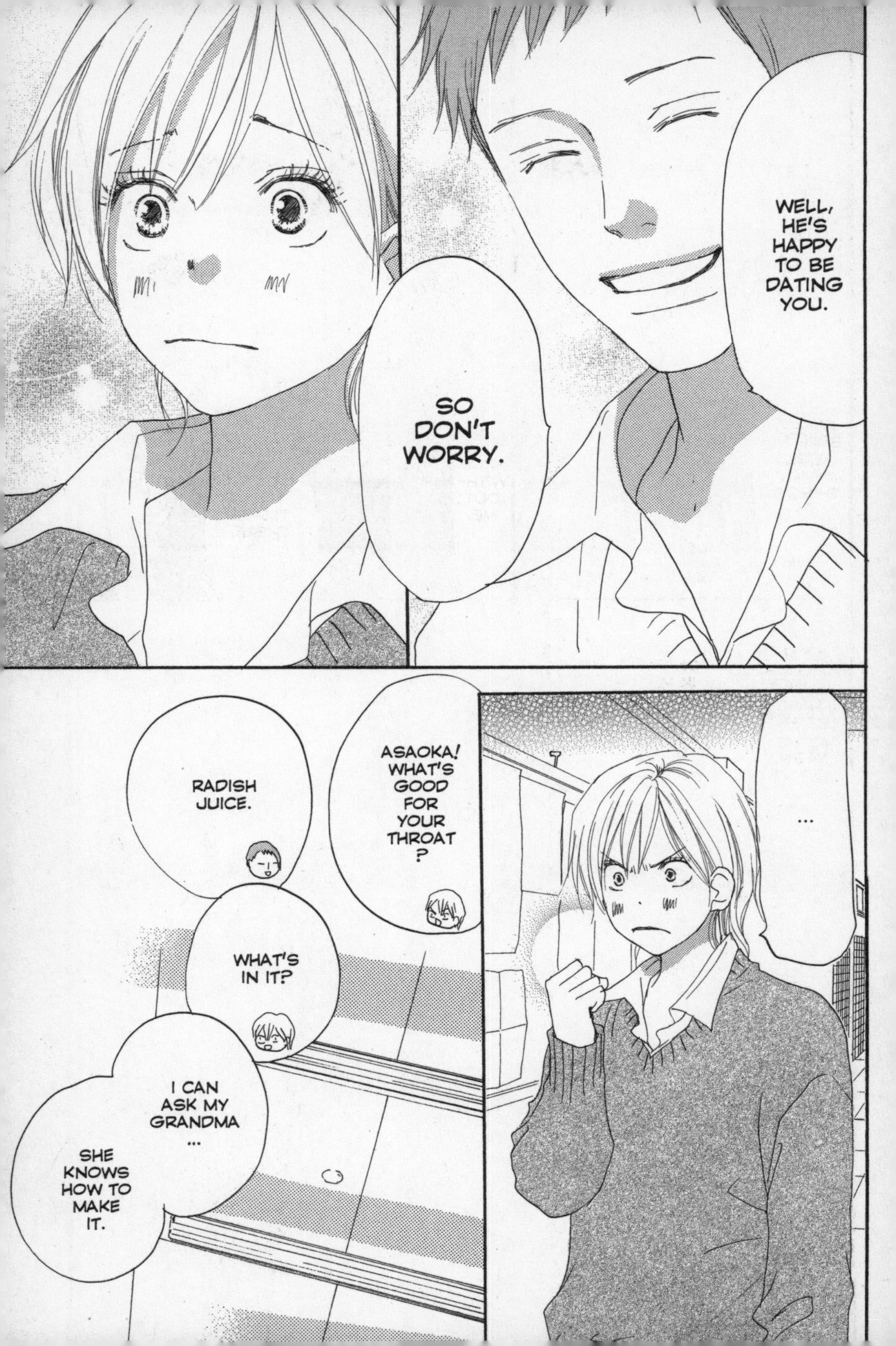
WELL, HE'S HAPPY TO BE DATING YOU.
SO DON'T WORRY.
...
ASAOKA! WHAT'S GOOD FOR YOUR THROAT?
RADISH JUICE.
WHAT'S IN IT?
I CAN ASK MY GRANDMA...
SHE KNOWS HOW TO MAKE IT.

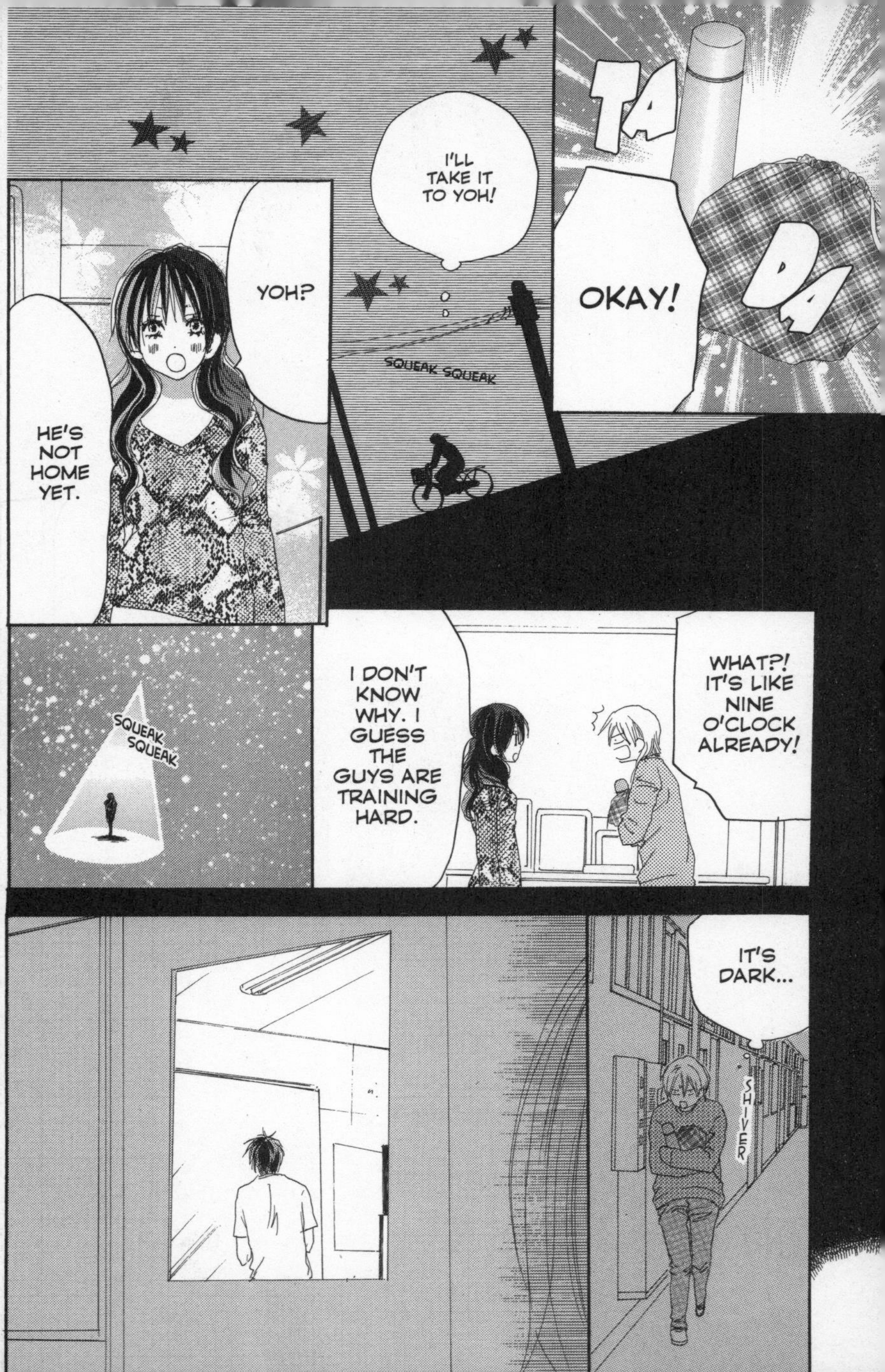
TA
DA
OKAY!
I'LL TAKE IT TO YOH!
SQUEAK SQUEAK
YOH?
HE'S NOT HOME YET.
WHAT?! IT'S LIKE NINE O'CLOCK ALREADY!
I DON'T KNOW WHY. I GUESS THE GUYS ARE TRAINING HARD.
SQUEAK SQUEAK
IT'S DARK...
SHIVER

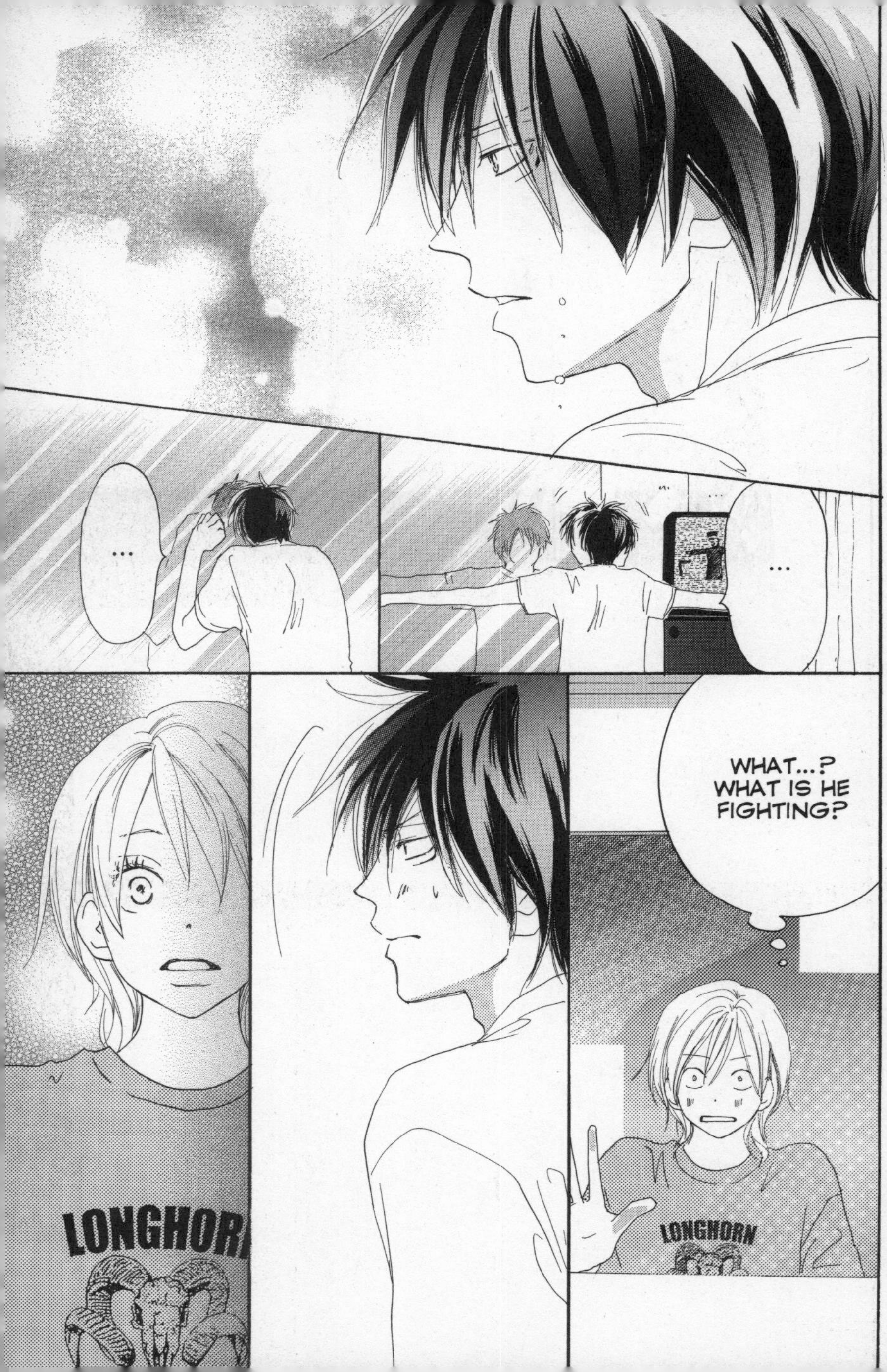
...
...
WHAT...? WHAT IS HE FIGHTING?
LONGHORN

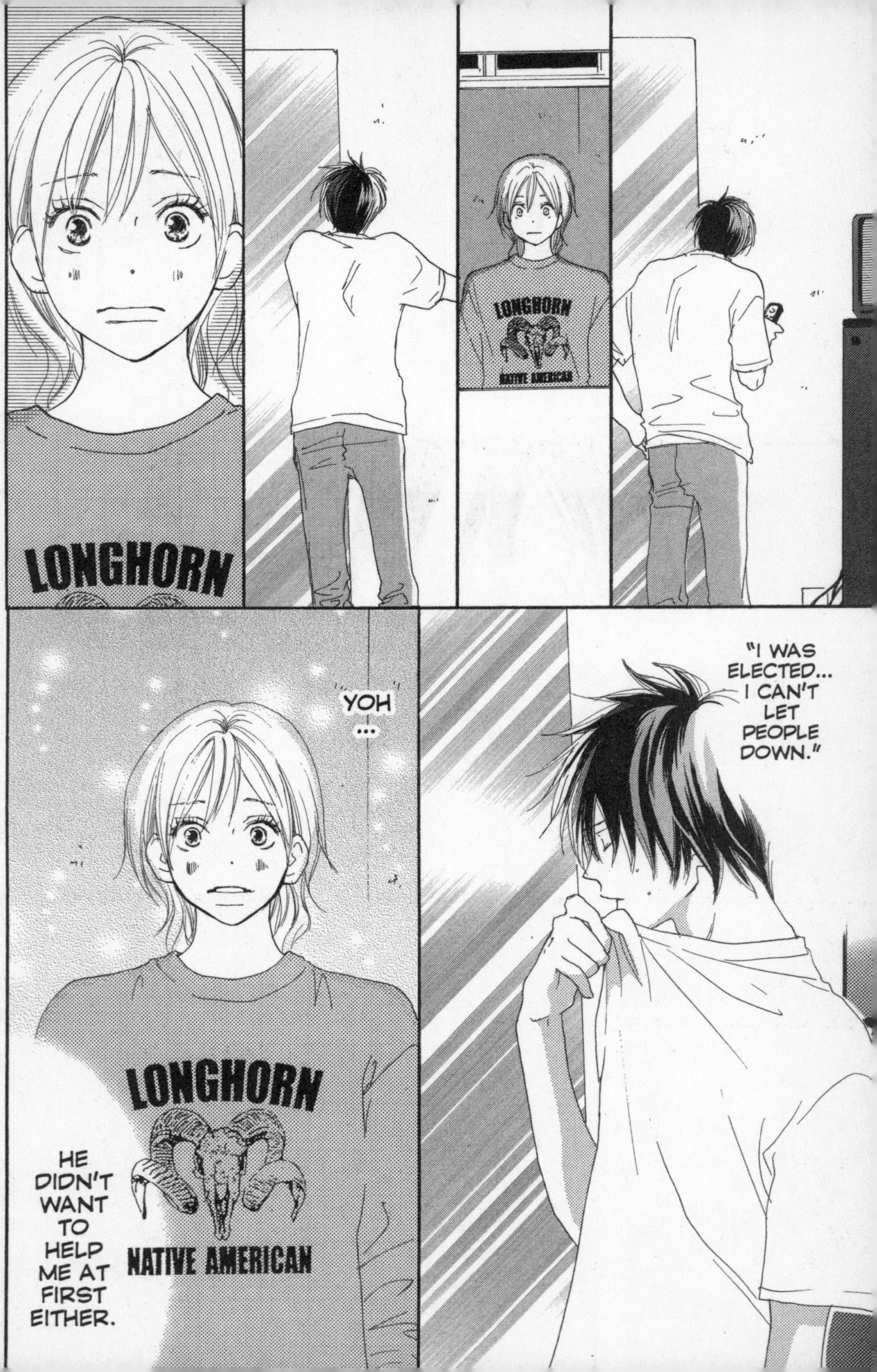
LONGHORN
NATIVE AMERICAN
LONGHORN
"I WAS ELECTED... I CAN'T LET PEOPLE DOWN."
YOH ...
LONGHORN
NATIVE AMERICAN
HE DIDN'T WANT TO HELP ME AT FIRST EITHER.

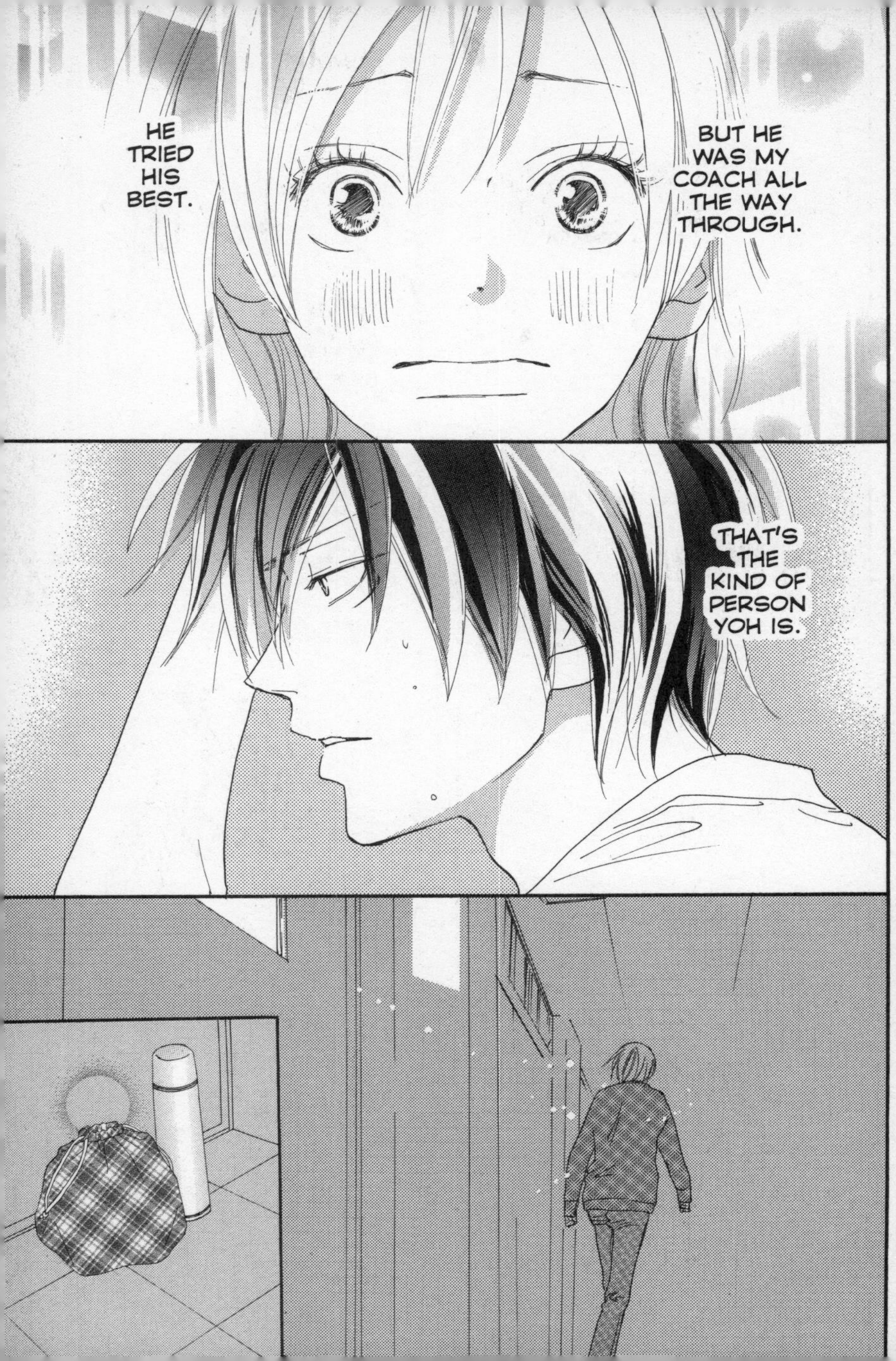
BUT HE WAS MY COACH ALL THE WAY THROUGH.
HE TRIED HIS BEST.
THAT'S THE KIND OF PERSON YOH IS.

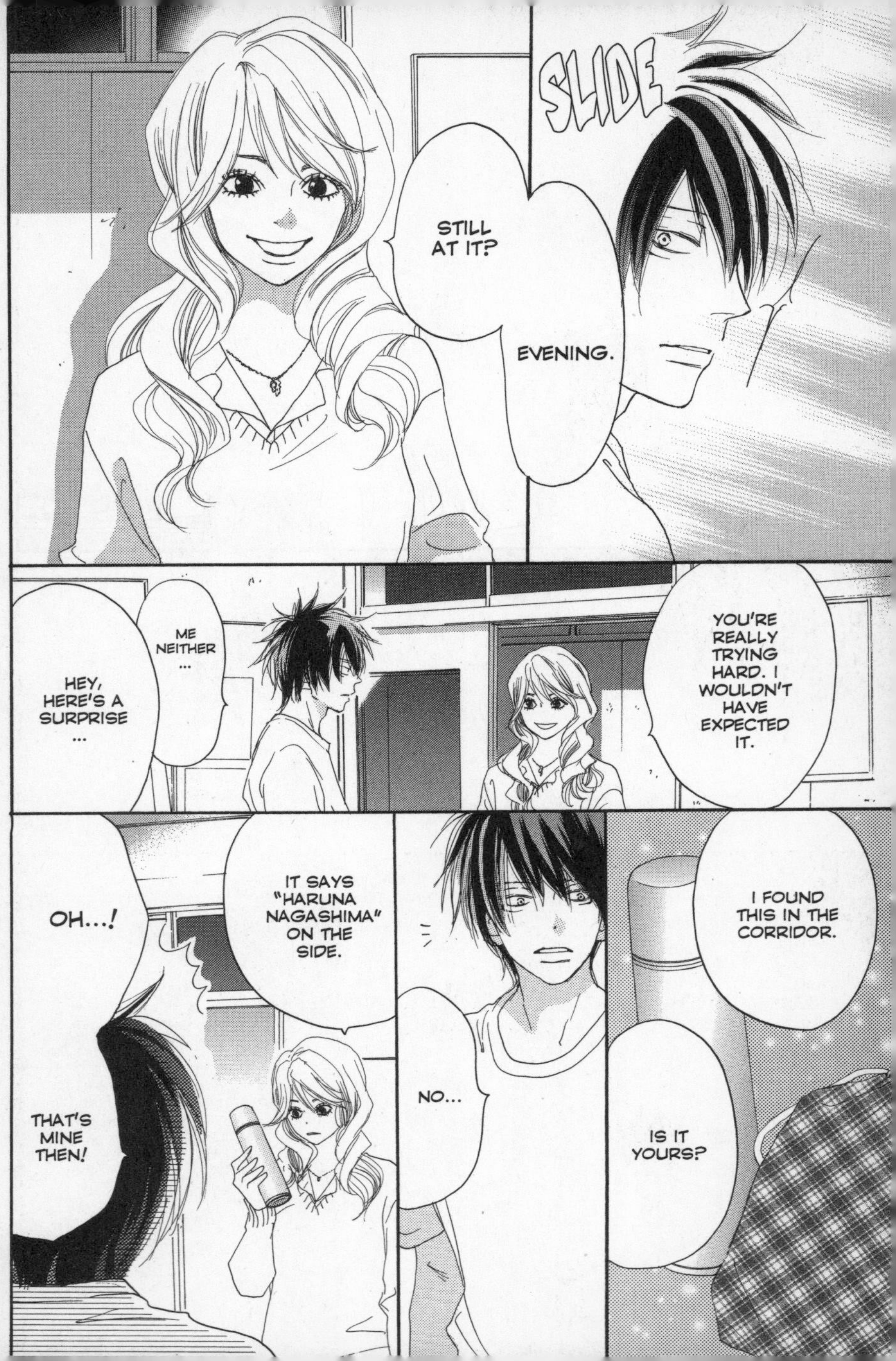
SLIDE
STILL AT IT?
EVENING.
YOU'RE REALLY TRYING HARD. I WOULDN'T HAVE EXPECTED IT.
ME NEITHER ...
HEY, HERE'S A SURPRISE ...
I FOUND THIS IN THE CORRIDOR.
IS IT YOURS?
NO...
IT SAYS "HARUNA NAGASHIMA" ON THE SIDE.
OH...!
THAT'S MINE THEN!

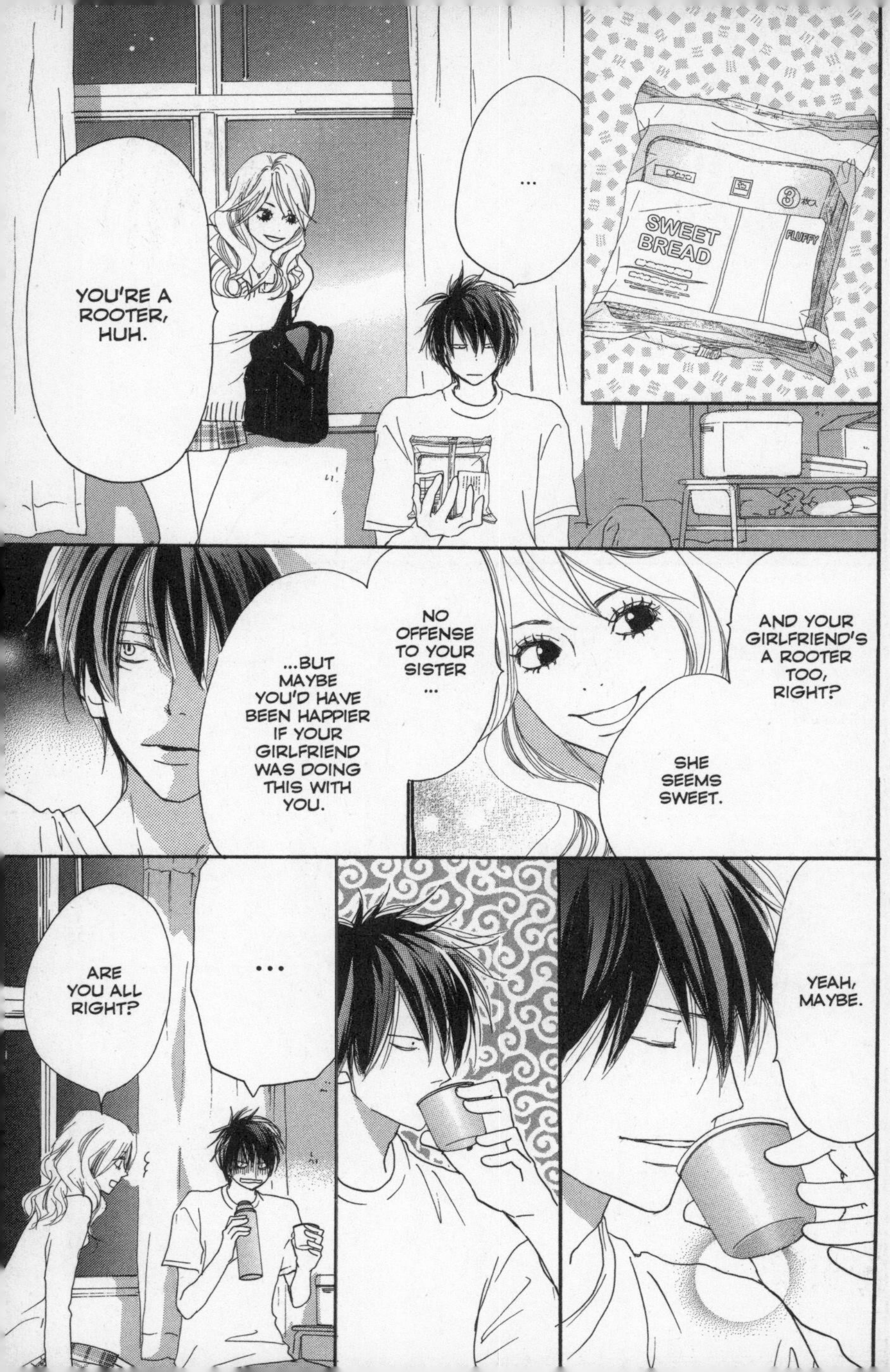
SWEET BREAD
FLUFFY
...
YOU'RE A ROOTER, HUH.
AND YOUR GIRLFRIEND'S A ROOTER TOO, RIGHT?
SHE SEEMS SWEET.
NO OFFENSE TO YOUR SISTER ...
...BUT MAYBE YOU'D HAVE BEEN HAPPIER IF YOUR GIRLFRIEND WAS DOING THIS WITH YOU.
YEAH, MAYBE.
...
ARE YOU ALL RIGHT?

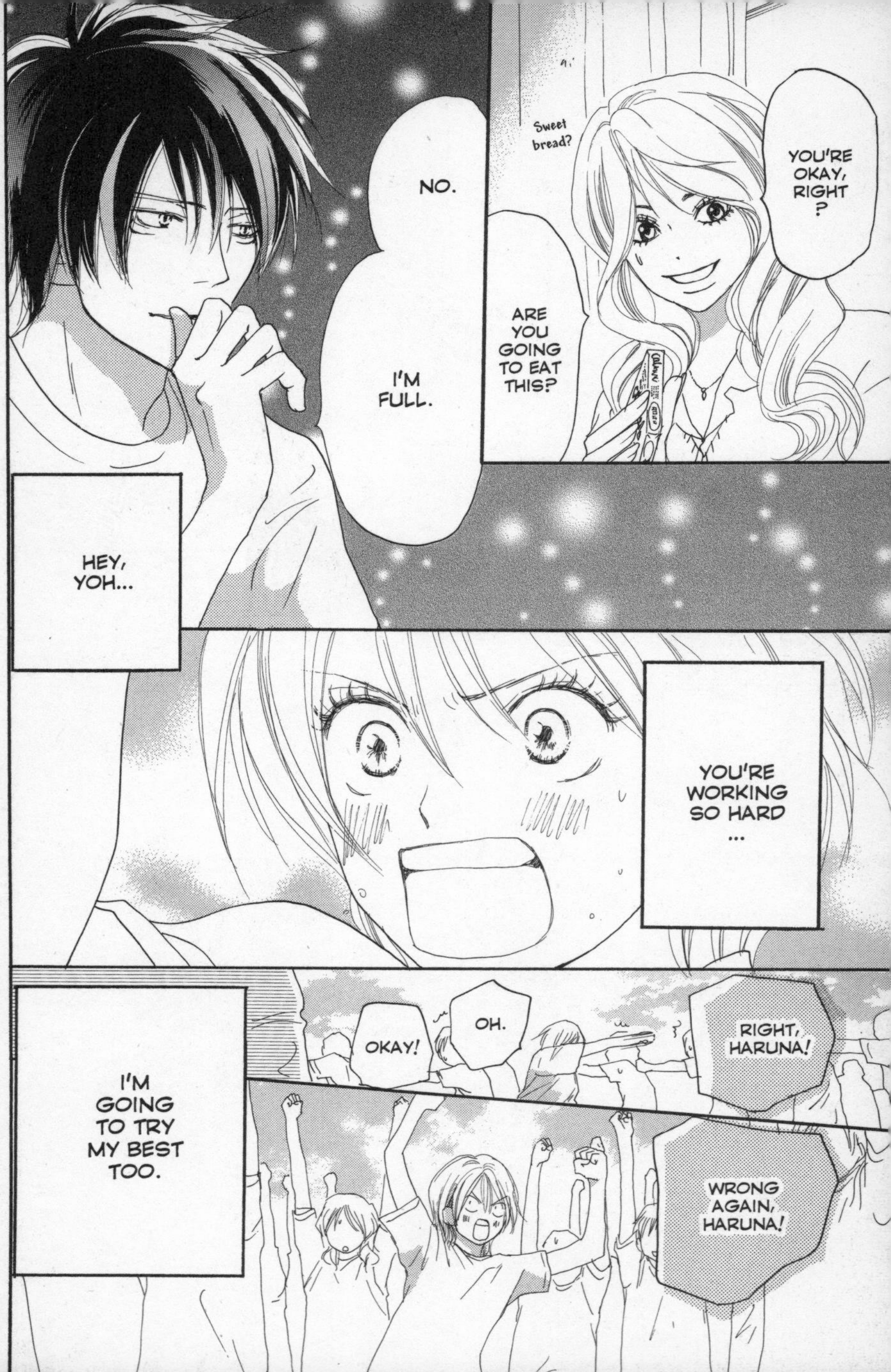
YOU'RE OKAY, RIGHT?
Sweet bread?
ARE YOU GOING TO EAT THIS?
NO.
I'M FULL.
HEY, YOH...
YOU'RE WORKING SO HARD...
RIGHT, HARUNA!
OH.
OKAY!
WRONG AGAIN, HARUNA!
I'M GOING TO TRY MY BEST TOO.

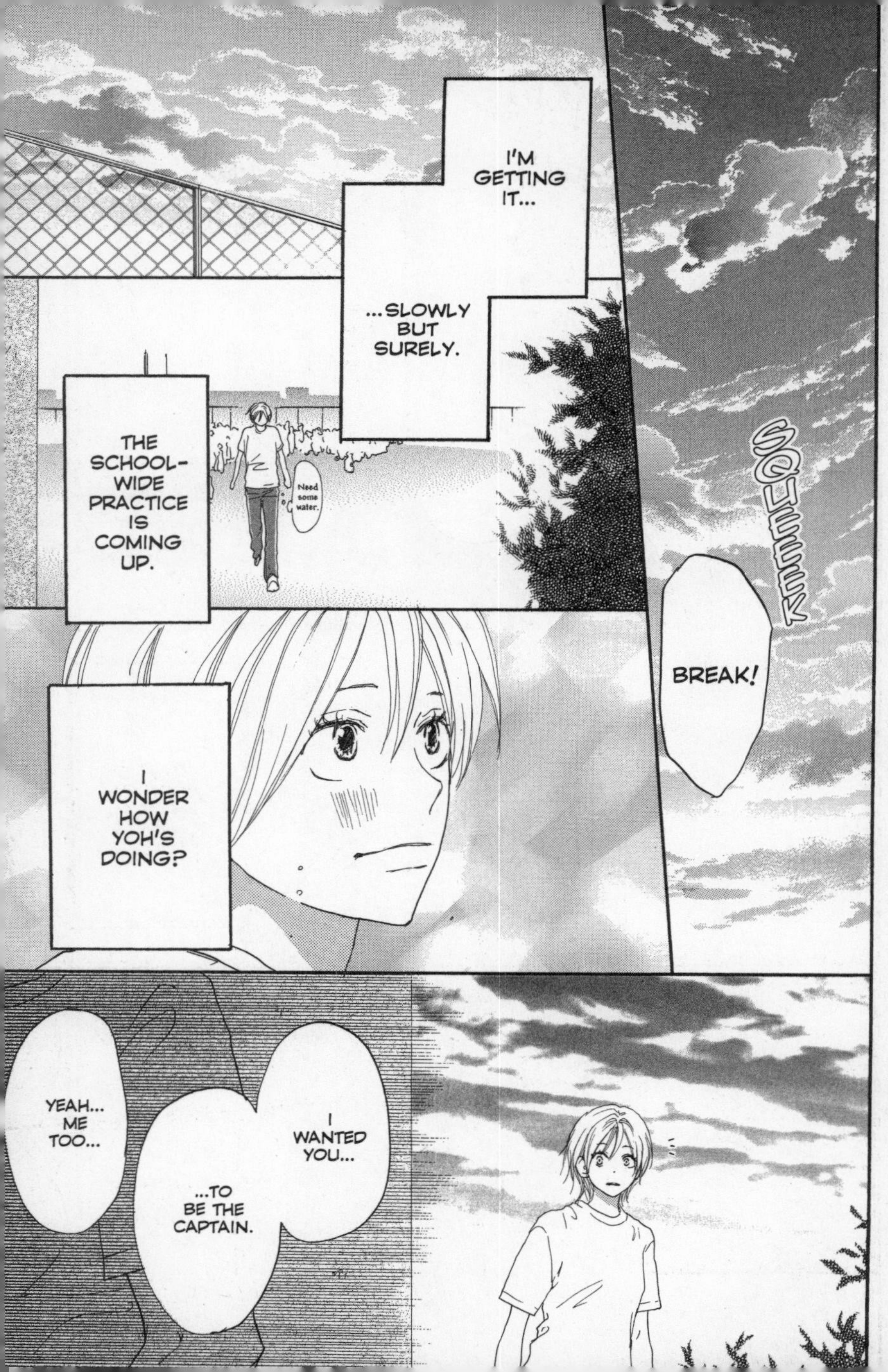
SQUEEEEK
BREAK!
I'M GETTING IT...
...SLOWLY BUT SURELY.
THE SCHOOL-WIDE PRACTICE IS COMING UP.
Need some water.
I WONDER HOW YOH'S DOING?
I WANTED YOU...
...TO BE THE CAPTAIN.
YEAH... ME TOO...

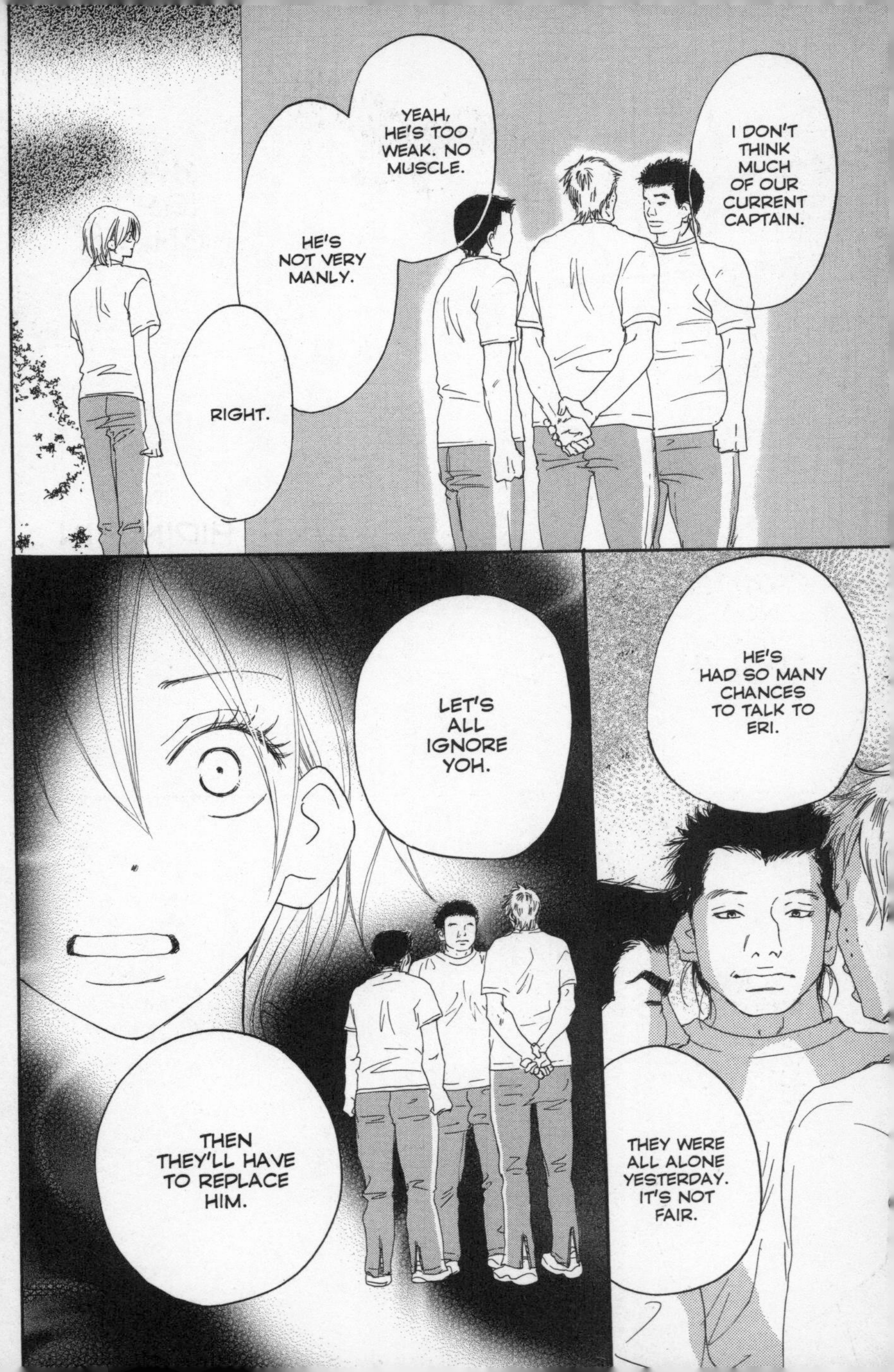
I DON'T THINK MUCH OF OUR CURRENT CAPTAIN.
YEAH, HE'S TOO WEAK. NO MUSCLE.
HE'S NOT VERY MANLY.
RIGHT.
HE'S HAD SO MANY CHANCES TO TALK TO ERI.
THEY WERE ALL ALONE YESTERDAY. IT'S NOT FAIR.
LET'S ALL IGNORE YOH.
THEN THEY'LL HAVE TO REPLACE HIM.

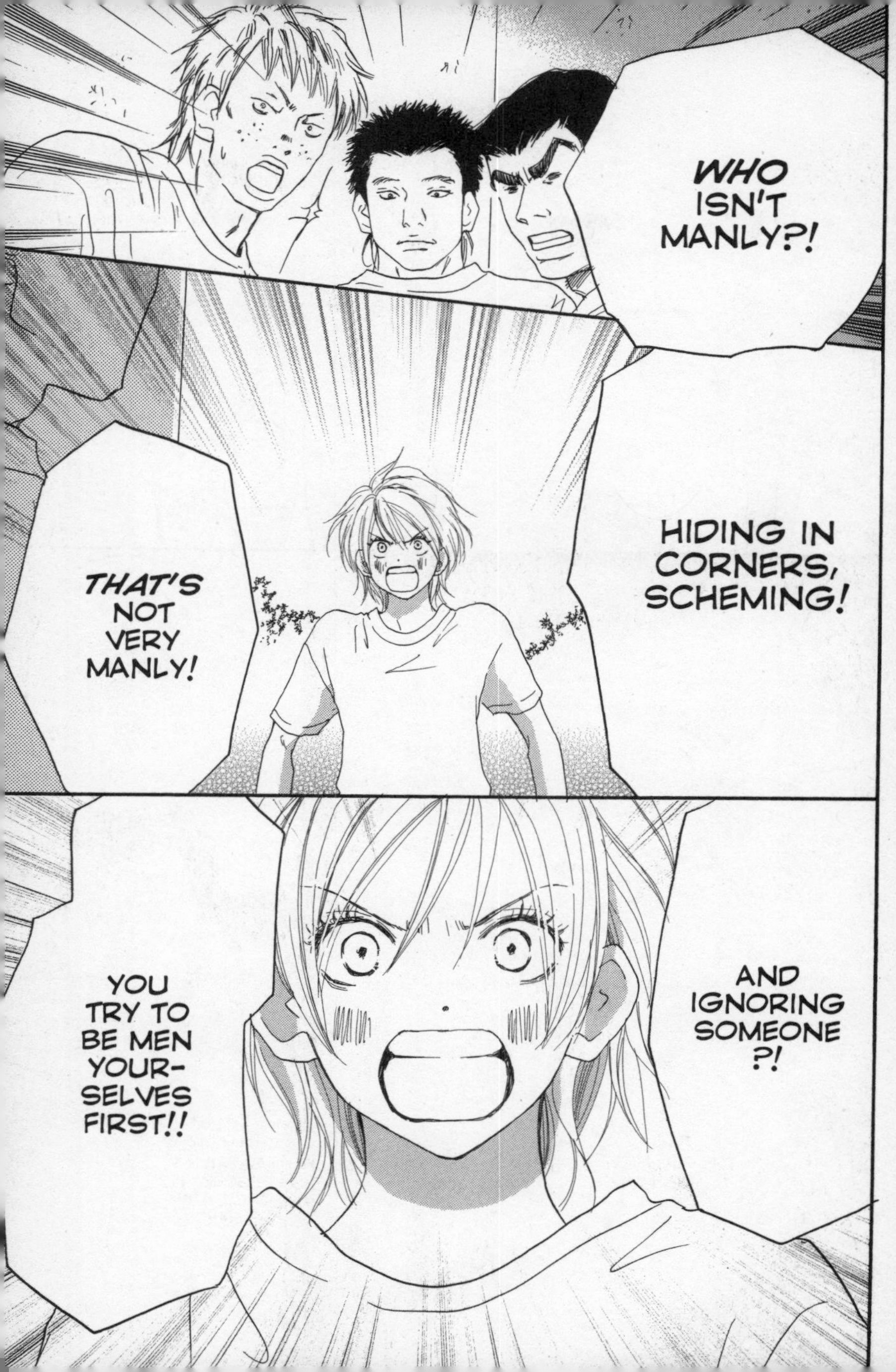
WHO ISN'T MANLY?!
HIDING IN CORNERS, SCHEMING!
THAT'S NOT VERY MANLY!
AND IGNORING SOMEONE ?!
YOU TRY TO BE MEN YOUR-SELVES FIRST!!

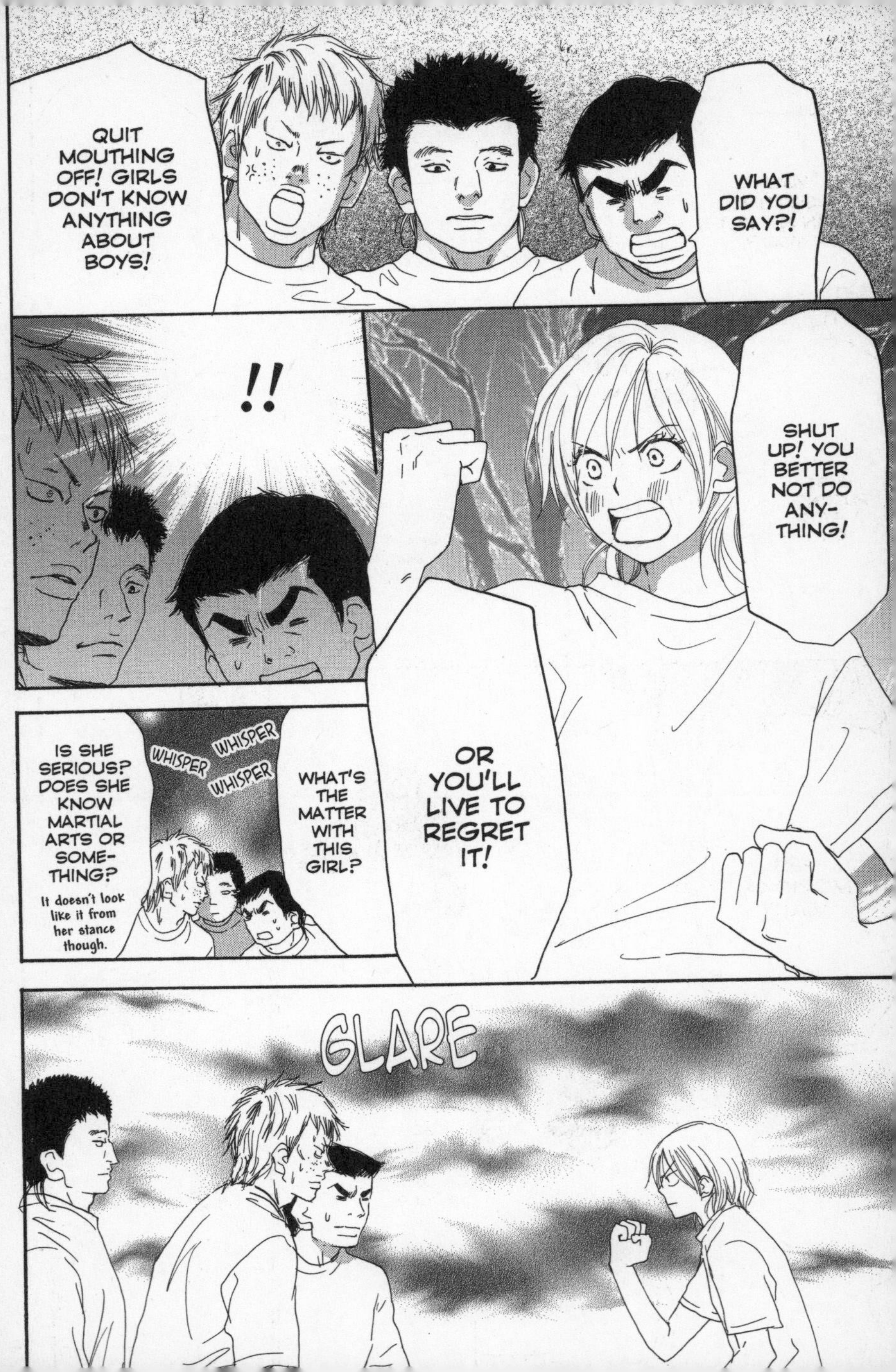
WHAT DID YOU SAY?!
QUIT MOUTHING OFF! GIRLS DON'T KNOW ANYTHING ABOUT BOYS!
SHUT UP! YOU BETTER NOT DO ANY-THING!
OR YOU'LL LIVE TO REGRET IT!
!!
WHAT'S THE MATTER WITH THIS GIRL?
WHISPER
WHISPER
WHISPER
IS SHE SERIOUS? DOES SHE KNOW MARTIAL ARTS OR SOME-THING?
It doesn't look like it from her stance though.
GLARE

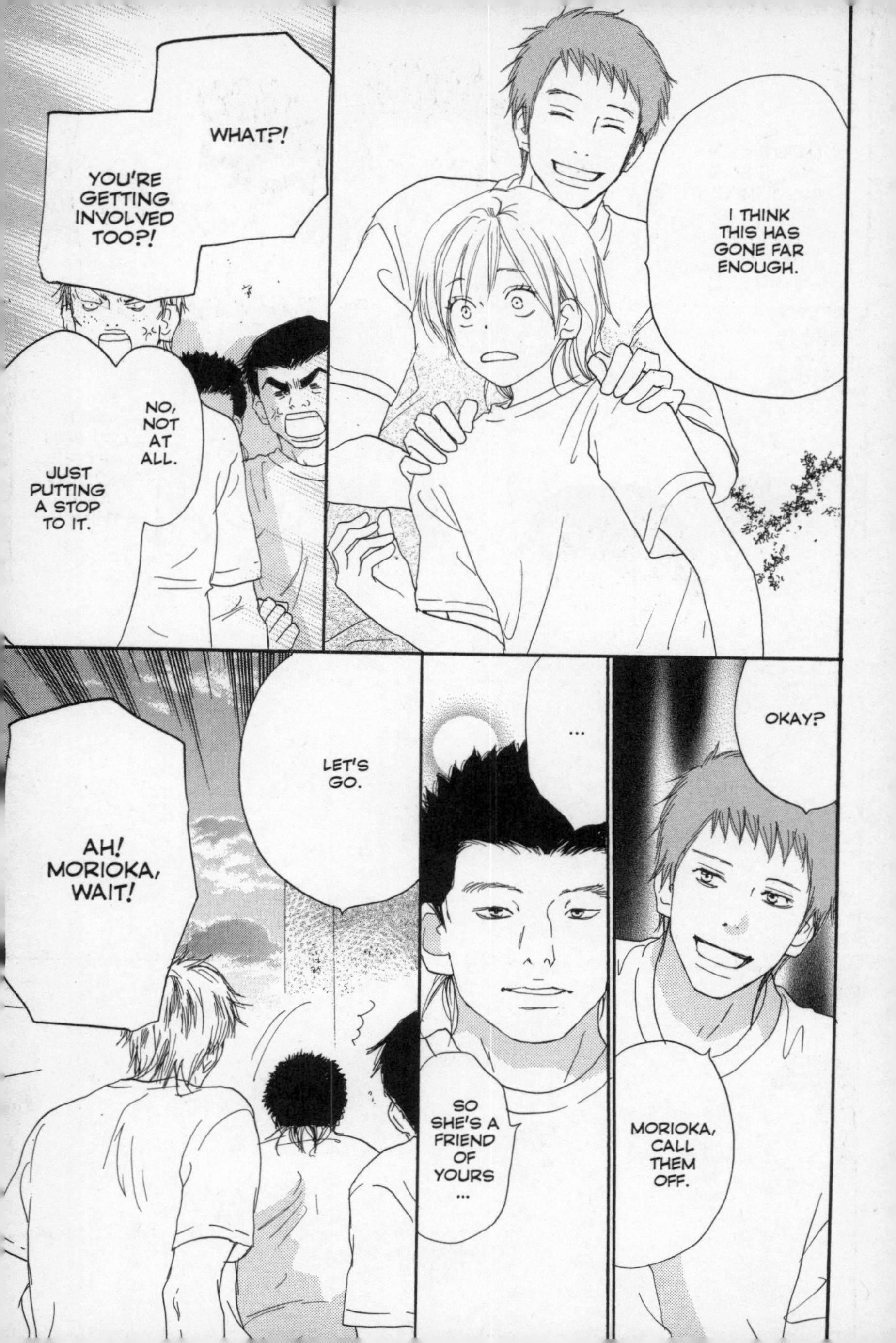
I THINK THIS HAS GONE FAR ENOUGH.
WHAT?!
YOU'RE GETTING INVOLVED TOO?!
NO, NOT AT ALL.
JUST PUTTING A STOP TO IT.
OKAY?
MORIOKA, CALL THEM OFF.
...
SO SHE'S A FRIEND OF YOURS ...
LET'S GO.
AH! MORIOKA, WAIT!

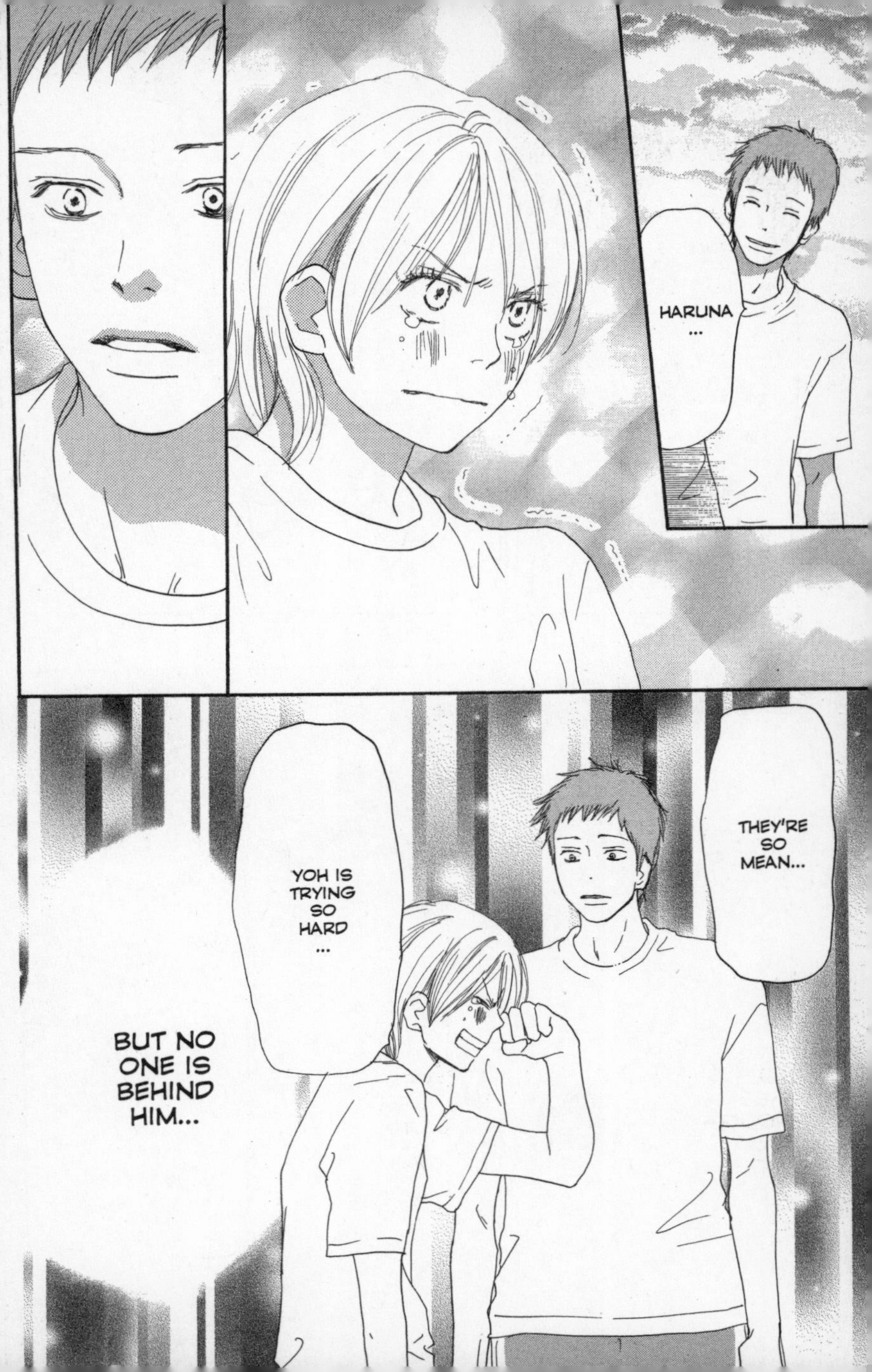
HARUNA ...
THEY'RE SO MEAN...
YOH IS TRYING SO HARD ...
BUT NO ONE IS BEHIND HIM...

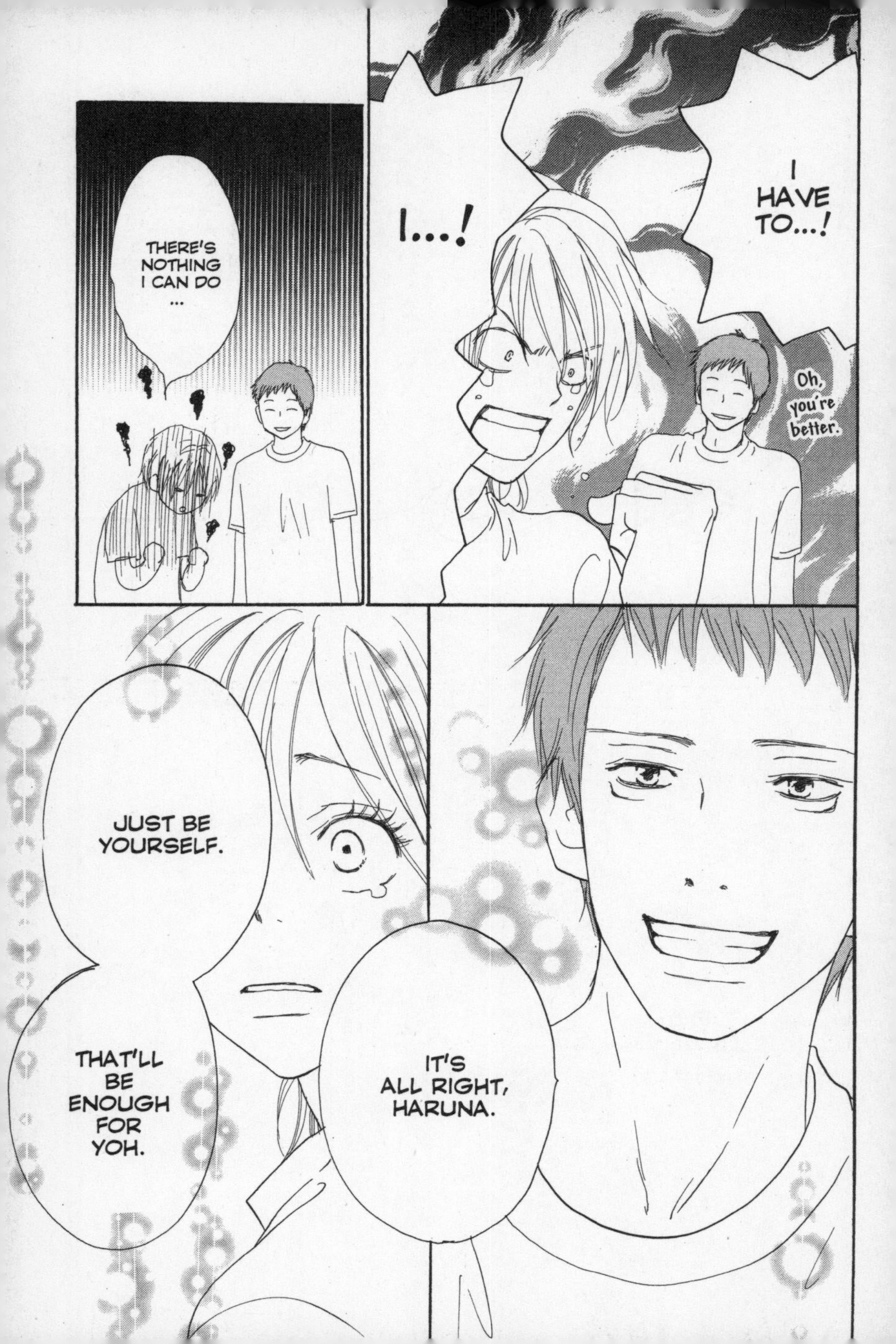
I HAVE TO...!
I...!
Oh, you're better.
THERE'S NOTHING I CAN DO ...
IT'S ALL RIGHT, HARUNA.
JUST BE YOURSELF.
THAT'LL BE ENOUGH FOR YOH.

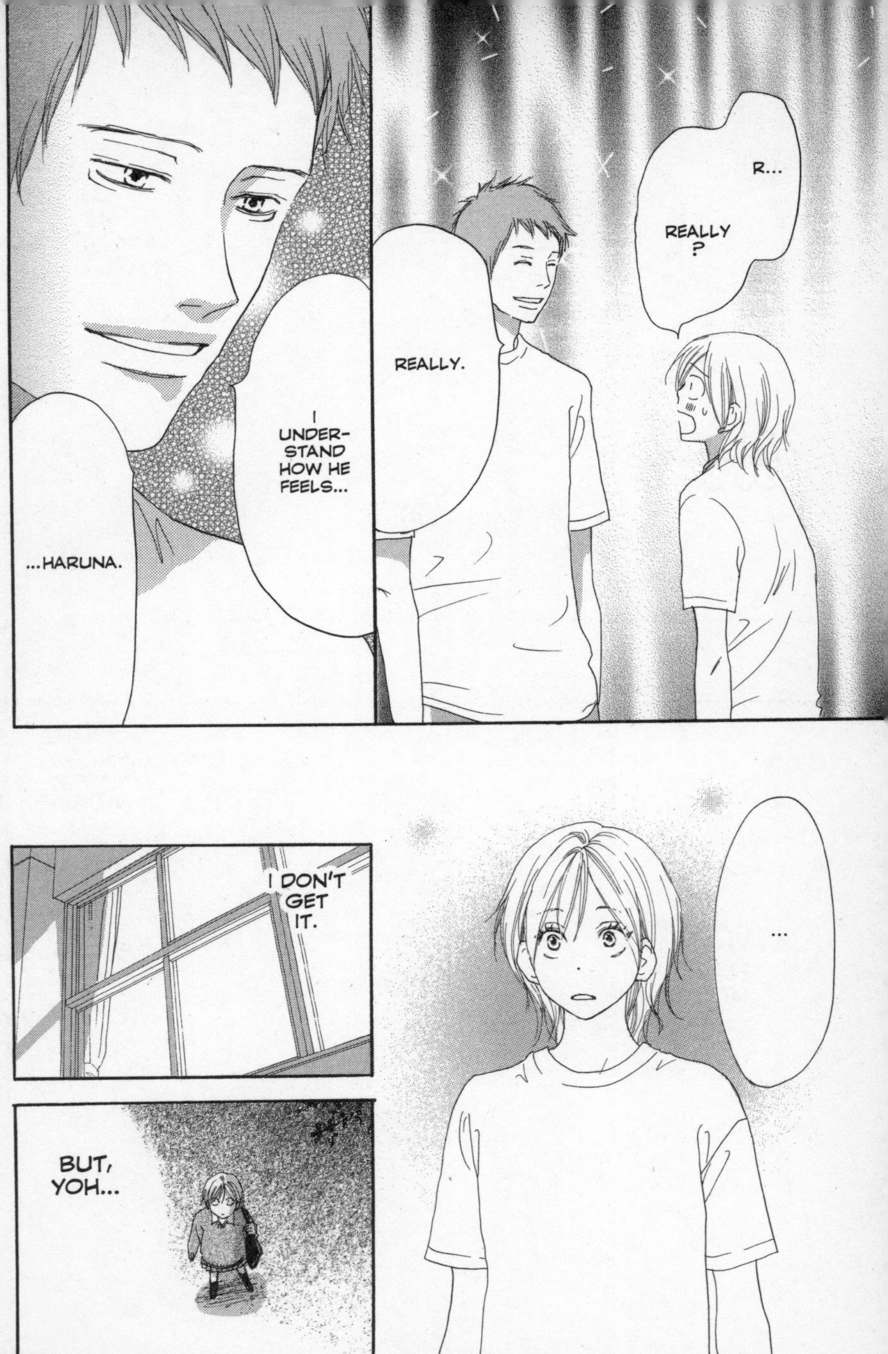
R...
REALLY?
REALLY.
I UNDERSTAND HOW HE FEELS...
...HARUNA.
...
I DON'T GET IT.
BUT, YOH...

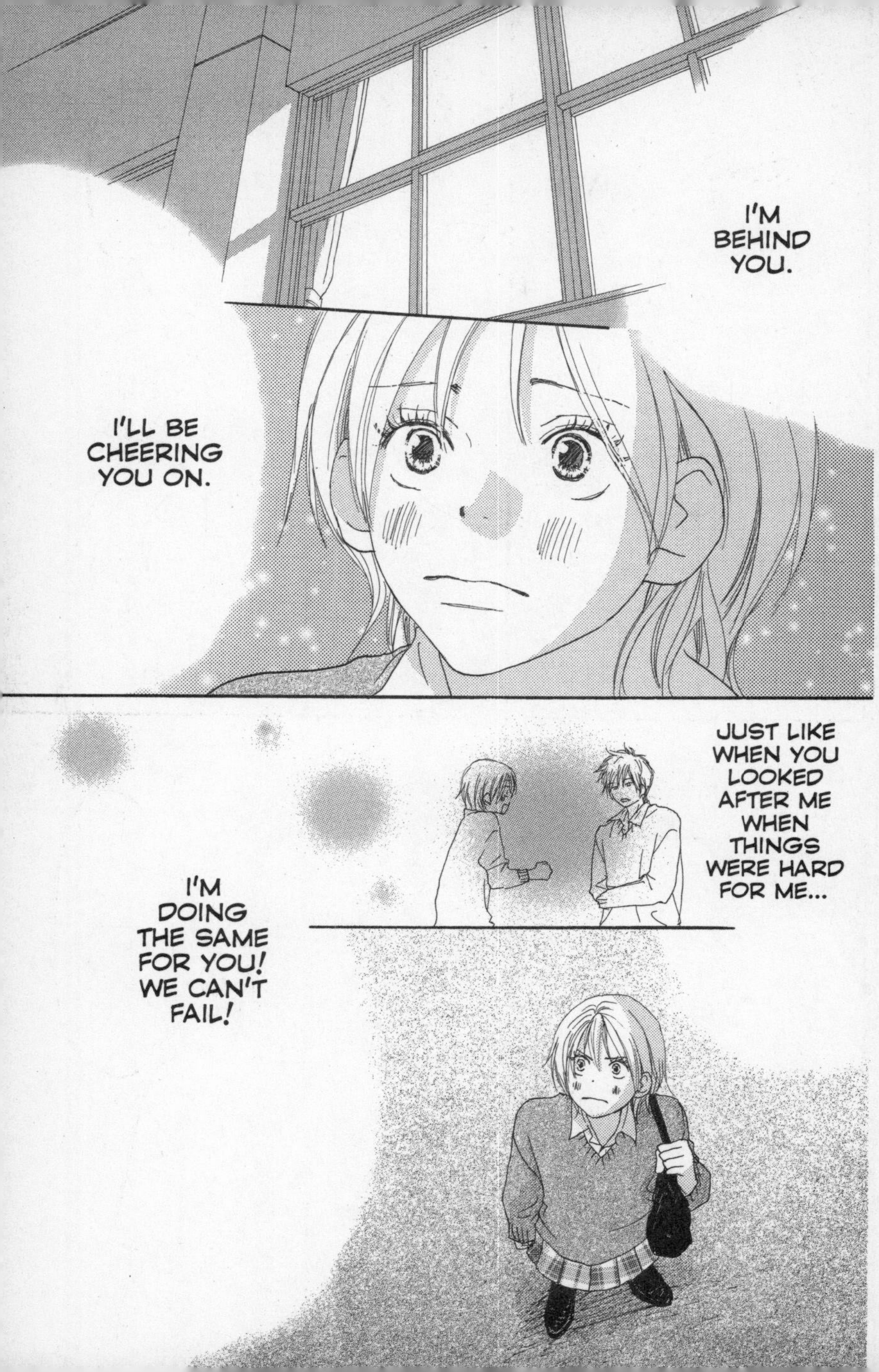
I'M BEHIND YOU.
I'LL BE CHEERING YOU ON.
JUST LIKE WHEN YOU LOOKED AFTER ME WHEN THINGS WERE HARD FOR ME...
I'M DOING THE SAME FOR YOU! WE CAN'T FAIL!

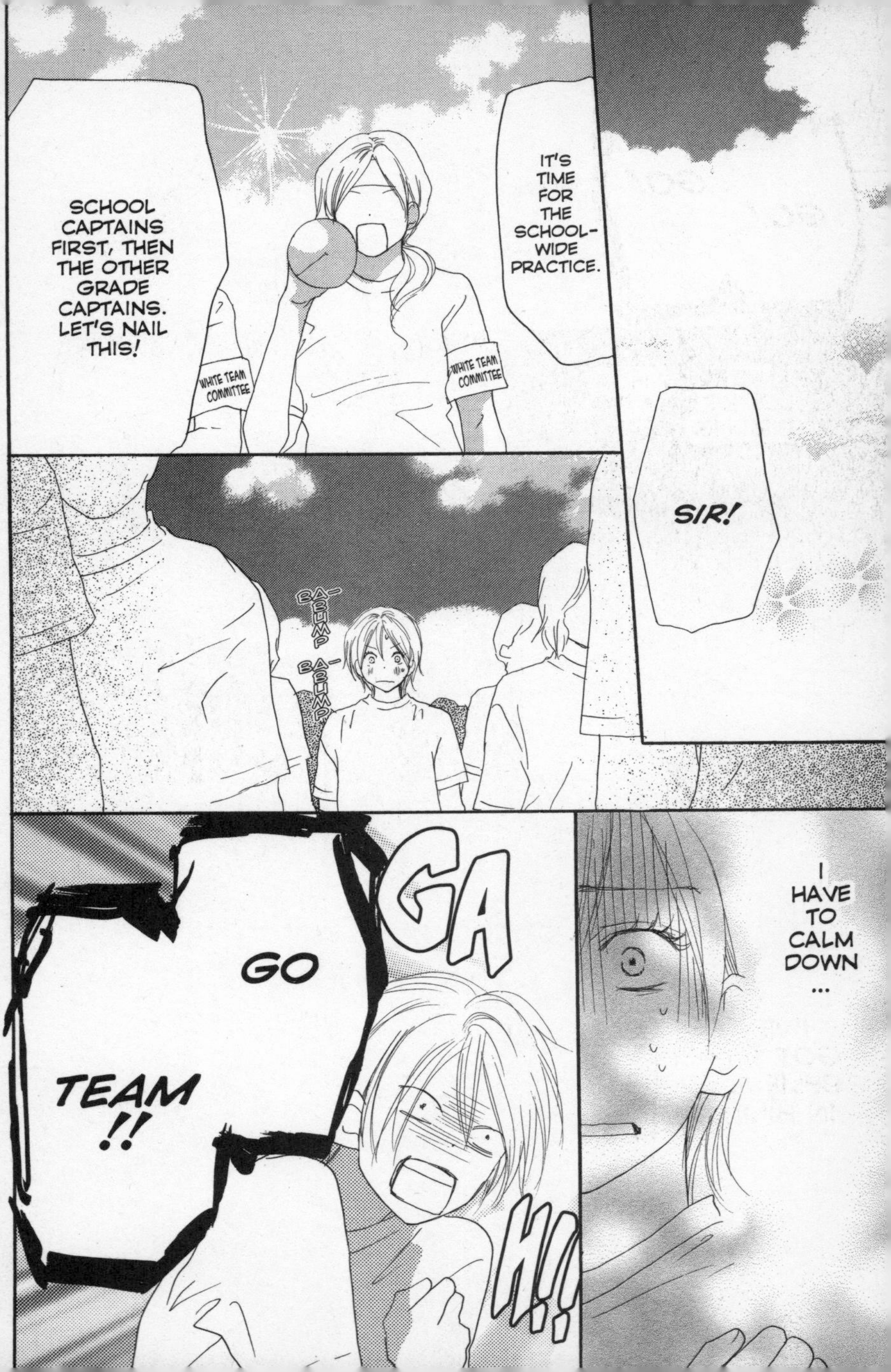

IT'S TIME FOR THE SCHOOL-WIDE PRACTICE.
SCHOOL CAPTAINS FIRST, THEN THE OTHER GRADE CAPTAINS. LET'S NAIL THIS!
WHITE TEAM COMMITTEE
WHITE TEAM COMMITTEE
SIR!
BA-BUMP
BA-BUMP
I HAVE TO CALM DOWN...
GA
H!!
GO TEAM!!

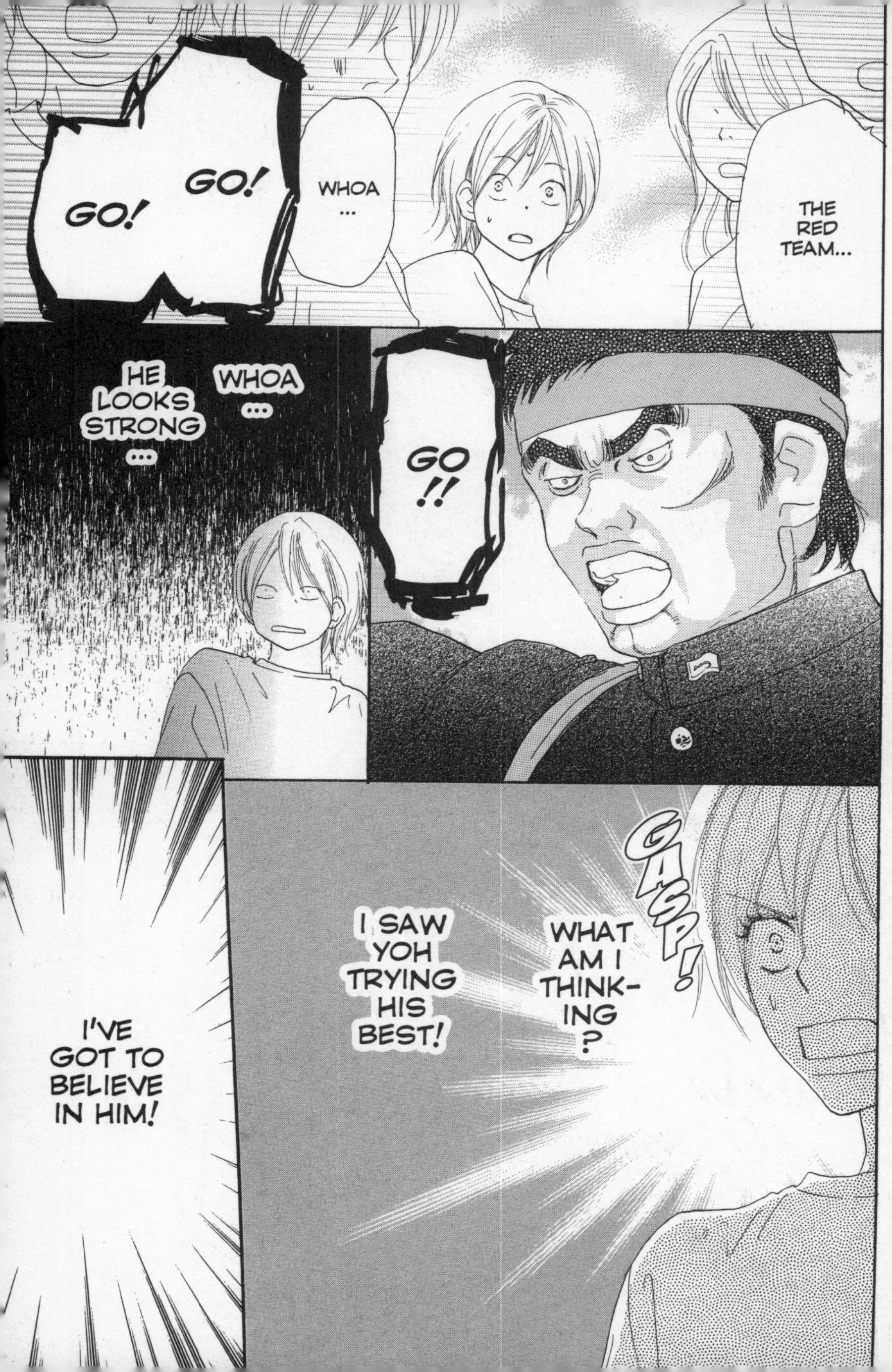
THE RED TEAM...
WHOA ...
GO!
GO!
GO !!
WHOA ...
HE LOOKS STRONG ...
GASP!
WHAT AM I THINKING-ING ?
I SAW YOH TRYING HIS BEST!
I'VE GOT TO BELIEVE IN HIM!

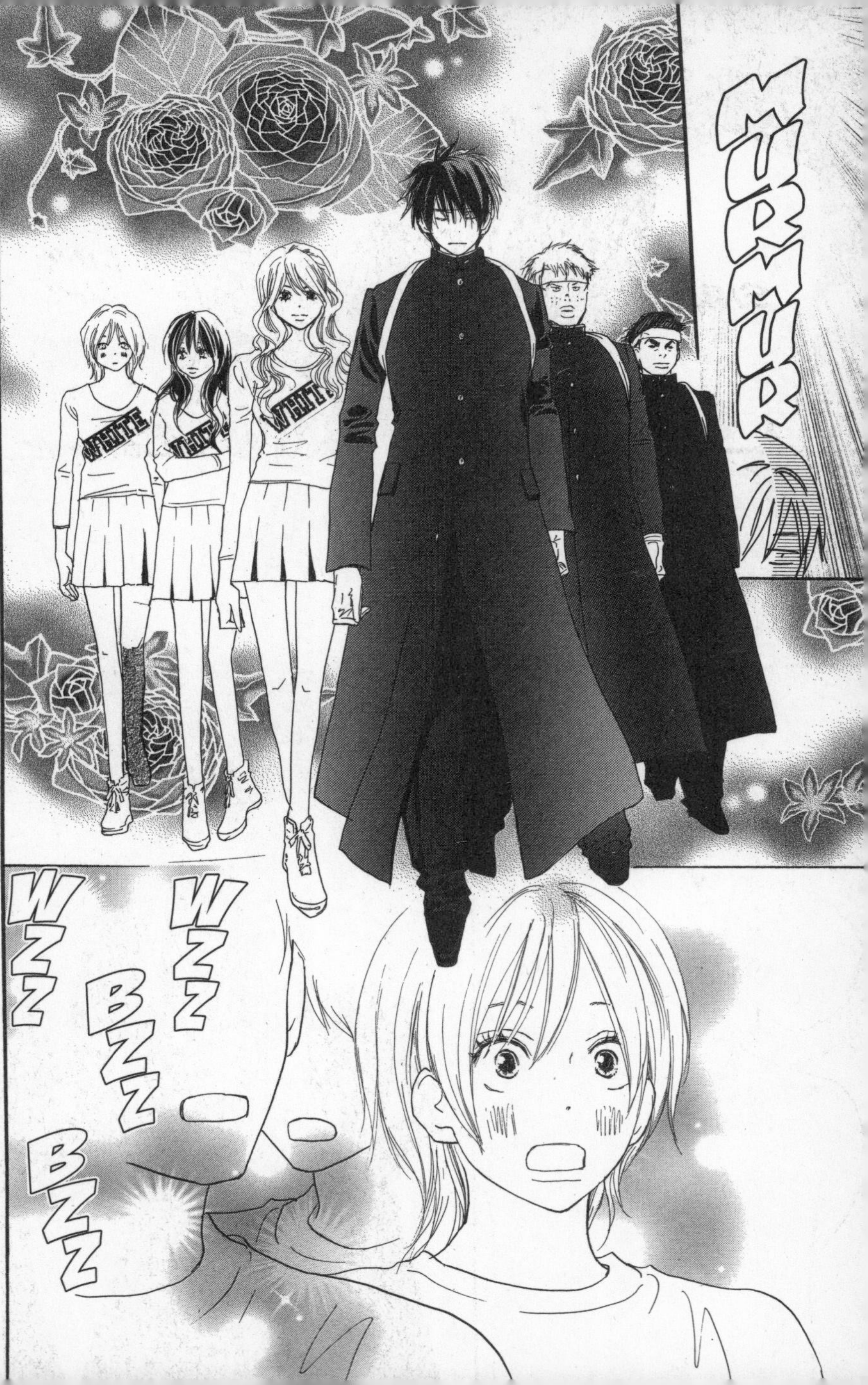
MURMUR
WZZ
BZZ
WZZ
BZZ

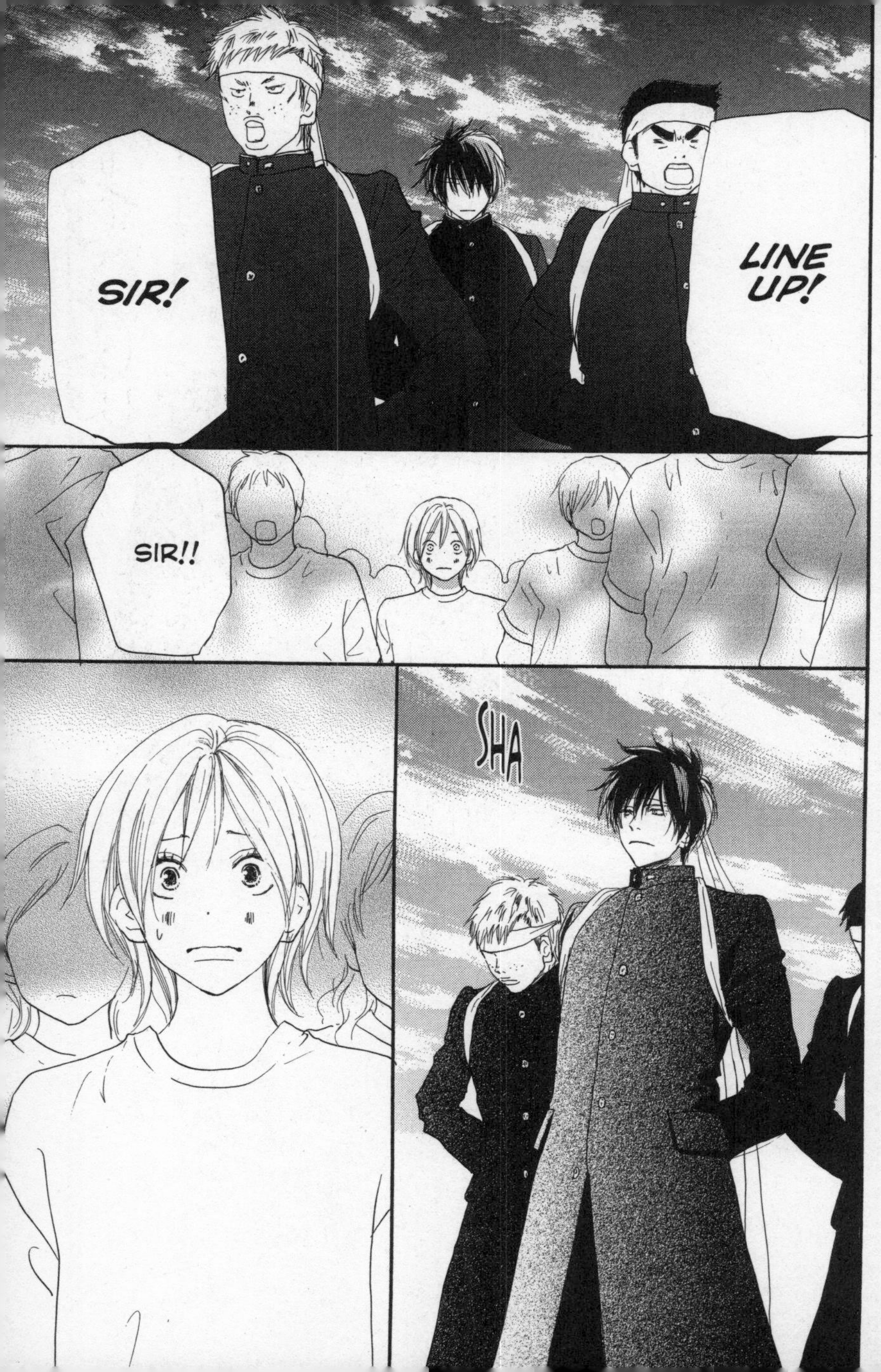
LINE UP!
SIR!
SIR!!
SHA

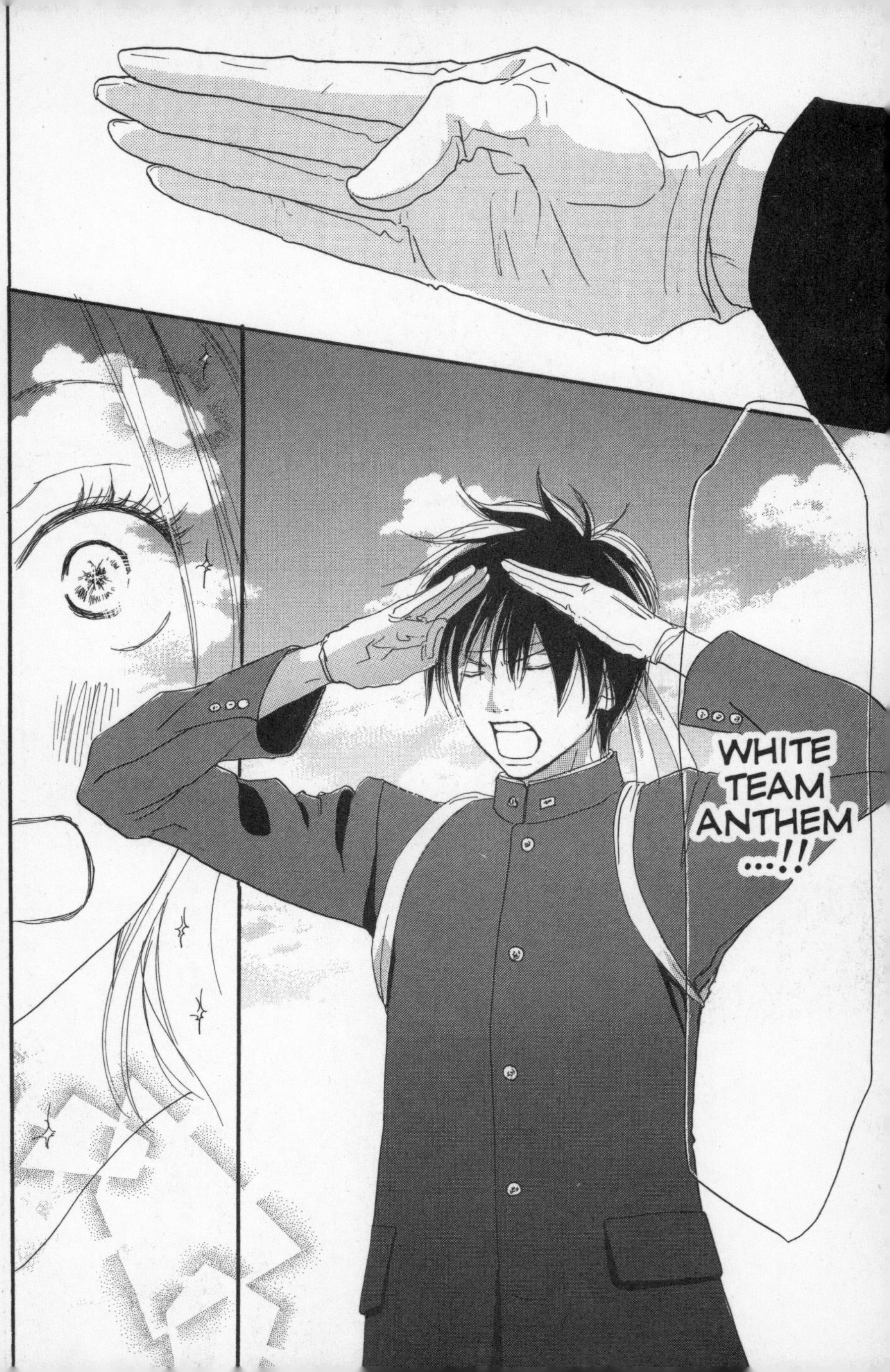
WHITE TEAM ANTHEM ...!!

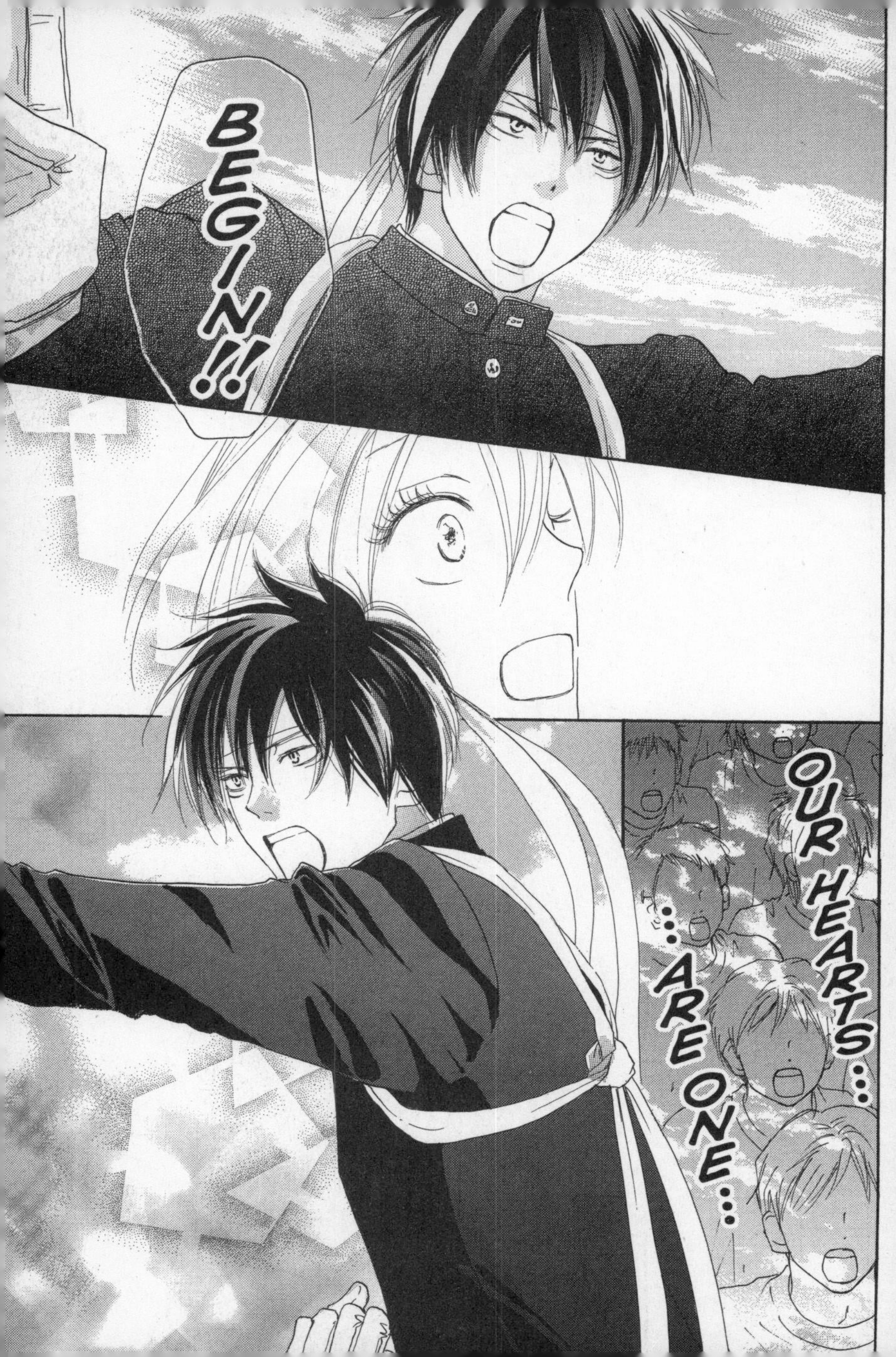
BEGIN!!
OUR HEARTS...
...ARE ONE...

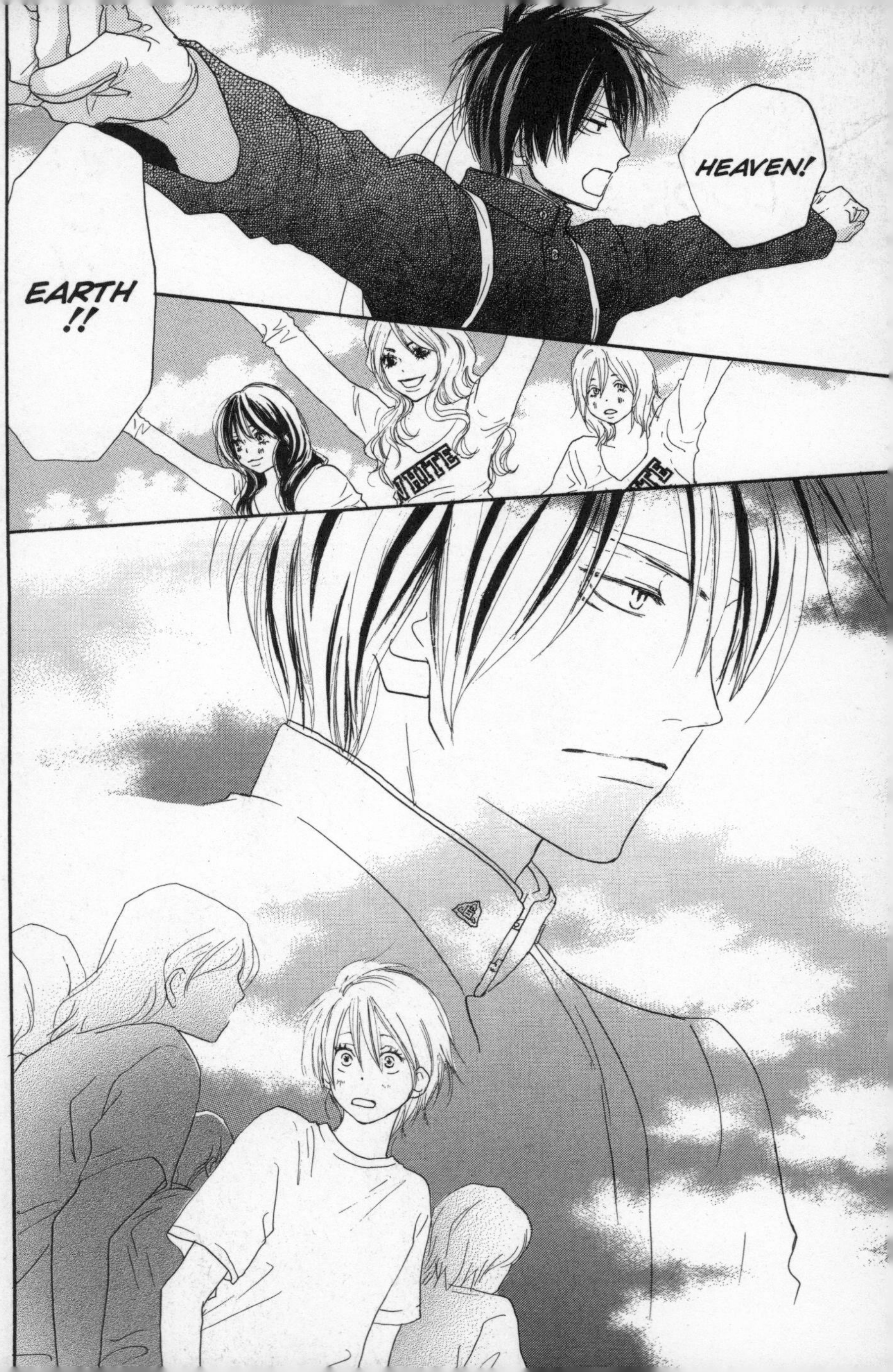
HEAVEN!
EARTH !!

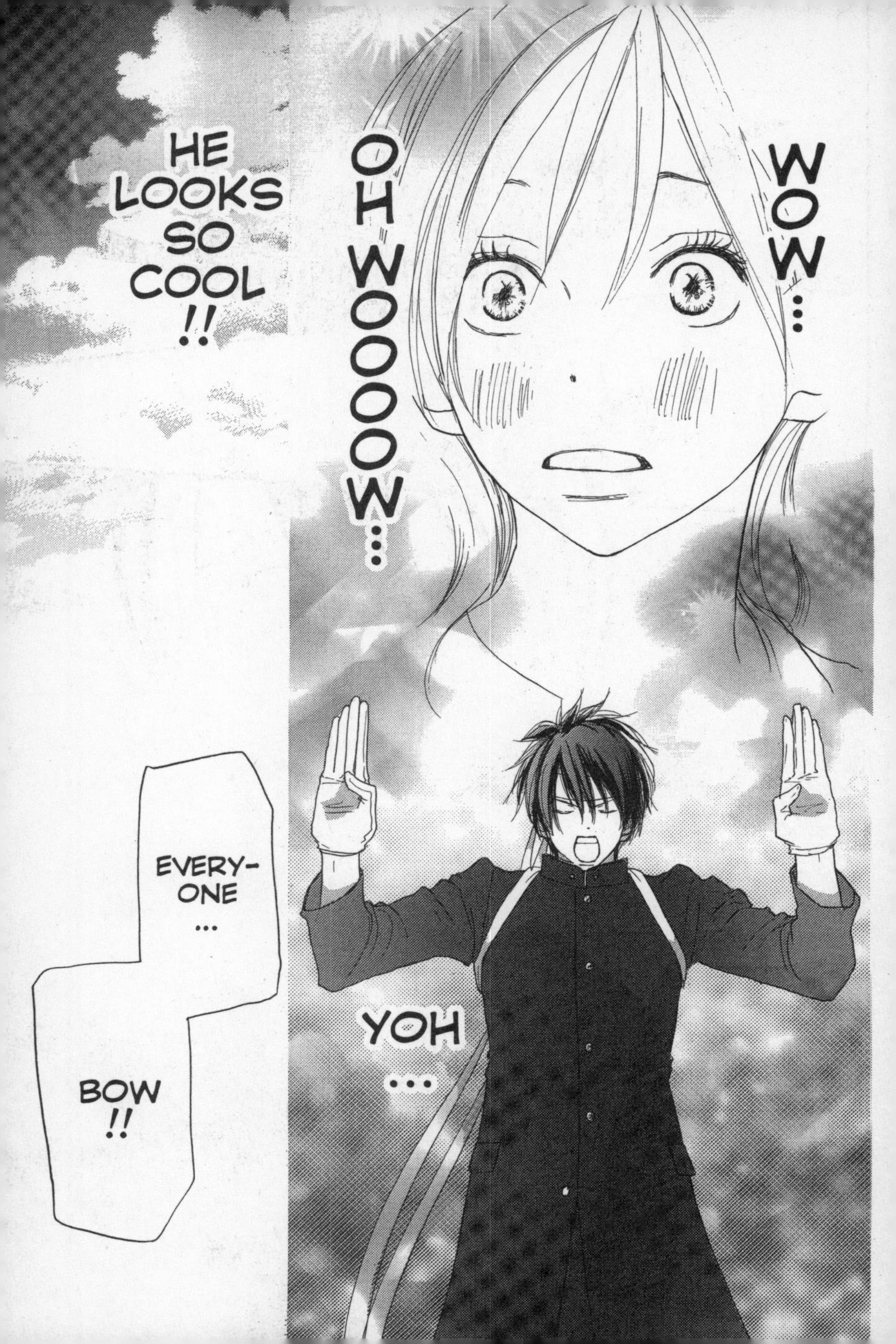
WOW...
OH WOOOOOW...
YOH...
HE LOOKS SO COOL!!
EVERY-ONE ... BOW!!

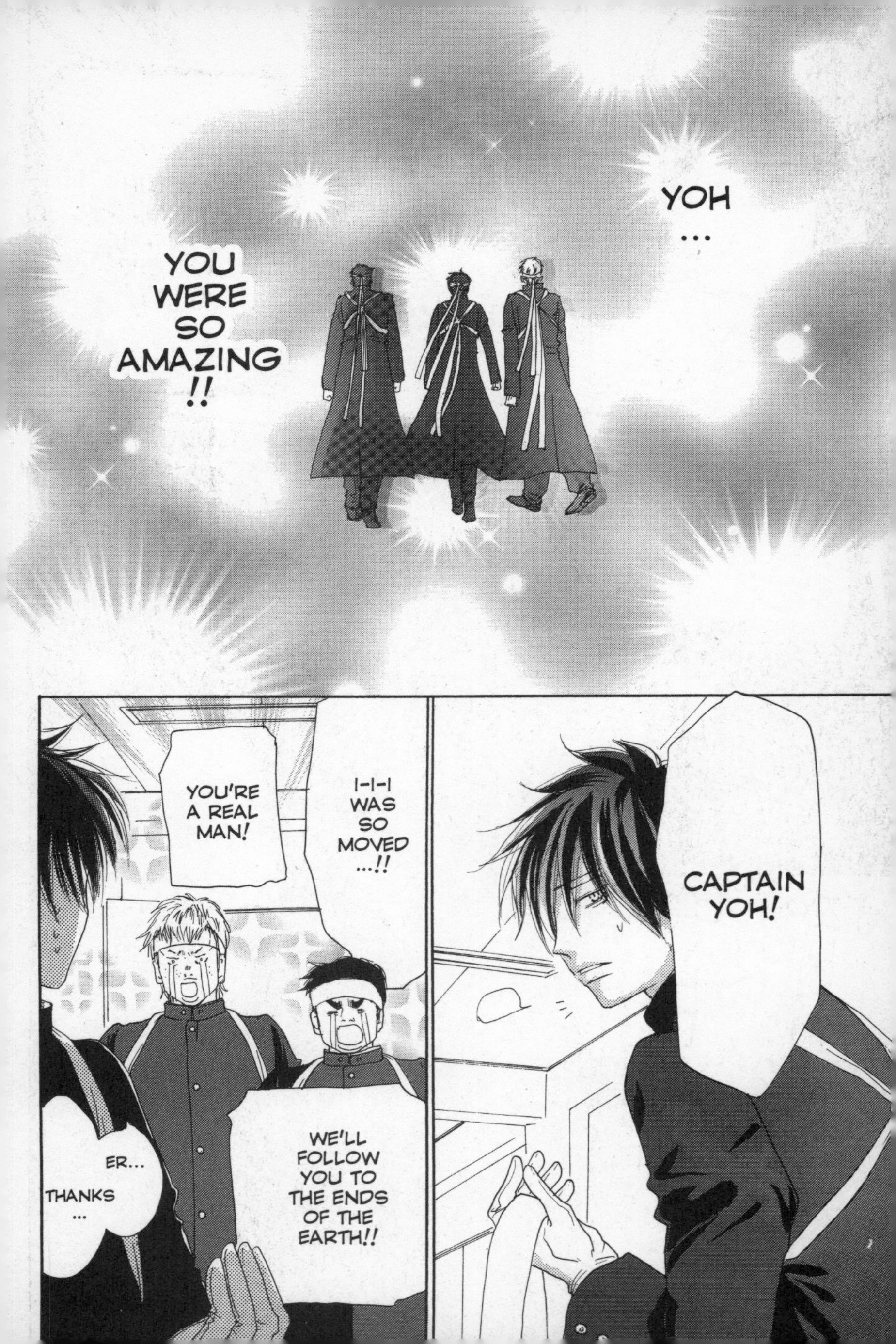
YOH ...
YOU WERE SO AMAZING!!
CAPTAIN YOH!
I-I-I WAS SO MOVED ...!!
YOU'RE A REAL MAN!
WE'LL FOLLOW YOU TO THE ENDS OF THE EARTH!!
ER... THANKS ...

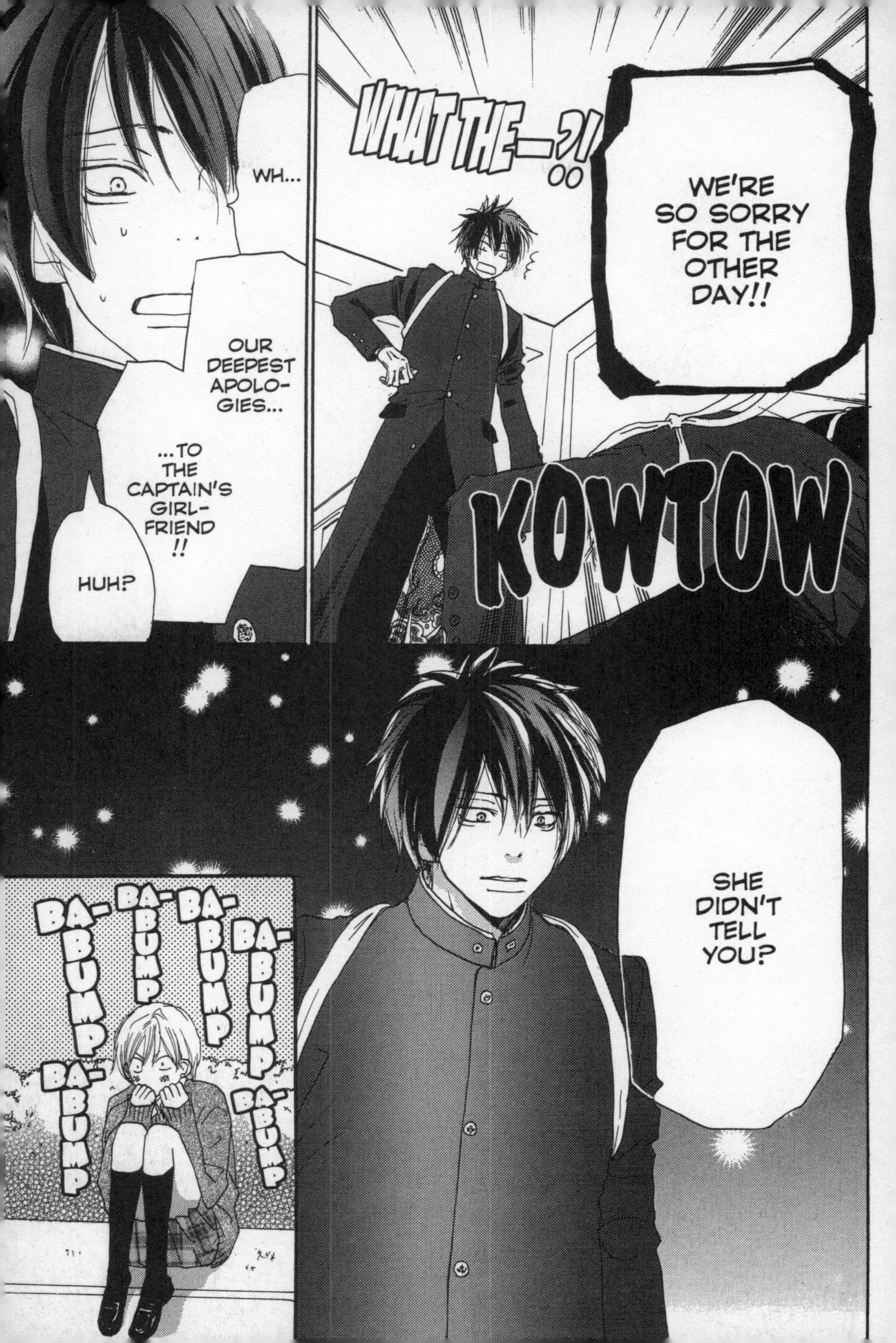
WE'RE SO SORRY FOR THE OTHER DAY!!
WHAT THE—?!
KOWTOW
WH...
OUR DEEPEST APOLOGIES...
...TO THE CAPTAIN'S GIRLFRIEND!!
HUH?
SHE DIDN'T TELL YOU?
BA-BUMP
BA-BUMP
BA-BUMP
BA-BUMP
BA-BUMP
BA-BUMP

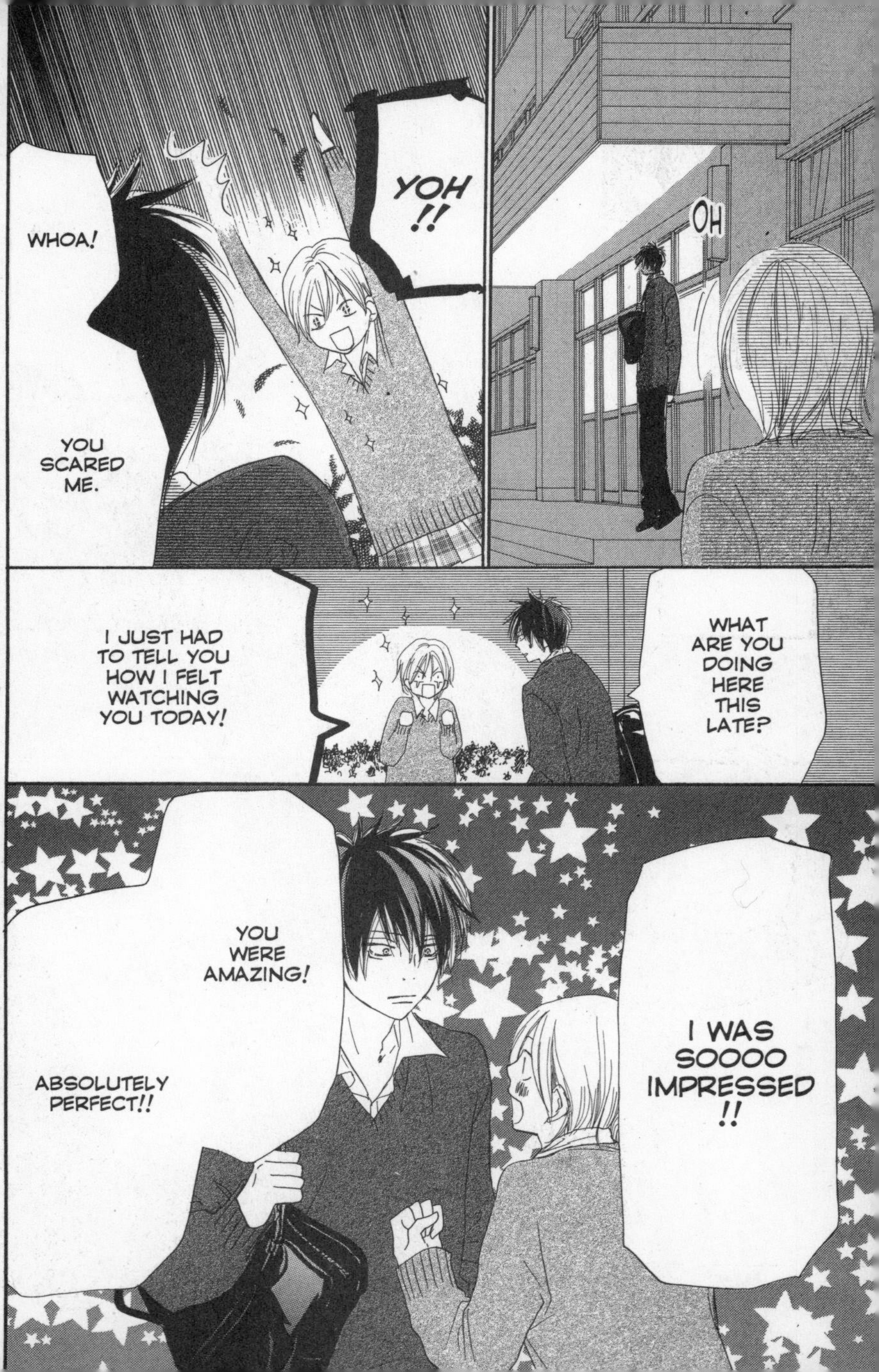
OH
YOH!!
WHOA!
YOU SCARED ME.
WHAT ARE YOU DOING HERE THIS LATE?
I JUST HAD TO TELL YOU HOW I FELT WATCHING YOU TODAY!
I WAS SOOOO IMPRESSED!!
YOU WERE AMAZING!
ABSOLUTELY PERFECT!!

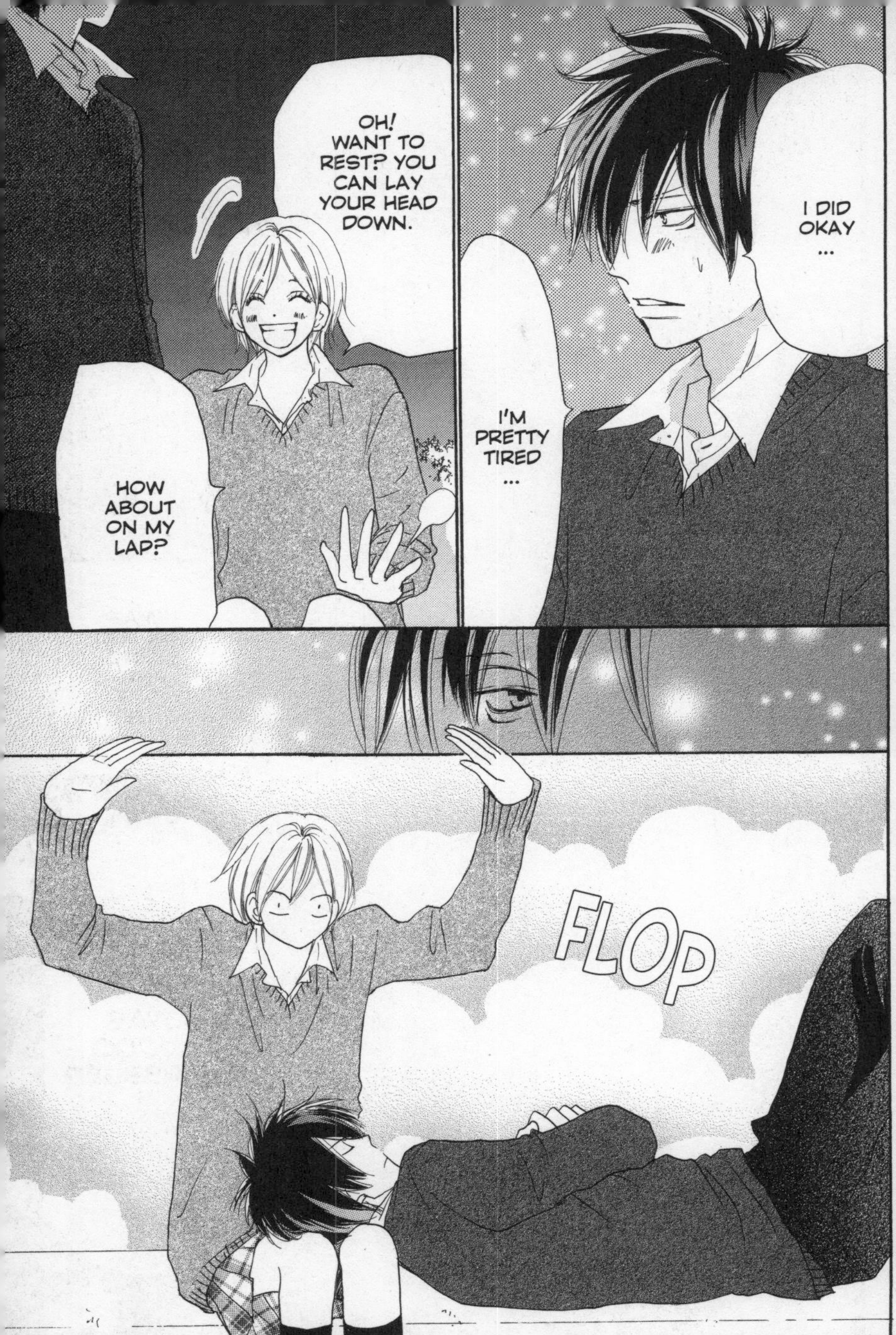
I DID OKAY ...
I'M PRETTY TIRED ...
OH! WANT TO REST? YOU CAN LAY YOUR HEAD DOWN.
HOW ABOUT ON MY LAP?
FLOP

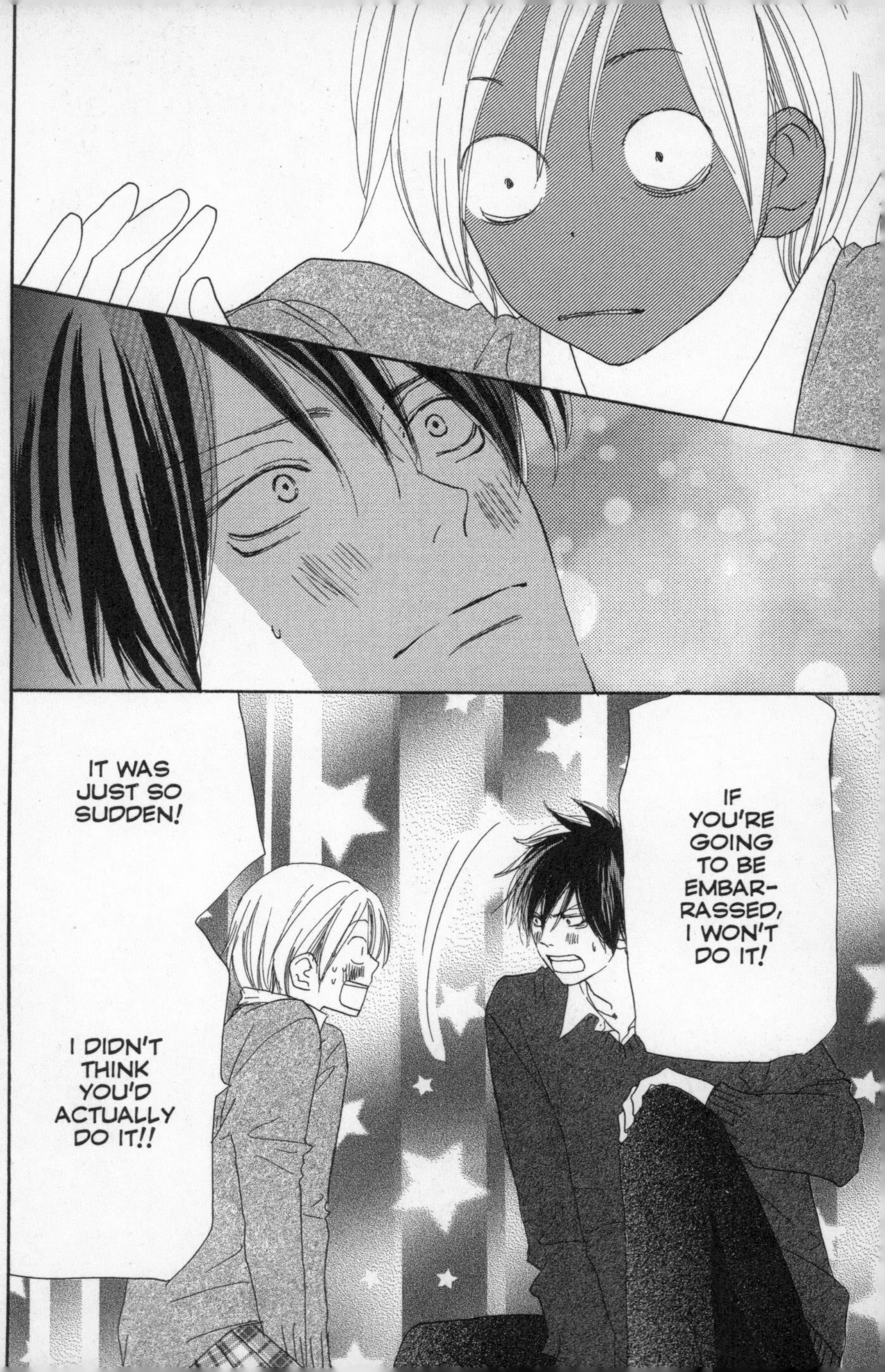
IF YOU'RE GOING TO BE EMBARRASSED, I WON'T DO IT!
IT WAS JUST SO SUDDEN!
I DIDN'T THINK YOU'D ACTUALLY DO IT!!

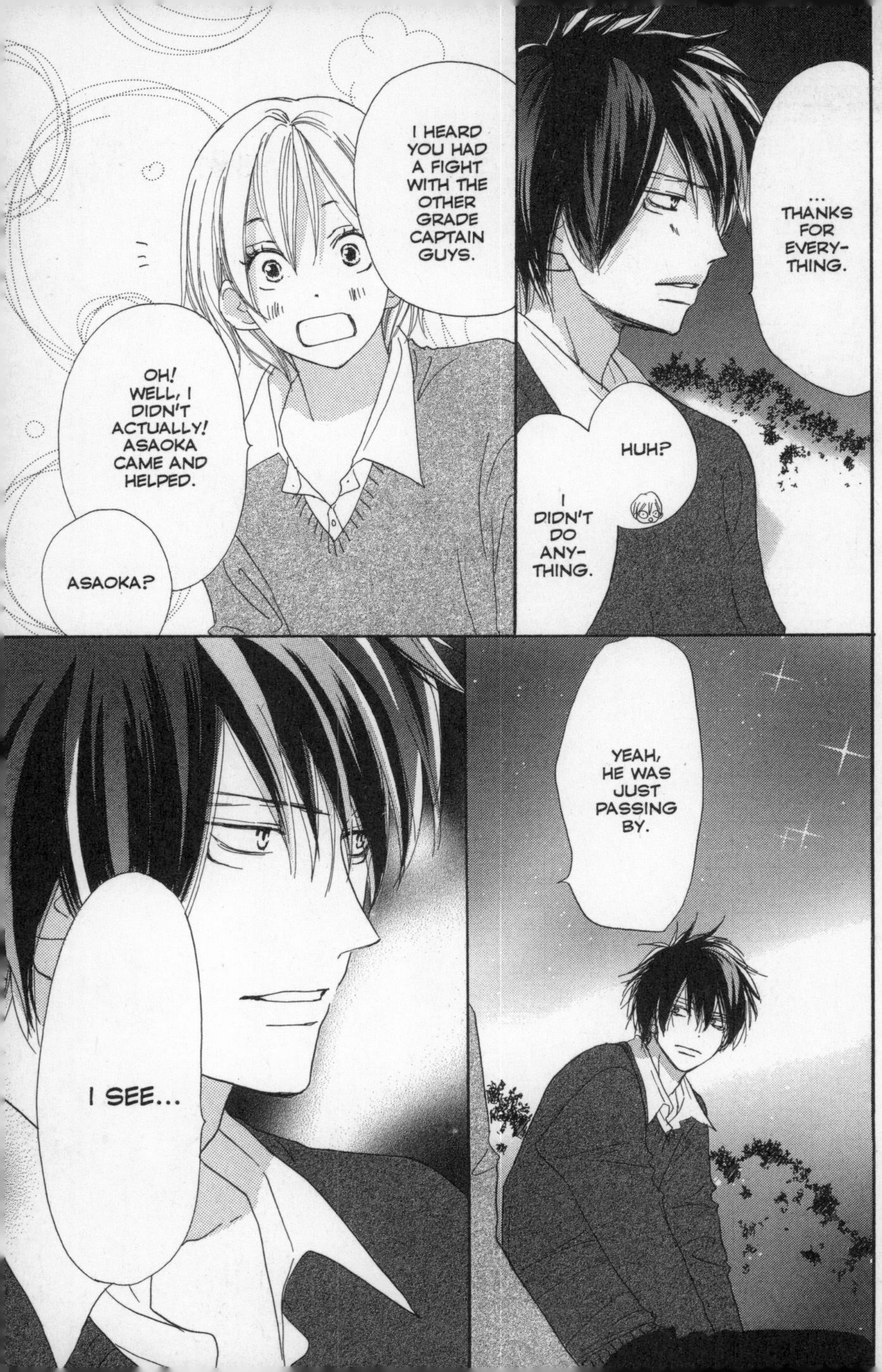
...THANKS FOR EVERY-THING.
HUH?
I DIDN'T DO ANY-THING.
I HEARD YOU HAD A FIGHT WITH THE OTHER GRADE CAPTAIN GUYS.
OH! WELL, I DIDN'T ACTUALLY! ASAOKA CAME AND HELPED.
ASAOKA?
YEAH, HE WAS JUST PASSING BY.
I SEE...

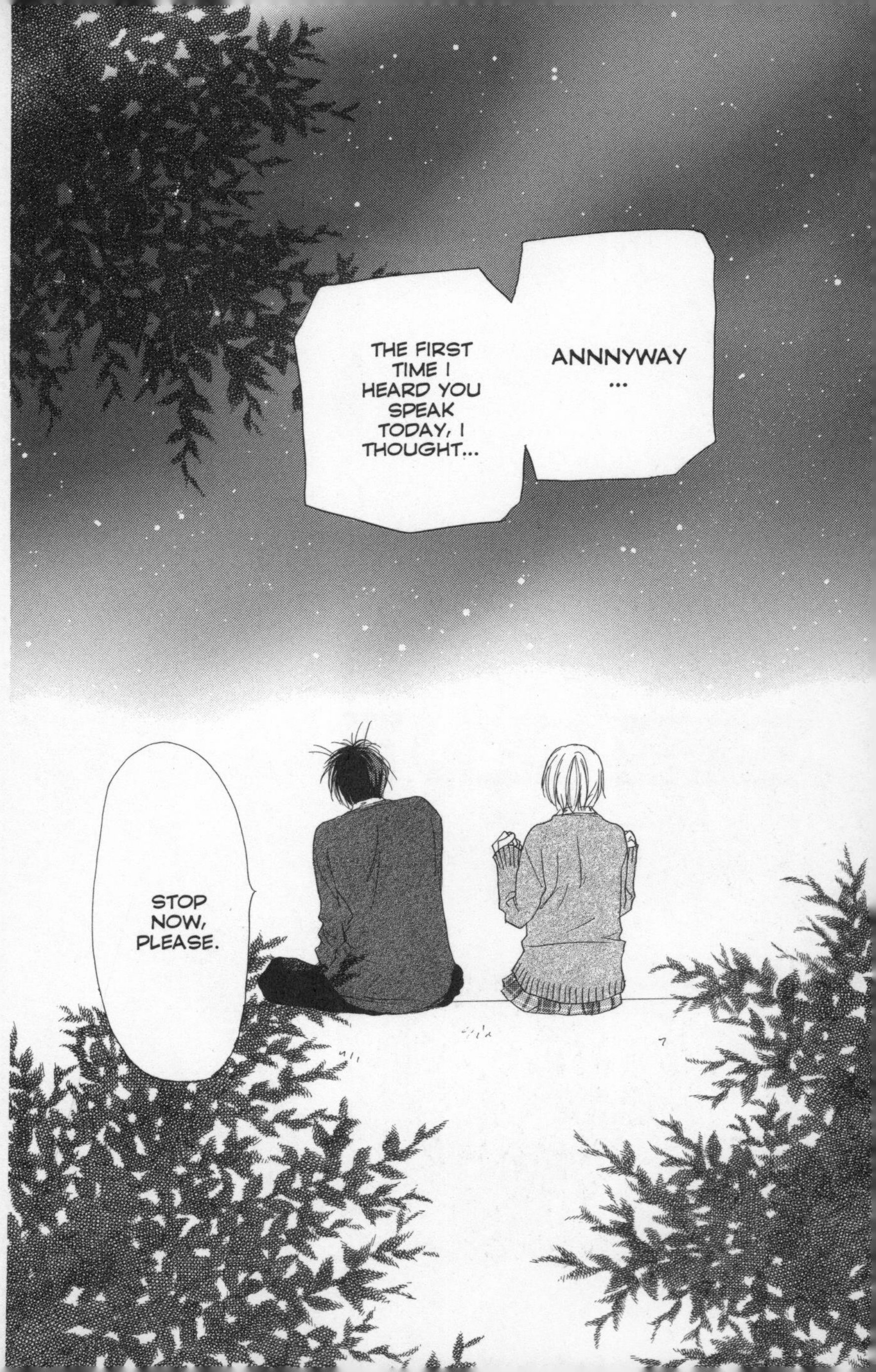
ANNNYWAY ...
THE FIRST TIME I HEARD YOU SPEAK TODAY, I THOUGHT...
STOP NOW, PLEASE.

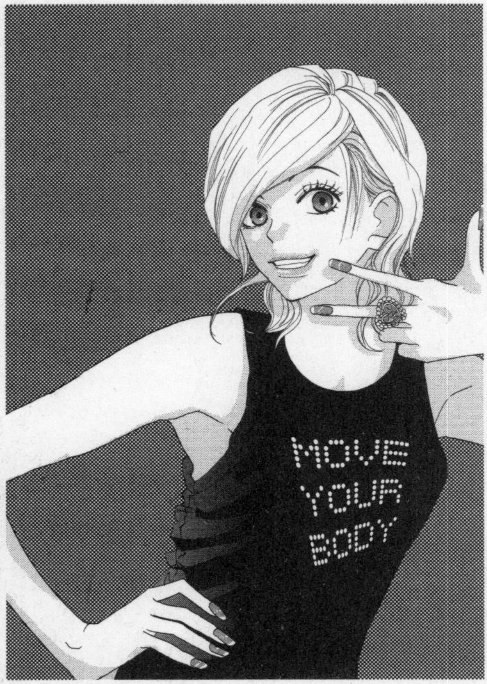
MOVE
YOUR
BODY

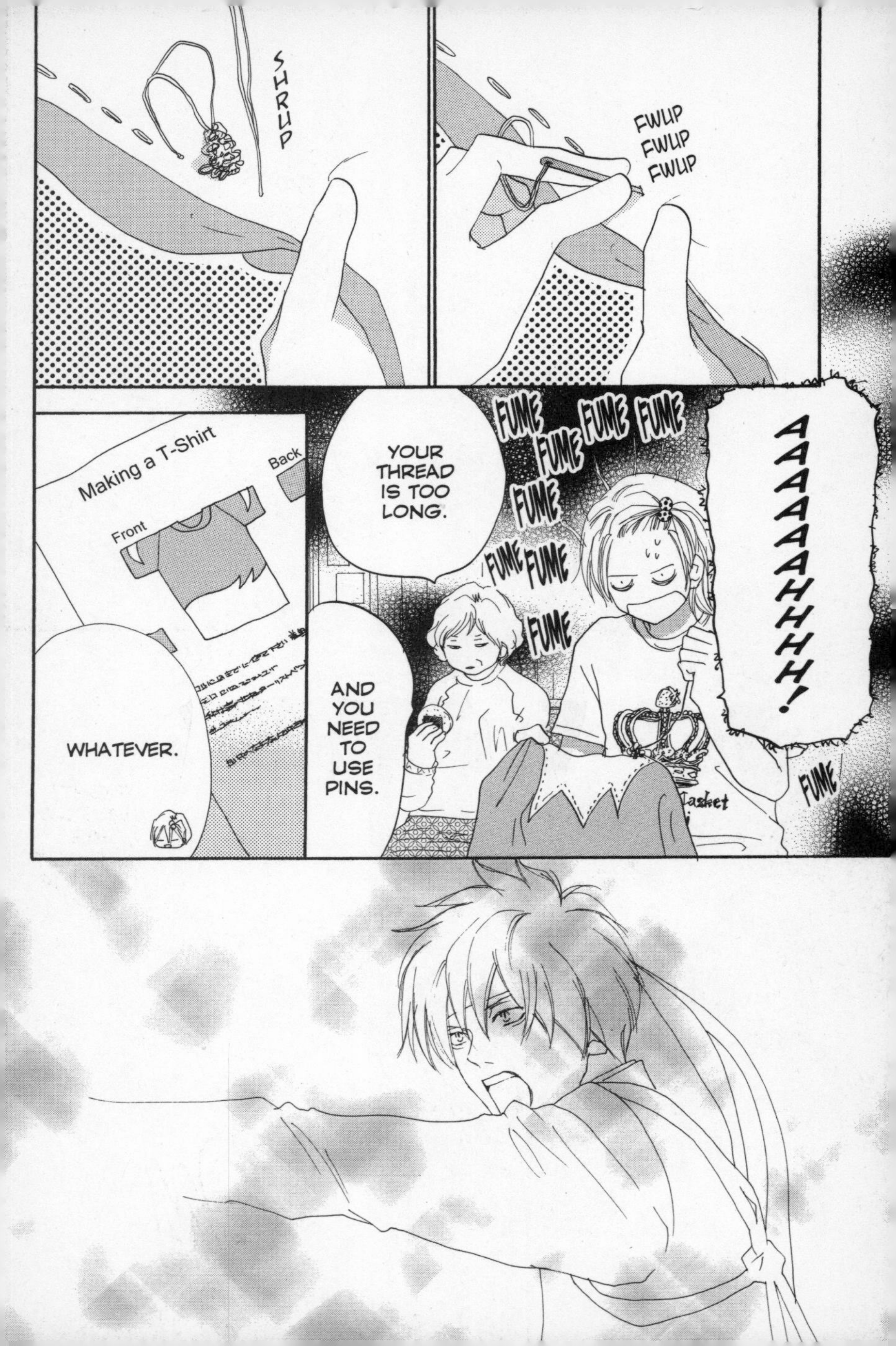
FWUP
FWUP
FWUP
SHRUP
AAAAAAHHHH!
FUME FUME FUME FUME FUME FUME FUME FUME FUME
YOUR THREAD IS TOO LONG.
AND YOU NEED TO USE PINS.
FUME
Making a T-Shirt
Back
Front
WHATEVER.

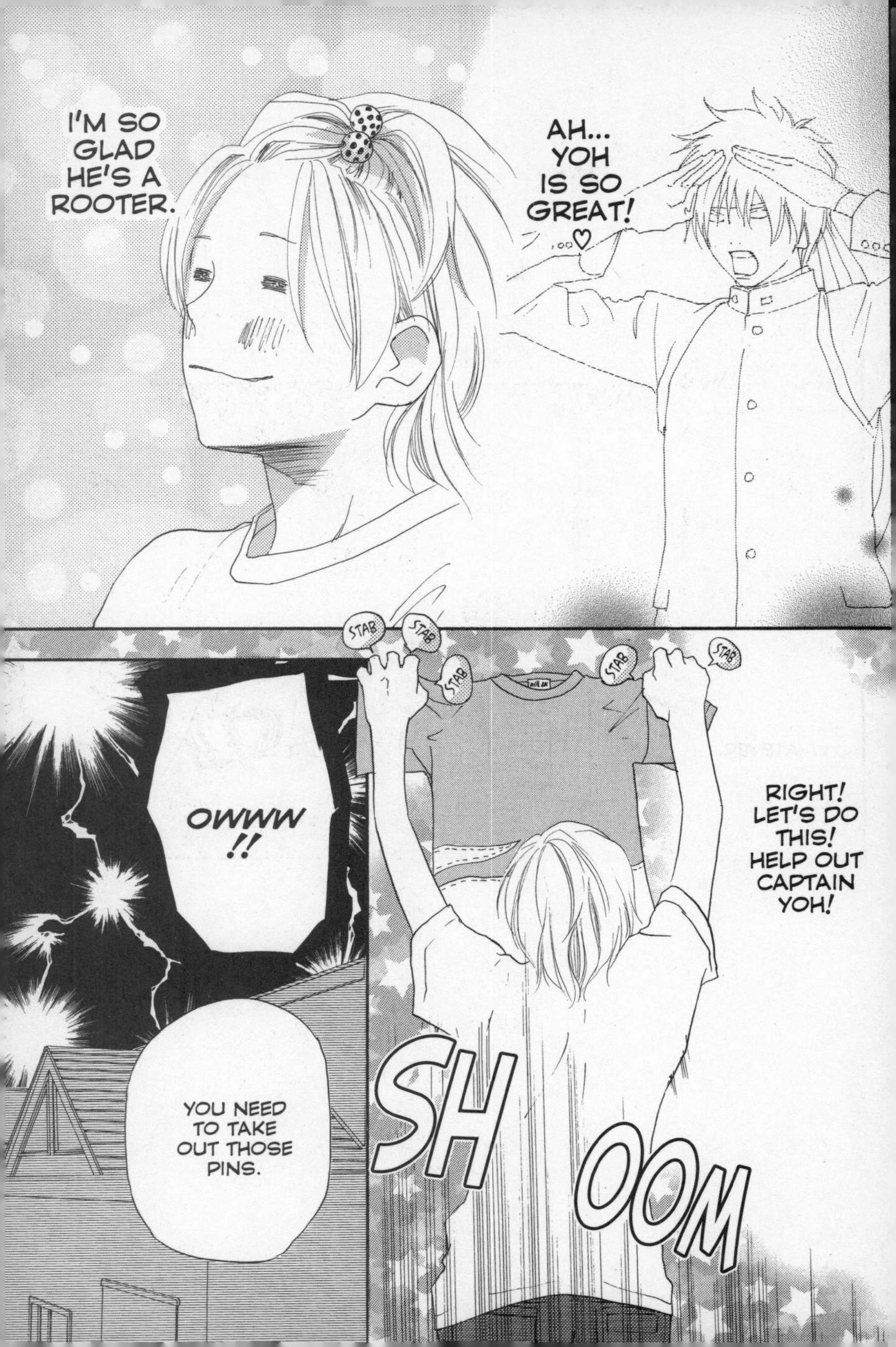
AH... YOH IS SO GREAT!
I'M SO GLAD HE'S A ROOTER.
STAB
STAB
STAB
STAB
STAB
RIGHT! LET'S DO THIS! HELP OUT CAPTAIN YOH!
SHOOM
OWWW!!
YOU NEED TO TAKE OUT THOSE PINS.

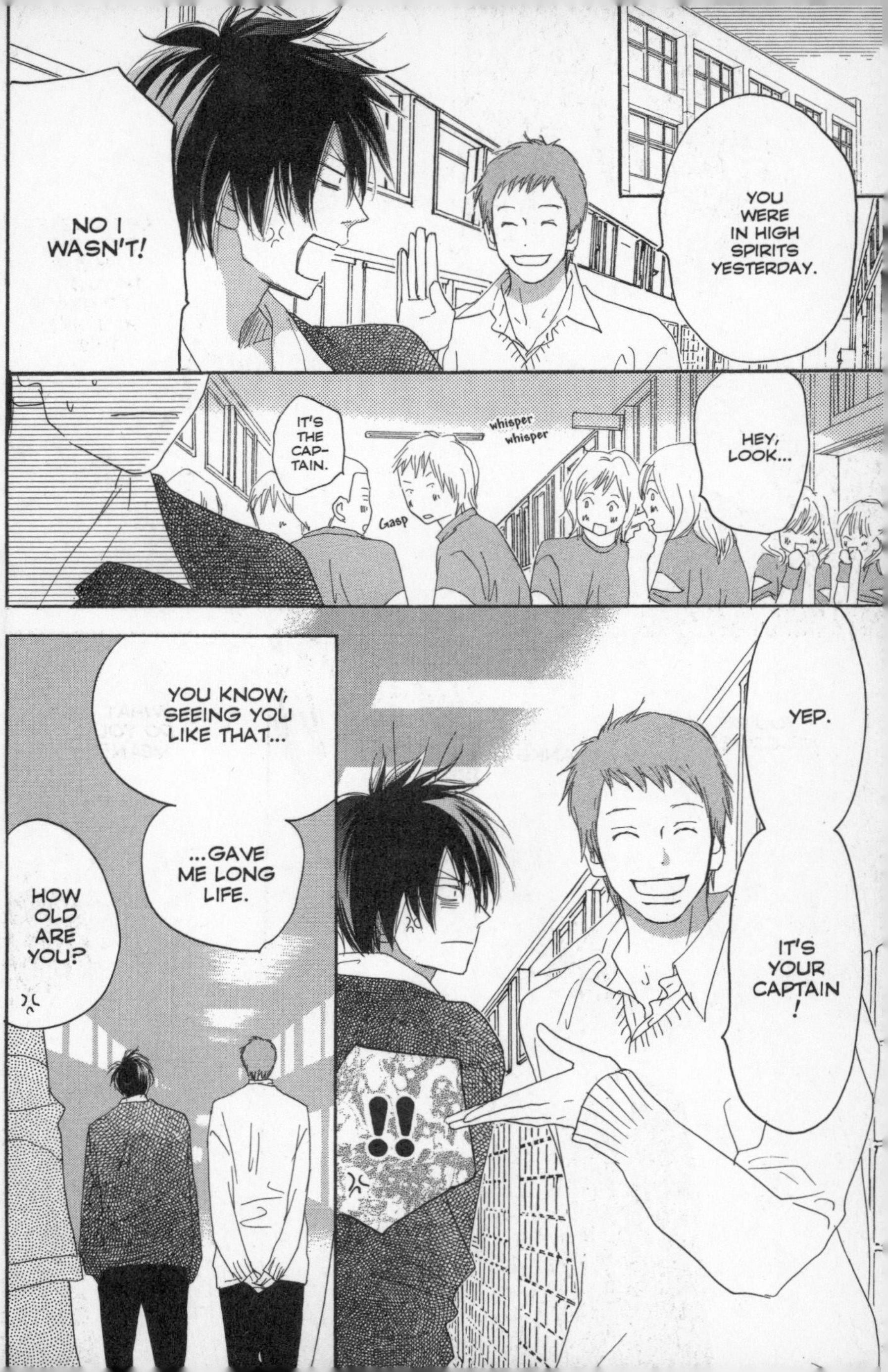
YOU WERE IN HIGH SPIRITS YESTERDAY.
NO I WASN'T!
HEY, LOOK...
whisper whisper
IT'S THE CAP-TAIN.
Gasp
YEP.
IT'S YOUR CAPTAIN!
YOU KNOW, SEEING YOU LIKE THAT...
...GAVE ME LONG LIFE.
HOW OLD ARE YOU?

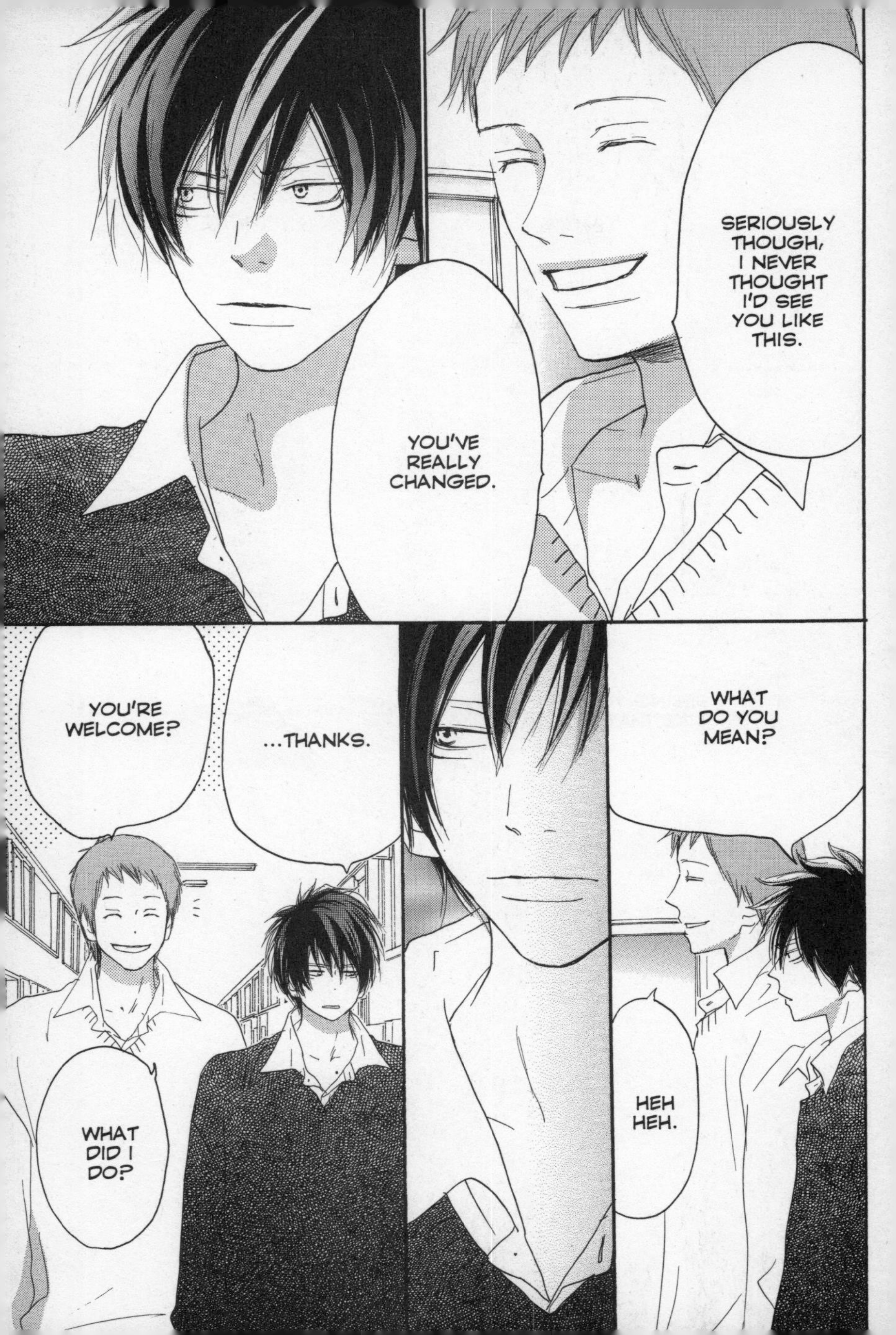
SERIOUSLY THOUGH, I NEVER THOUGHT I'D SEE YOU LIKE THIS.
YOU'VE REALLY CHANGED.
WHAT DO YOU MEAN?
HEH HEH.
...THANKS.
YOU'RE WELCOME?
WHAT DID I DO?

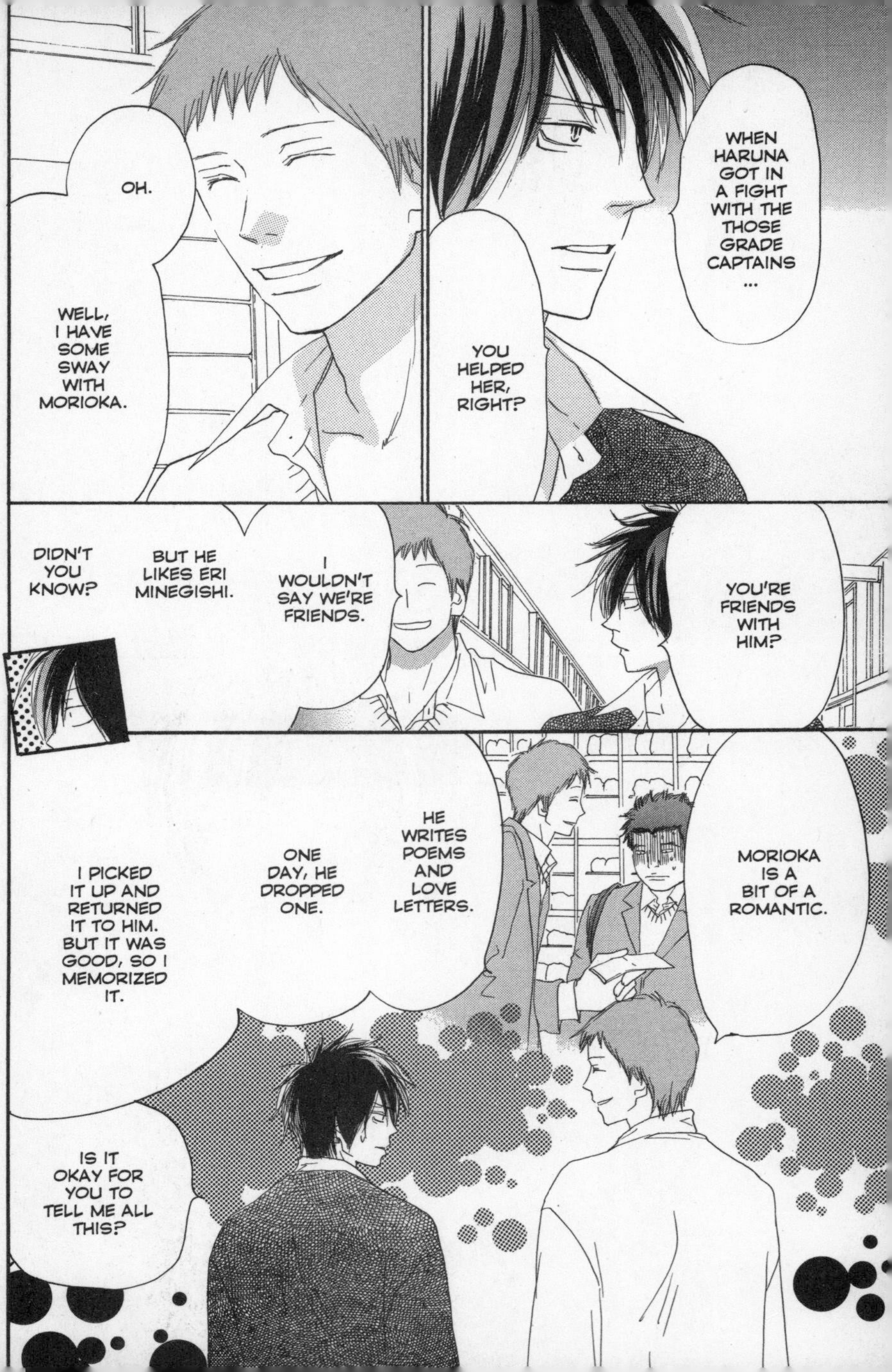
WHEN HARUNA GOT IN A FIGHT WITH THE THOSE GRADE CAPTAINS ...
YOU HELPED HER, RIGHT?
OH.
WELL, I HAVE SOME SWAY WITH MORIOKA.
YOU'RE FRIENDS WITH HIM?
I WOULDN'T SAY WE'RE FRIENDS.
BUT HE LIKES ERI MINEGISHI.
DIDN'T YOU KNOW?
MORIOKA IS A BIT OF A ROMANTIC.
HE WRITES POEMS AND LOVE LETTERS.
ONE DAY, HE DROPPED ONE.
I PICKED IT UP AND RETURNED IT TO HIM. BUT IT WAS GOOD, SO I MEMORIZED IT.
IS IT OKAY FOR YOU TO TELL ME ALL THIS?

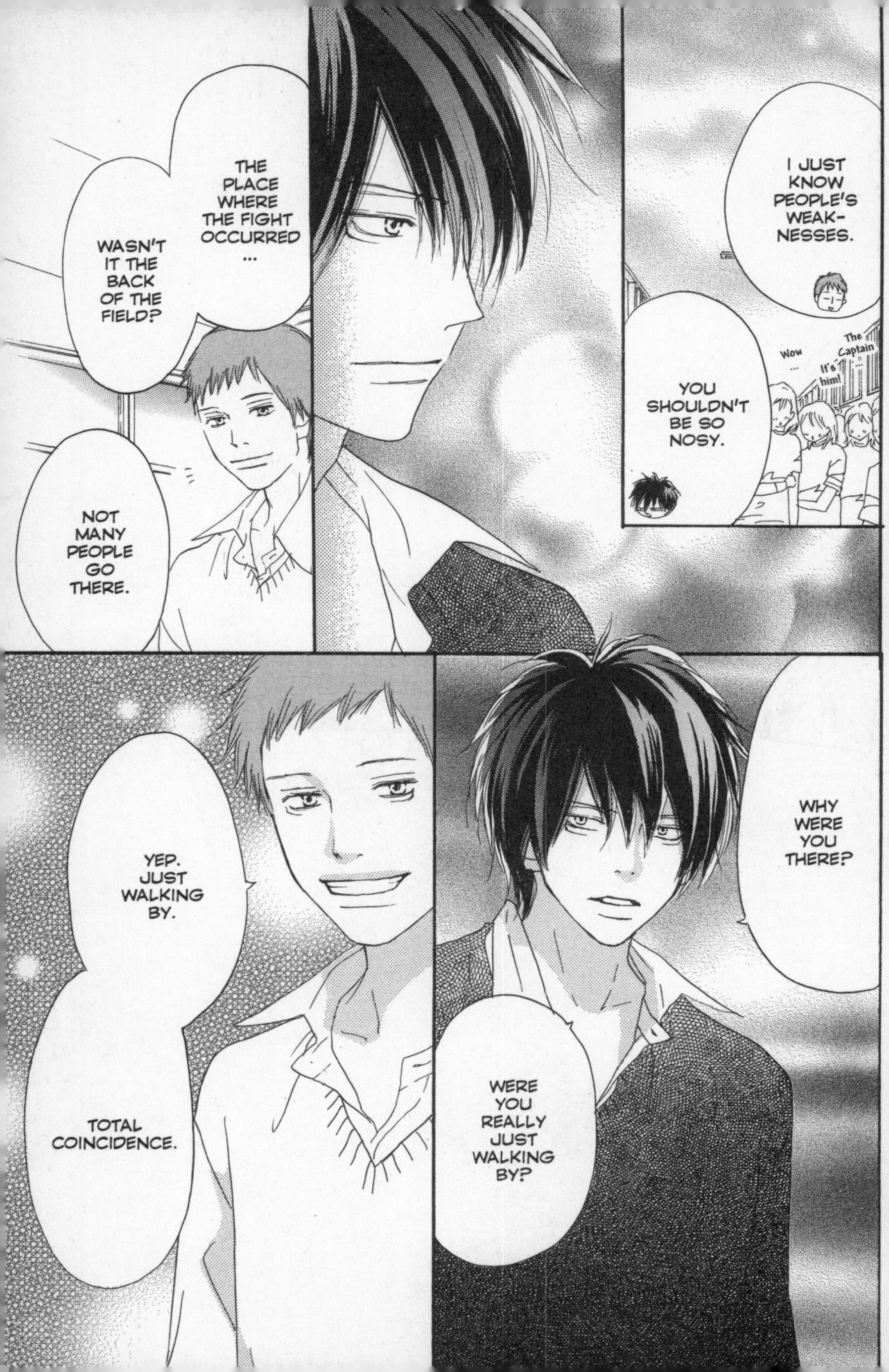
I JUST KNOW PEOPLE'S WEAK-NESSES.
The Captain ...
It's him!
Wow ...
YOU SHOULDN'T BE SO NOSY.
THE PLACE WHERE THE FIGHT OCCURRED ...
WASN'T IT THE BACK OF THE FIELD?
NOT MANY PEOPLE GO THERE.
WHY WERE YOU THERE?
WERE YOU REALLY JUST WALKING BY?
YEP. JUST WALKING BY.
TOTAL COINCIDENCE.

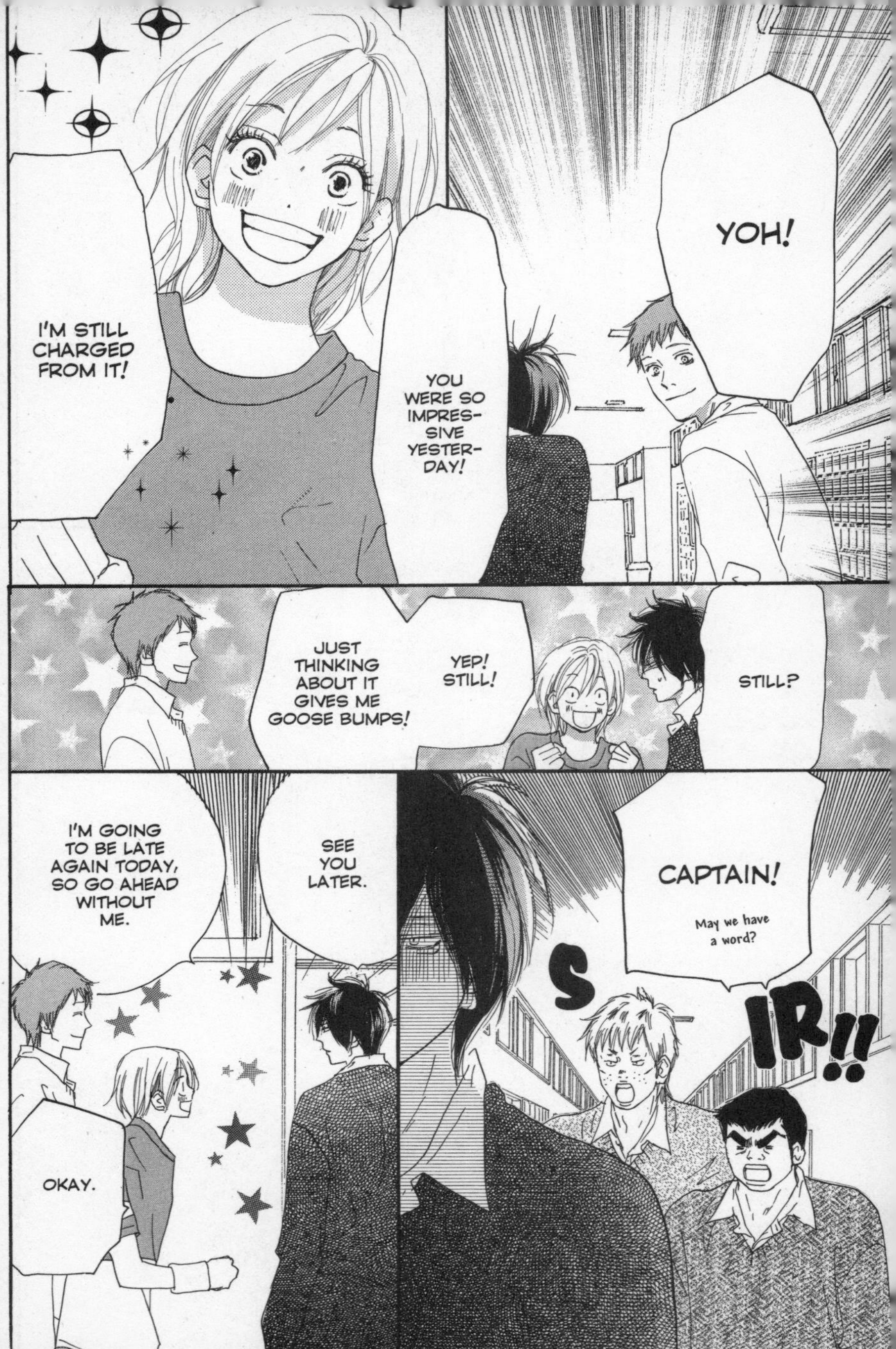
YOH!
YOU WERE SO IMPRESSIVE YESTERDAY!
I'M STILL CHARGED FROM IT!
STILL?
YEP! STILL!
JUST THINKING ABOUT IT GIVES ME GOOSE BUMPS!
CAPTAIN!
May we have a word?
S
IR!!
SEE YOU LATER.
I'M GOING TO BE LATE AGAIN TODAY, SO GO AHEAD WITHOUT ME.
OKAY.

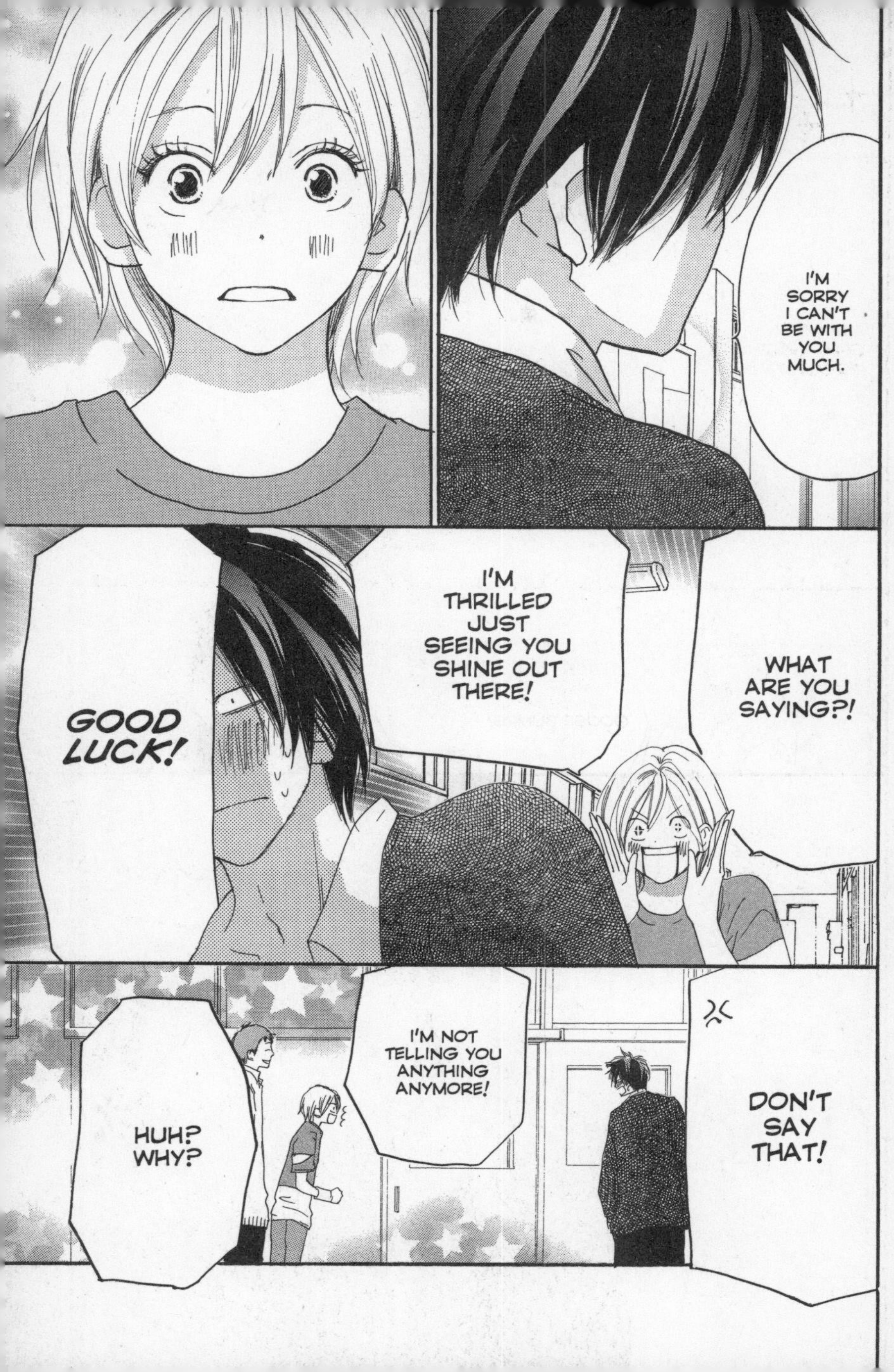
I'M SORRY I CAN'T BE WITH YOU MUCH.
WHAT ARE YOU SAYING?!
I'M THRILLED JUST SEEING YOU SHINE OUT THERE!
GOOD LUCK!
DON'T SAY THAT!
I'M NOT TELLING YOU ANYTHING ANYMORE!
HUH? WHY?

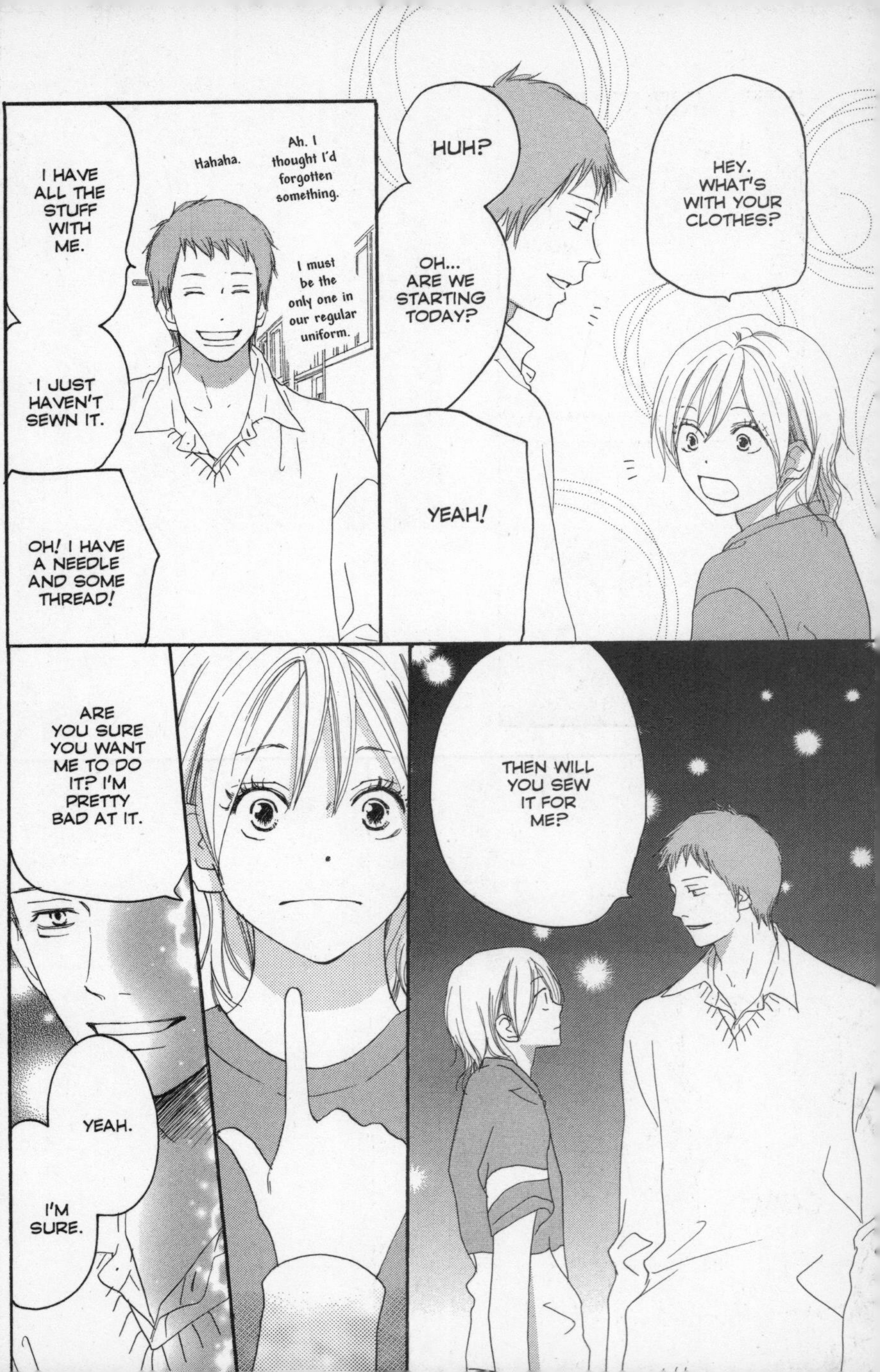
HEY. WHAT'S WITH YOUR CLOTHES?
HUH?
OH... ARE WE STARTING TODAY?
YEAH!
Ah. I thought I'd forgotten something.
Hahaha.
I must be the only one in our regular uniform.
I HAVE ALL THE STUFF WITH ME.
I JUST HAVEN'T SEWN IT.
OH! I HAVE A NEEDLE AND SOME THREAD!
THEN WILL YOU SEW IT FOR ME?
ARE YOU SURE YOU WANT ME TO DO IT? I'M PRETTY BAD AT IT.
YEAH.
I'M SURE.

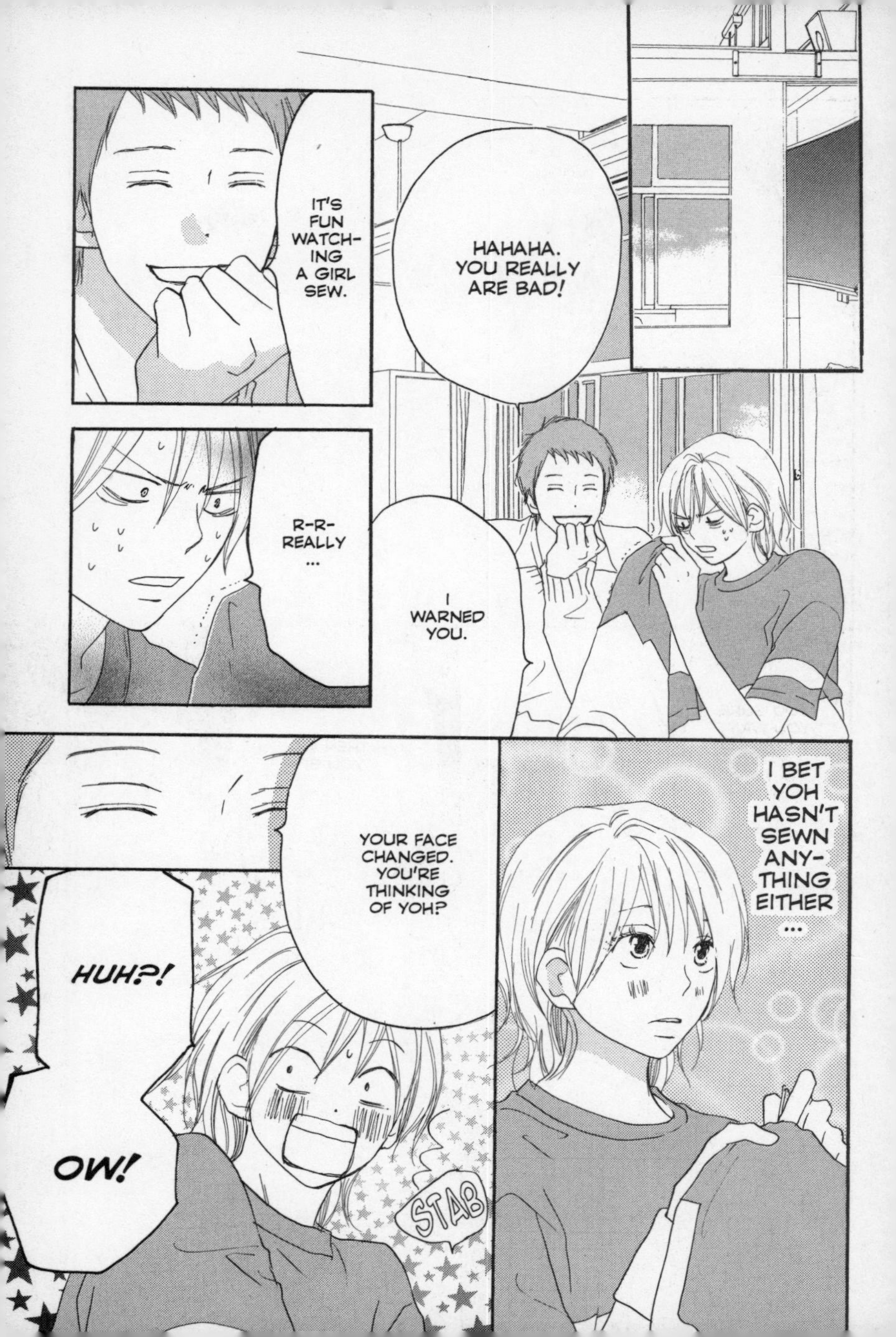
IT'S FUN WATCHING-ING A GIRL SEW.
HAHAHA. YOU REALLY ARE BAD!
I WARNED YOU.
R-R-REALLY ...
I BET YOH HASN'T SEWN ANY-THING EITHER ...
YOUR FACE CHANGED. YOU'RE THINKING OF YOH?
HUH?!
STAB
OW!

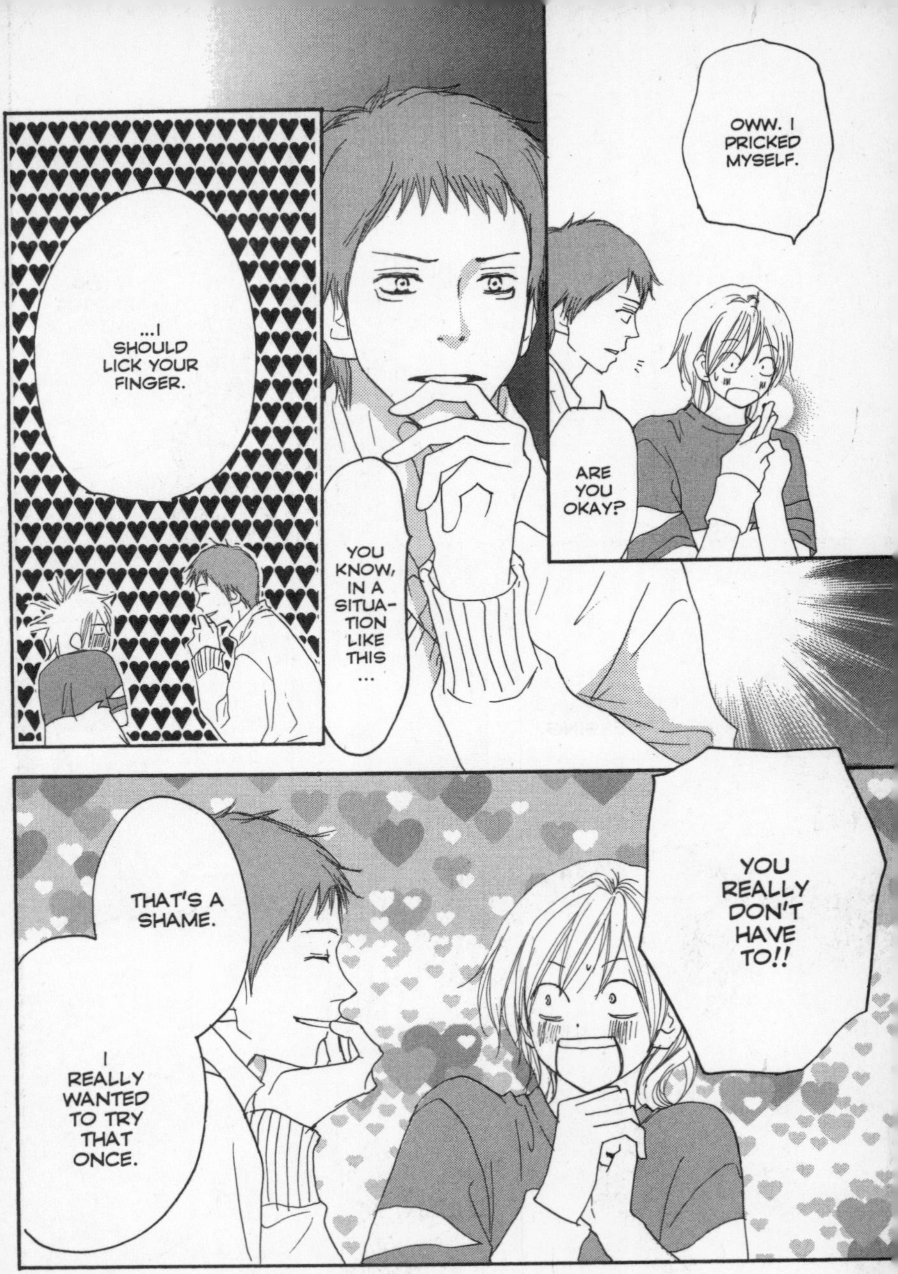
OWW. I PRICKED MYSELF.
ARE YOU OKAY?
YOU KNOW, IN A SITUATION LIKE THIS...
...I SHOULD LICK YOUR FINGER.
YOU REALLY DON'T HAVE TO!!
THAT'S A SHAME.
I REALLY WANTED TO TRY THAT ONCE.

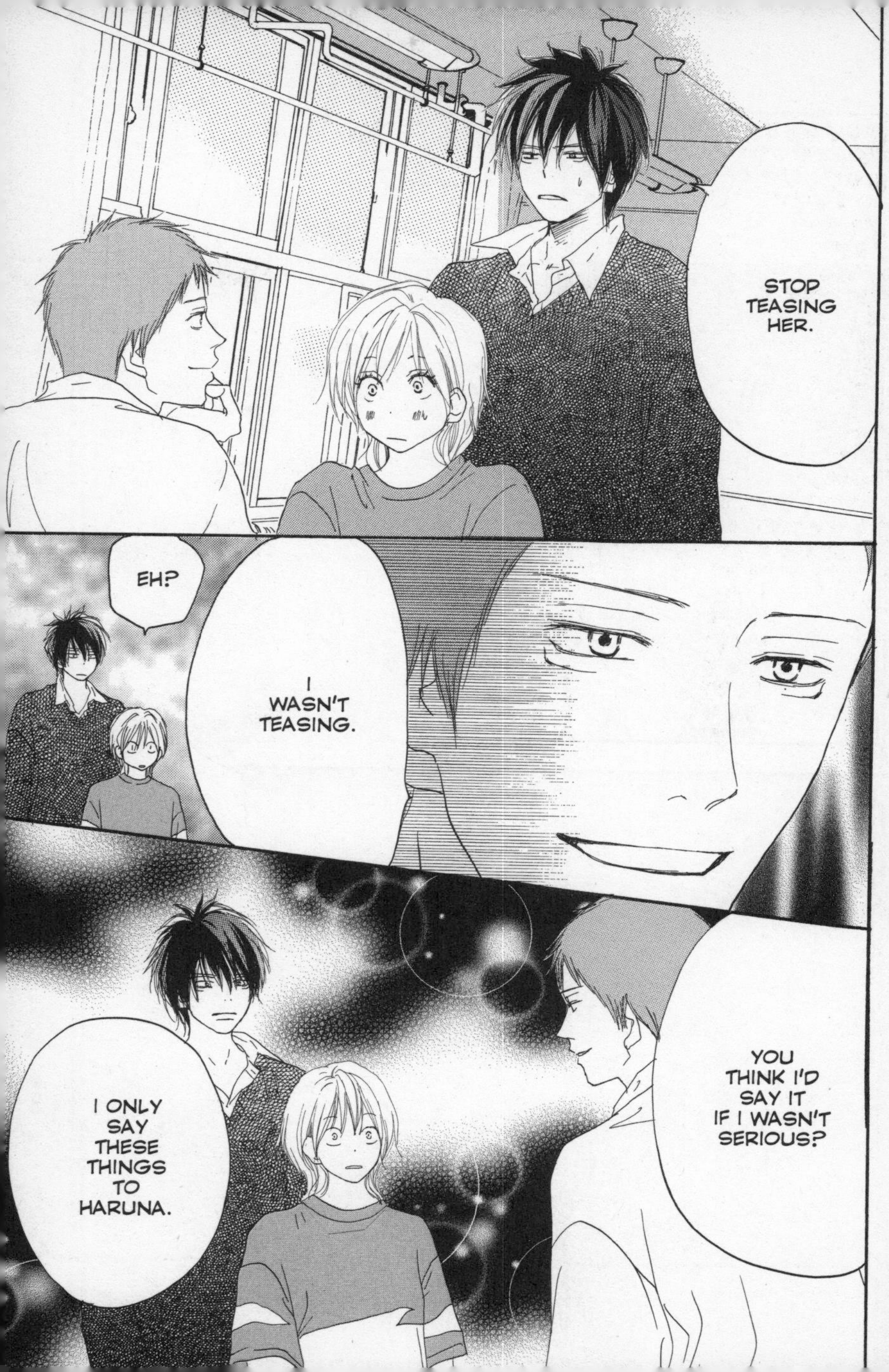
STOP TEASING HER.
EH?
I WASN'T TEASING.
YOU THINK I'D SAY IT IF I WASN'T SERIOUS?
I ONLY SAY THESE THINGS TO HARUNA.

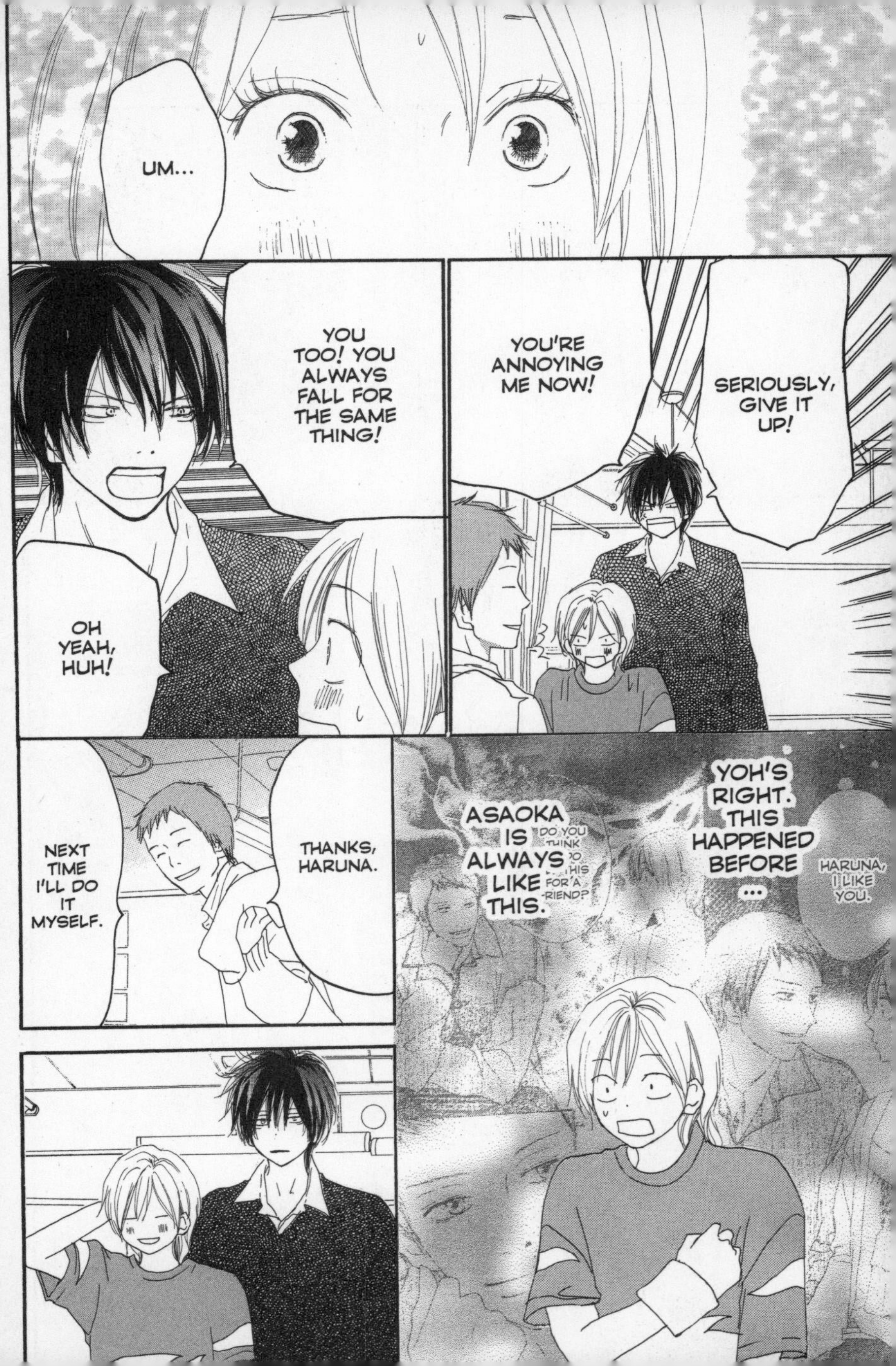
UM...
SERIOUSLY, GIVE IT UP!
YOU'RE ANNOYING ME NOW!
YOU TOO! YOU ALWAYS FALL FOR THE SAME THING!
OH YEAH, HUH!
YOH'S RIGHT. THIS HAPPENED BEFORE...
HARUNA, I LIKE YOU.
ASAOKA IS ALWAYS LIKE THIS.
THANKS, HARUNA.
NEXT TIME I'LL DO IT MYSELF.

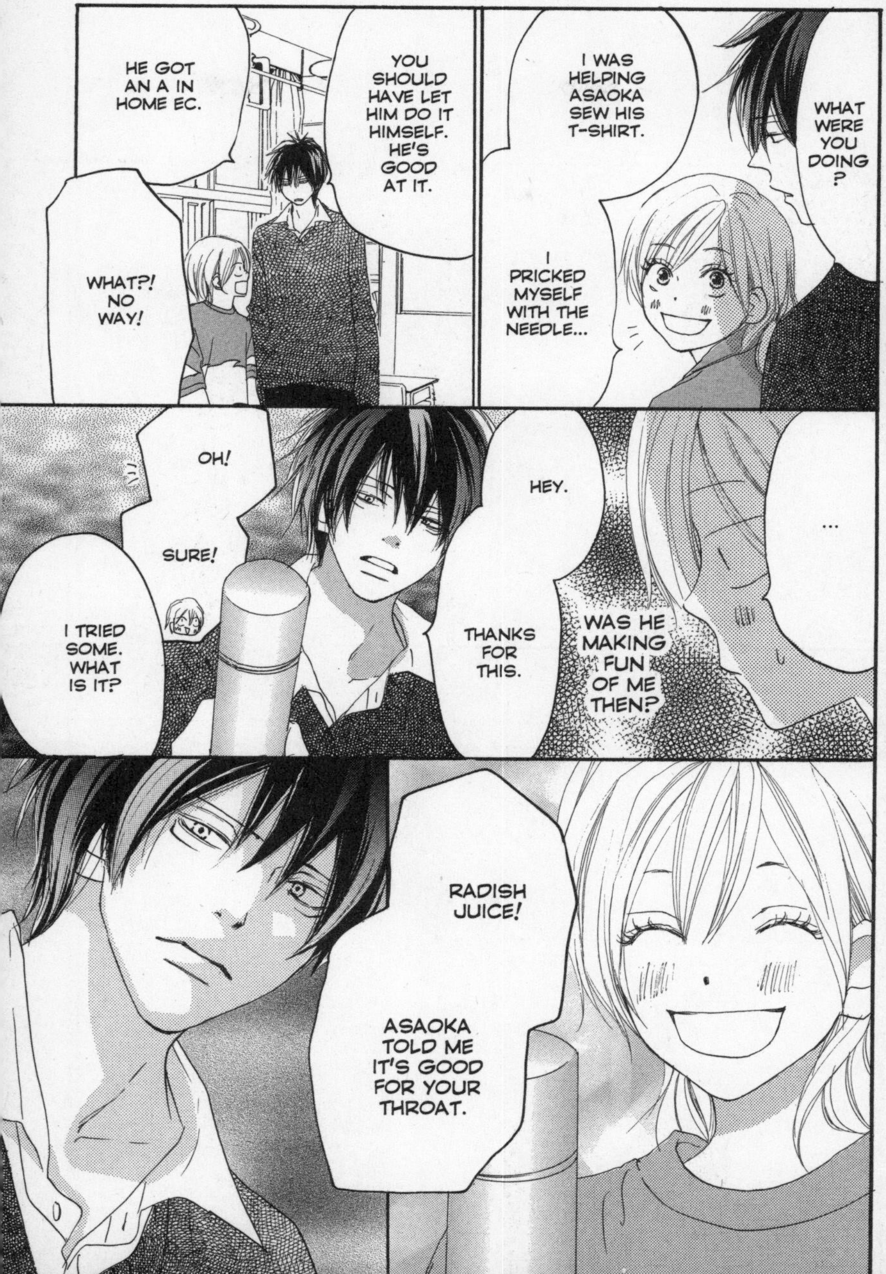
WHAT WERE YOU DOING?
I WAS HELPING ASAOKA SEW HIS T-SHIRT.
I PRICKED MYSELF WITH THE NEEDLE...
YOU SHOULD HAVE LET HIM DO IT HIMSELF. HE'S GOOD AT IT.
HE GOT AN A IN HOME EC.
WHAT?! NO WAY!
...
WAS HE MAKING FUN OF ME THEN?
HEY.
THANKS FOR THIS.
OH!
SURE!
I TRIED SOME. WHAT IS IT?
RADISH JUICE!
ASAOKA TOLD ME IT'S GOOD FOR YOUR THROAT.

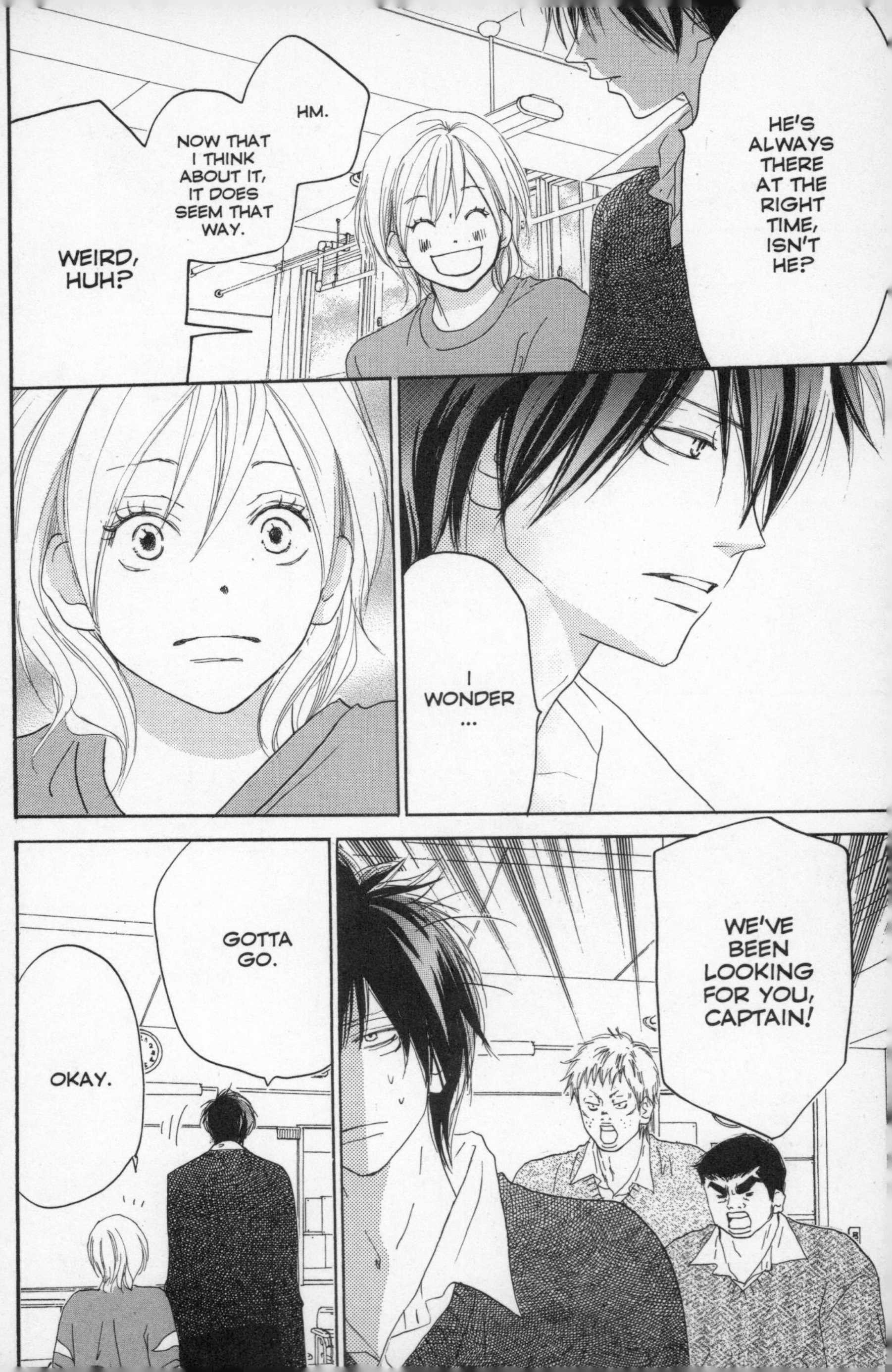
HE'S ALWAYS THERE AT THE RIGHT TIME, ISN'T HE?
HM.
NOW THAT I THINK ABOUT IT, IT DOES SEEM THAT WAY.
WEIRD, HUH?
I WONDER...
WE'VE BEEN LOOKING FOR YOU, CAPTAIN!
GOTTA GO.
OKAY.

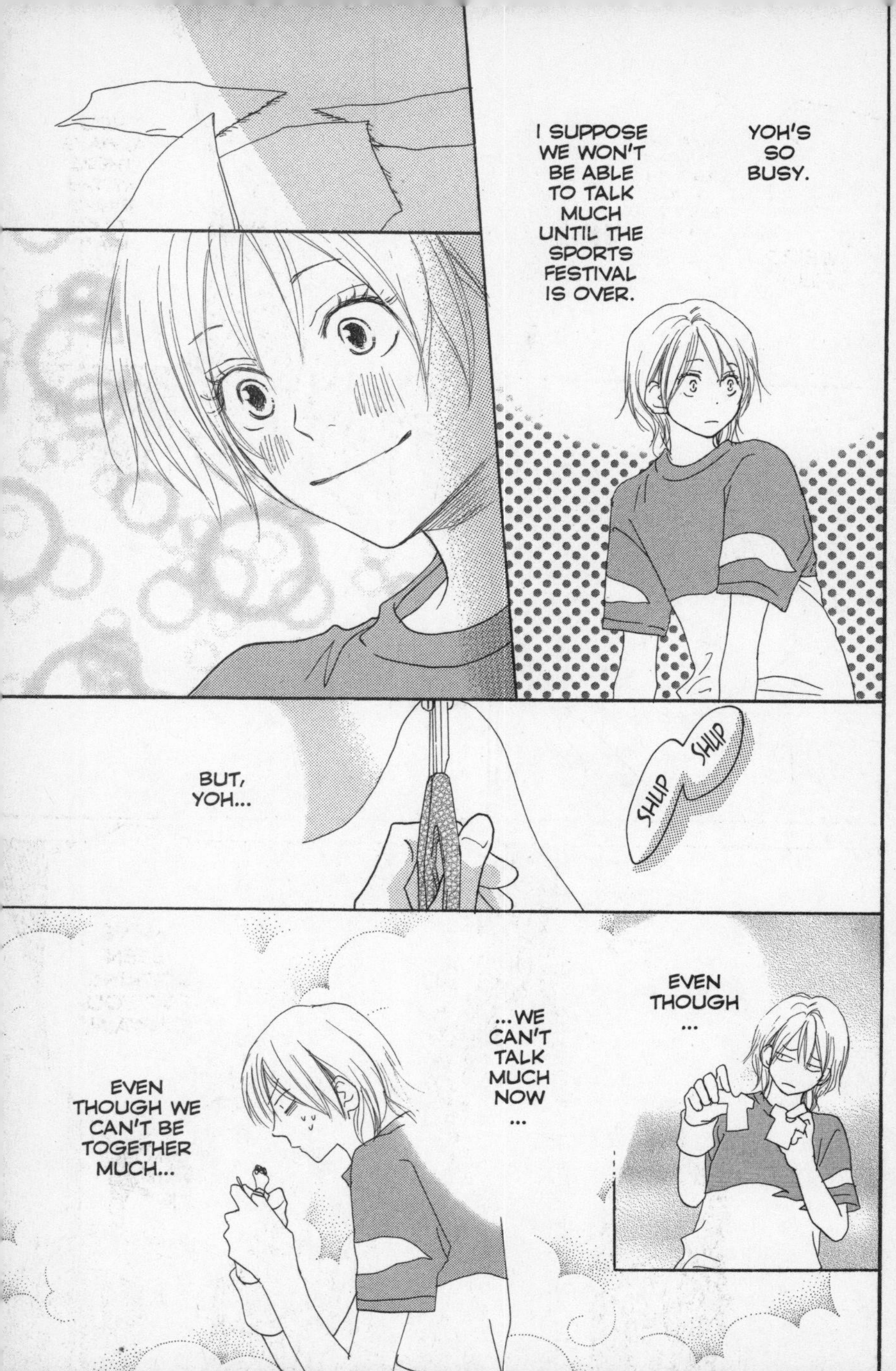
YOH'S SO BUSY.
I SUPPOSE WE WON'T BE ABLE TO TALK MUCH UNTIL THE SPORTS FESTIVAL IS OVER.
SHUP SHUP
BUT, YOH...
EVEN THOUGH ...
...WE CAN'T TALK MUCH NOW ...
EVEN THOUGH WE CAN'T BE TOGETHER MUCH...

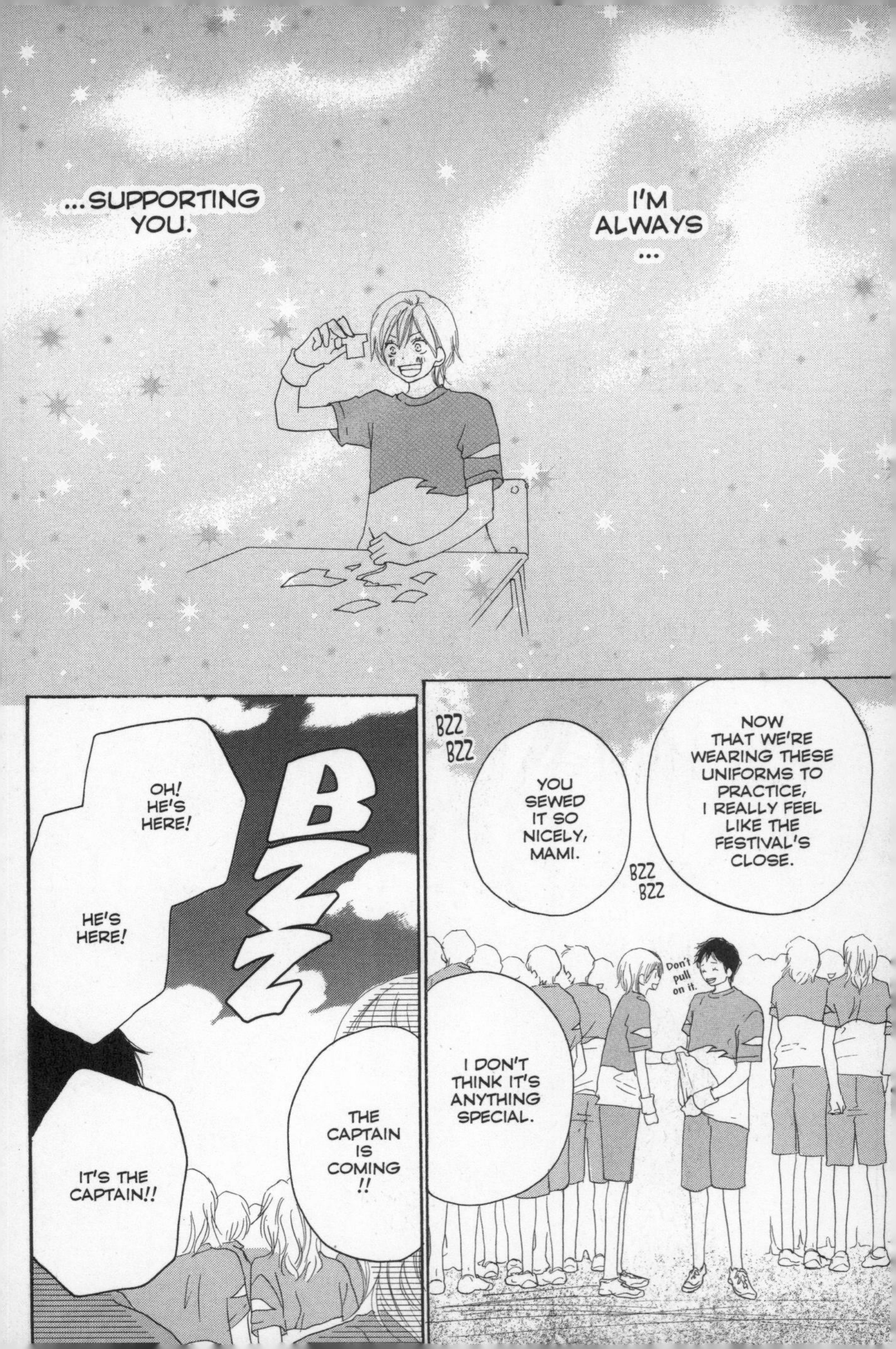
I'M ALWAYS ...
...SUPPORTING YOU.
NOW THAT WE'RE WEARING THESE UNIFORMS TO PRACTICE, I REALLY FEEL LIKE THE FESTIVAL'S CLOSE.
YOU SEWED IT SO NICELY, MAMI.
BZZ BZZ
BZZ BZZ
Don't pull on it.
I DON'T THINK IT'S ANYTHING SPECIAL.
BZZ
OH! HE'S HERE!
HE'S HERE!
THE CAPTAIN IS COMING!!
IT'S THE CAPTAIN!!

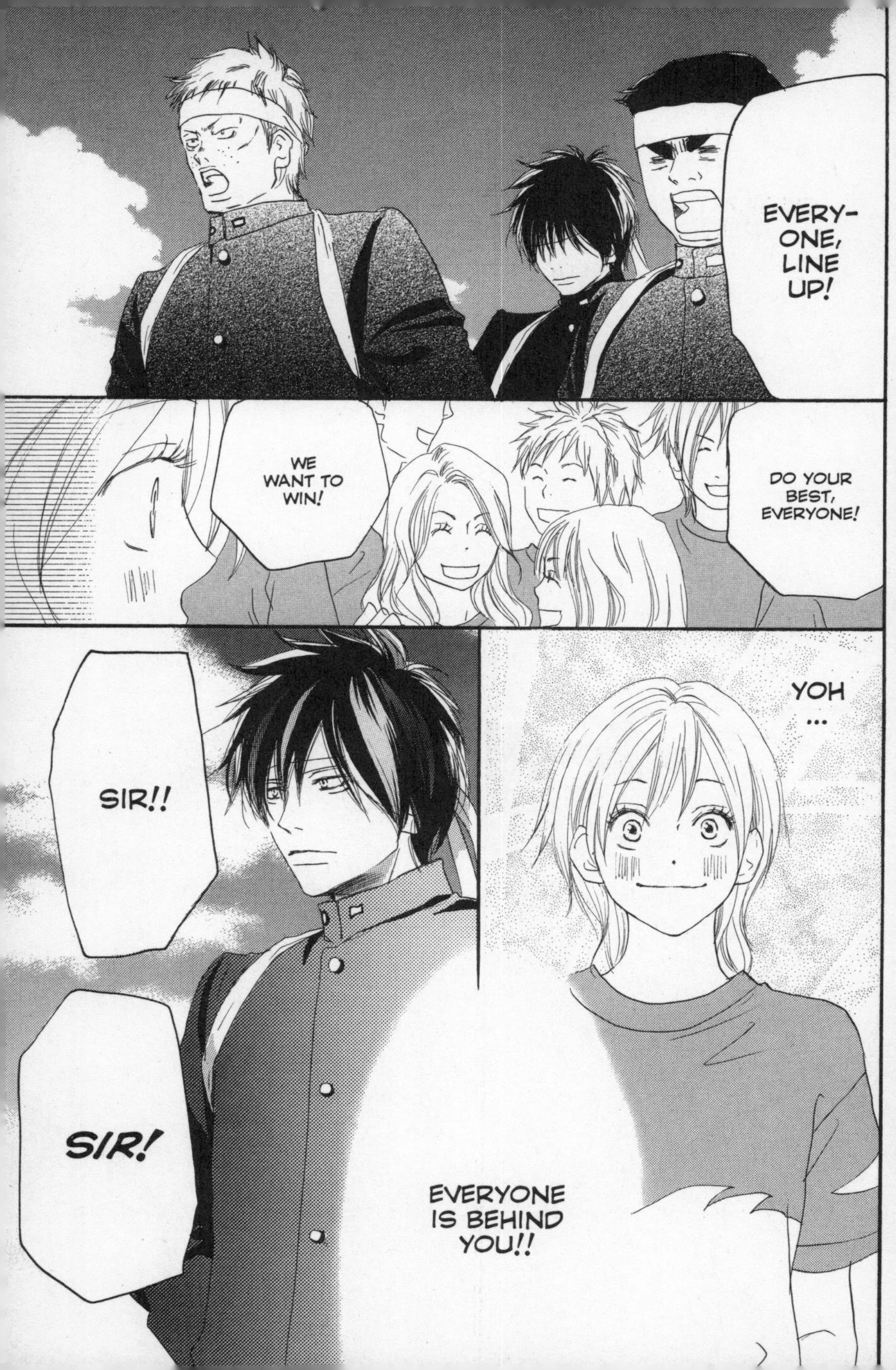

EVERY-ONE, LINE UP!
DO YOUR BEST, EVERYONE!
WE WANT TO WIN!
YOH ...
SIR!!
EVERYONE IS BEHIND YOU!!
SIR!

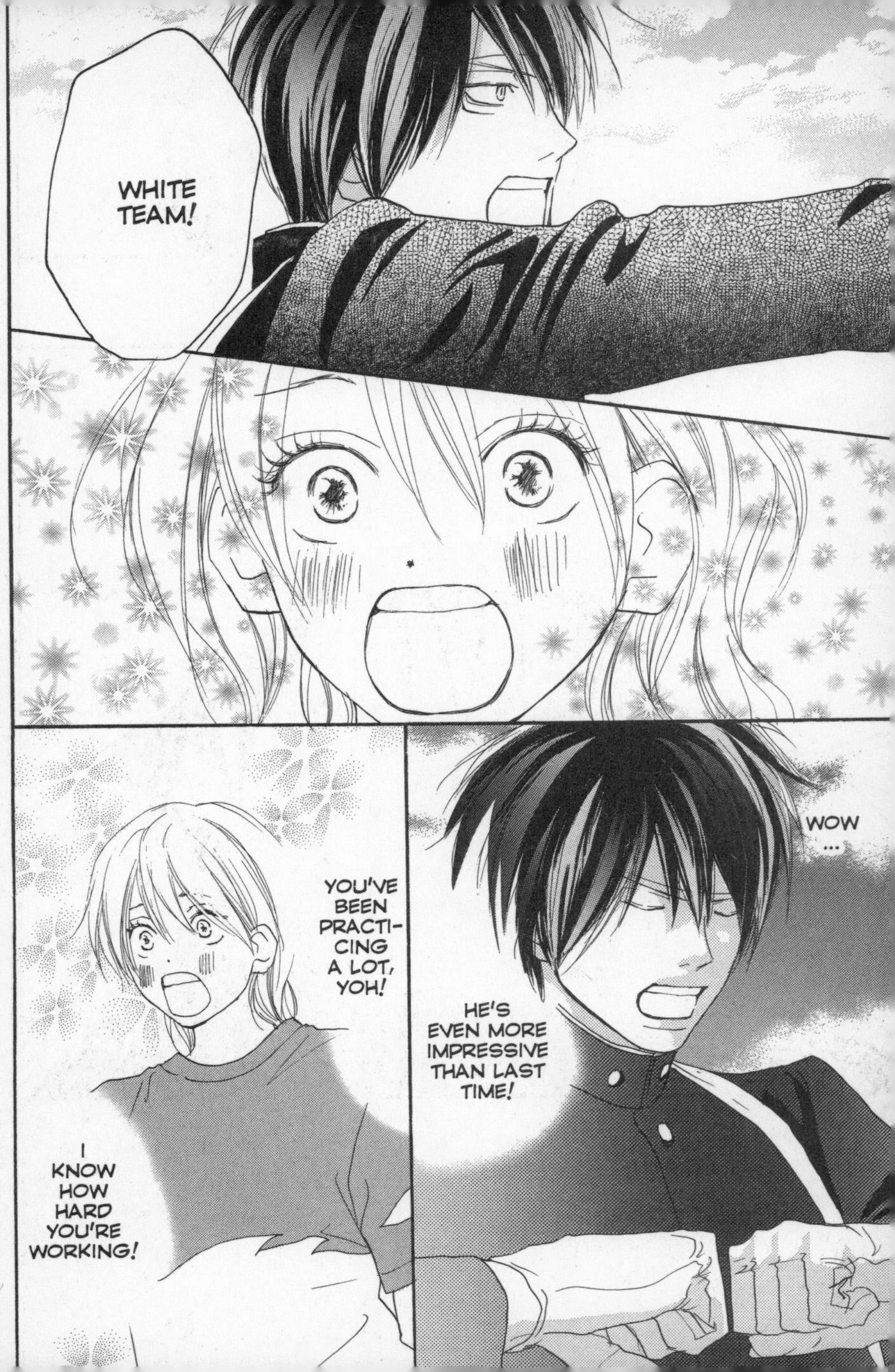
WHITE TEAM!
WOW ...
HE'S EVEN MORE IMPRESSIVE THAN LAST TIME!
YOU'VE BEEN PRACTI-CING A LOT, YOH!
I KNOW HOW HARD YOU'RE WORKING!

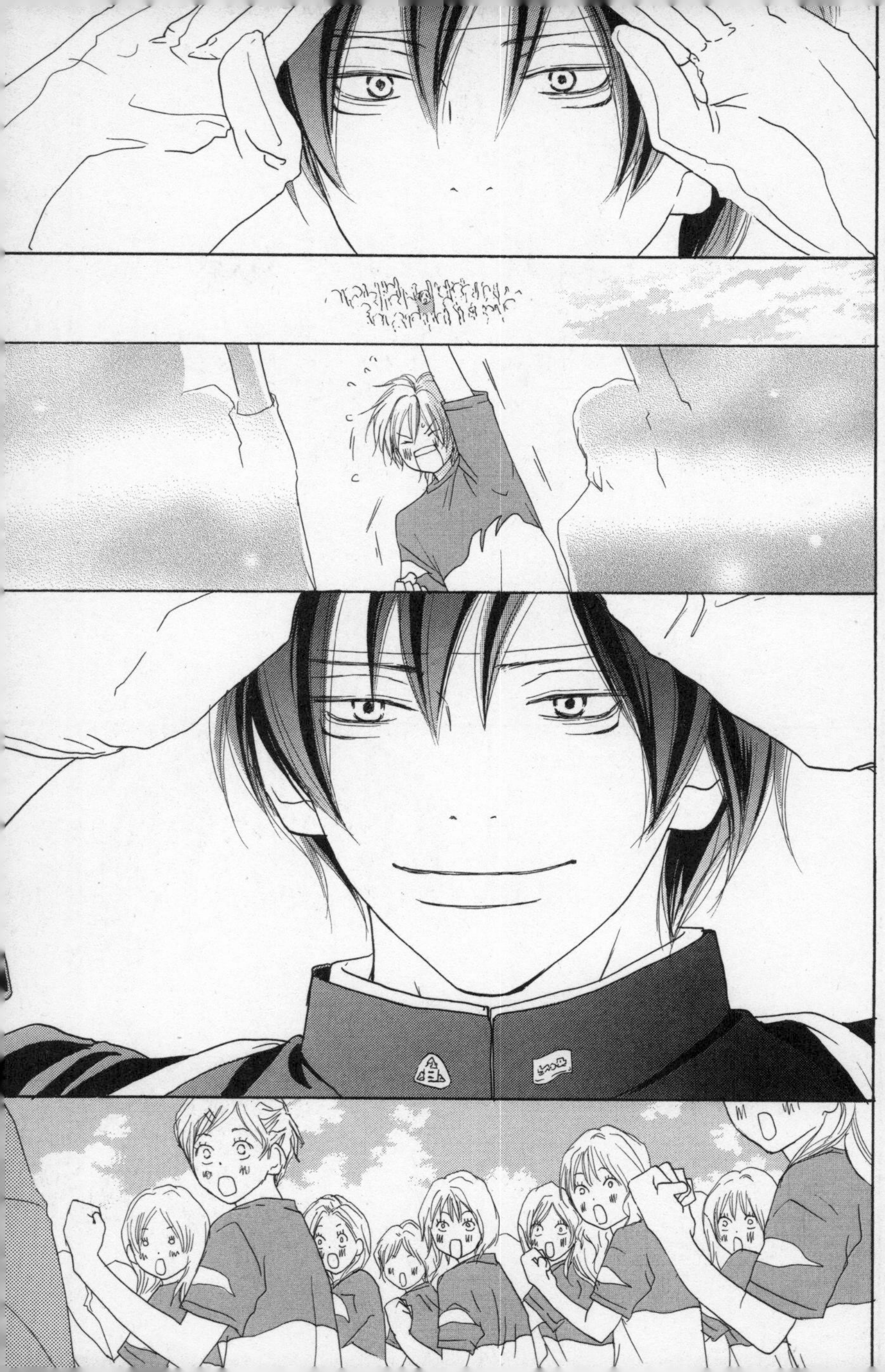

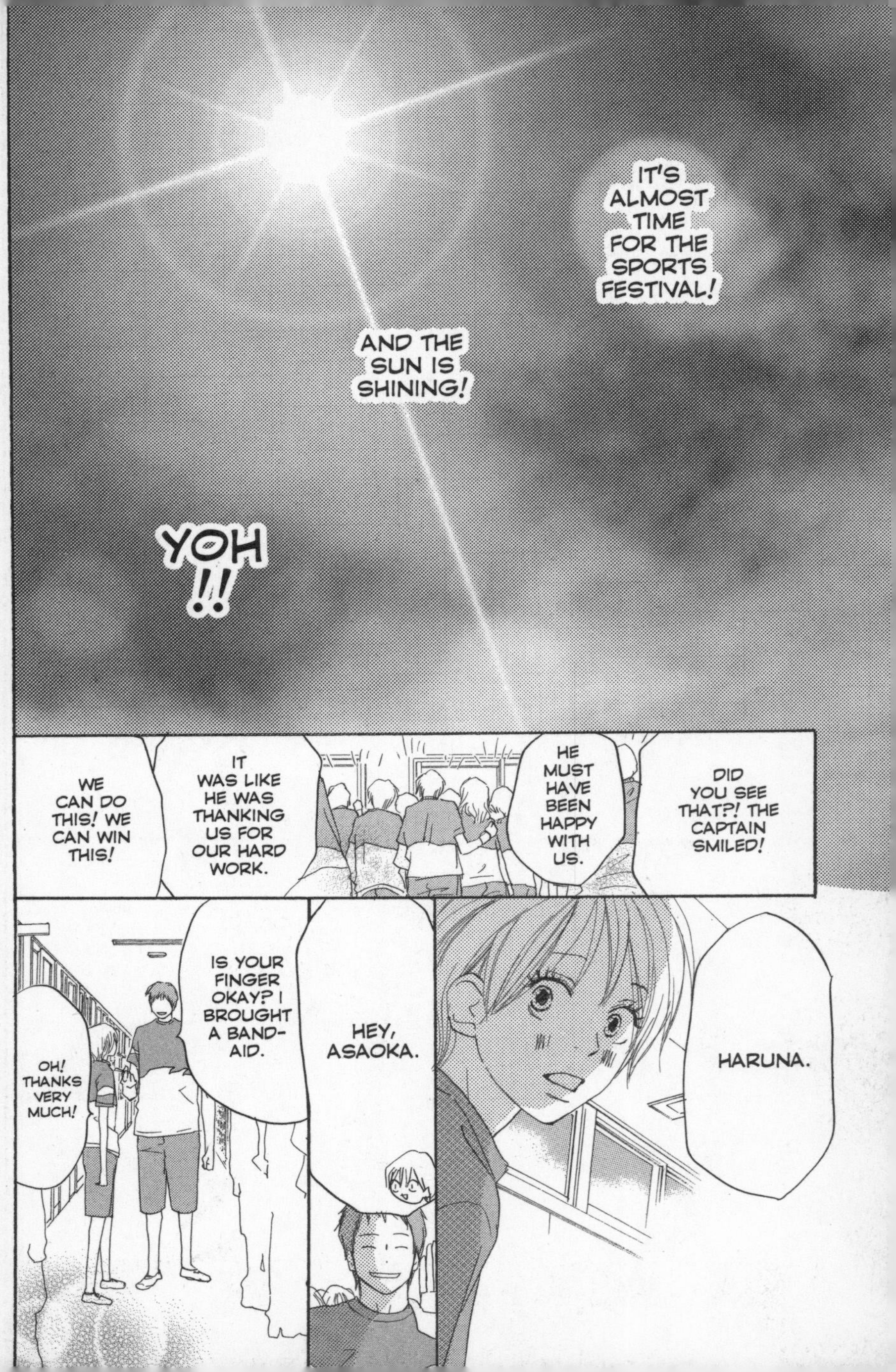
IT'S ALMOST TIME FOR THE SPORTS FESTIVAL!
AND THE SUN IS SHINING!
YOH !!
DID YOU SEE THAT?! THE CAPTAIN SMILED!
HE MUST HAVE BEEN HAPPY WITH US.
IT WAS LIKE HE WAS THANKING US FOR OUR HARD WORK.
WE CAN DO THIS! WE CAN WIN THIS!
HARUNA.
HEY, ASAOKA.
IS YOUR FINGER OKAY? I BROUGHT A BAND-AID.
OH! THANKS VERY MUCH!

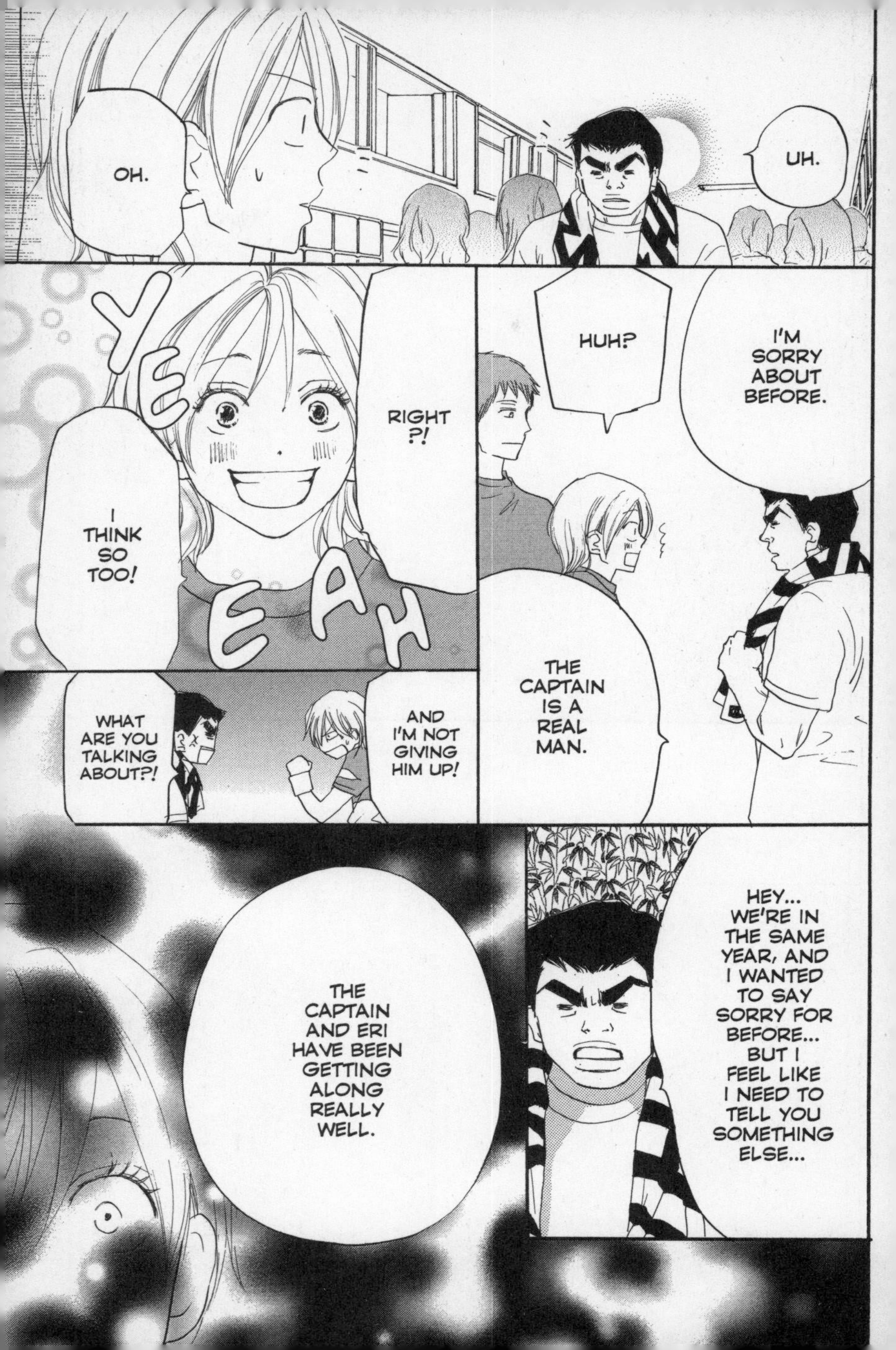
UH.
OH.
I'M SORRY ABOUT BEFORE.
HUH?
THE CAPTAIN IS A REAL MAN.
RIGHT?!
YEAH
I THINK SO TOO!
AND I'M NOT GIVING HIM UP!
WHAT ARE YOU TALKING ABOUT?!
HEY... WE'RE IN THE SAME YEAR, AND I WANTED TO SAY SORRY FOR BEFORE... BUT I FEEL LIKE I NEED TO TELL YOU SOMETHING ELSE...
THE CAPTAIN AND ERI HAVE BEEN GETTING ALONG REALLY WELL.

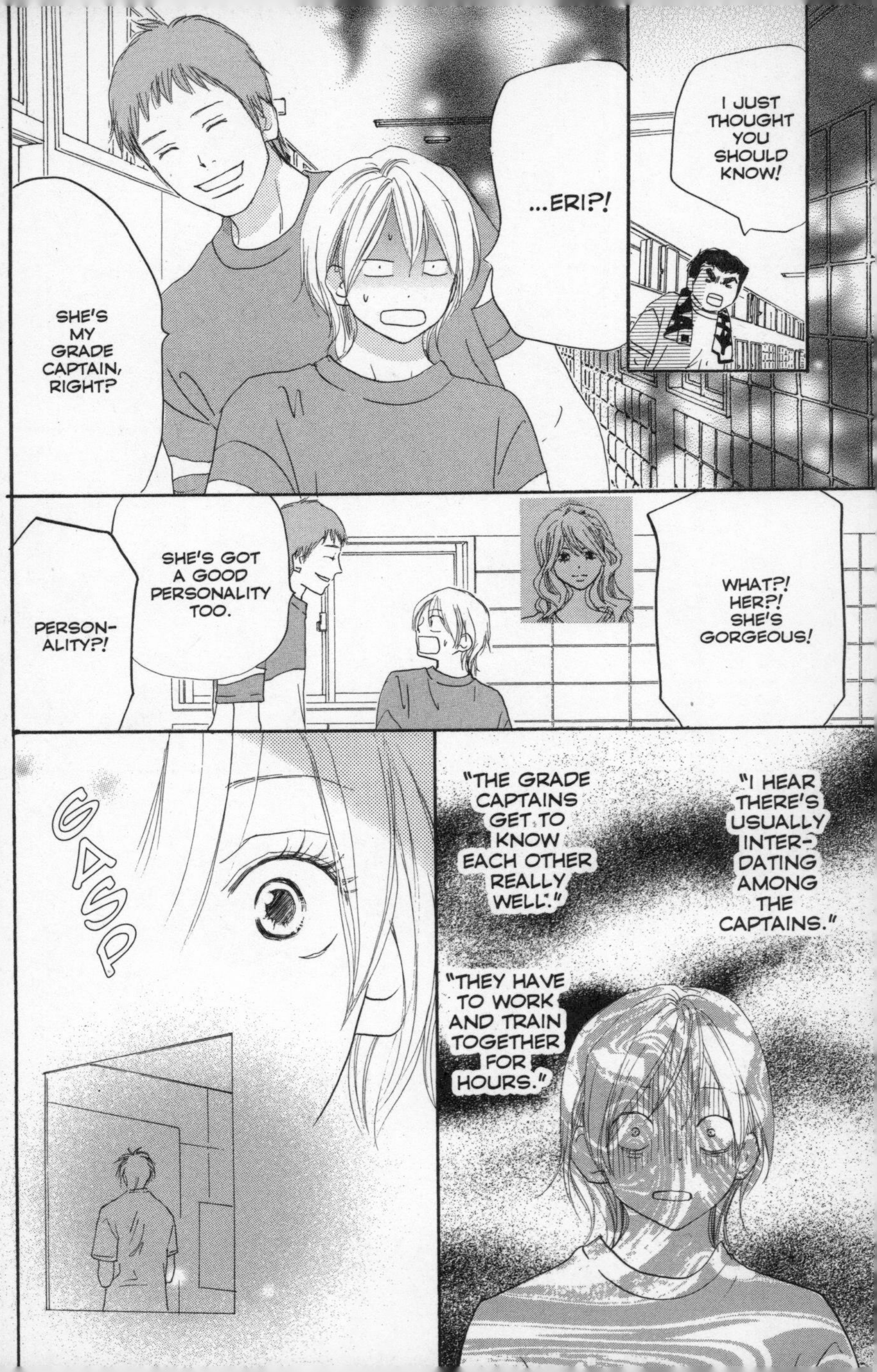
I JUST THOUGHT YOU SHOULD KNOW!
...ERI?!
SHE'S MY GRADE CAPTAIN, RIGHT?
WHAT?! HER?! SHE'S GORGEOUS!
SHE'S GOT A GOOD PERSONALITY TOO.
PERSON-ALITY?!
"I HEAR THERE'S USUALLY INTER-DATING AMONG THE CAPTAINS."
"THE GRADE CAPTAINS GET TO KNOW EACH OTHER REALLY WELL."
"THEY HAVE TO WORK AND TRAIN TOGETHER FOR HOURS."
GASP

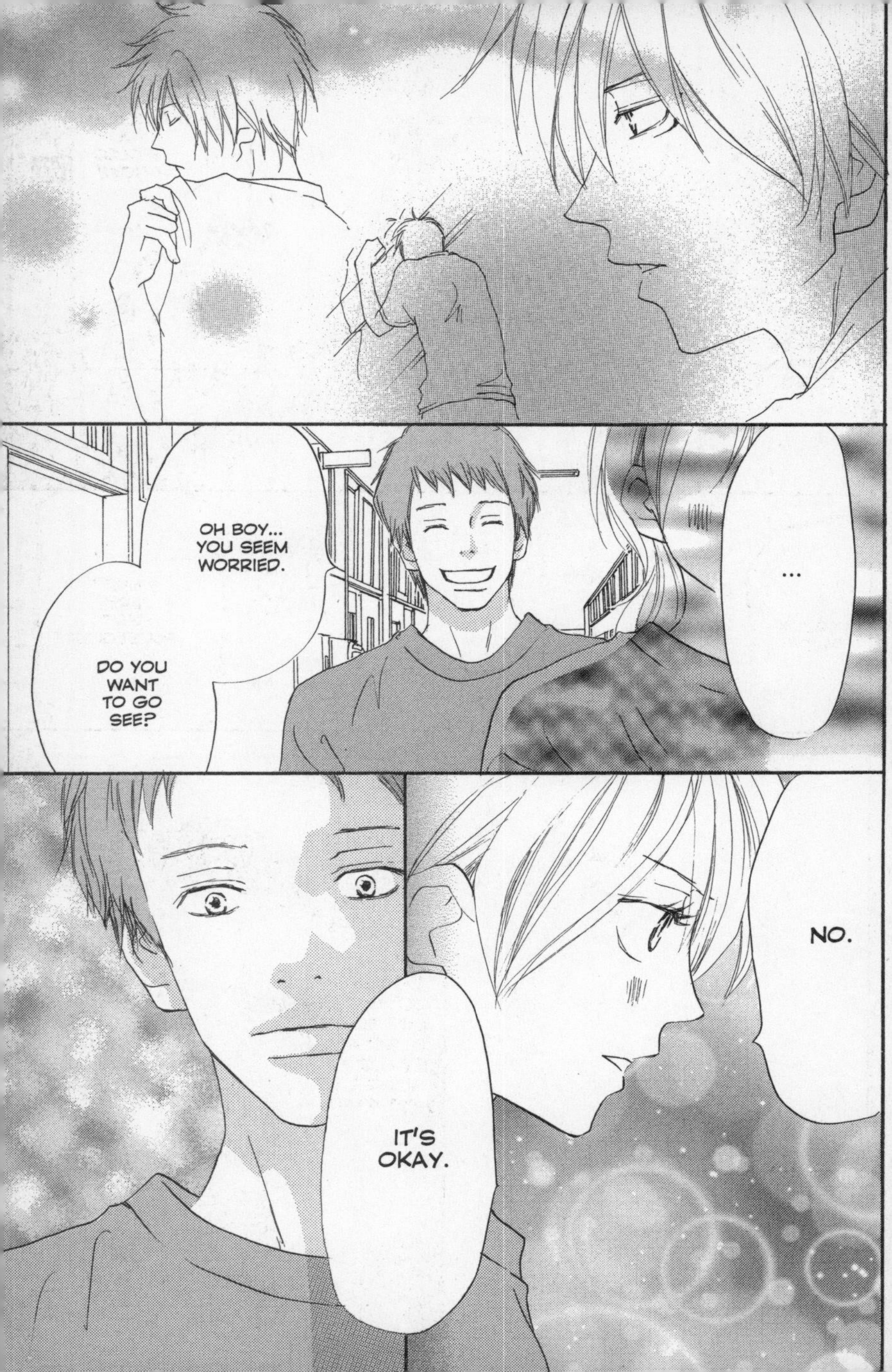
...
OH BOY... YOU SEEM WORRIED.
DO YOU WANT TO GO SEE?
NO.
IT'S OKAY.

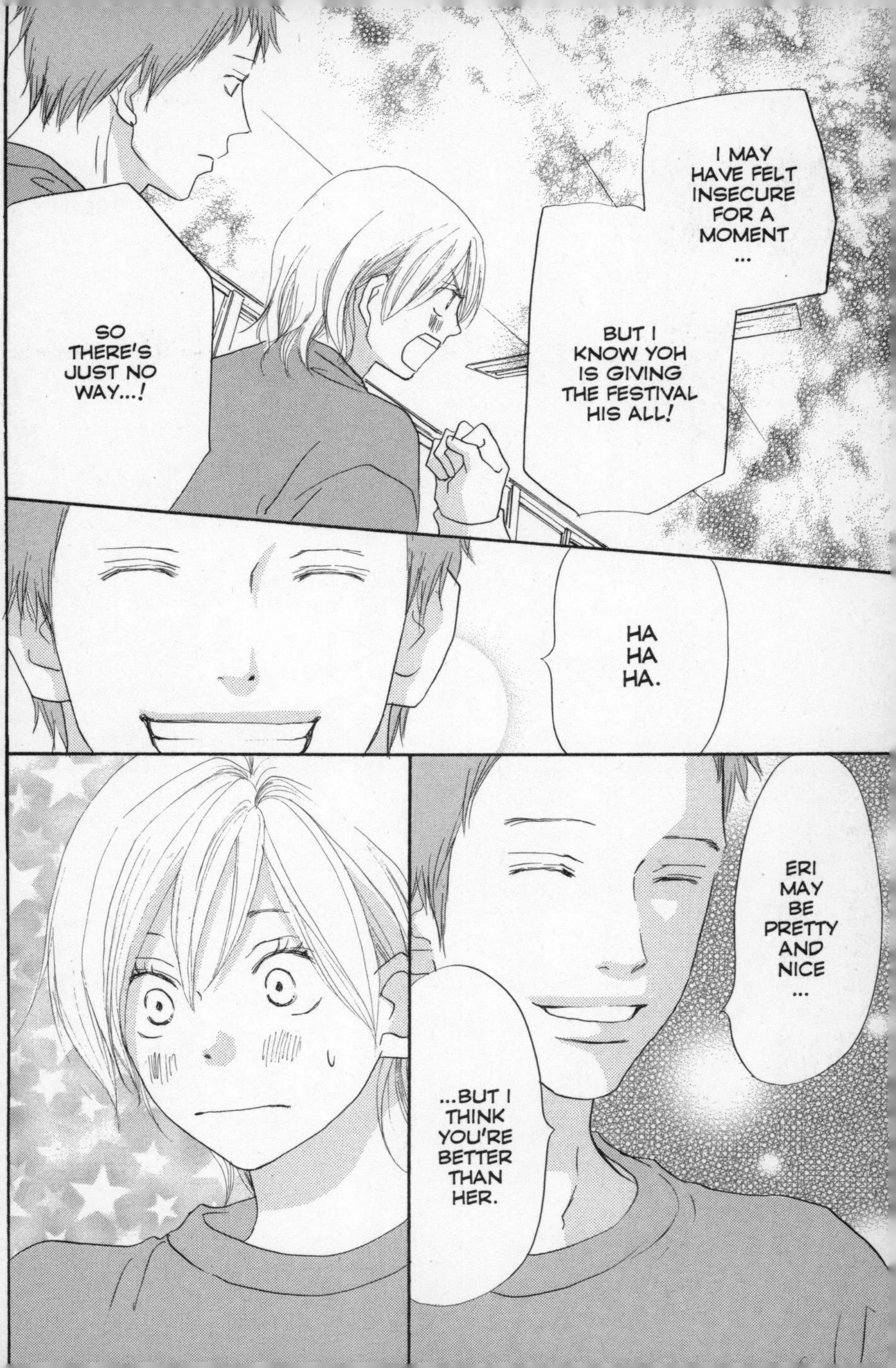
I MAY HAVE FELT INSECURE FOR A MOMENT ...
BUT I KNOW YOH IS GIVING THE FESTIVAL HIS ALL!
SO THERE'S JUST NO WAY...!
HA HA HA.
ERI MAY BE PRETTY AND NICE ...
...BUT I THINK YOU'RE BETTER THAN HER.

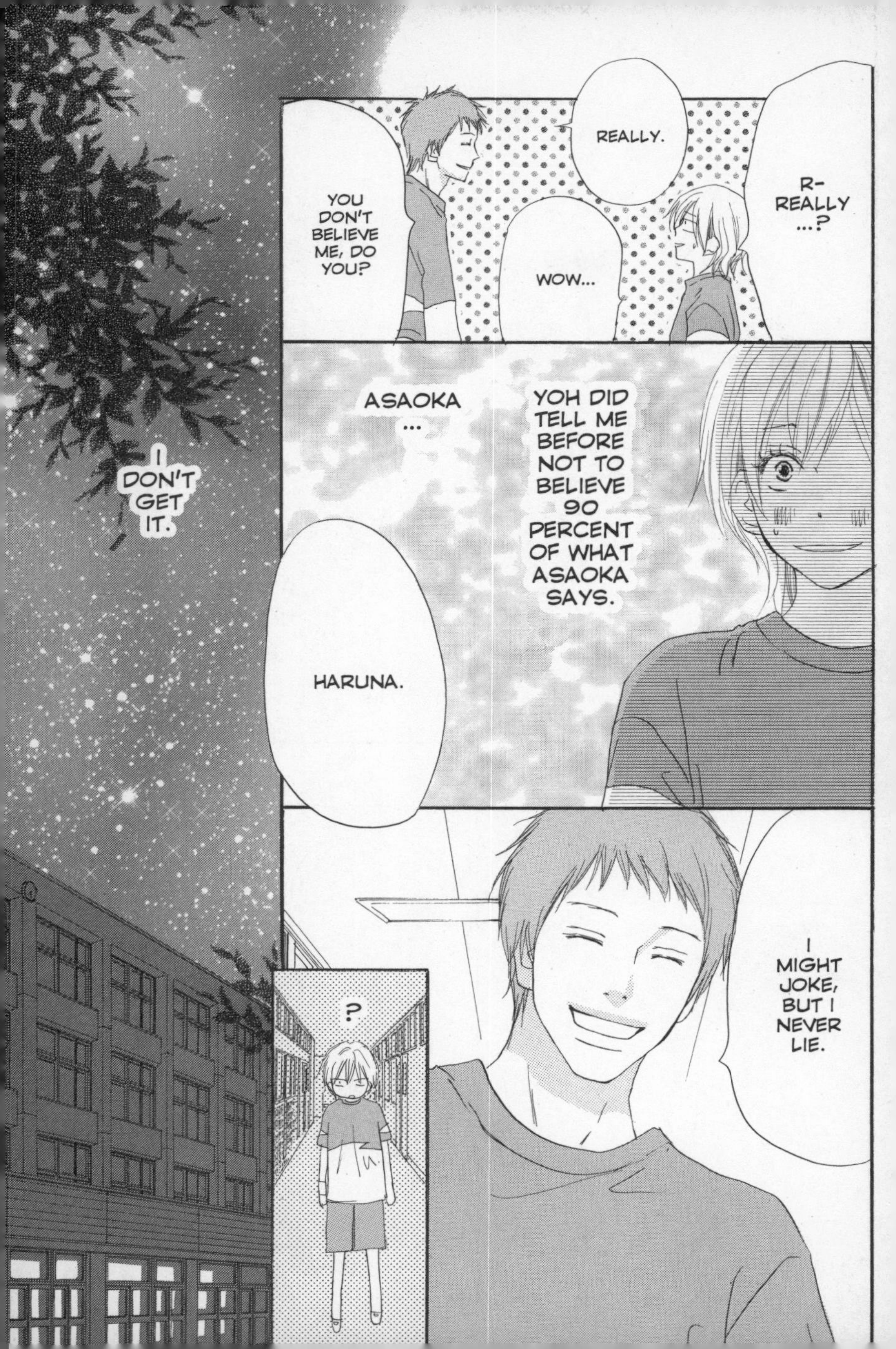
R-REALLY ...?
REALLY.
WOW...
YOU DON'T BELIEVE ME, DO YOU?
YOH DID TELL ME BEFORE NOT TO BELIEVE 90 PERCENT OF WHAT ASAOKA SAYS.
ASAOKA ...
HARUNA.
I MIGHT JOKE, BUT I NEVER LIE.
?
I DON'T GET IT.

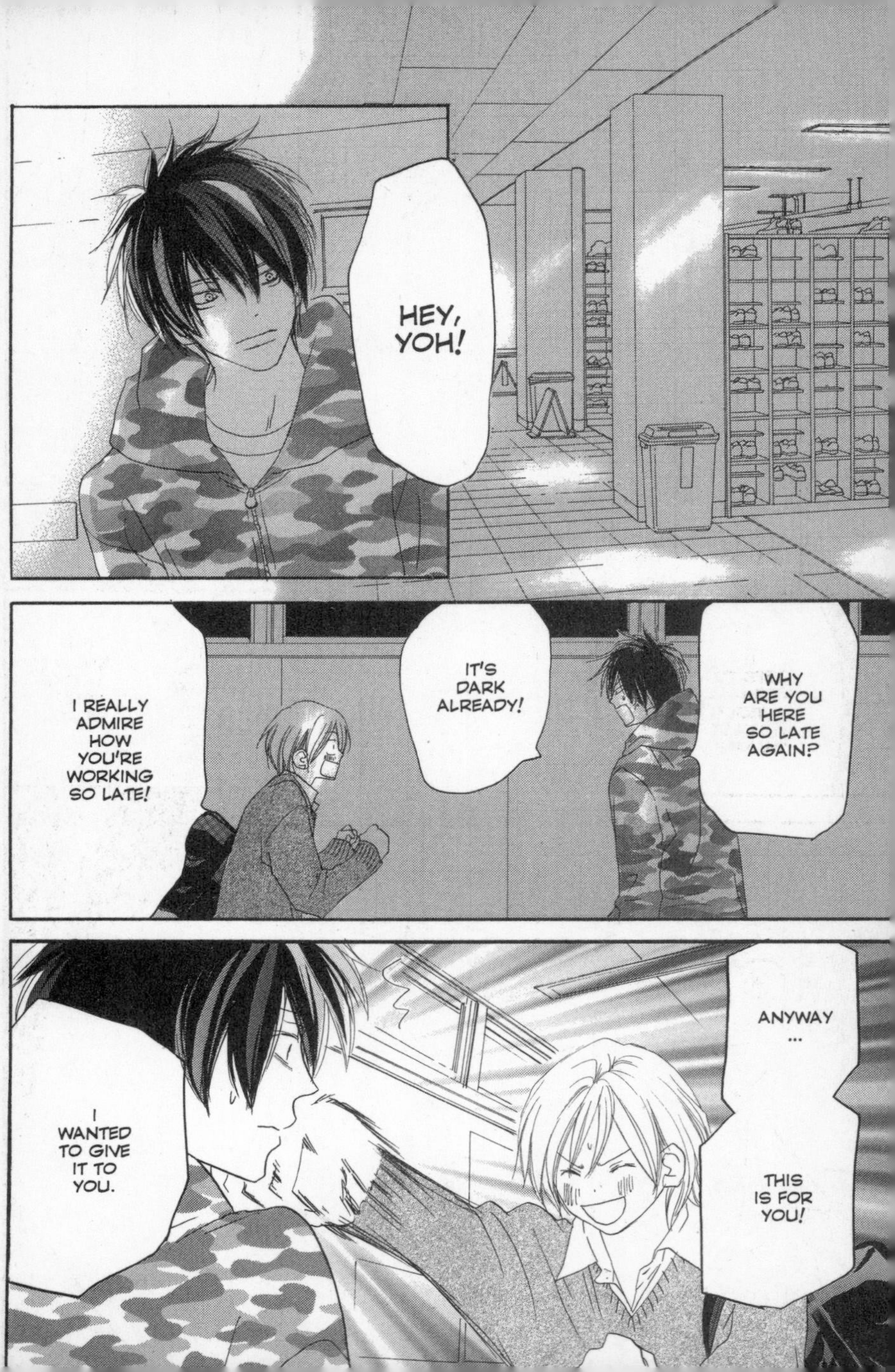
HEY, YOH!
WHY ARE YOU HERE SO LATE AGAIN?
IT'S DARK ALREADY!
I REALLY ADMIRE HOW YOU'RE WORKING SO LATE!
ANYWAY ...
THIS IS FOR YOU!
I WANTED TO GIVE IT TO YOU.

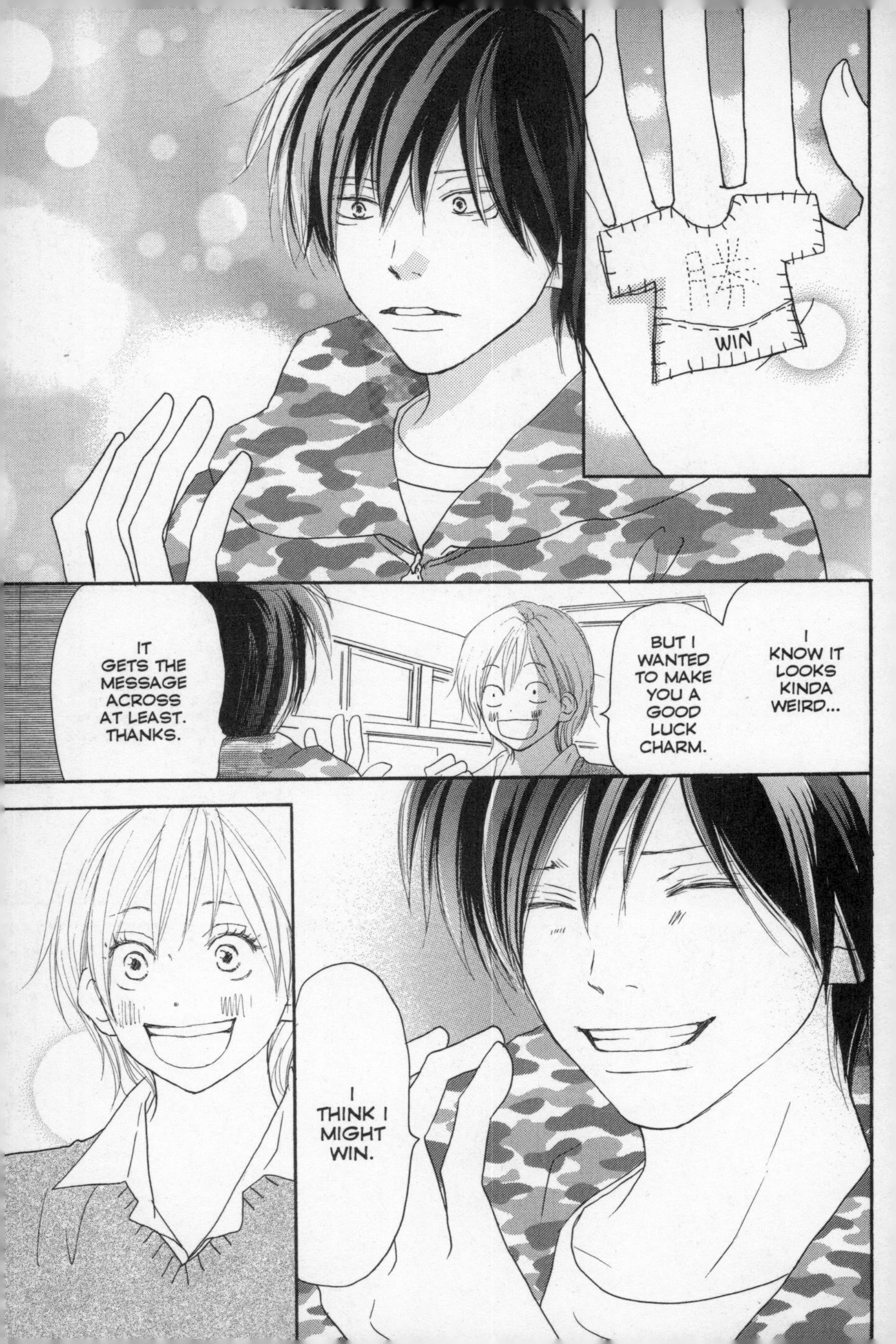
勝
WIN
I KNOW IT LOOKS KINDA WEIRD...
BUT I WANTED TO MAKE YOU A GOOD LUCK CHARM.
IT GETS THE MESSAGE ACROSS AT LEAST. THANKS.
I THINK I MIGHT WIN.

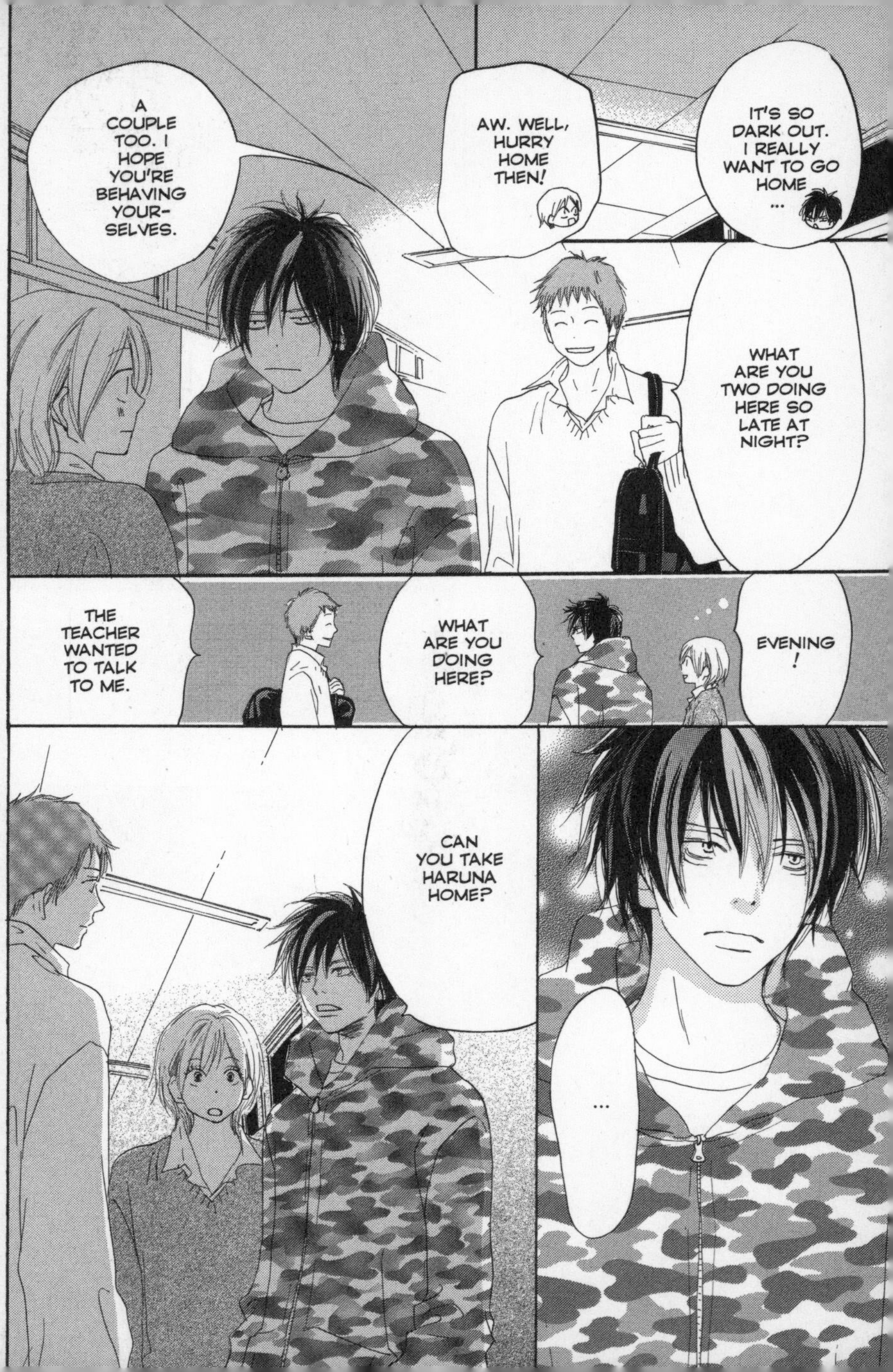
IT'S SO DARK OUT. I REALLY WANT TO GO HOME ...
AW. WELL, HURRY HOME THEN!
A COUPLE TOO. I HOPE YOU'RE BEHAVING YOUR-SELVES.
WHAT ARE YOU TWO DOING HERE SO LATE AT NIGHT?
EVENING!
WHAT ARE YOU DOING HERE?
THE TEACHER WANTED TO TALK TO ME.
...
CAN YOU TAKE HARUNA HOME?

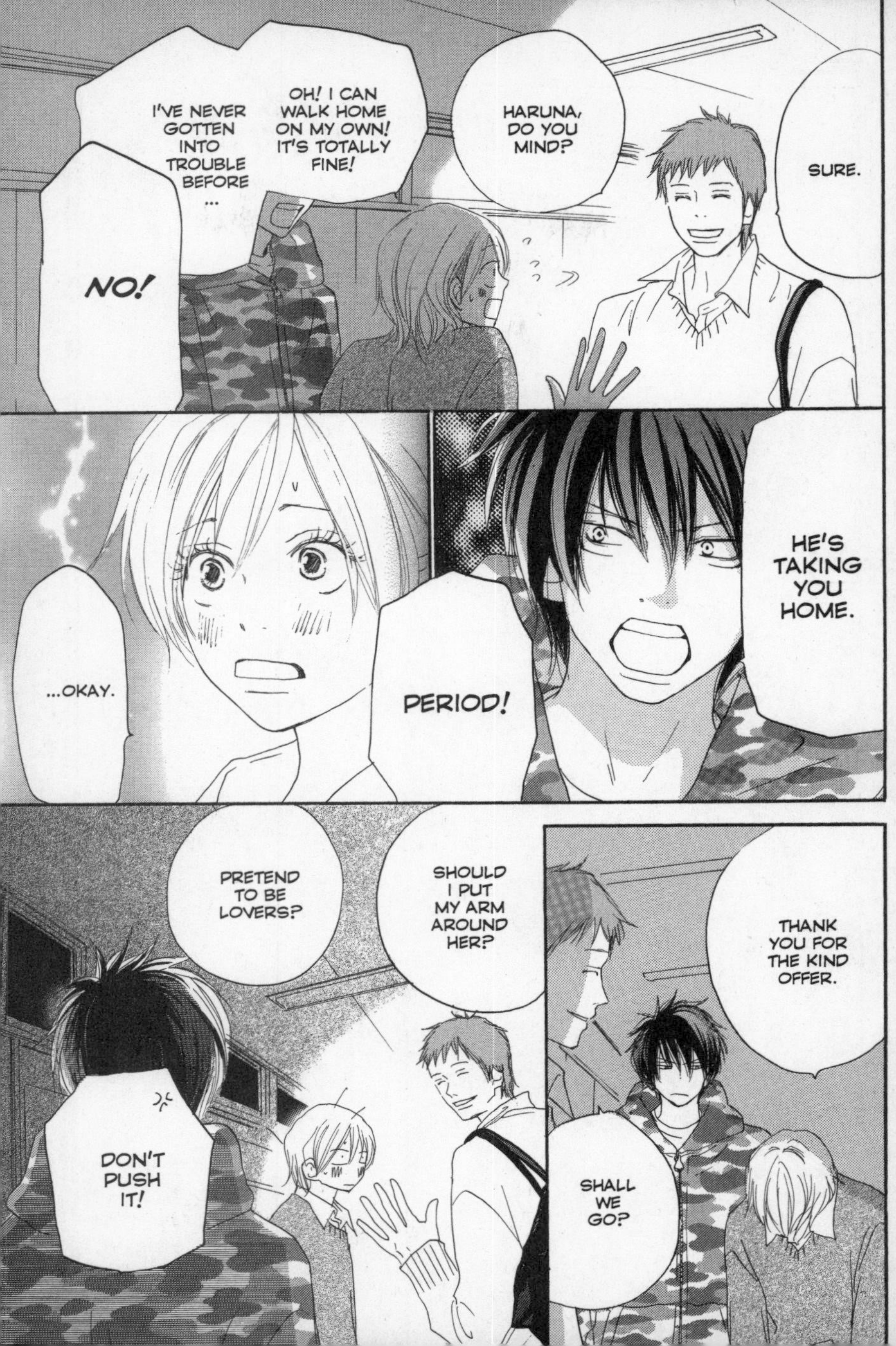
SURE.
HARUNA, DO YOU MIND?
OH! I CAN WALK HOME ON MY OWN! IT'S TOTALLY FINE!
I'VE NEVER GOTTEN INTO TROUBLE BEFORE ...
NO!
HE'S TAKING YOU HOME.
PERIOD!
...OKAY.
THANK YOU FOR THE KIND OFFER.
SHALL WE GO?
SHOULD I PUT MY ARM AROUND HER?
PRETEND TO BE LOVERS?
DON'T PUSH IT!

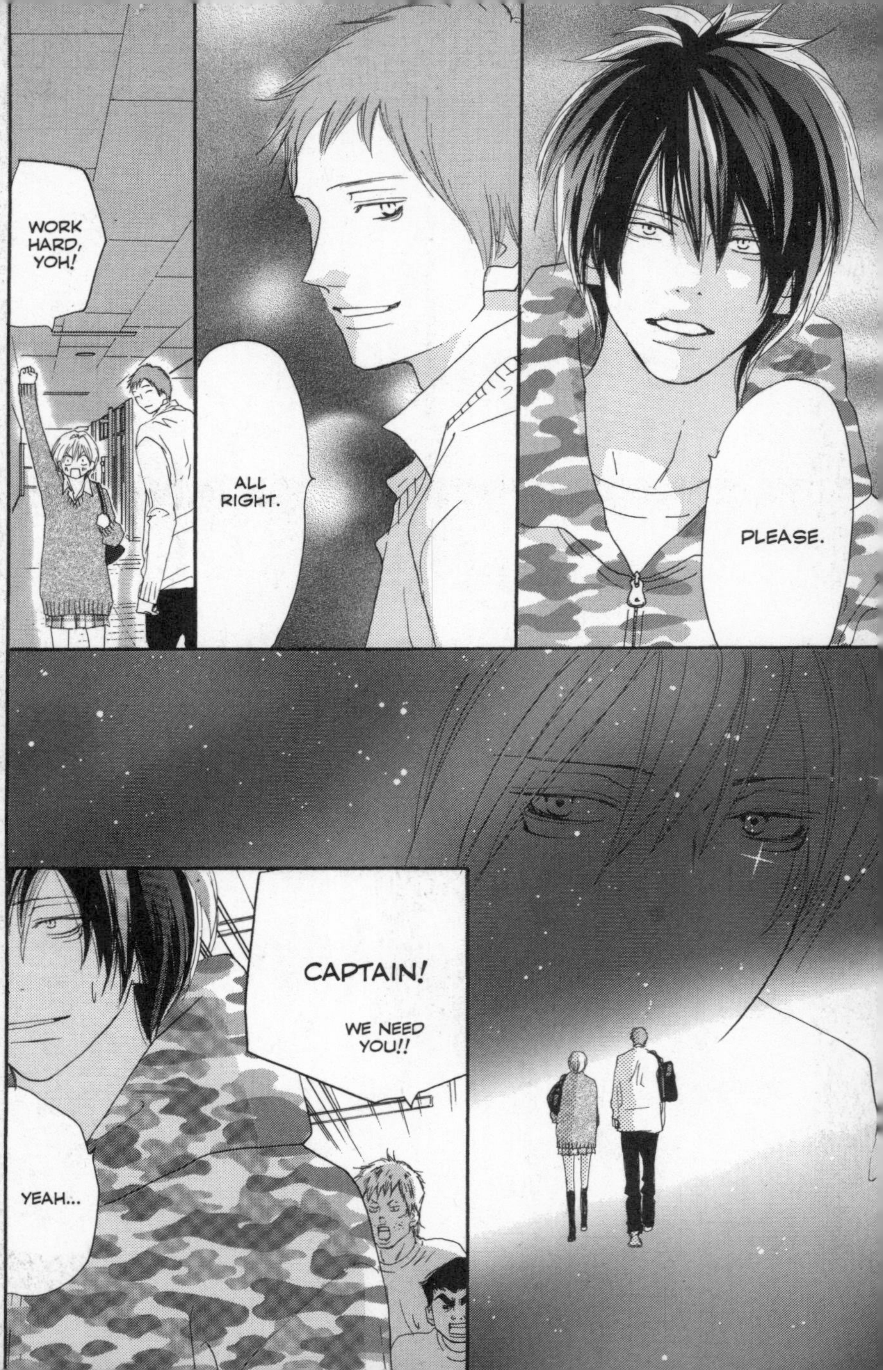
PLEASE.
ALL RIGHT.
WORK HARD, YOH!
CAPTAIN!
WE NEED YOU!!
YEAH...

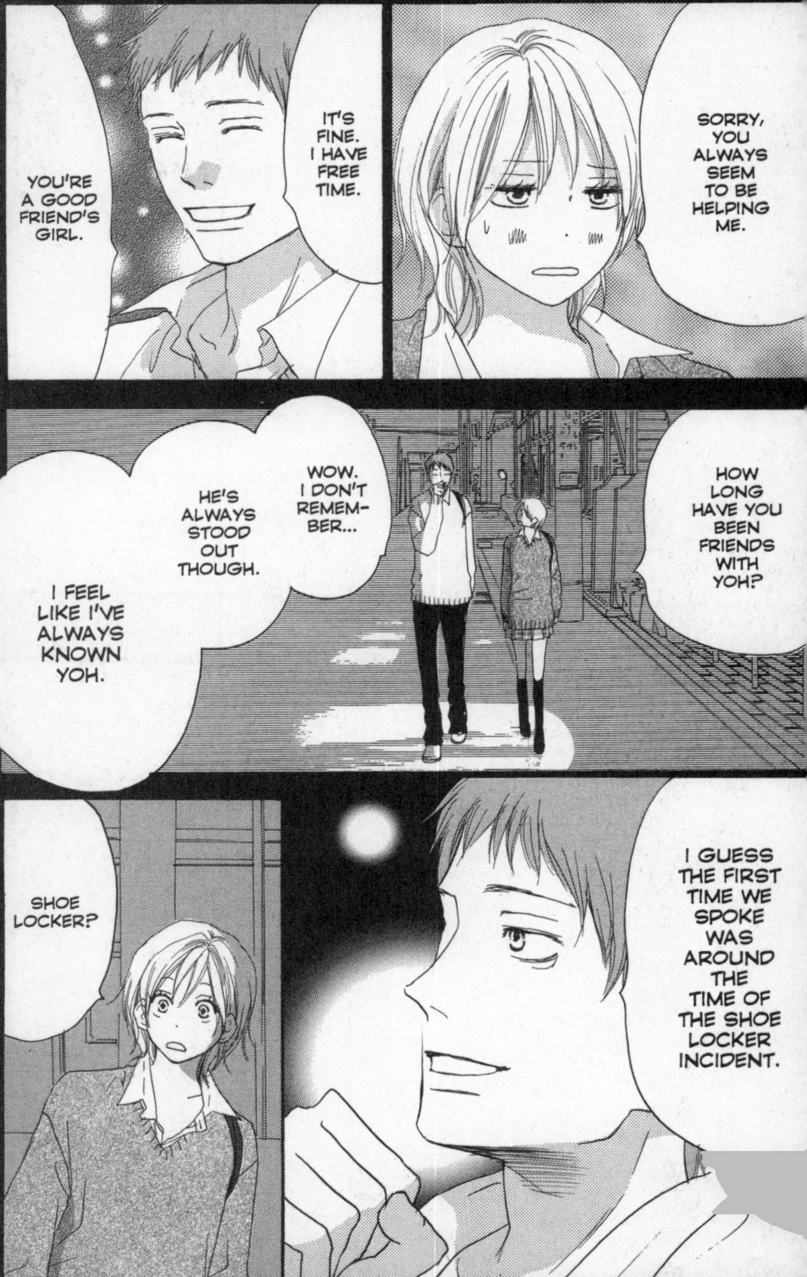
SORRY, YOU ALWAYS SEEM TO BE HELPING ME.
IT'S FINE. I HAVE FREE TIME.
YOU'RE A GOOD FRIEND'S GIRL.
HOW LONG HAVE YOU BEEN FRIENDS WITH YOH?
WOW. I DON'T REMEMBER...
HE'S ALWAYS STOOD OUT THOUGH.
I FEEL LIKE I'VE ALWAYS KNOWN YOH.
I GUESS THE FIRST TIME WE SPOKE WAS AROUND THE TIME OF THE SHOE LOCKER INCIDENT.
SHOE LOCKER?

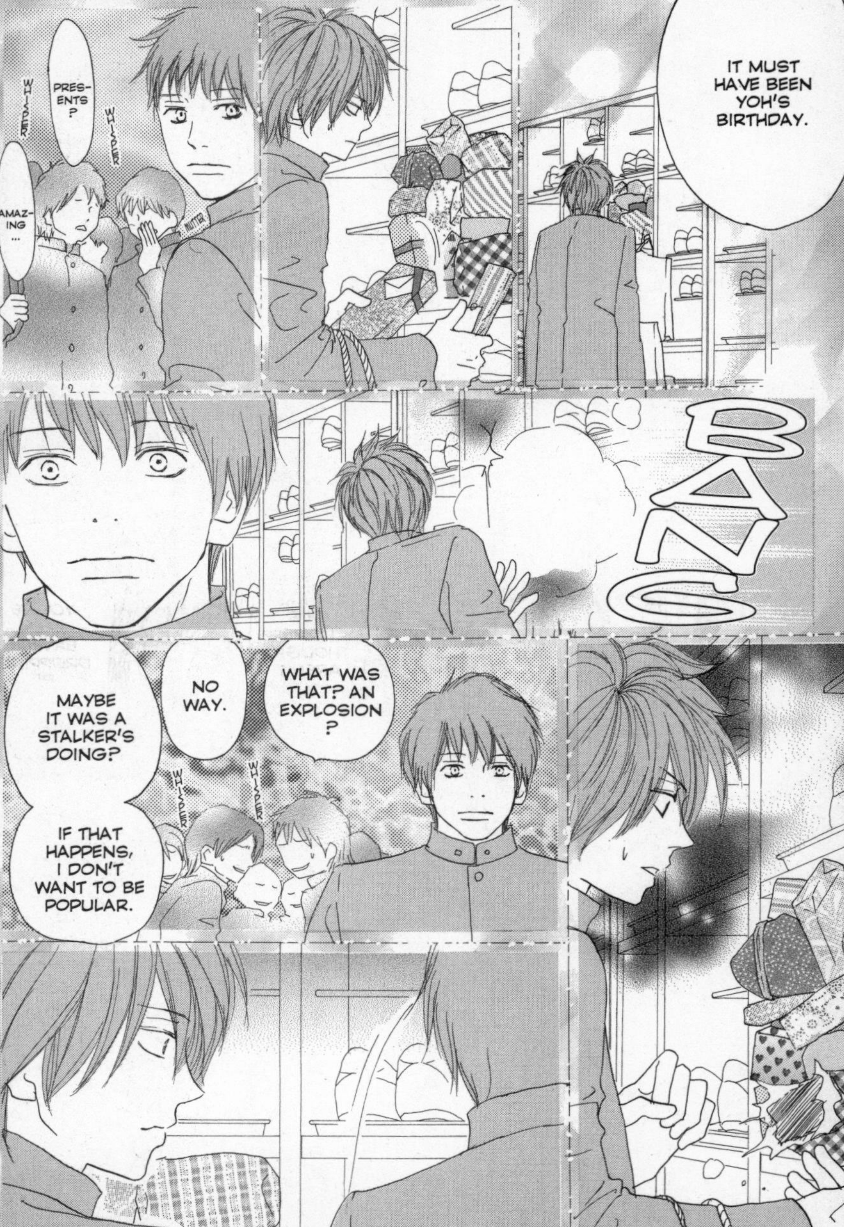
IT MUST HAVE BEEN YOH'S BIRTHDAY.
MUTTER
WHISPER
PRESENTS?
WHISPER
AMAZING...
BANG
WHAT WAS THAT? AN EXPLOSION?
NO WAY.
WHISPER
WHISPER
MAYBE IT WAS A STALKER'S DOING?
IF THAT HAPPENS, I DON'T WANT TO BE POPULAR.

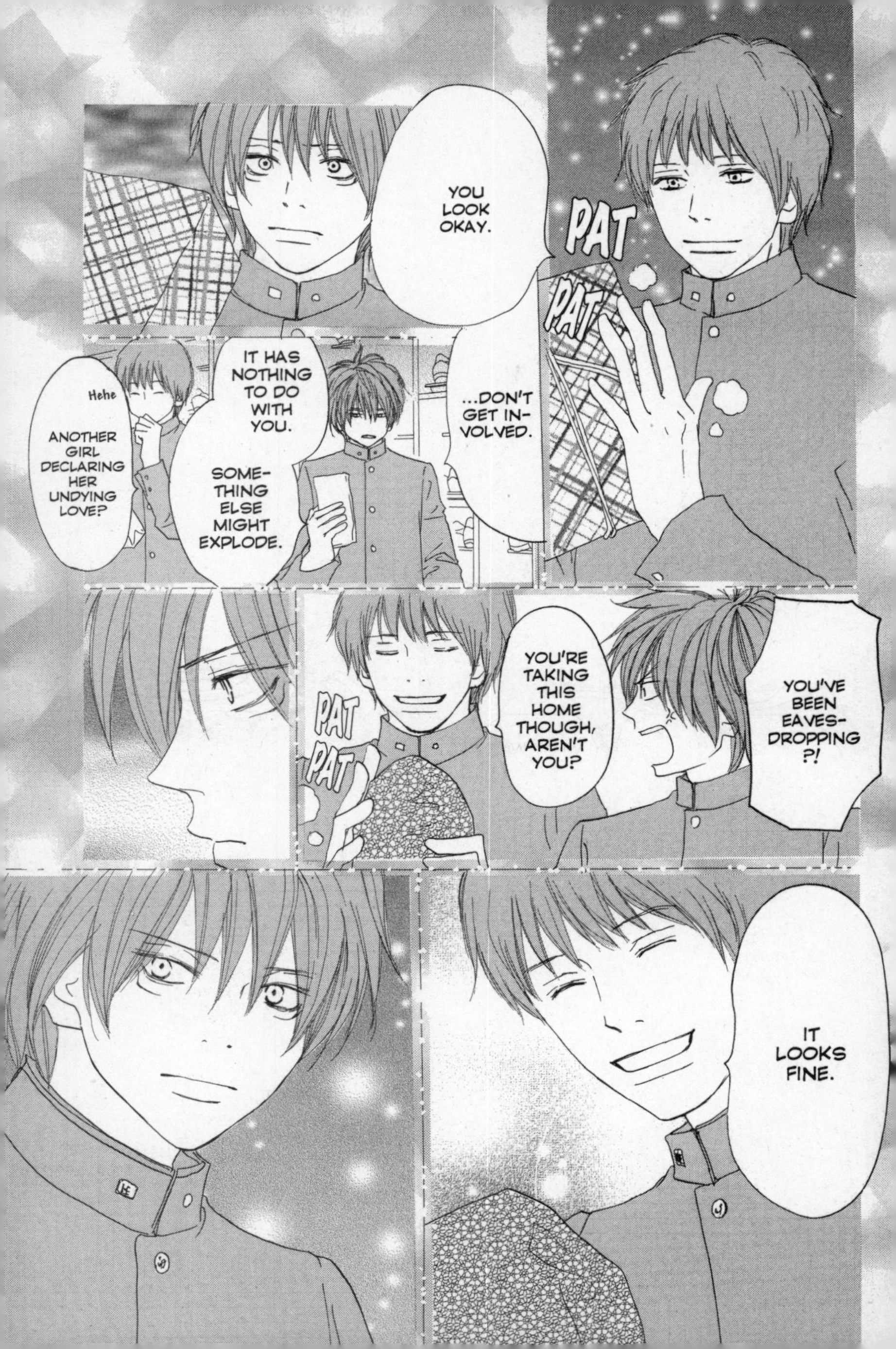
PAT
PAT
YOU LOOK OKAY.
...DON'T GET IN-VOLVED.
IT HAS NOTHING TO DO WITH YOU.
SOME-THING ELSE MIGHT EXPLODE.
Hehe
ANOTHER GIRL DECLARING HER UNDYING LOVE?
YOU'VE BEEN EAVES-DROPPING?!
YOU'RE TAKING THIS HOME THOUGH, AREN'T YOU?
PAT
PAT
IT LOOKS FINE.

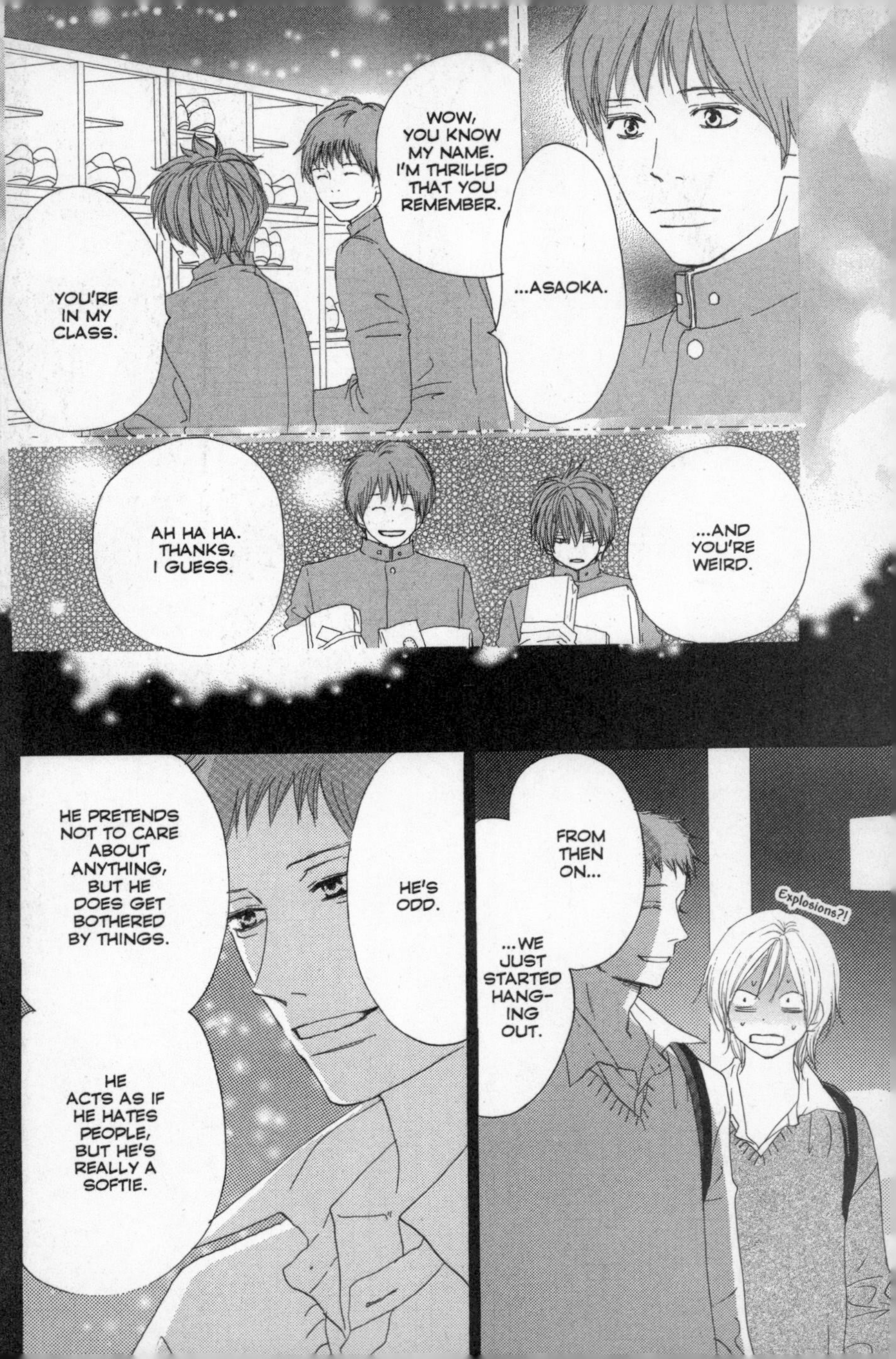
...ASAOKA.
WOW, YOU KNOW MY NAME. I'M THRILLED THAT YOU REMEMBER.
YOU'RE IN MY CLASS.
...AND YOU'RE WEIRD.
AH HA HA. THANKS, I GUESS.
FROM THEN ON...
...WE JUST STARTED HANG-ING OUT.
Explosions?!
HE'S ODD.
HE PRETENDS NOT TO CARE ABOUT ANYTHING, BUT HE DOES GET BOTHERED BY THINGS.
HE ACTS AS IF HE HATES PEOPLE, BUT HE'S REALLY A SOFTIE.

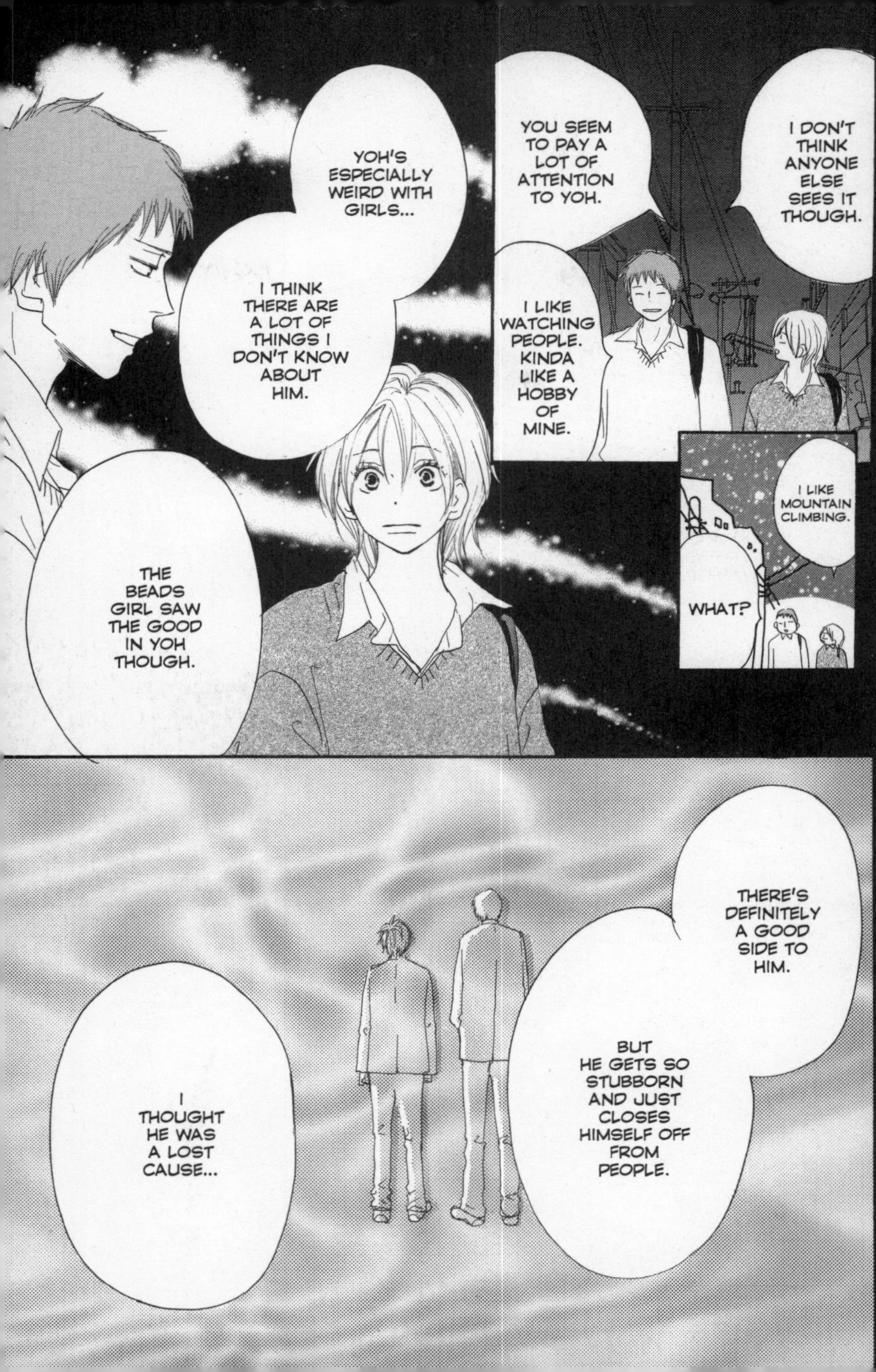
I DON'T THINK ANYONE ELSE SEES IT THOUGH.
YOU SEEM TO PAY A LOT OF ATTENTION TO YOH.
I LIKE WATCHING PEOPLE. KINDA LIKE A HOBBY OF MINE.
I LIKE MOUNTAIN CLIMBING.
WHAT?
YOH'S ESPECIALLY WEIRD WITH GIRLS...
I THINK THERE ARE A LOT OF THINGS I DON'T KNOW ABOUT HIM.
THE BEADS GIRL SAW THE GOOD IN YOH THOUGH.
THERE'S DEFINITELY A GOOD SIDE TO HIM.
BUT HE GETS SO STUBBORN AND JUST CLOSES HIMSELF OFF FROM PEOPLE.
I THOUGHT HE WAS A LOST CAUSE...

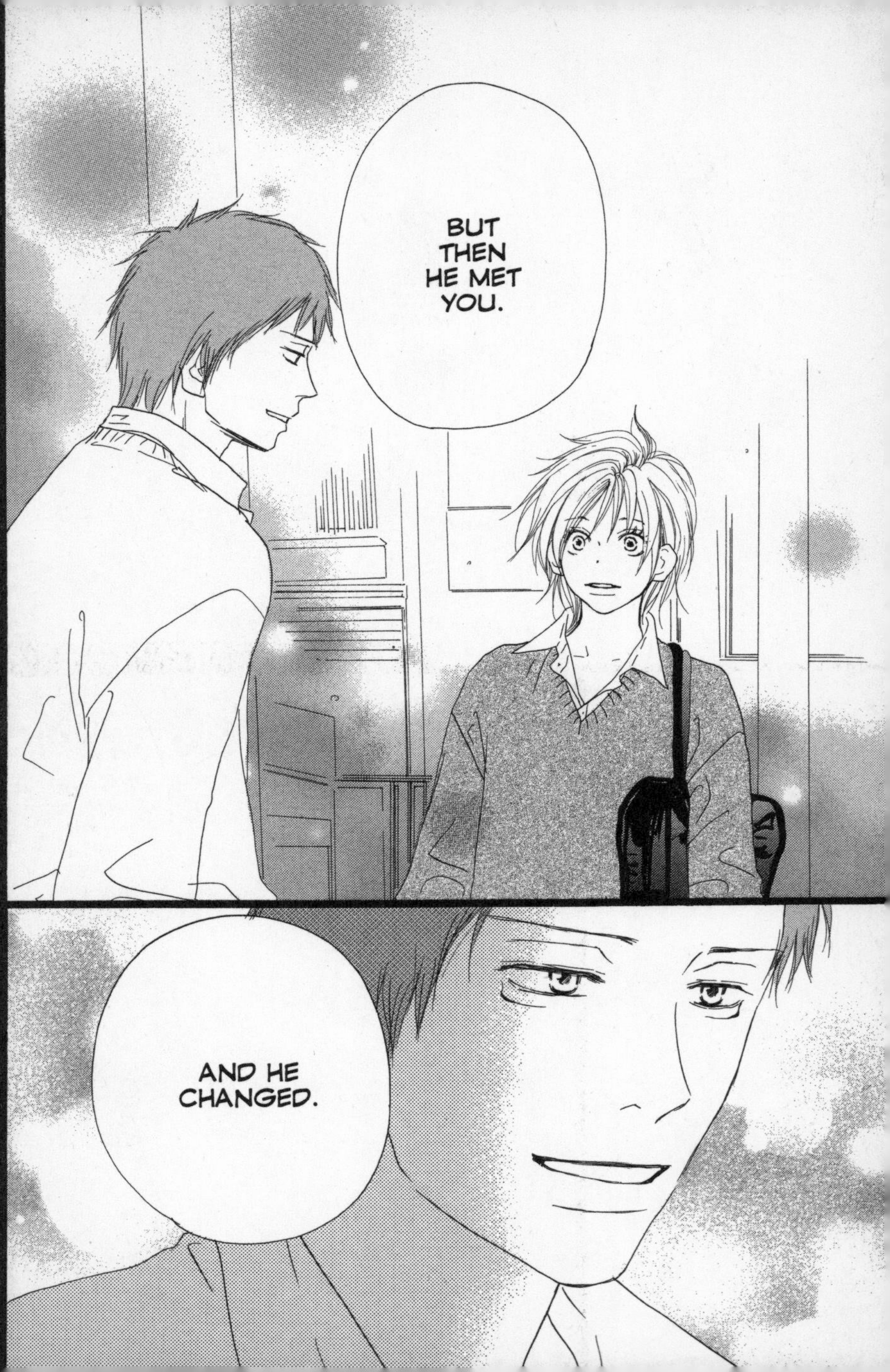
BUT THEN HE MET YOU.
AND HE CHANGED.

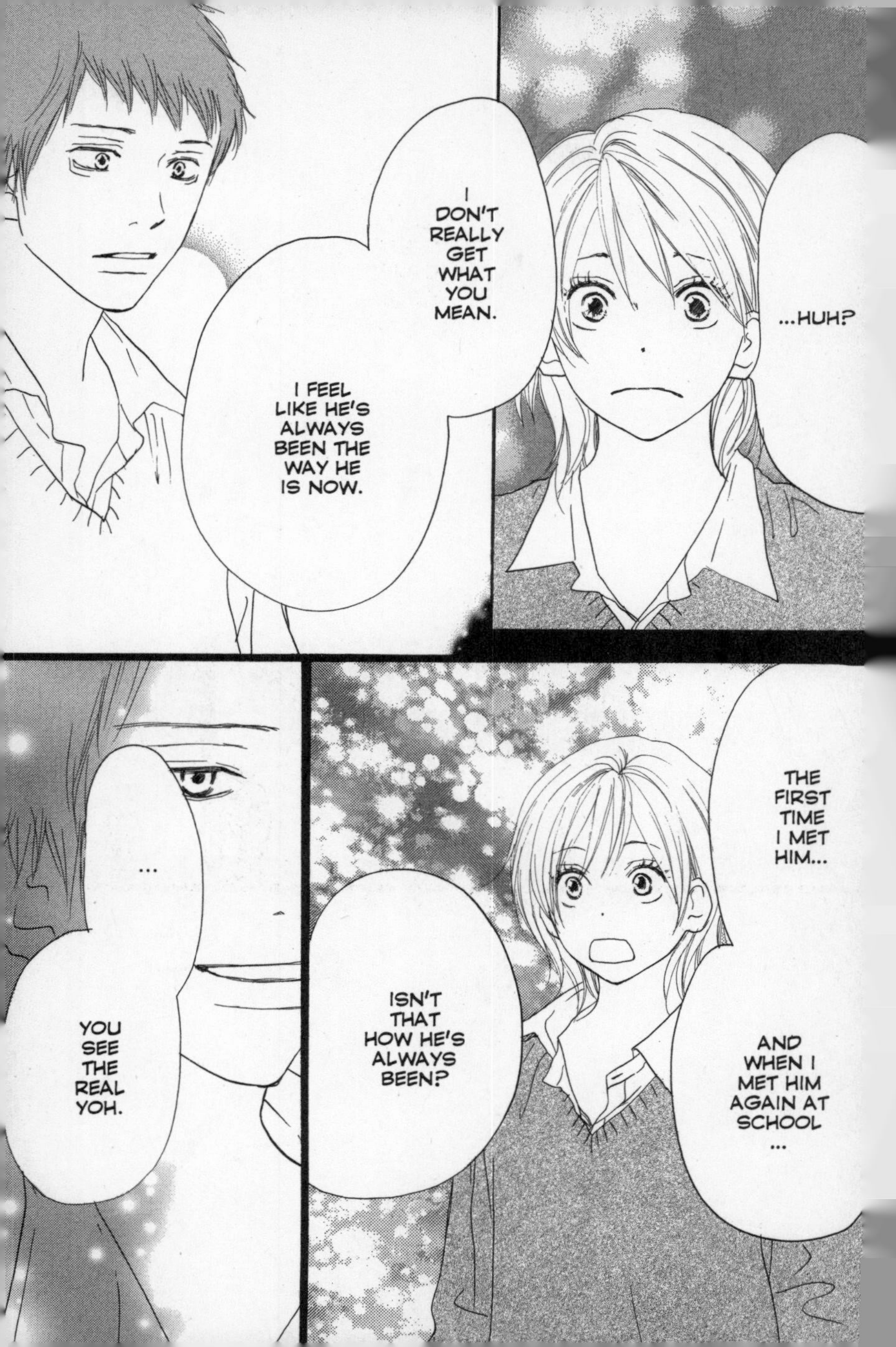
...HUH?
I DON'T REALLY GET WHAT YOU MEAN.
I FEEL LIKE HE'S ALWAYS BEEN THE WAY HE IS NOW.
THE FIRST TIME I MET HIM...
AND WHEN I MET HIM AGAIN AT SCHOOL...
ISN'T THAT HOW HE'S ALWAYS BEEN?
...
YOU SEE THE REAL YOH.

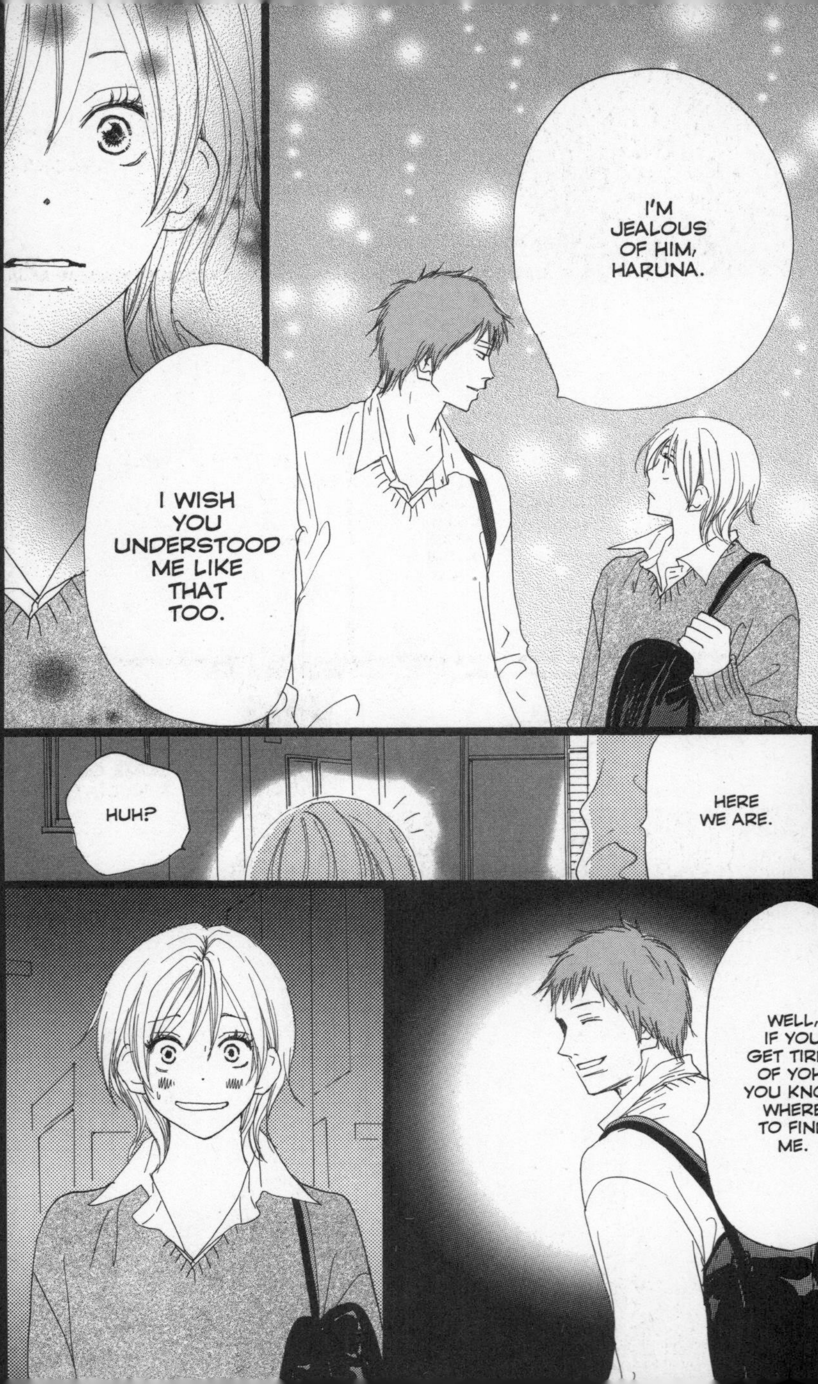
I'M JEALOUS OF HIM, HARUNA.
I WISH YOU UNDERSTOOD ME LIKE THAT TOO.
HERE WE ARE.
HUH?
WELL, IF YOU GET TIRED OF YOH, YOU KNOW WHERE TO FIND ME.

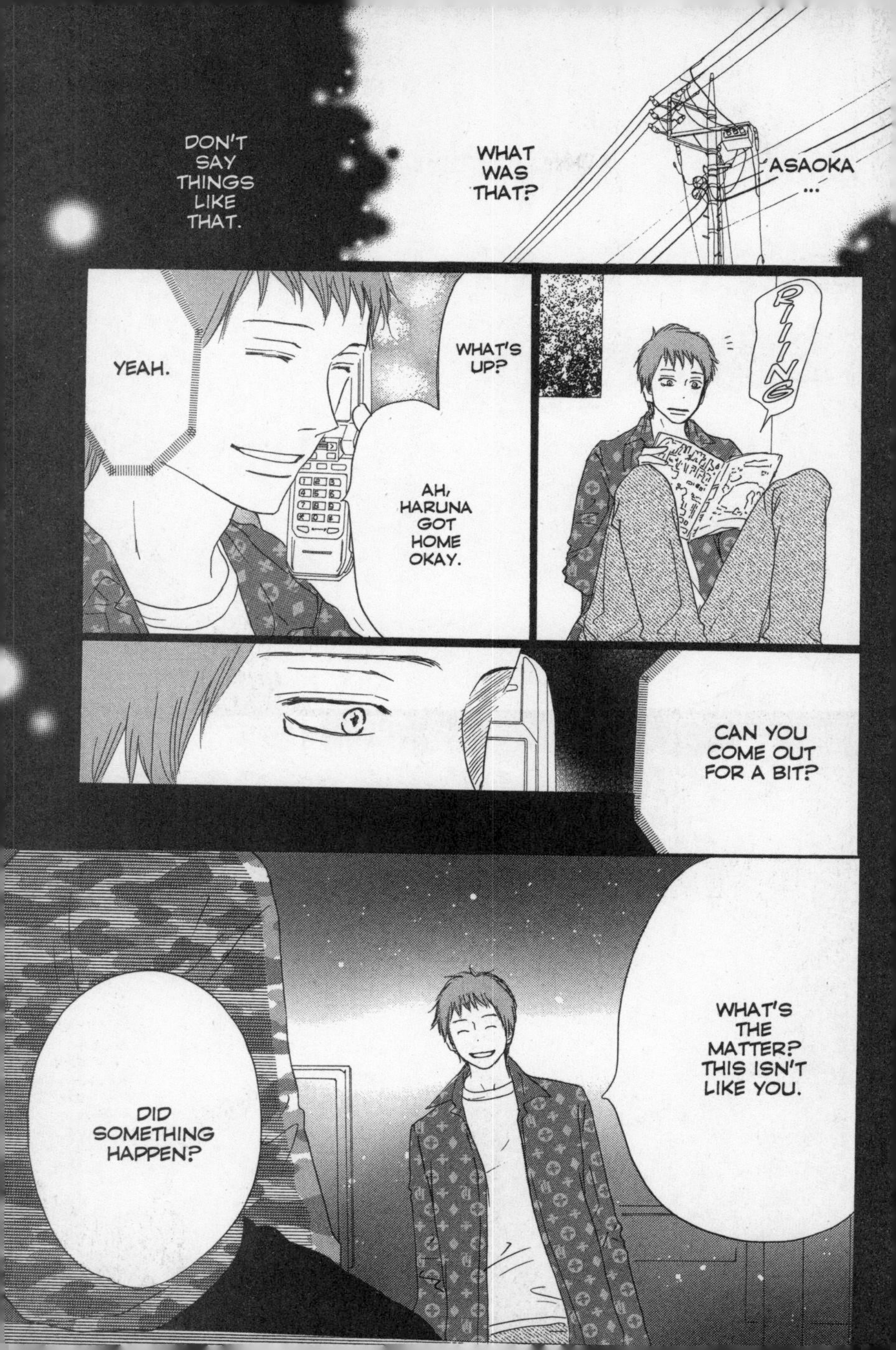
ASAOKA ...
WHAT WAS THAT?
DON'T SAY THINGS LIKE THAT.
RIIING
WHAT'S UP?
YEAH.
AH, HARUNA GOT HOME OKAY.
CAN YOU COME OUT FOR A BIT?
WHAT'S THE MATTER? THIS ISN'T LIKE YOU.
DID SOMETHING HAPPEN?

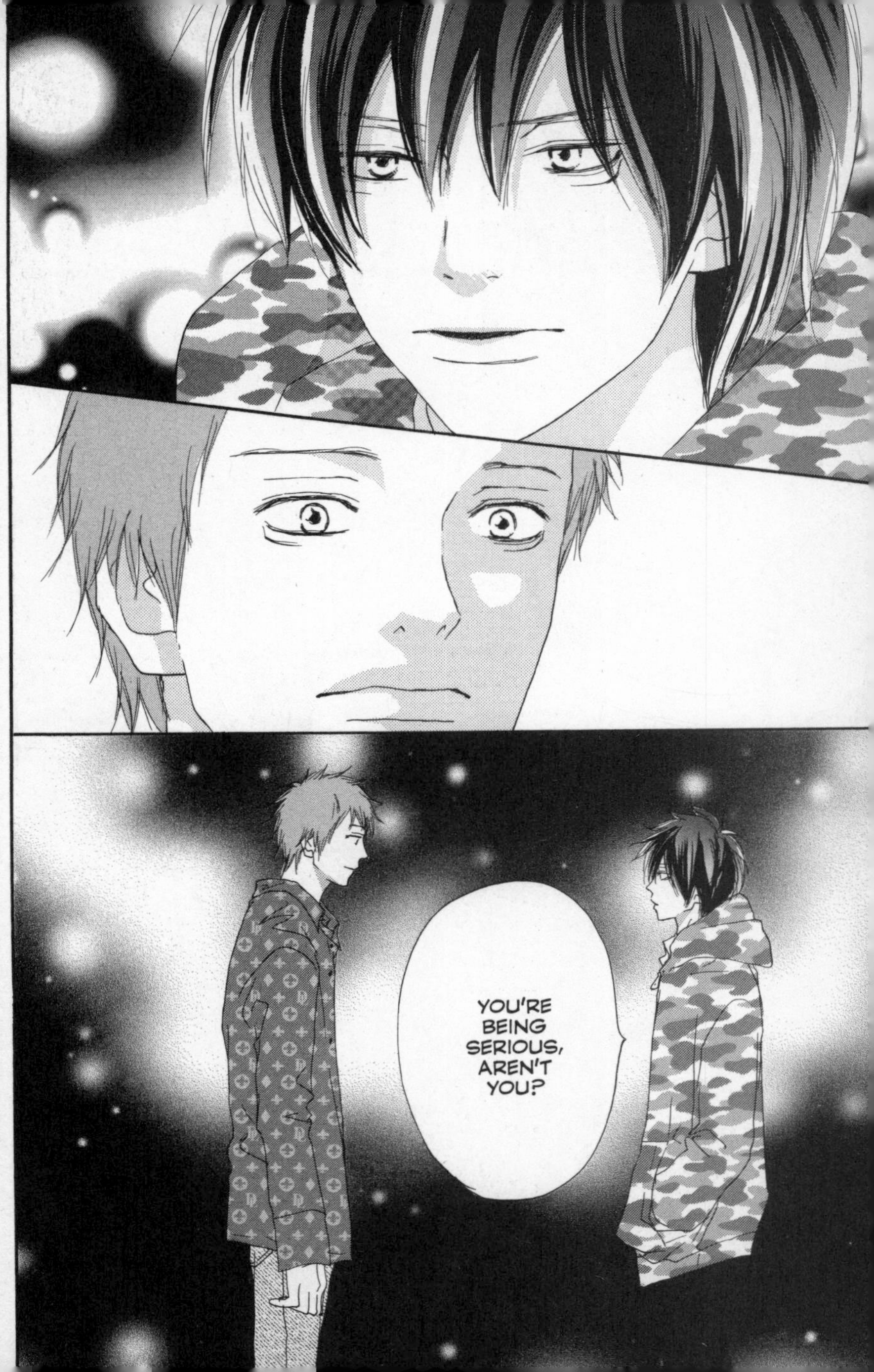
YOU'RE BEING SERIOUS, AREN'T YOU?

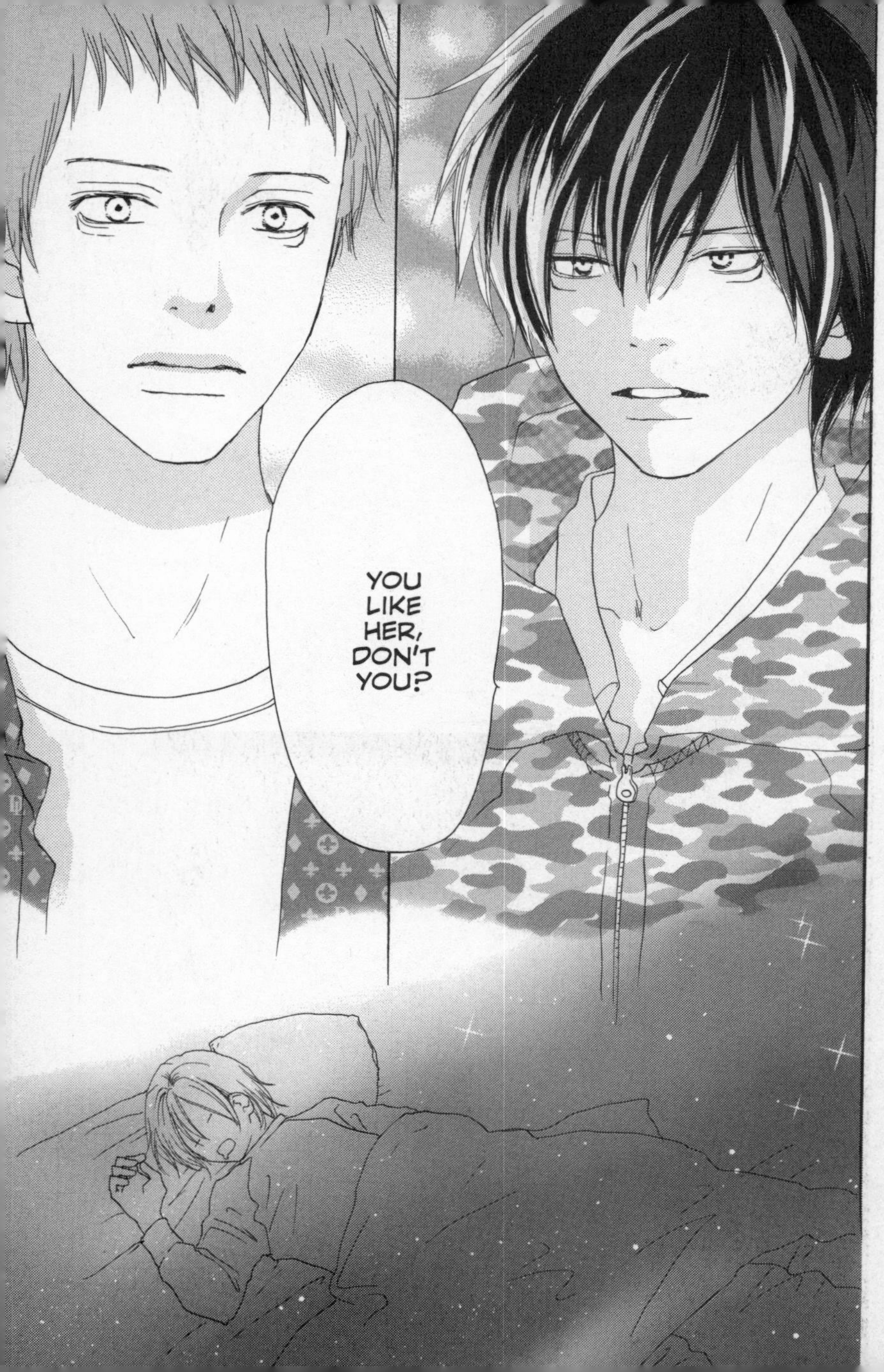
YOU LIKE HER, DON'T YOU?

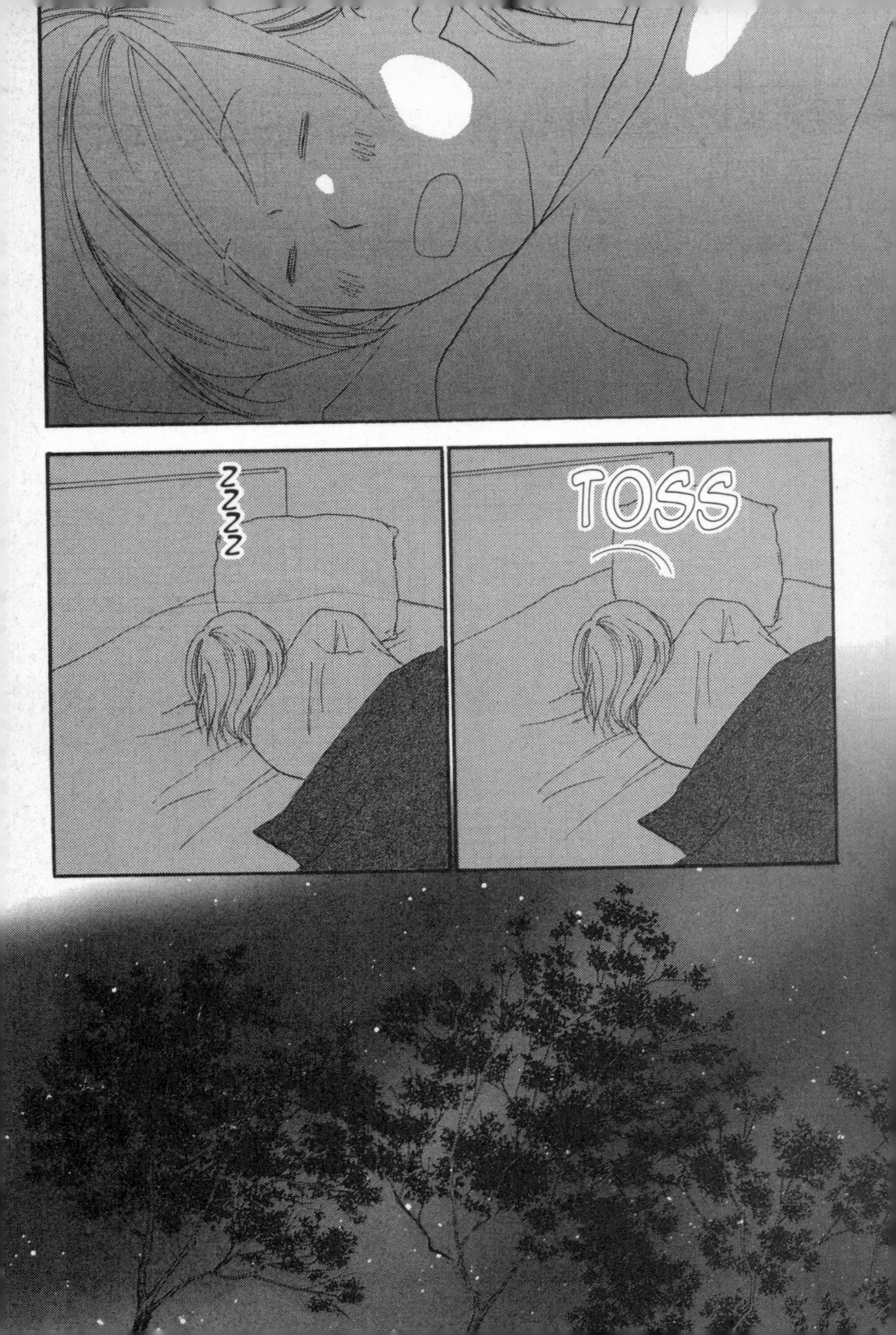
TOSS
ZZZZ

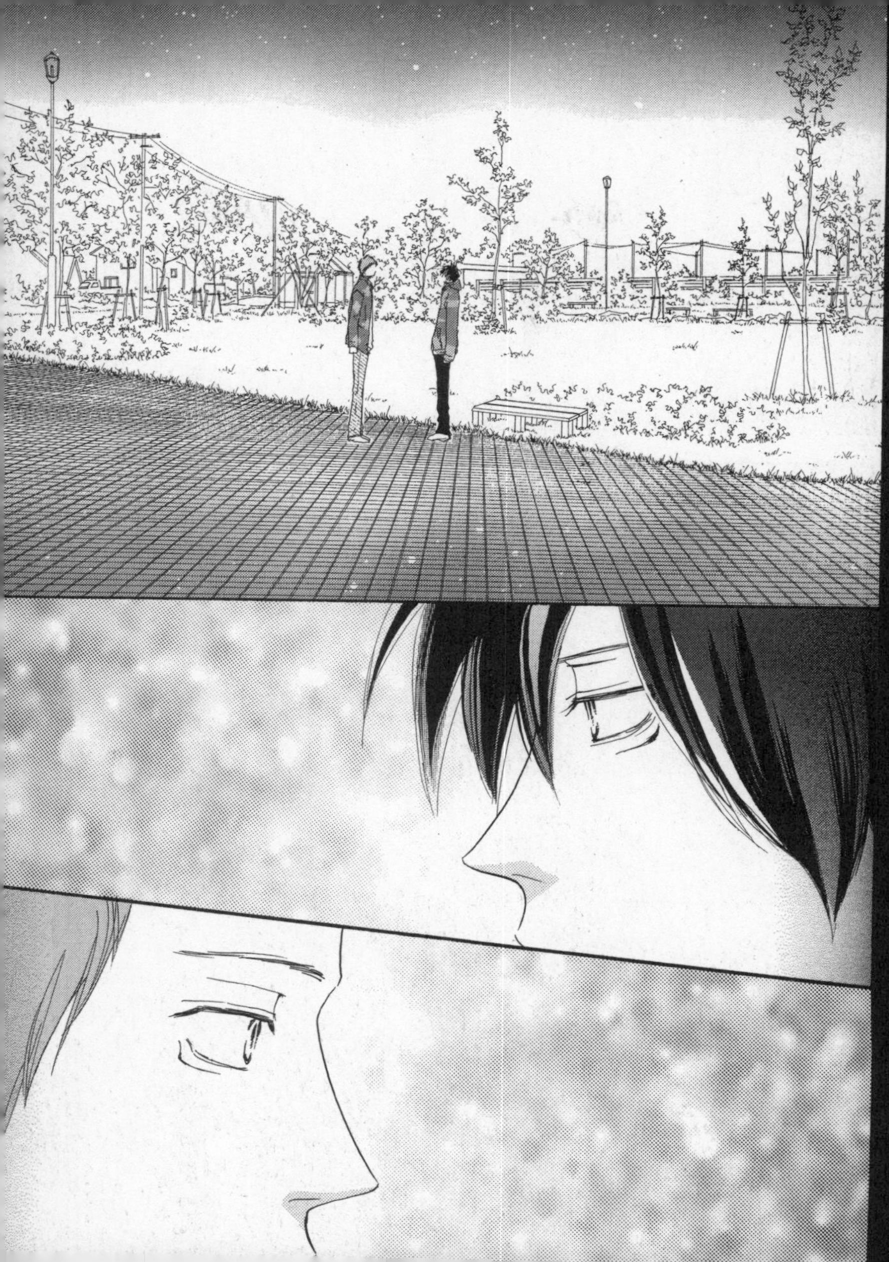

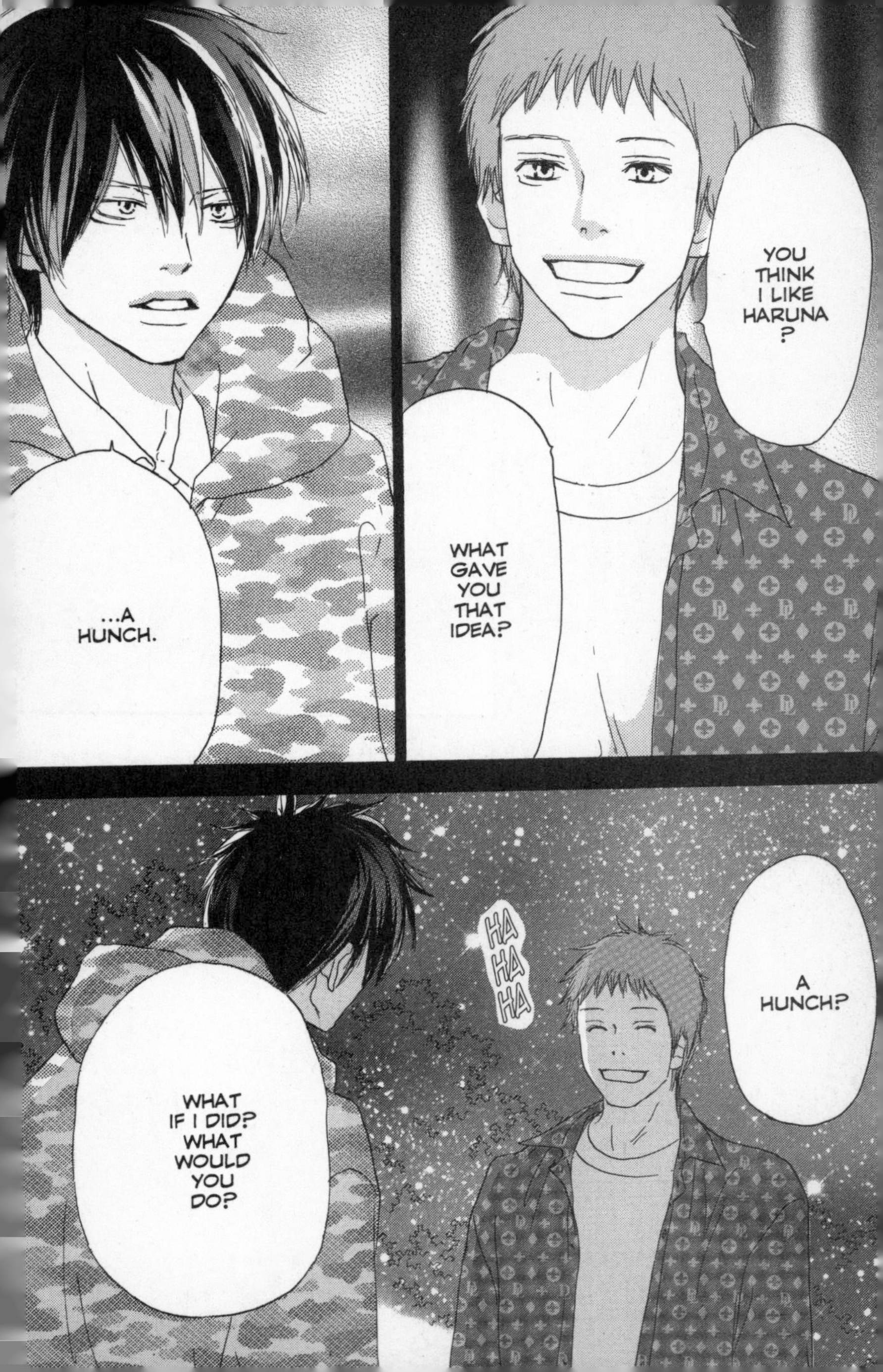
YOU THINK I LIKE HARUNA?
WHAT GAVE YOU THAT IDEA?
...A HUNCH.
A HUNCH?
HA HA HA
WHAT IF I DID? WHAT WOULD YOU DO?

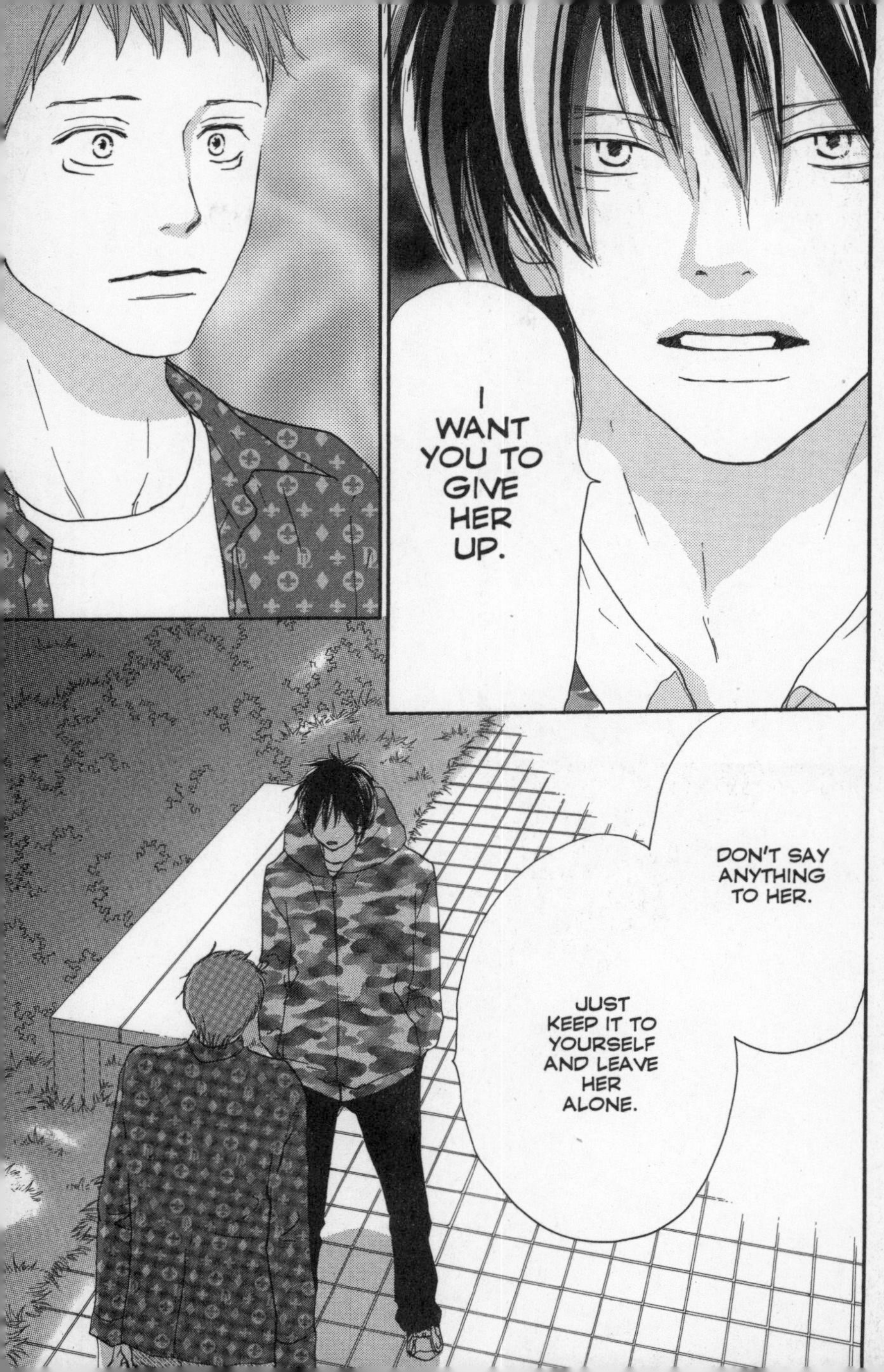
I WANT YOU TO GIVE HER UP.
DON'T SAY ANYTHING TO HER.
JUST KEEP IT TO YOURSELF AND LEAVE HER ALONE.

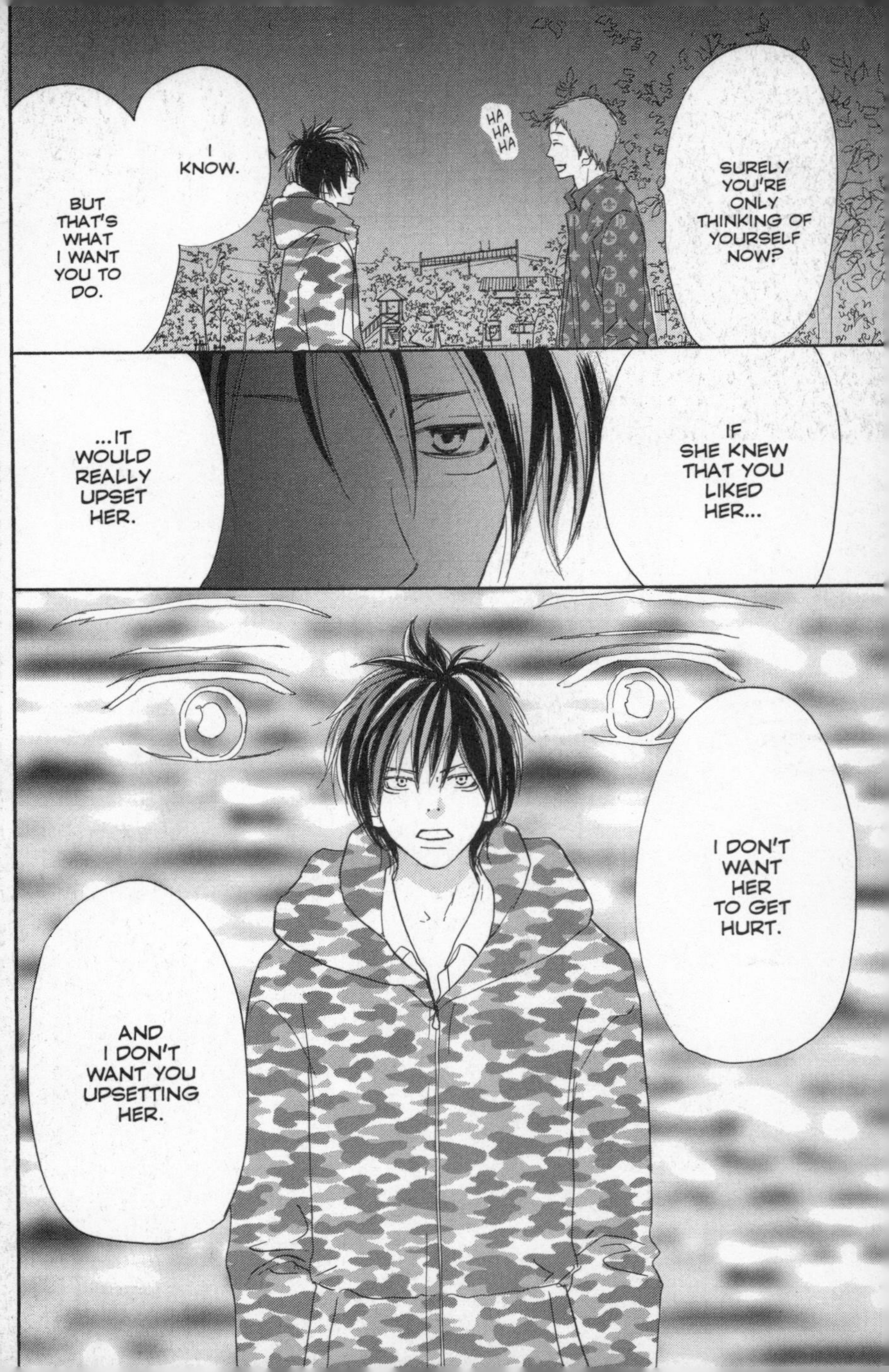
SURELY YOU'RE ONLY THINKING OF YOURSELF NOW?
HA HA HA
I KNOW.
BUT THAT'S WHAT I WANT YOU TO DO.
IF SHE KNEW THAT YOU LIKED HER...
...IT WOULD REALLY UPSET HER.
I DON'T WANT HER TO GET HURT.
AND I DON'T WANT YOU UPSETTING HER.

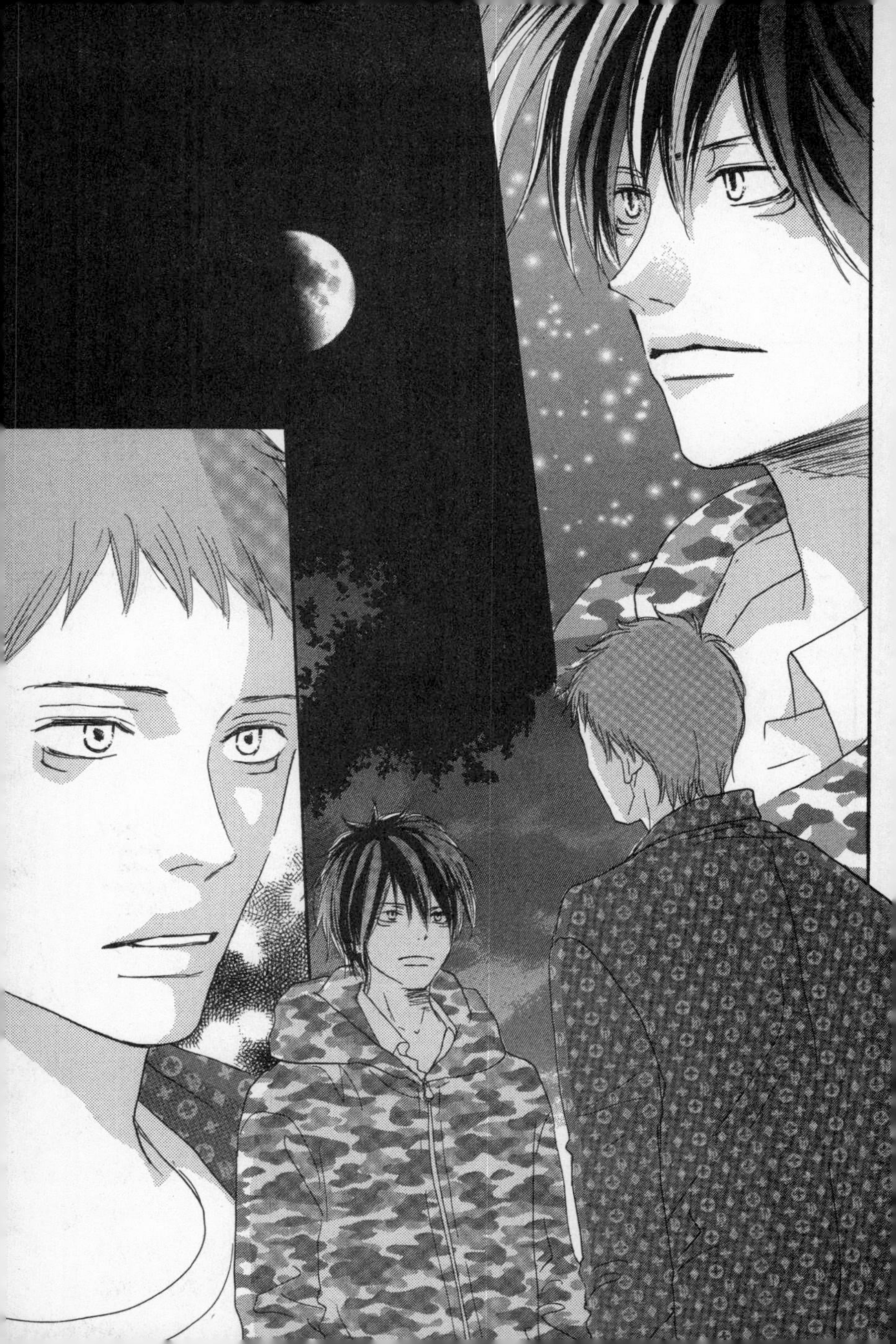

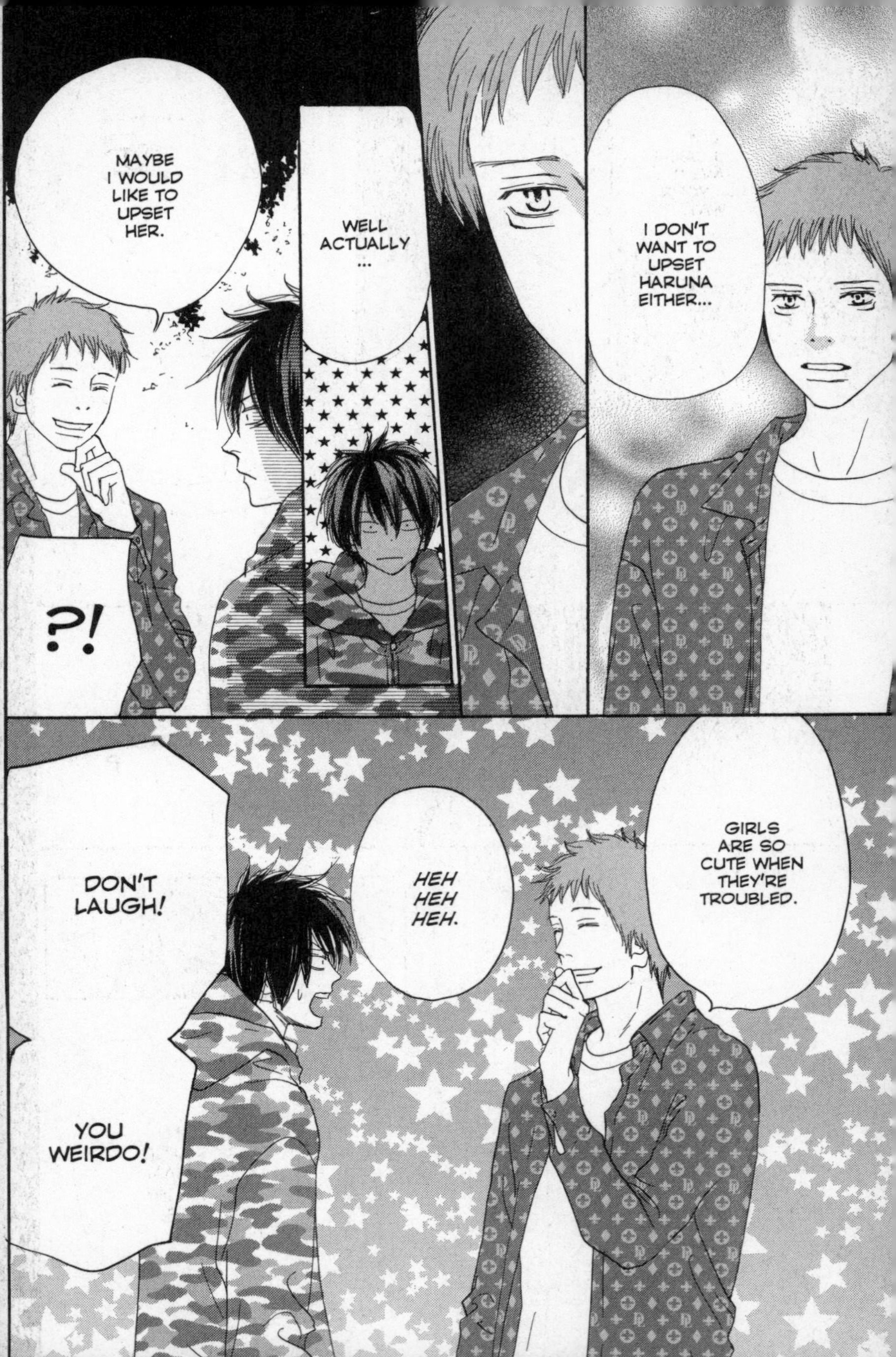
I DON'T WANT TO UPSET HARUNA EITHER...
WELL ACTUALLY ...
MAYBE I WOULD LIKE TO UPSET HER.
?!
GIRLS ARE SO CUTE WHEN THEY'RE TROUBLED.
HEH HEH HEH.
DON'T LAUGH!
YOU WEIRDO!

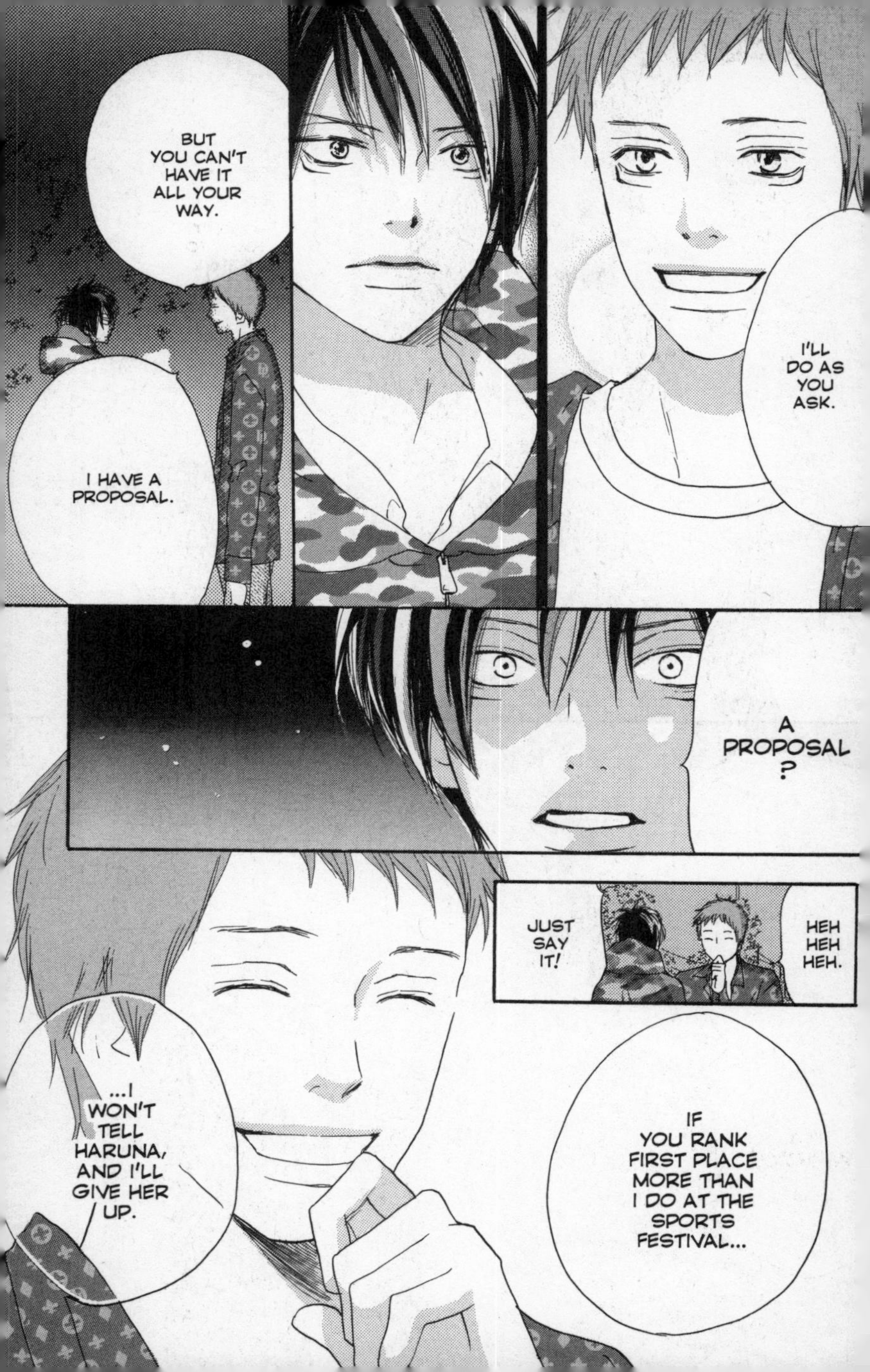
I'LL DO AS YOU ASK.
BUT YOU CAN'T HAVE IT ALL YOUR WAY.
I HAVE A PROPOSAL.
A PROPOSAL?
HEH HEH HEH.
JUST SAY IT!
IF YOU RANK FIRST PLACE MORE THAN I DO AT THE SPORTS FESTIVAL...
...I WON'T TELL HARUNA, AND I'LL GIVE HER UP.

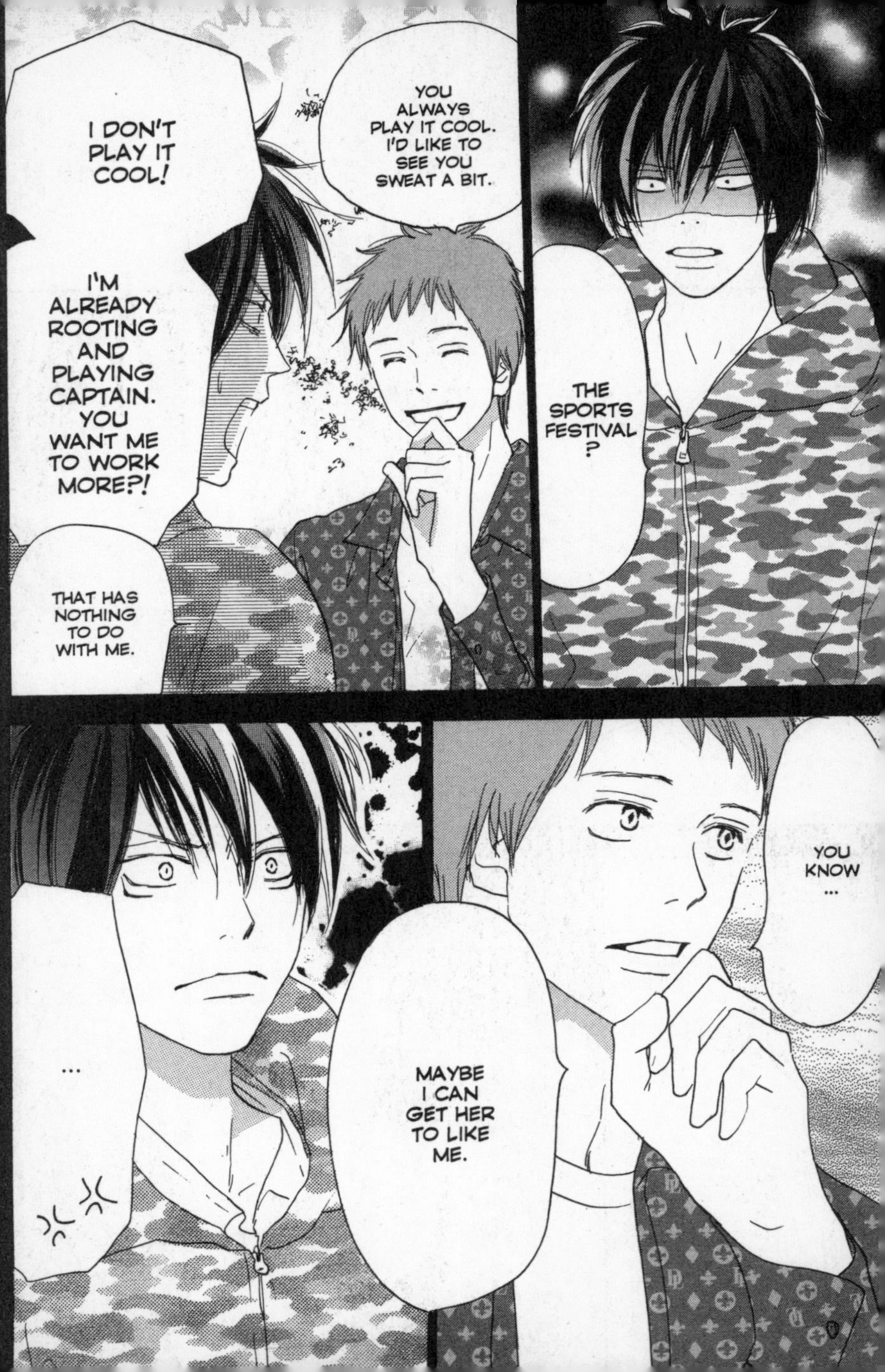
THE SPORTS FESTIVAL?
YOU ALWAYS PLAY IT COOL. I'D LIKE TO SEE YOU SWEAT A BIT.
I DON'T PLAY IT COOL!
I'M ALREADY ROOTING AND PLAYING CAPTAIN. YOU WANT ME TO WORK MORE?!
THAT HAS NOTHING TO DO WITH ME.
YOU KNOW...
MAYBE I CAN GET HER TO LIKE ME.
...

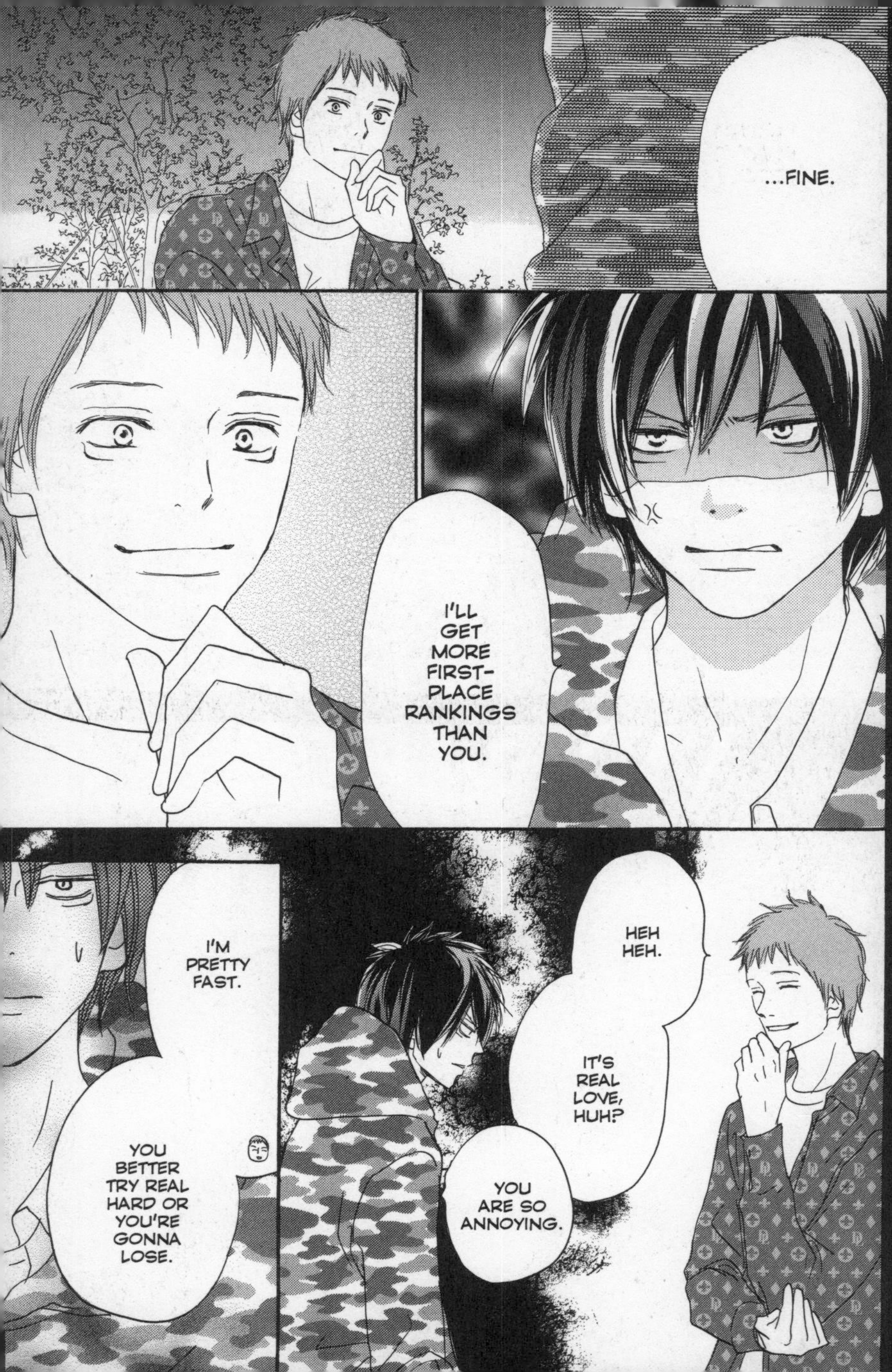
...FINE.
I'LL GET MORE FIRST-PLACE RANKINGS THAN YOU.
HEH HEH.
IT'S REAL LOVE, HUH?
YOU ARE SO ANNOYING.
I'M PRETTY FAST.
YOU BETTER TRY REAL HARD OR YOU'RE GONNA LOSE.

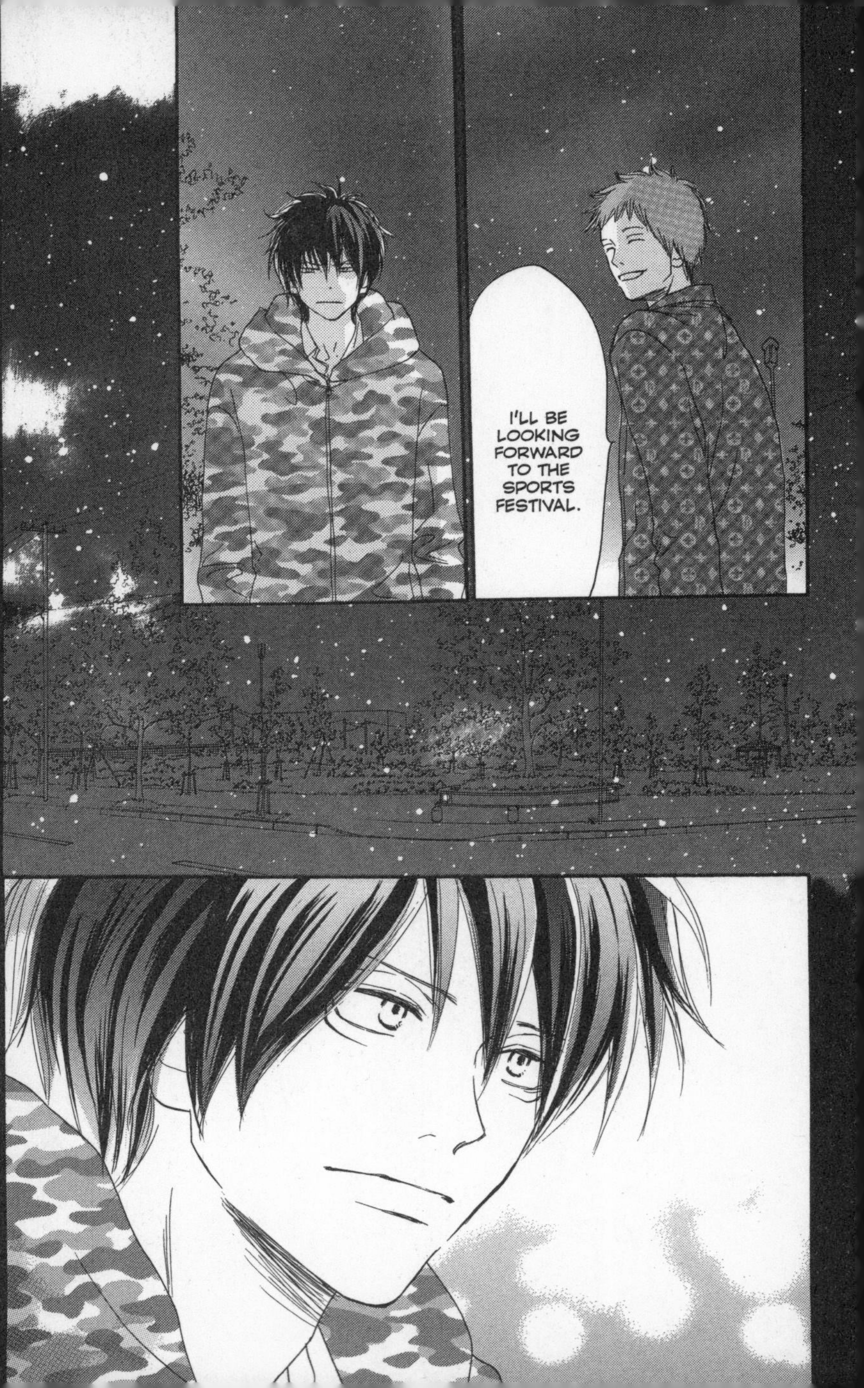
I'LL BE LOOKING FORWARD TO THE SPORTS FESTIVAL.

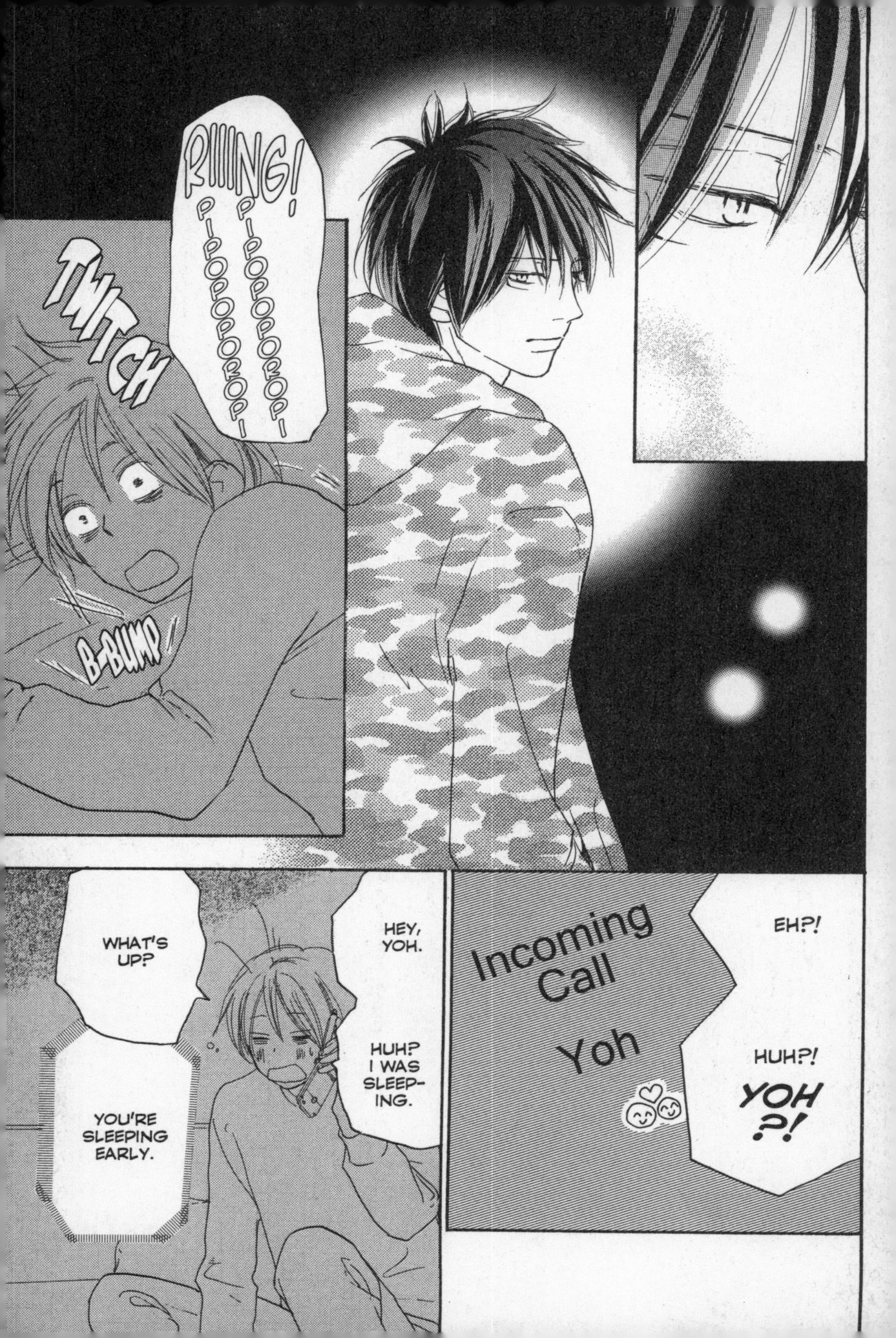
RIIING!
PIPOPOPOROPI PIPOPOPOROPI
TWITCH
B-BUMP
EH?!
HUH?!
YOH ?!
Incoming Call
Yoh
HEY, YOH.
HUH? I WAS SLEEP-ING.
WHAT'S UP?
YOU'RE SLEEPING EARLY.

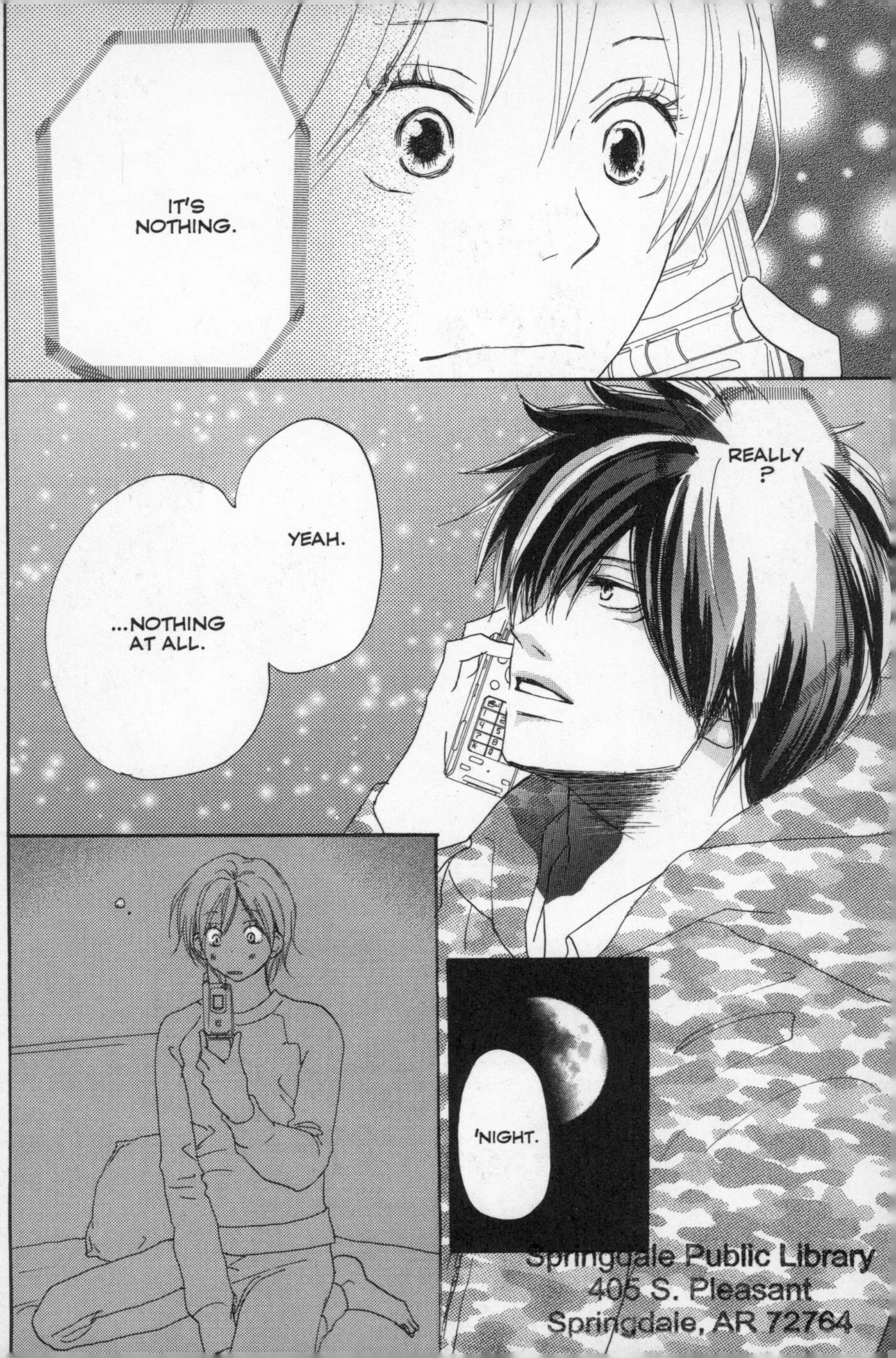
IT'S NOTHING.
REALLY?
YEAH.
...NOTHING AT ALL.
'NIGHT.

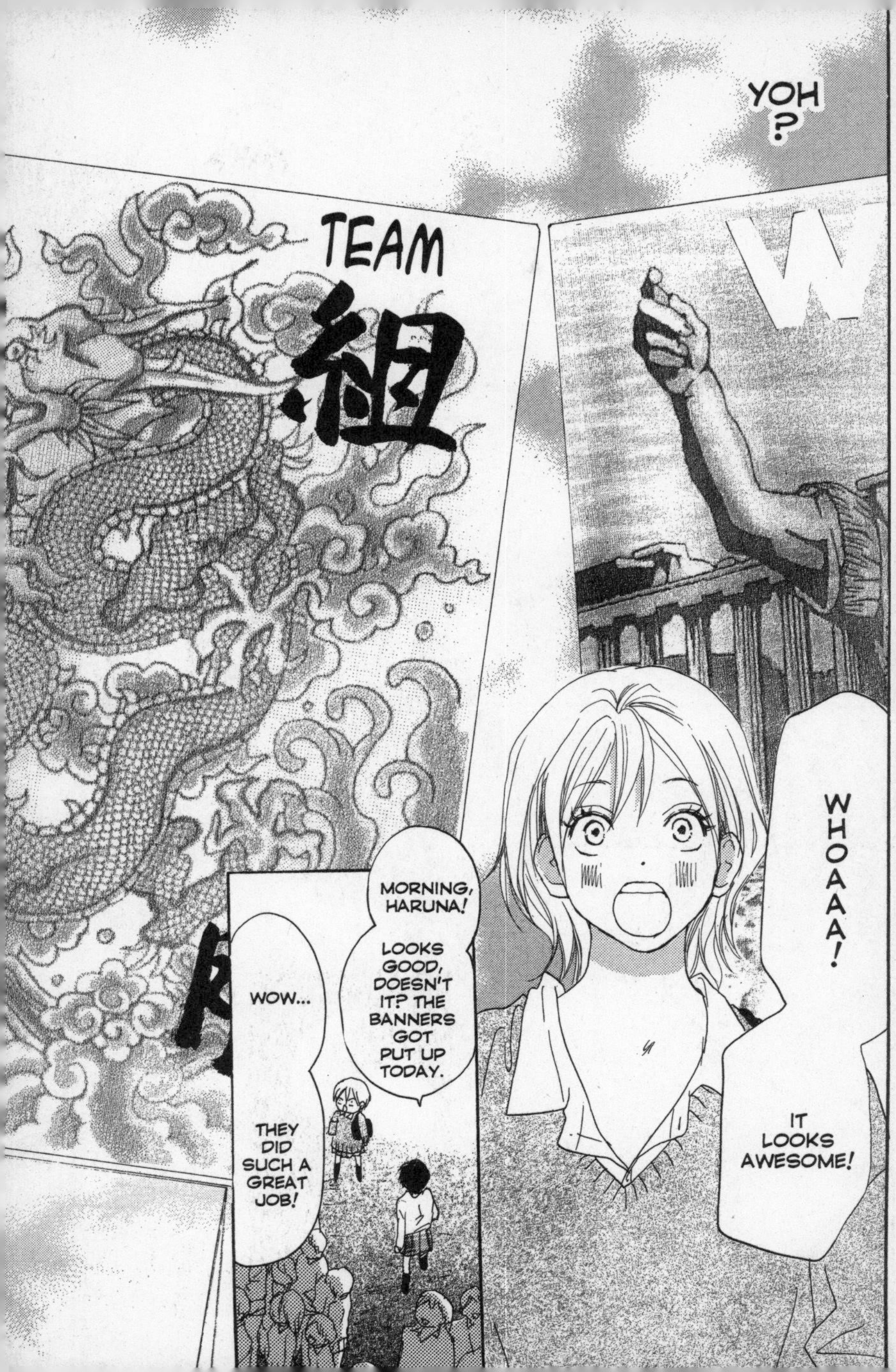
YOH?
WHOAAA!
IT LOOKS AWESOME!
TEAM
組
MORNING, HARUNA!
LOOKS GOOD, DOESN'T IT? THE BANNERS GOT PUT UP TODAY.
WOW...
THEY DID SUCH A GREAT JOB!

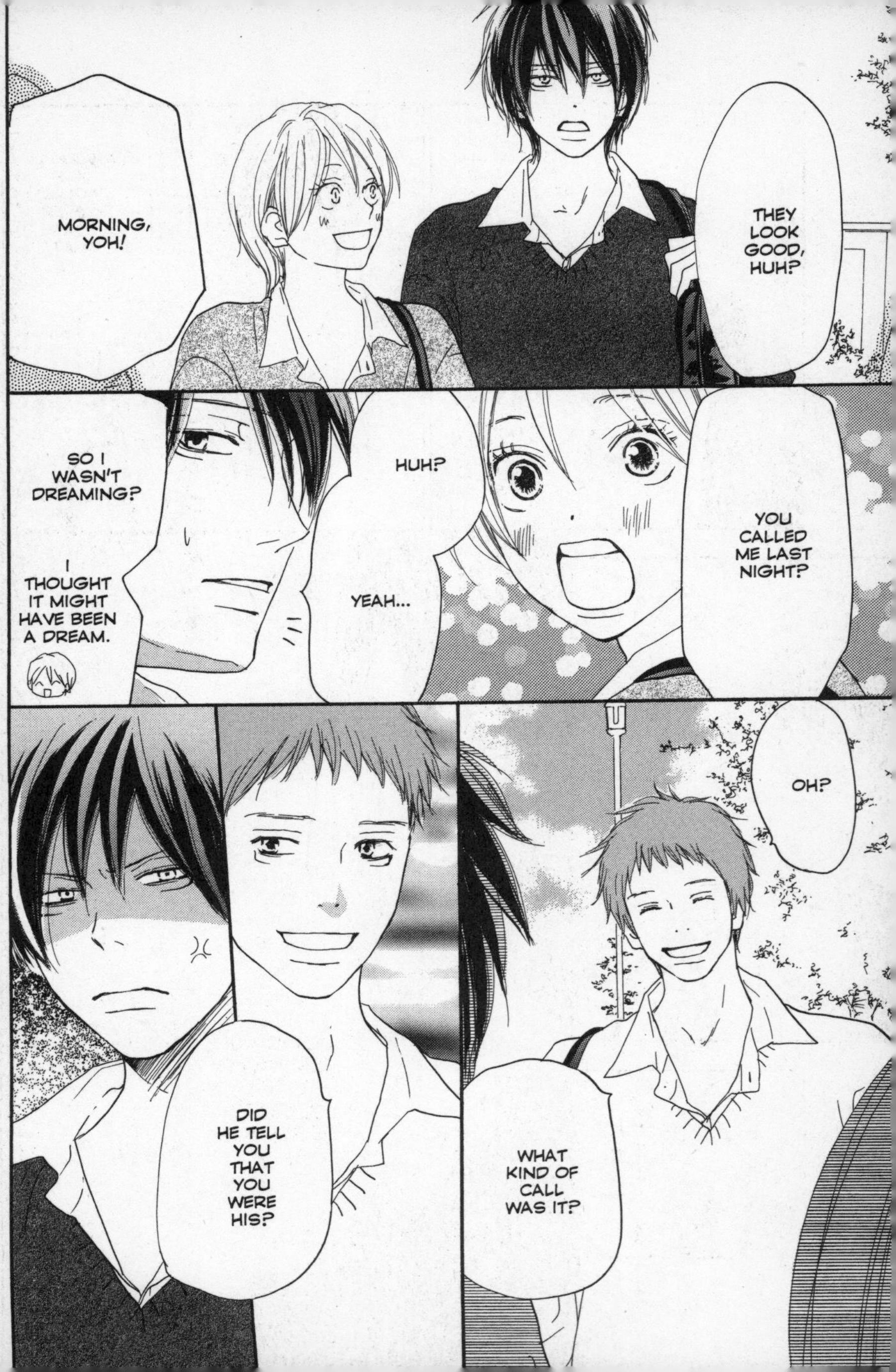
THEY LOOK GOOD, HUH?
MORNING, YOH!
YOU CALLED ME LAST NIGHT?
HUH?
YEAH...
SO I WASN'T DREAMING?
I THOUGHT IT MIGHT HAVE BEEN A DREAM.
OH?
WHAT KIND OF CALL WAS IT?
DID HE TELL YOU THAT YOU WERE HIS?

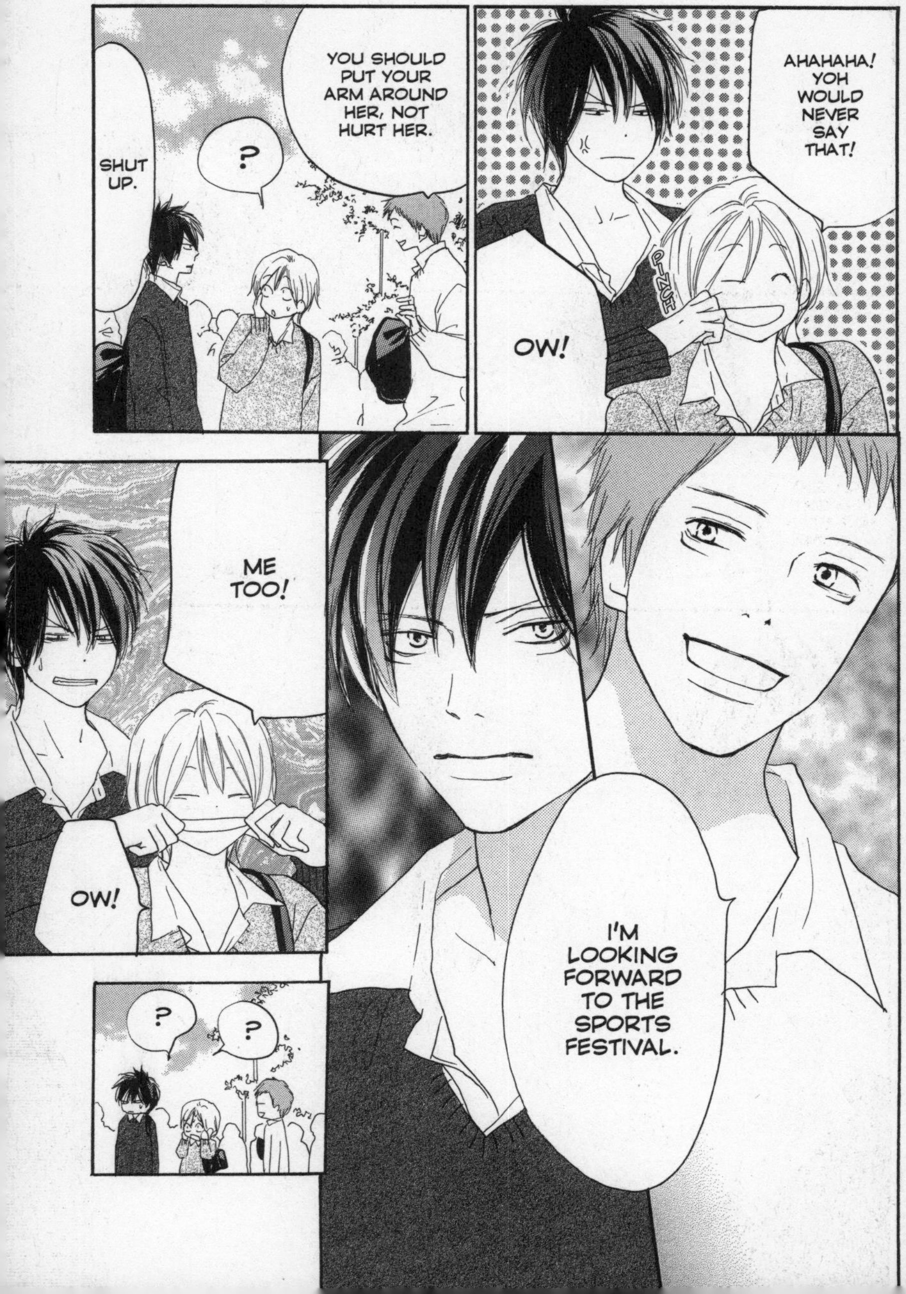
AHAHAHA! YOH WOULD NEVER SAY THAT!
PINCH
OW!
YOU SHOULD PUT YOUR ARM AROUND HER, NOT HURT HER.
?
SHUT UP.
I'M LOOKING FORWARD TO THE SPORTS FESTIVAL.
ME TOO!
OW!
?
?

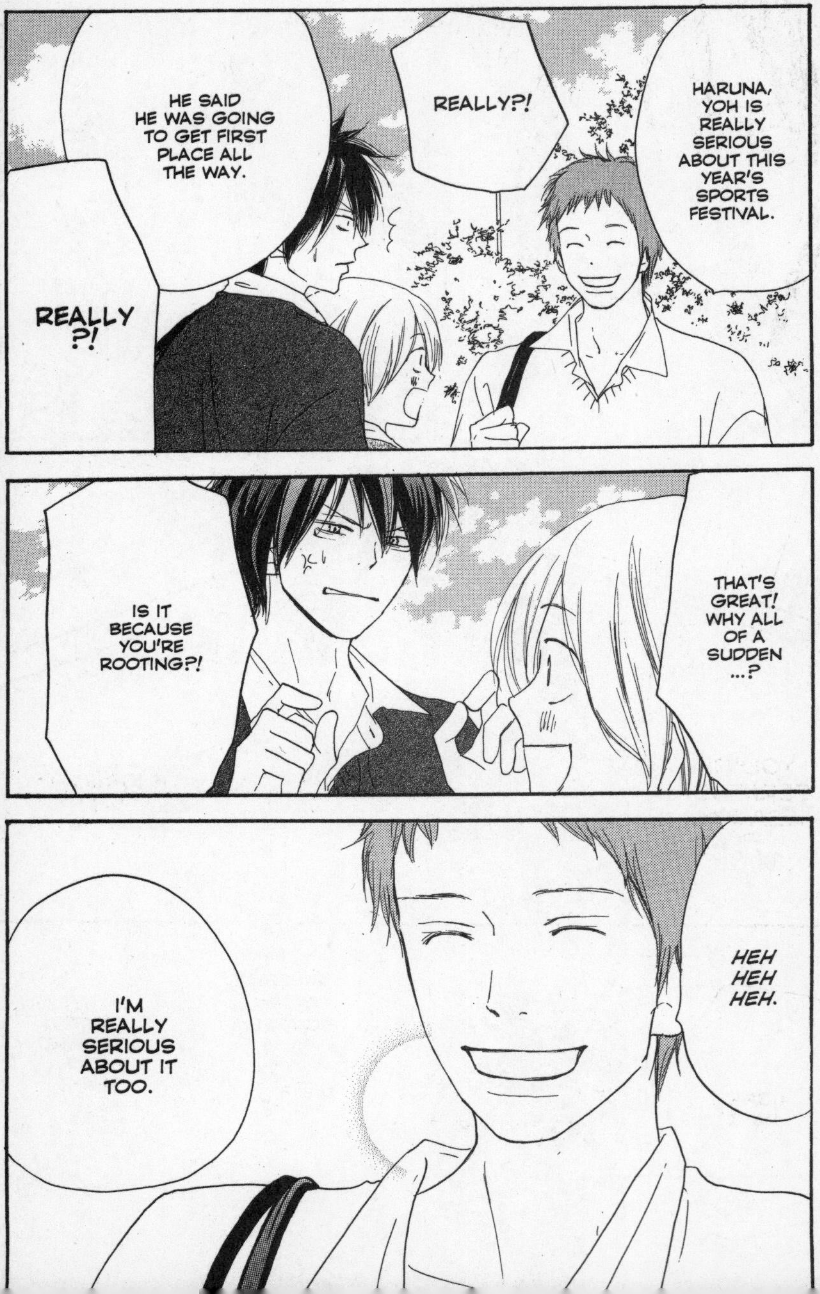
HARUNA, YOH IS REALLY SERIOUS ABOUT THIS YEAR'S SPORTS FESTIVAL.
REALLY?!
HE SAID HE WAS GOING TO GET FIRST PLACE ALL THE WAY.
REALLY ?!
THAT'S GREAT! WHY ALL OF A SUDDEN ...?
IS IT BECAUSE YOU'RE ROOTING?!
HEH HEH HEH.
I'M REALLY SERIOUS ABOUT IT TOO.

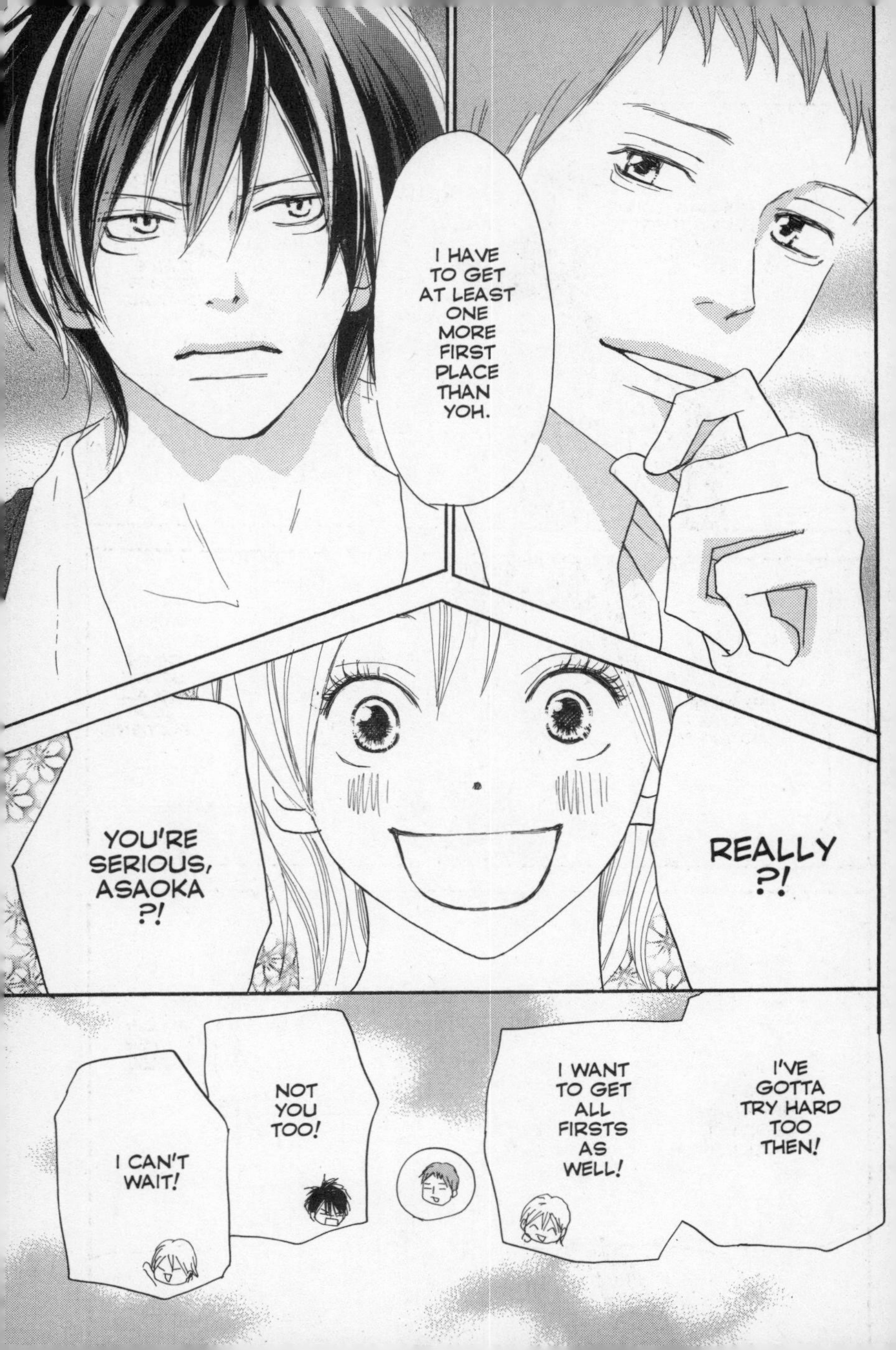
I HAVE TO GET AT LEAST ONE MORE FIRST PLACE THAN YOH.
REALLY ?!
YOU'RE SERIOUS, ASAOKA ?!
I'VE GOTTA TRY HARD TOO THEN!
I WANT TO GET ALL FIRSTS AS WELL!
NOT YOU TOO!
I CAN'T WAIT!

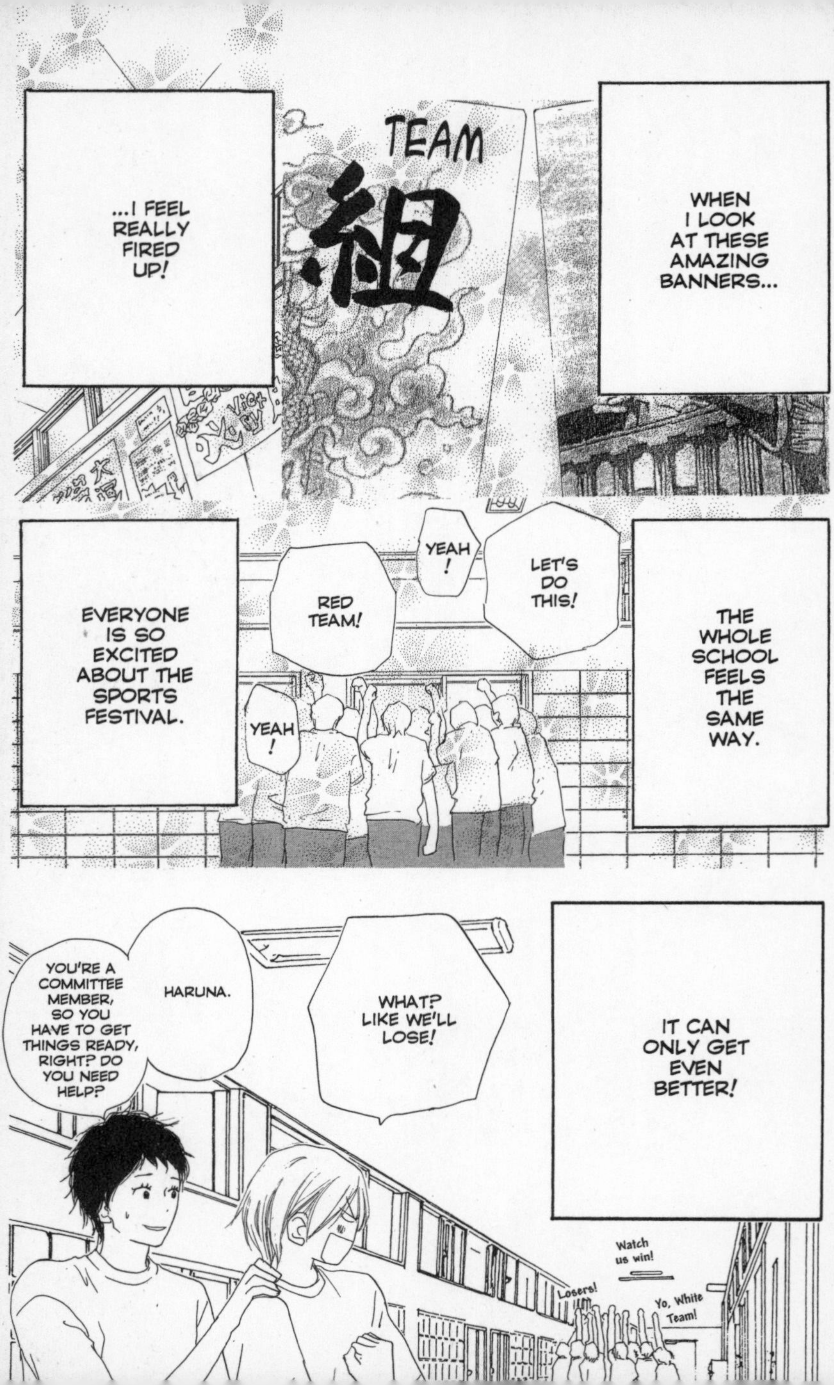

WHEN I LOOK AT THESE AMAZING BANNERS...
TEAM
組
...I FEEL REALLY FIRED UP!
THE WHOLE SCHOOL FEELS THE SAME WAY.
LET'S DO THIS!
YEAH!
RED TEAM!
YEAH!
EVERYONE IS SO EXCITED ABOUT THE SPORTS FESTIVAL.
IT CAN ONLY GET EVEN BETTER!
Watch us win!
Yo, White Team!
Losers!
WHAT? LIKE WE'LL LOSE!
HARUNA.
YOU'RE A COMMITTEE MEMBER, SO YOU HAVE TO GET THINGS READY, RIGHT? DO YOU NEED HELP?

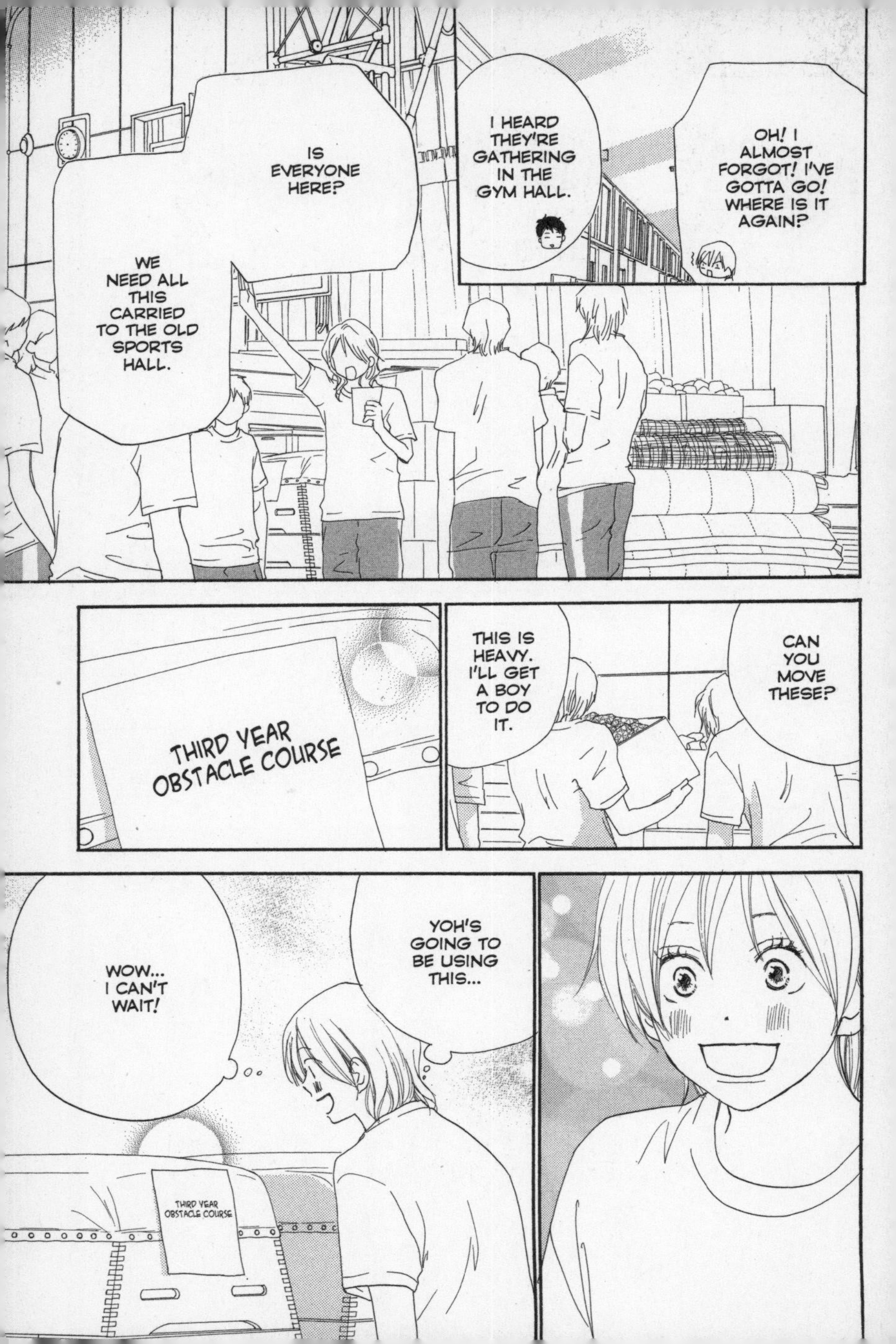
OH! I ALMOST FORGOT! I'VE GOTTA GO! WHERE IS IT AGAIN?
I HEARD THEY'RE GATHERING IN THE GYM HALL.
IS EVERYONE HERE?
WE NEED ALL THIS CARRIED TO THE OLD SPORTS HALL.
CAN YOU MOVE THESE?
THIS IS HEAVY. I'LL GET A BOY TO DO IT.
THIRD YEAR OBSTACLE COURSE
YOH'S GOING TO BE USING THIS...
WOW... I CAN'T WAIT!
THIRD YEAR OBSTACLE COURSE

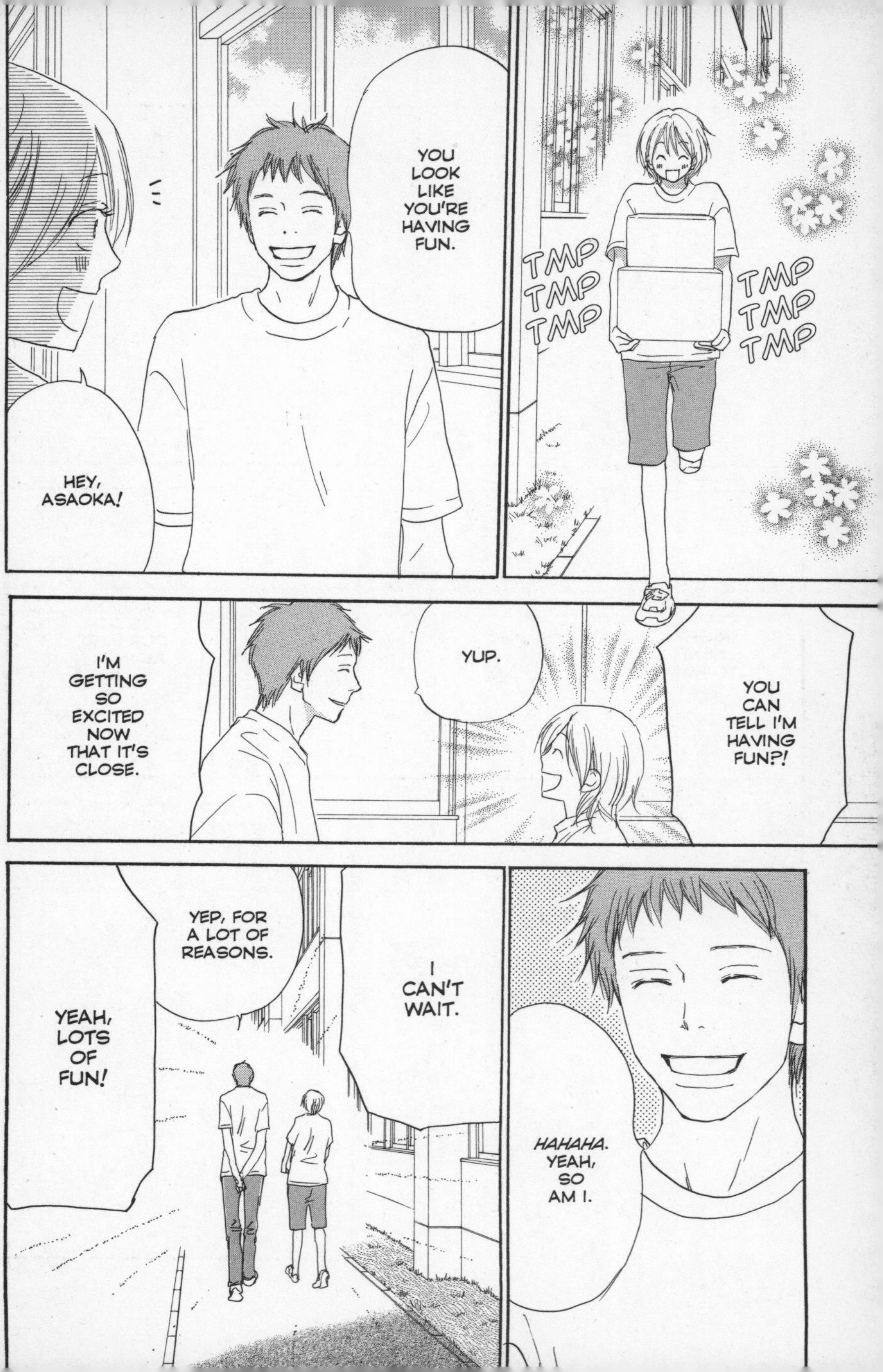
TMP TMP TMP
TMP TMP TMP
YOU LOOK LIKE YOU'RE HAVING FUN.
HEY, ASAOKA!
YOU CAN TELL I'M HAVING FUN?!
YUP.
I'M GETTING SO EXCITED NOW THAT IT'S CLOSE.
HAHAHA. YEAH, SO AM I.
I CAN'T WAIT.
YEP, FOR A LOT OF REASONS.
YEAH, LOTS OF FUN!

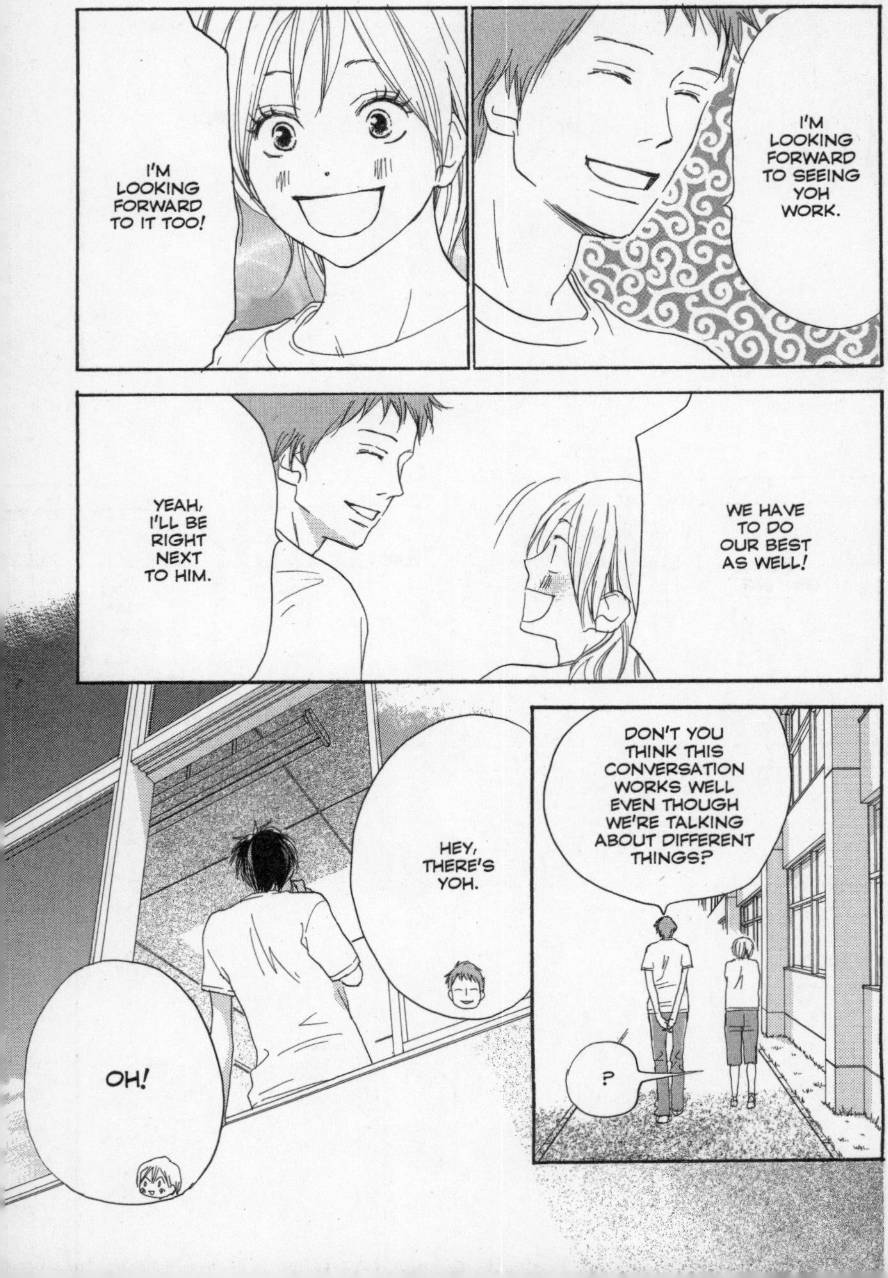
I'M LOOKING FORWARD TO SEEING YOH WORK.
I'M LOOKING FORWARD TO IT TOO!
WE HAVE TO DO OUR BEST AS WELL!
YEAH, I'LL BE RIGHT NEXT TO HIM.
DON'T YOU THINK THIS CONVERSATION WORKS WELL EVEN THOUGH WE'RE TALKING ABOUT DIFFERENT THINGS?
?
HEY, THERE'S YOH.
OH!

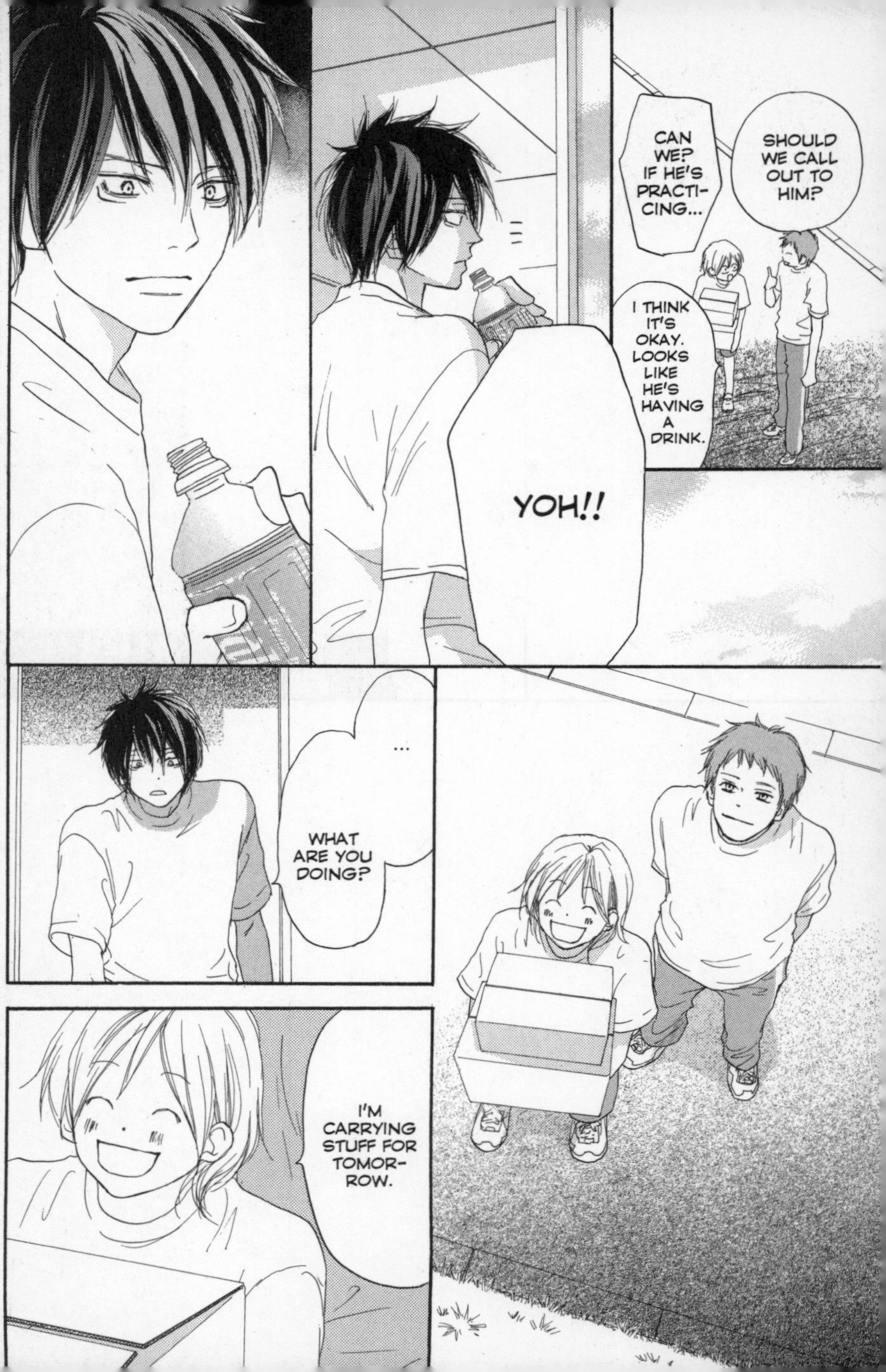
SHOULD WE CALL OUT TO HIM?
CAN WE? IF HE'S PRACTICING...
I THINK IT'S OKAY. LOOKS LIKE HE'S HAVING A DRINK.
YOH!!
...
WHAT ARE YOU DOING?
I'M CARRYING STUFF FOR TOMORROW.

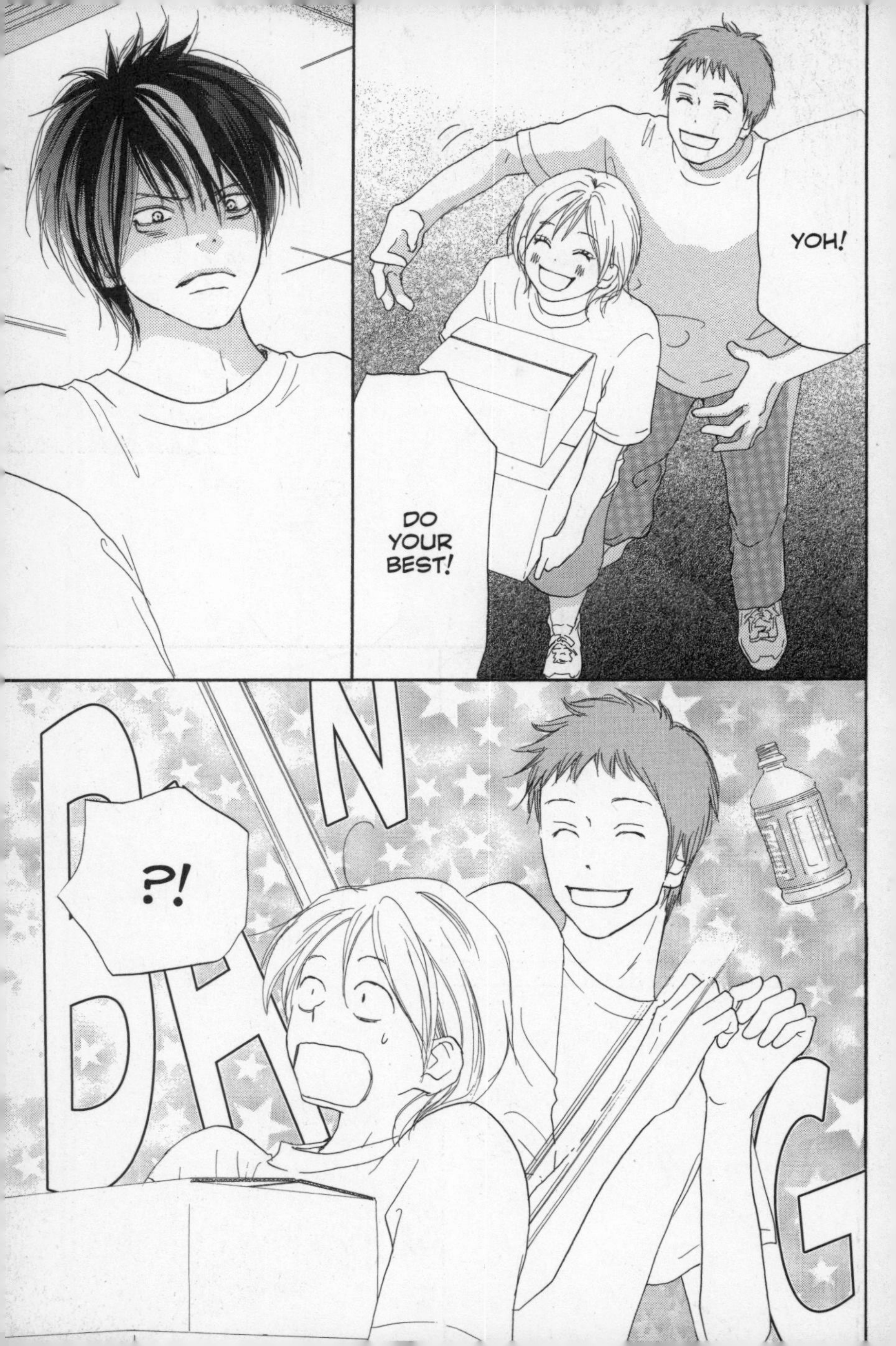
YOH!
DO YOUR BEST!
?!

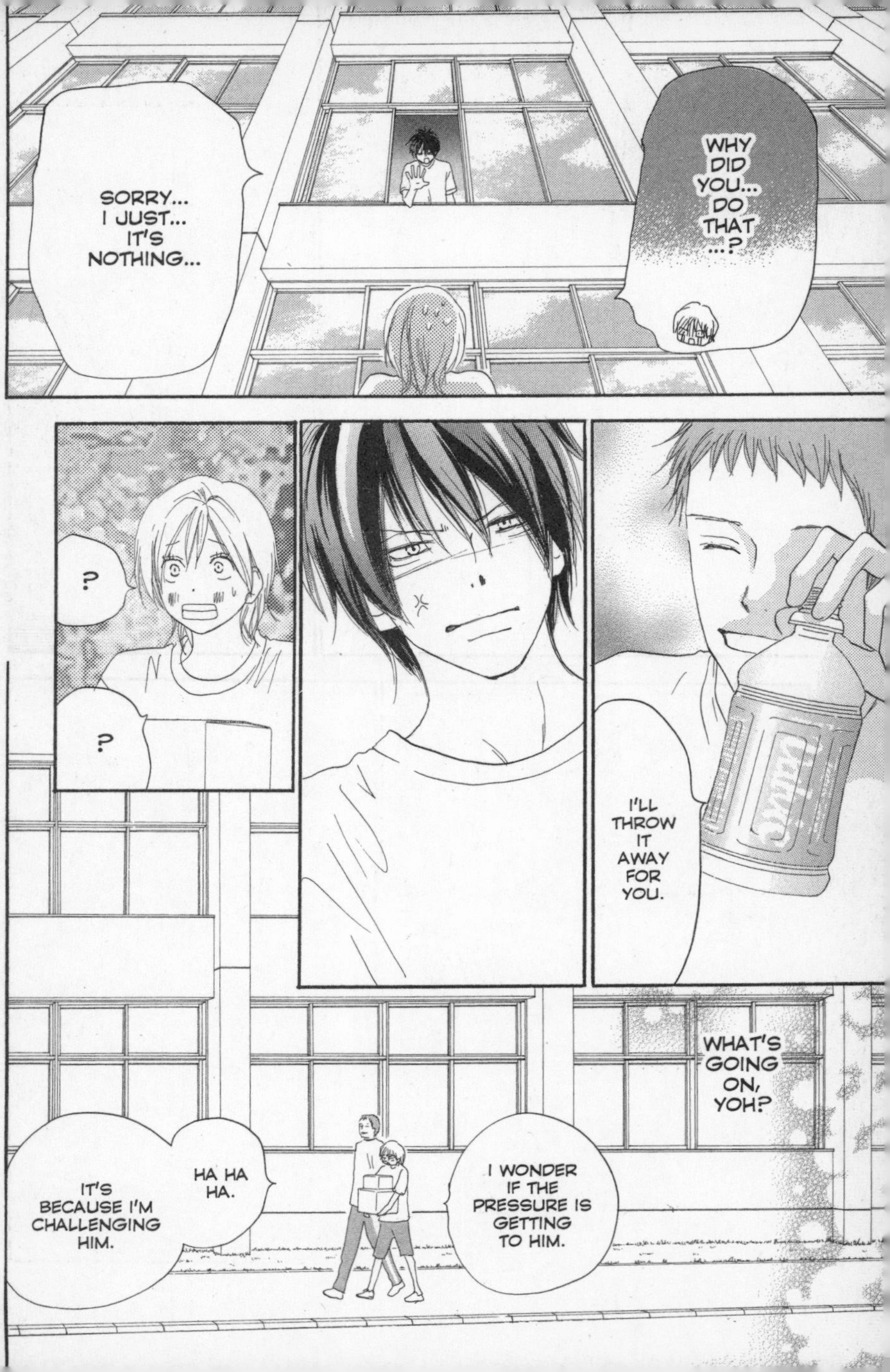
WHY DID YOU... DO THAT ...?
SORRY... I JUST... IT'S NOTHING...
I'LL THROW IT AWAY FOR YOU.
?
?
WHAT'S GOING ON, YOH?
I WONDER IF THE PRESSURE IS GETTING TO HIM.
HA HA HA.
IT'S BECAUSE I'M CHALLENGING HIM.

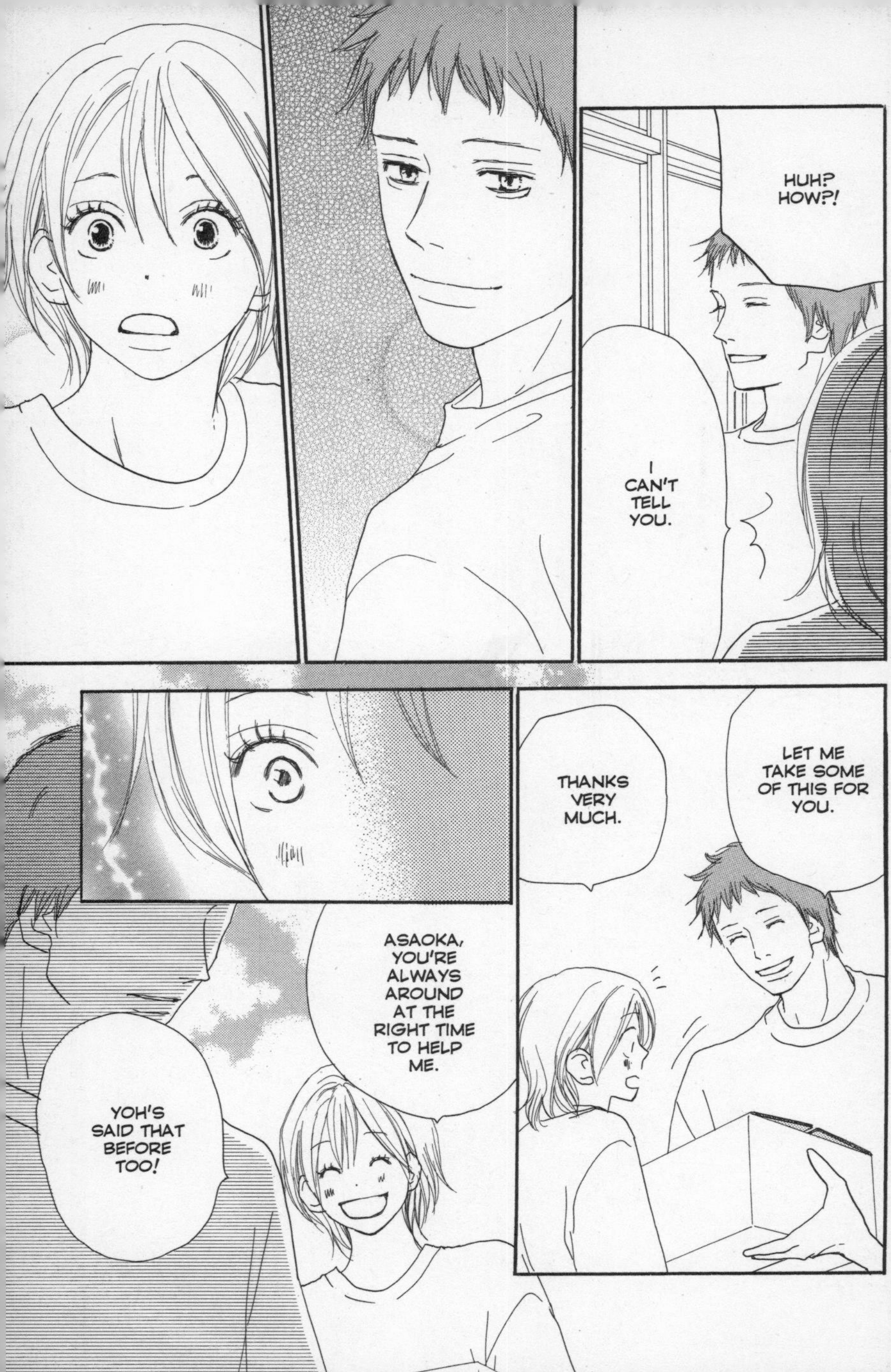
HUH? HOW?!
I CAN'T TELL YOU.
LET ME TAKE SOME OF THIS FOR YOU.
THANKS VERY MUCH.
ASAOKA, YOU'RE ALWAYS AROUND AT THE RIGHT TIME TO HELP ME.
YOH'S SAID THAT BEFORE TOO!

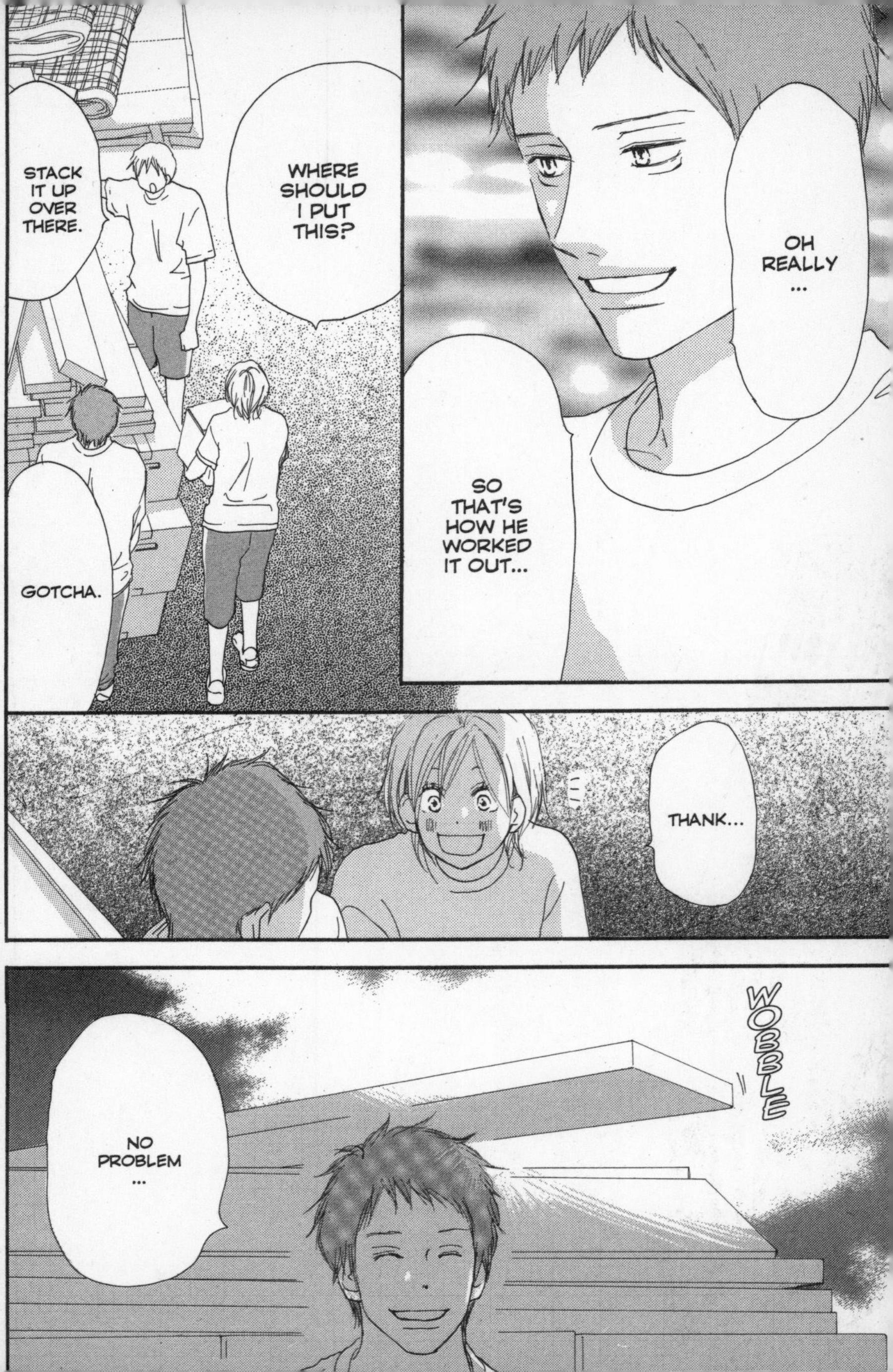
OH REALLY ...
SO THAT'S HOW HE WORKED IT OUT...
WHERE SHOULD I PUT THIS?
STACK IT UP OVER THERE.
GOTCHA.
THANK...
WOBBLE
NO PROBLEM ...

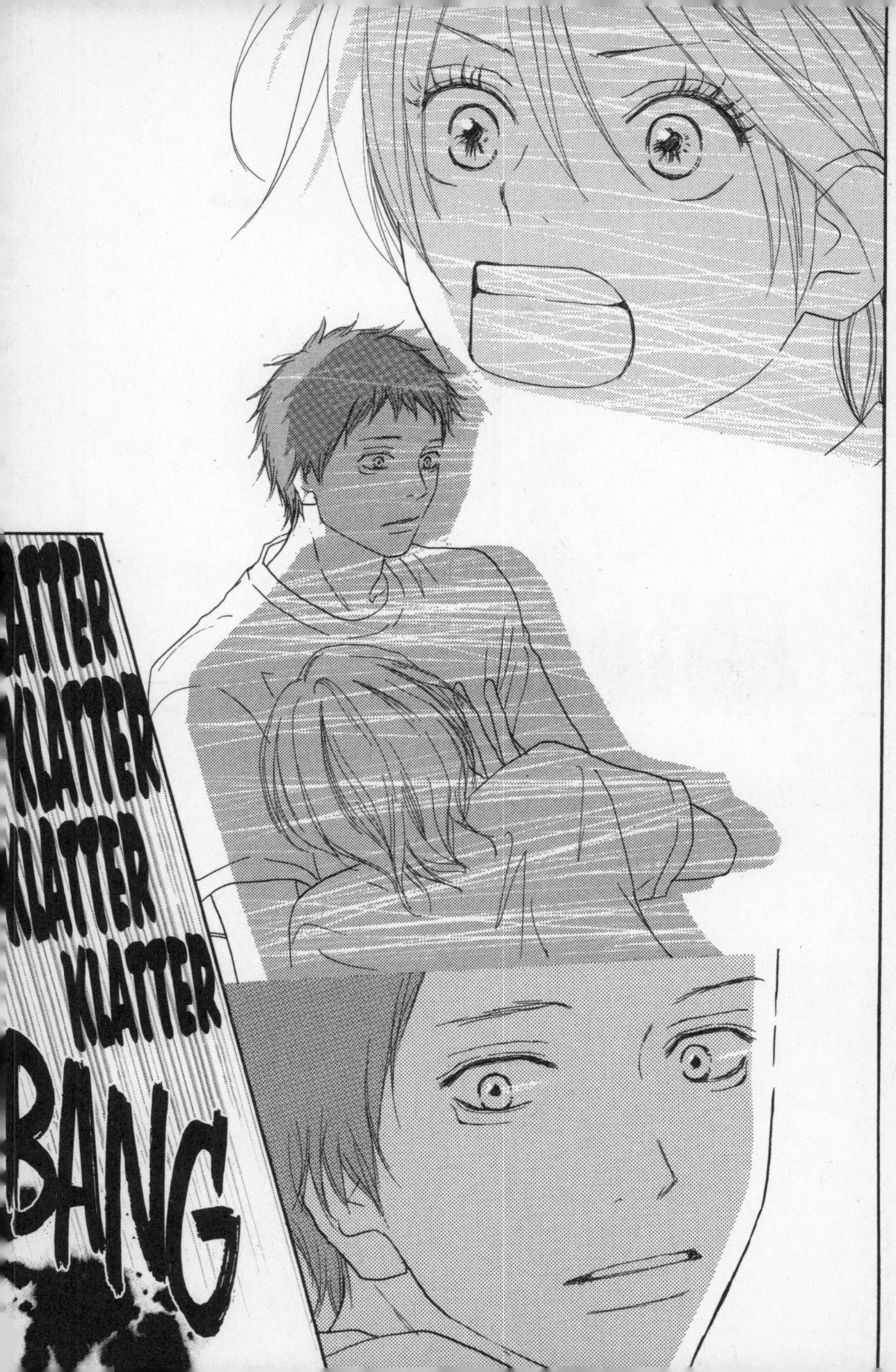
ATTER
KLATTER
KLATTER
KLATTER
BANG

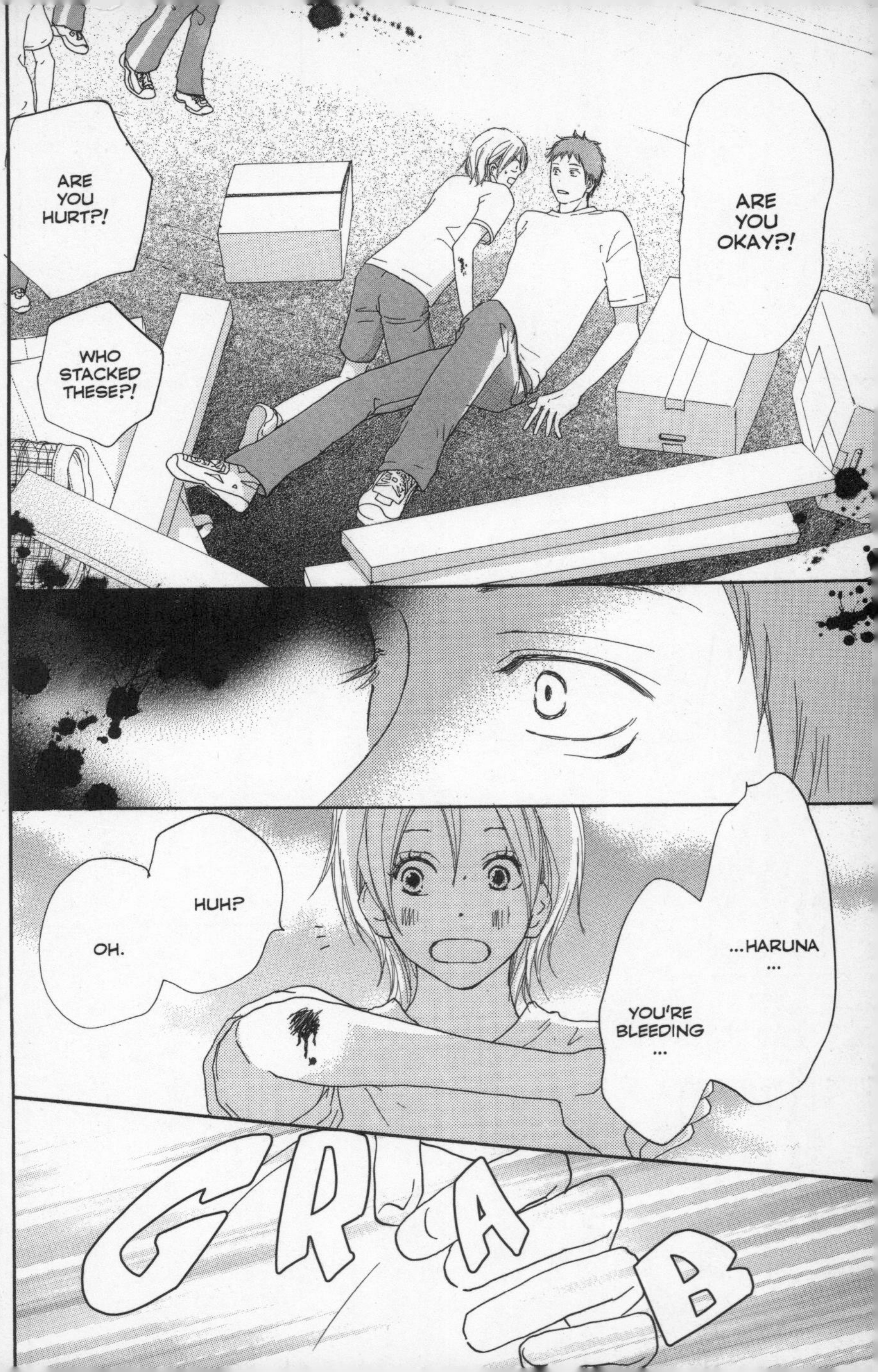
ARE YOU OKAY?!
ARE YOU HURT?!
WHO STACKED THESE?!
...HARUNA ...
YOU'RE BLEEDING ...
HUH?
OH.
GRAB

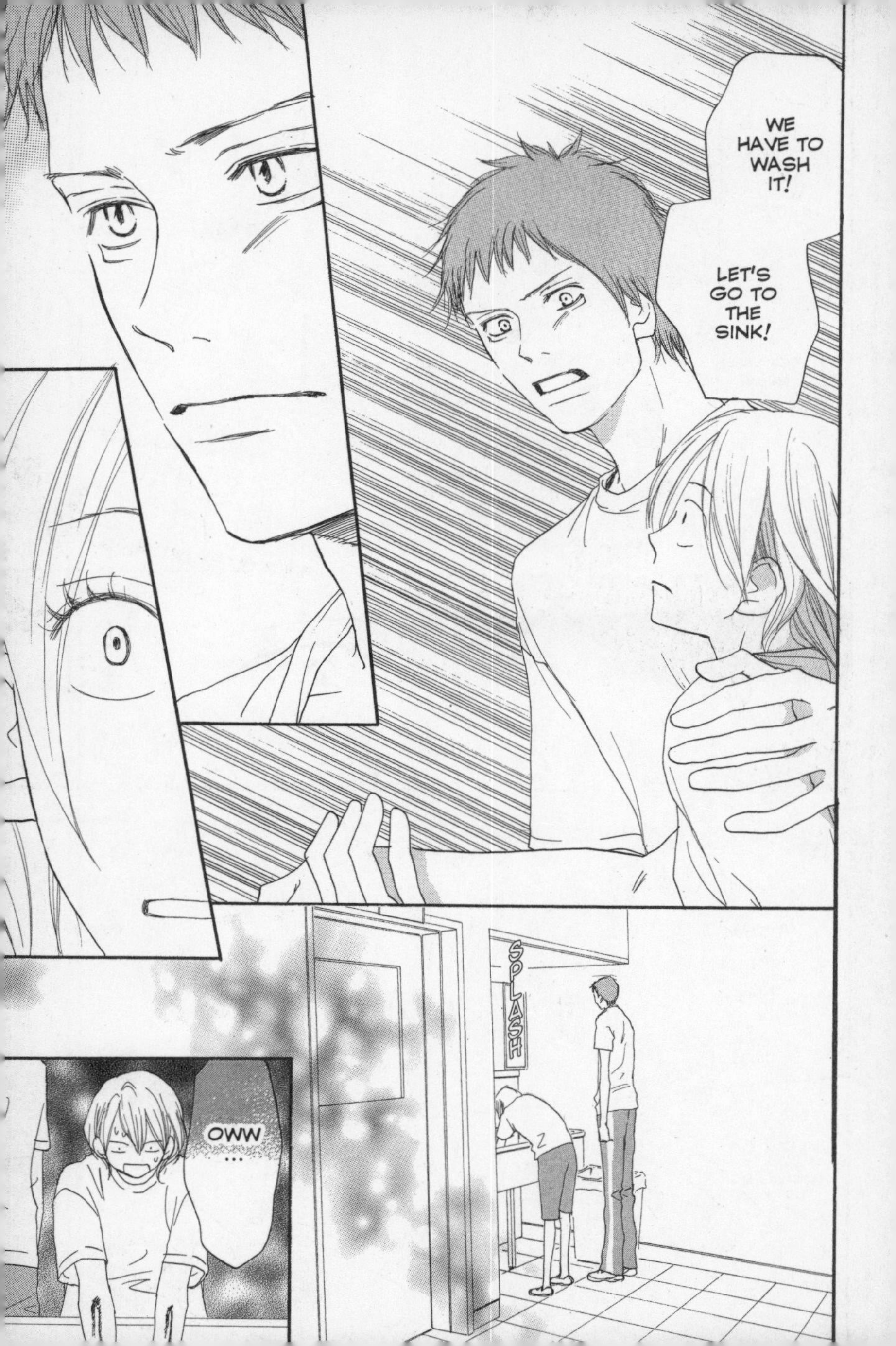
WE HAVE TO WASH IT!
LET'S GO TO THE SINK!
SPLASH
OWW ...

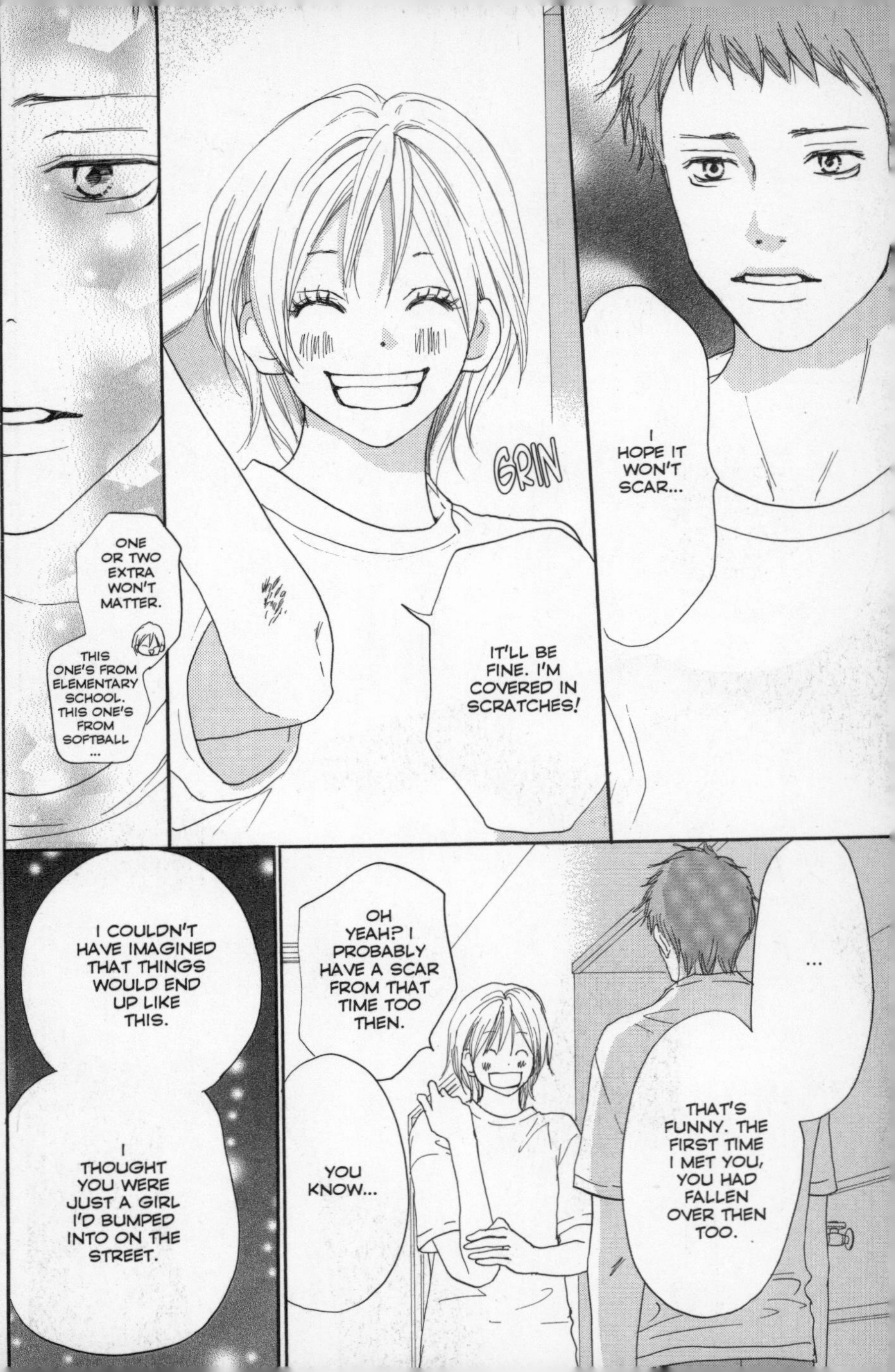
I HOPE IT WON'T SCAR...
GRIN
IT'LL BE FINE. I'M COVERED IN SCRATCHES!
ONE OR TWO EXTRA WON'T MATTER.
THIS ONE'S FROM ELEMENTARY SCHOOL. THIS ONE'S FROM SOFTBALL...
...
THAT'S FUNNY. THE FIRST TIME I MET YOU, YOU HAD FALLEN OVER THEN TOO.
OH YEAH? I PROBABLY HAVE A SCAR FROM THAT TIME TOO THEN.
YOU KNOW...
I COULDN'T HAVE IMAGINED THAT THINGS WOULD END UP LIKE THIS.
I THOUGHT YOU WERE JUST A GIRL I'D BUMPED INTO ON THE STREET.

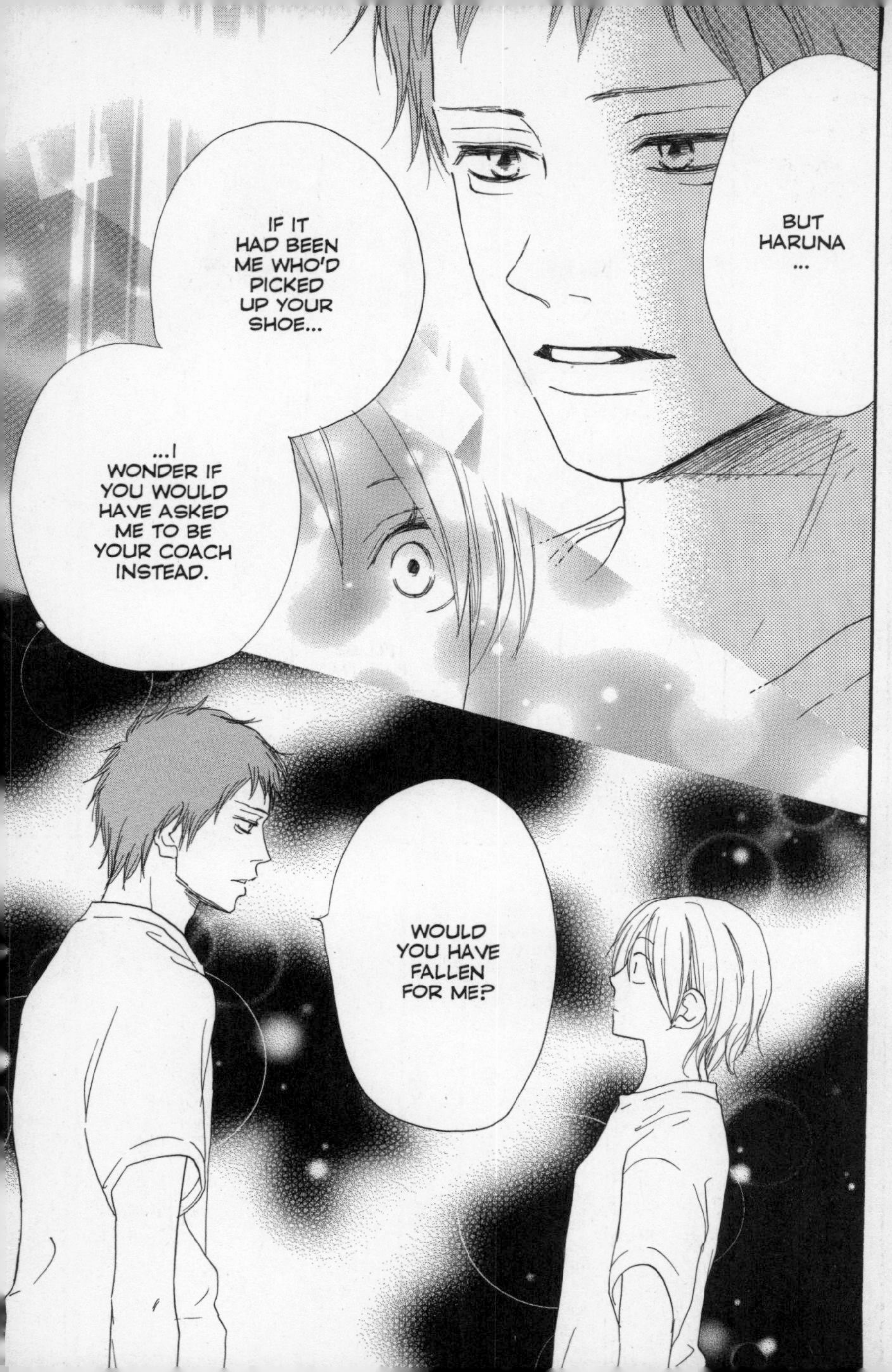
BUT HARUNA ...
IF IT HAD BEEN ME WHO'D PICKED UP YOUR SHOE...
...I WONDER IF YOU WOULD HAVE ASKED ME TO BE YOUR COACH INSTEAD.
WOULD YOU HAVE FALLEN FOR ME?

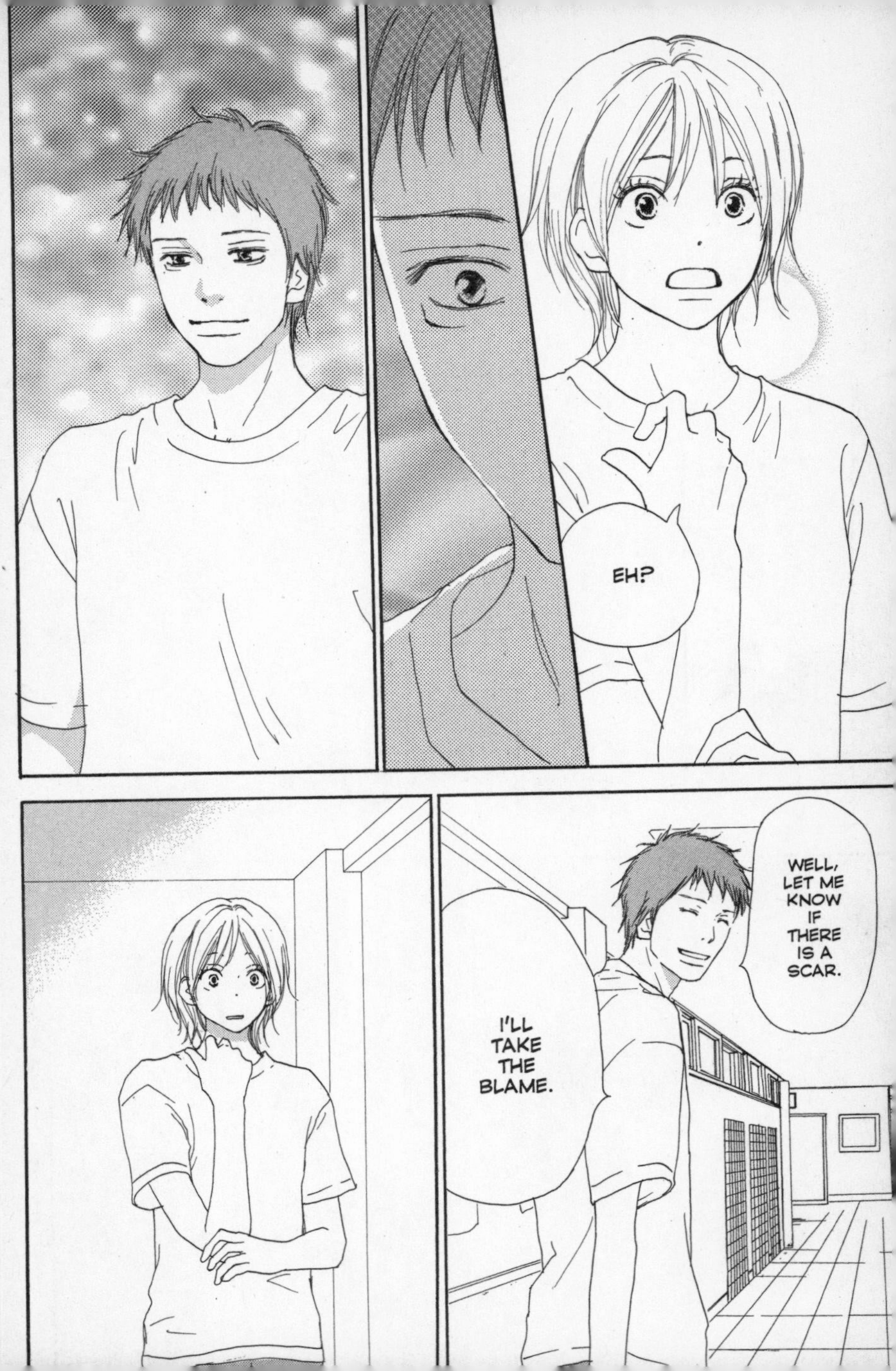
EH?
WELL, LET ME KNOW IF THERE IS A SCAR.
I'LL TAKE THE BLAME.

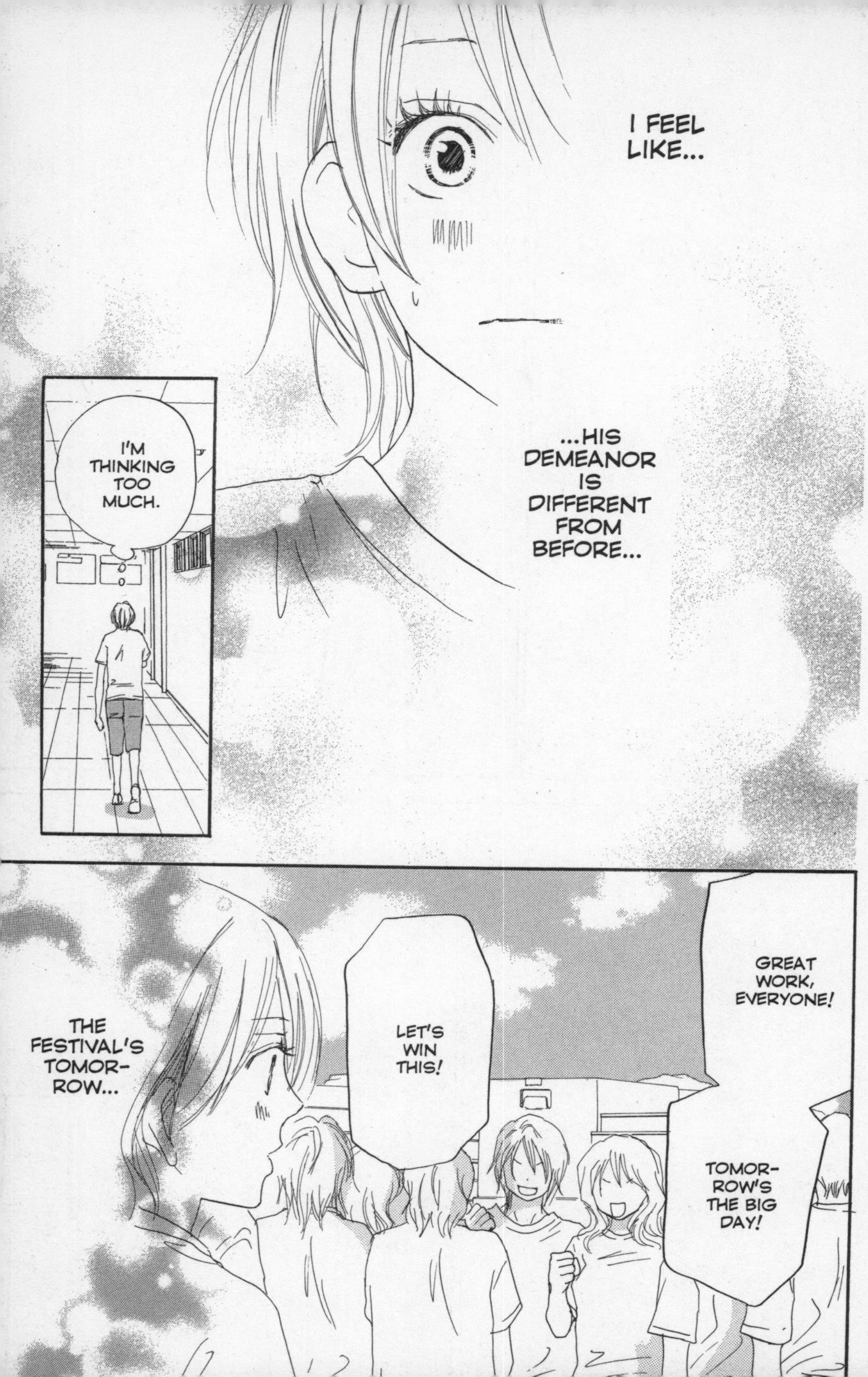
I FEEL LIKE...
...HIS DEMEANOR IS DIFFERENT FROM BEFORE...
I'M THINKING TOO MUCH.
GREAT WORK, EVERYONE!
LET'S WIN THIS!
TOMOR-ROW'S THE BIG DAY!
THE FESTIVAL'S TOMOR-ROW...

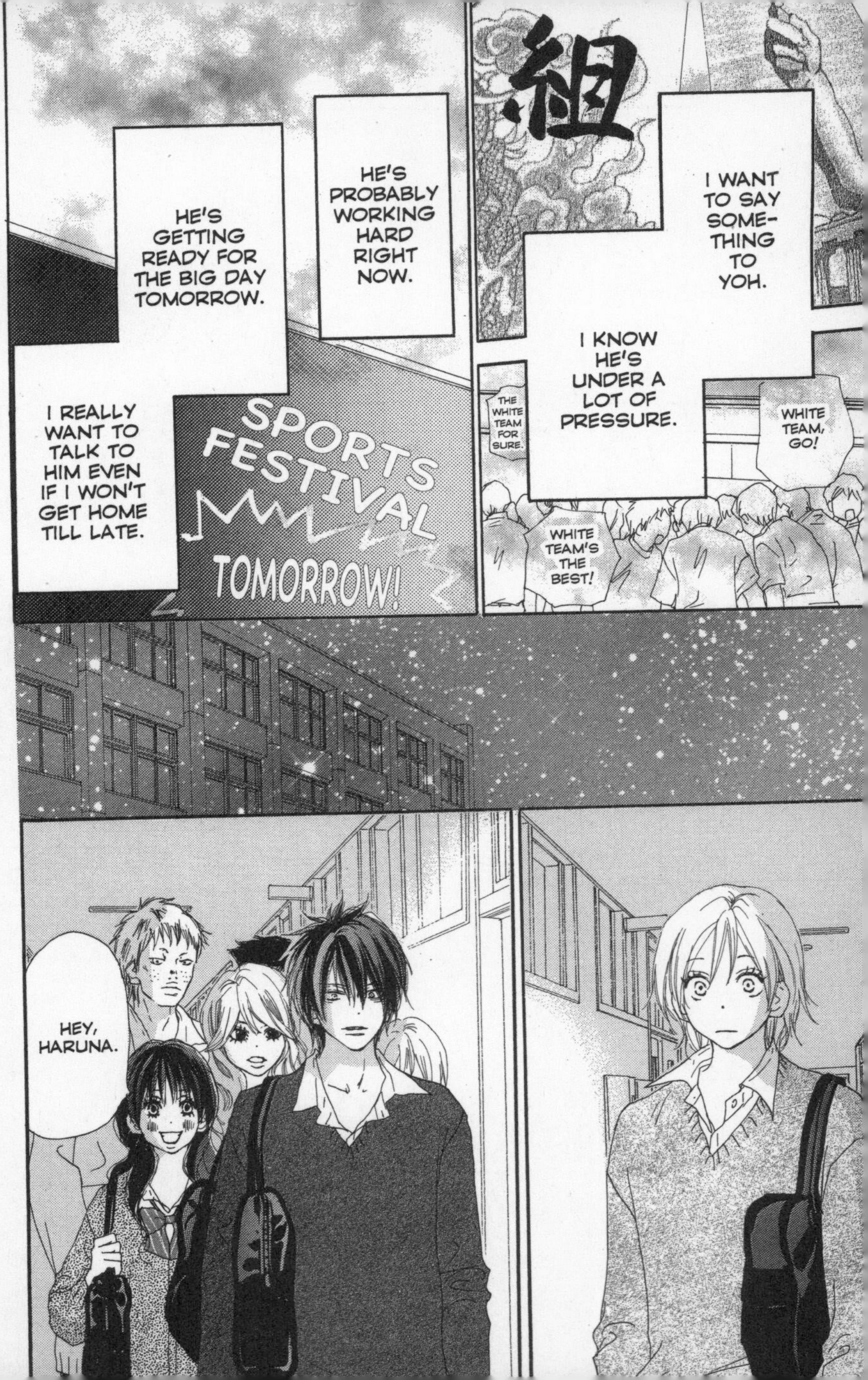
組
I WANT TO SAY SOME-THING TO YOH.
I KNOW HE'S UNDER A LOT OF PRESSURE.
WHITE TEAM, GO!
THE WHITE TEAM FOR SURE.
WHITE TEAM'S THE BEST!
HE'S PROBABLY WORKING HARD RIGHT NOW.
HE'S GETTING READY FOR THE BIG DAY TOMORROW.
I REALLY WANT TO TALK TO HIM EVEN IF I WON'T GET HOME TILL LATE.
SPORTS FESTIVAL TOMORROW!
HEY, HARUNA.

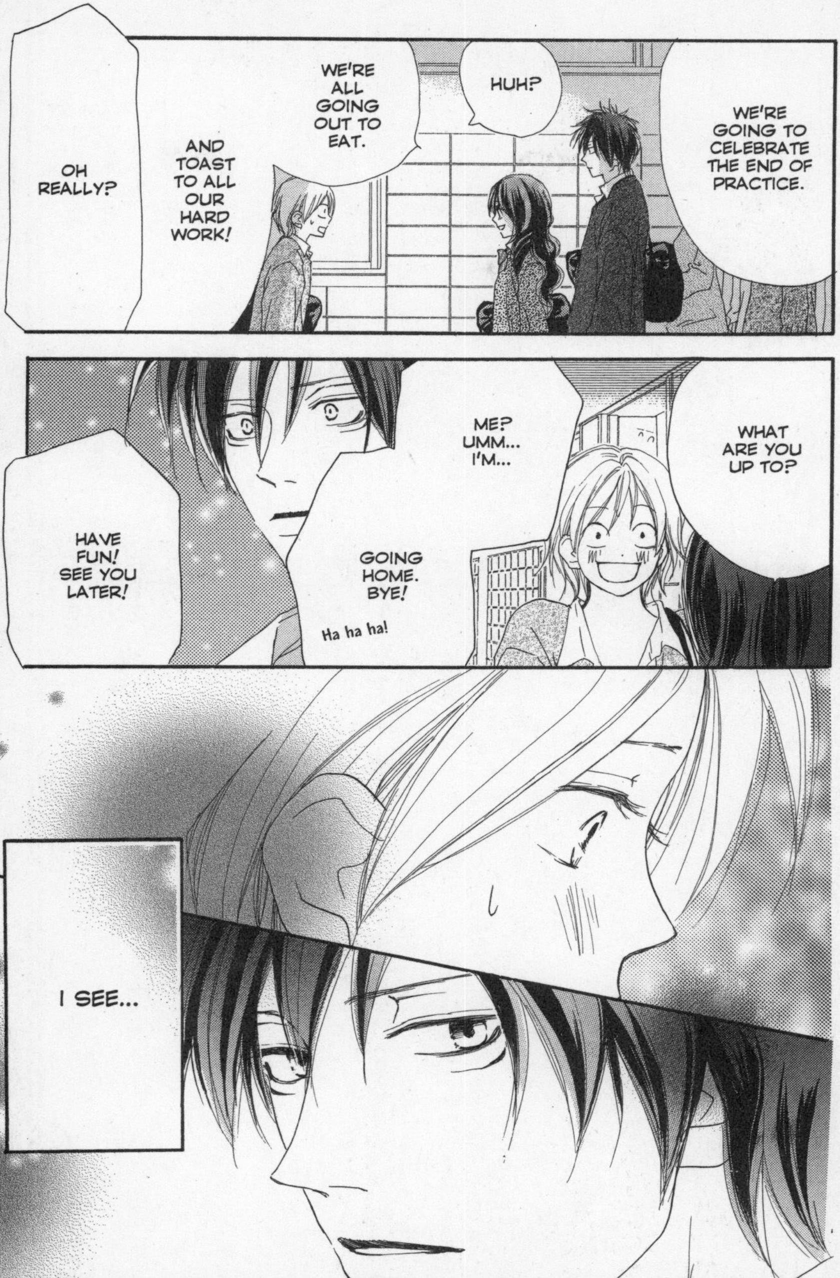
WE'RE GOING TO CELEBRATE THE END OF PRACTICE.
HUH?
WE'RE ALL GOING OUT TO EAT.
AND TOAST TO ALL OUR HARD WORK!
OH REALLY?
WHAT ARE YOU UP TO?
ME? UMM... I'M...
GOING HOME. BYE!
Ha ha ha!
HAVE FUN! SEE YOU LATER!
I SEE...

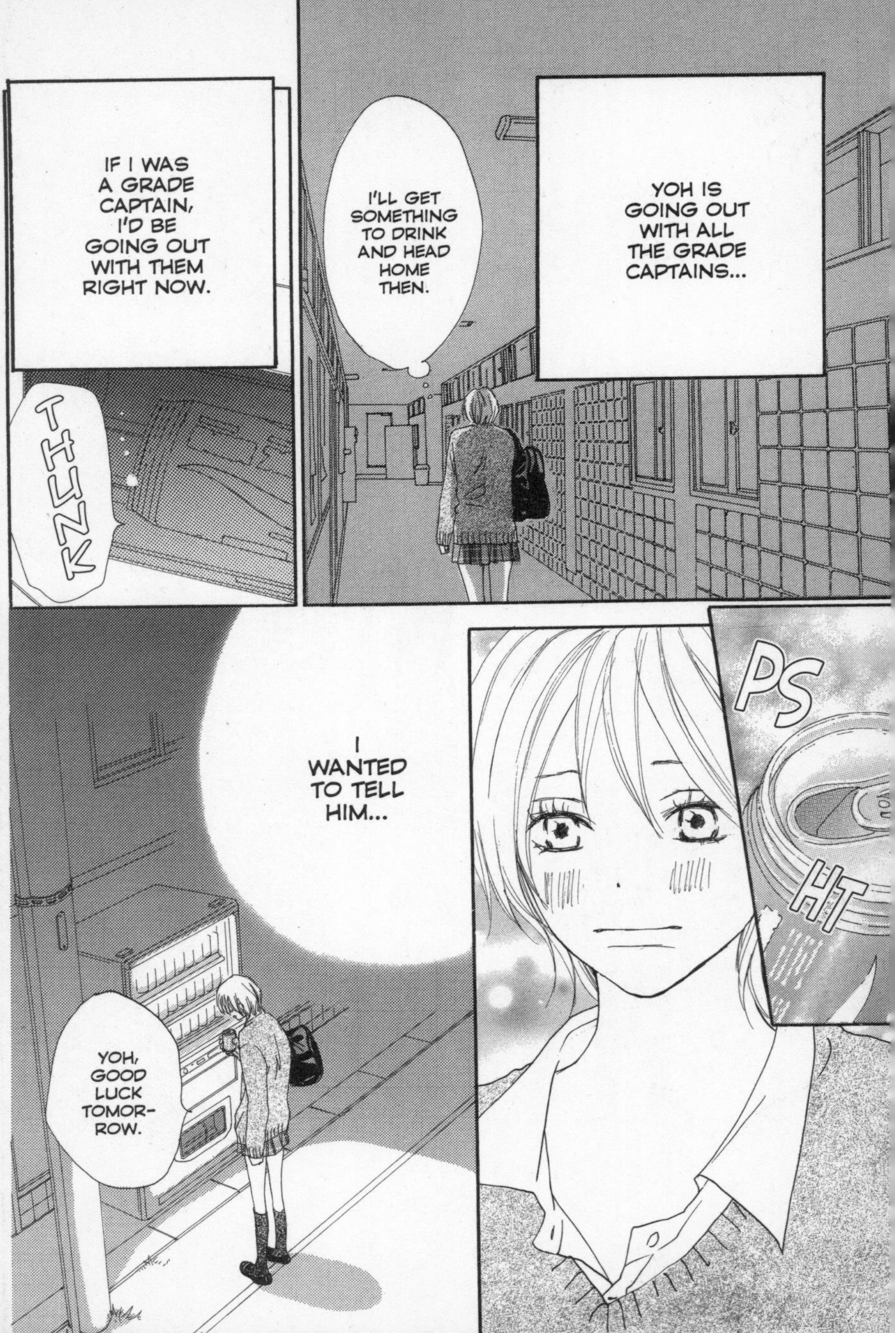
YOH IS GOING OUT WITH ALL THE GRADE CAPTAINS...
I'LL GET SOMETHING TO DRINK AND HEAD HOME THEN.
IF I WAS A GRADE CAPTAIN, I'D BE GOING OUT WITH THEM RIGHT NOW.
THUNK
PSHT
I WANTED TO TELL HIM...
YOH, GOOD LUCK TOMORROW.

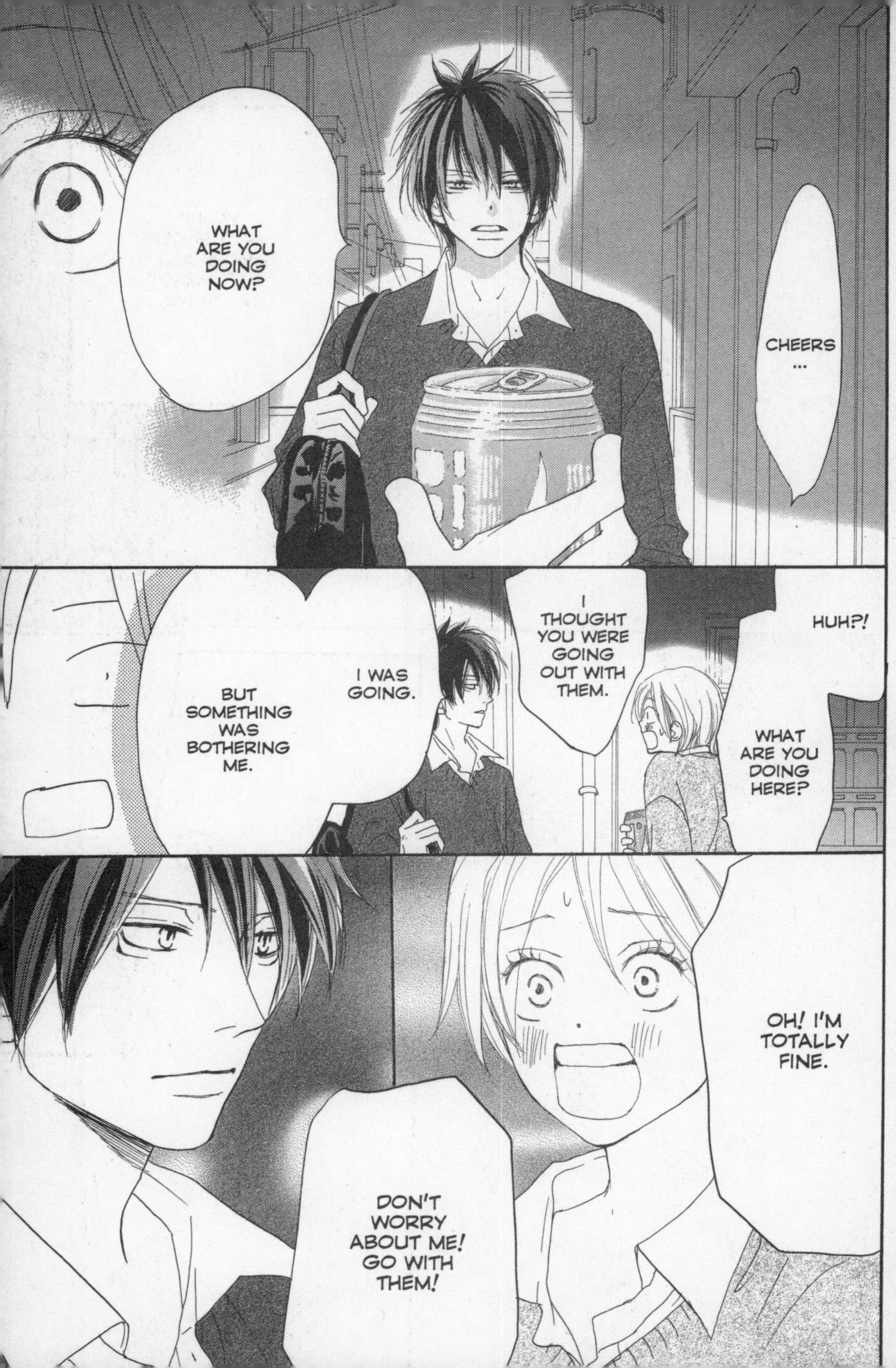
CHEERS ...
WHAT ARE YOU DOING NOW?
HUH?!
WHAT ARE YOU DOING HERE?
I THOUGHT YOU WERE GOING OUT WITH THEM.
I WAS GOING.
BUT SOMETHING WAS BOTHERING ME.
OH! I'M TOTALLY FINE.
DON'T WORRY ABOUT ME! GO WITH THEM!

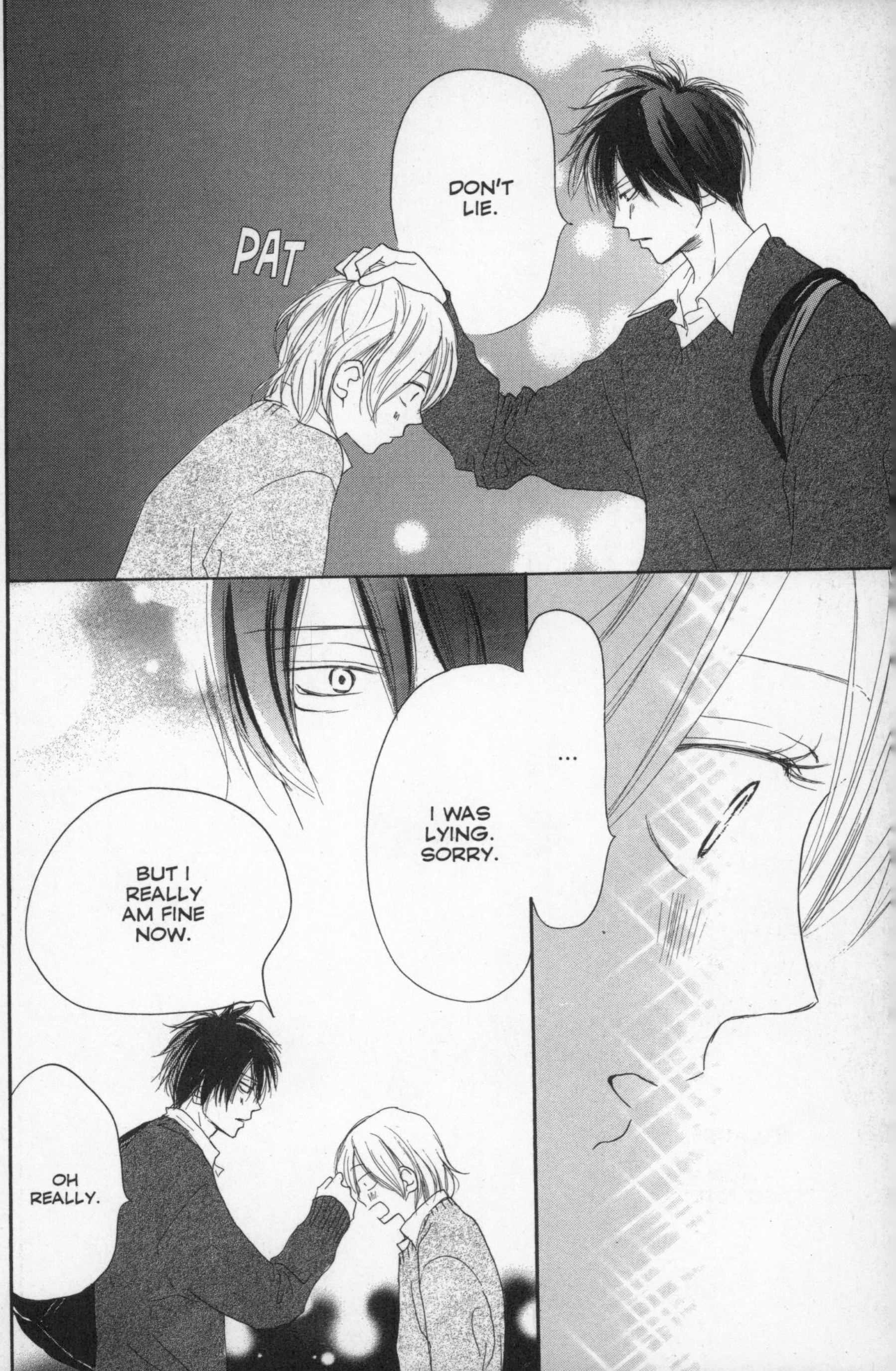
PAT
DON'T LIE.
...
I WAS LYING. SORRY.
BUT I REALLY AM FINE NOW.
OH REALLY.

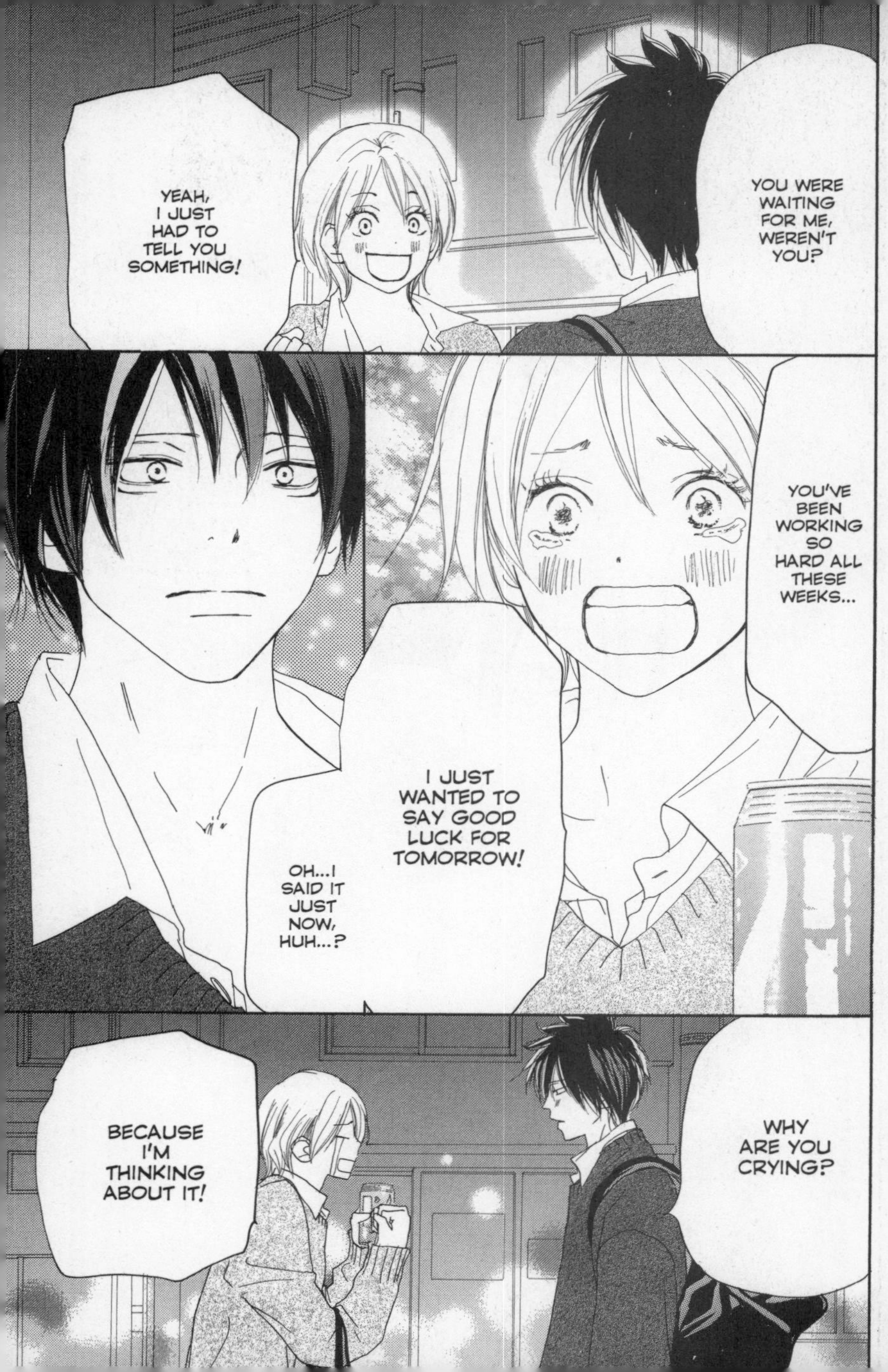
YOU WERE WAITING FOR ME, WEREN'T YOU?
YEAH, I JUST HAD TO TELL YOU SOMETHING!
YOU'VE BEEN WORKING SO HARD ALL THESE WEEKS...
I JUST WANTED TO SAY GOOD LUCK FOR TOMORROW!
OH...I SAID IT JUST NOW, HUH...?
WHY ARE YOU CRYING?
BECAUSE I'M THINKING ABOUT IT!

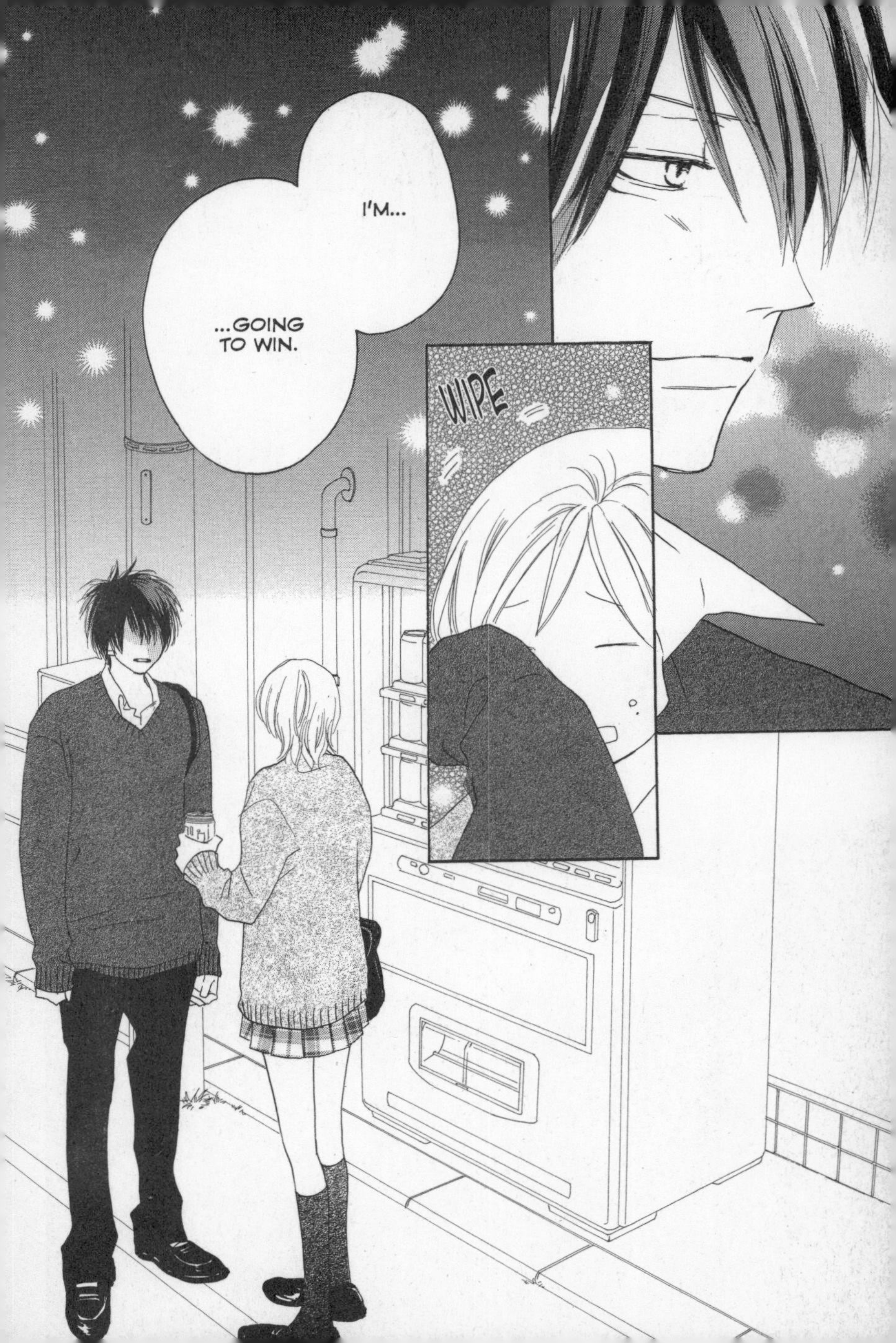
WIPE
I'M...
...GOING TO WIN.

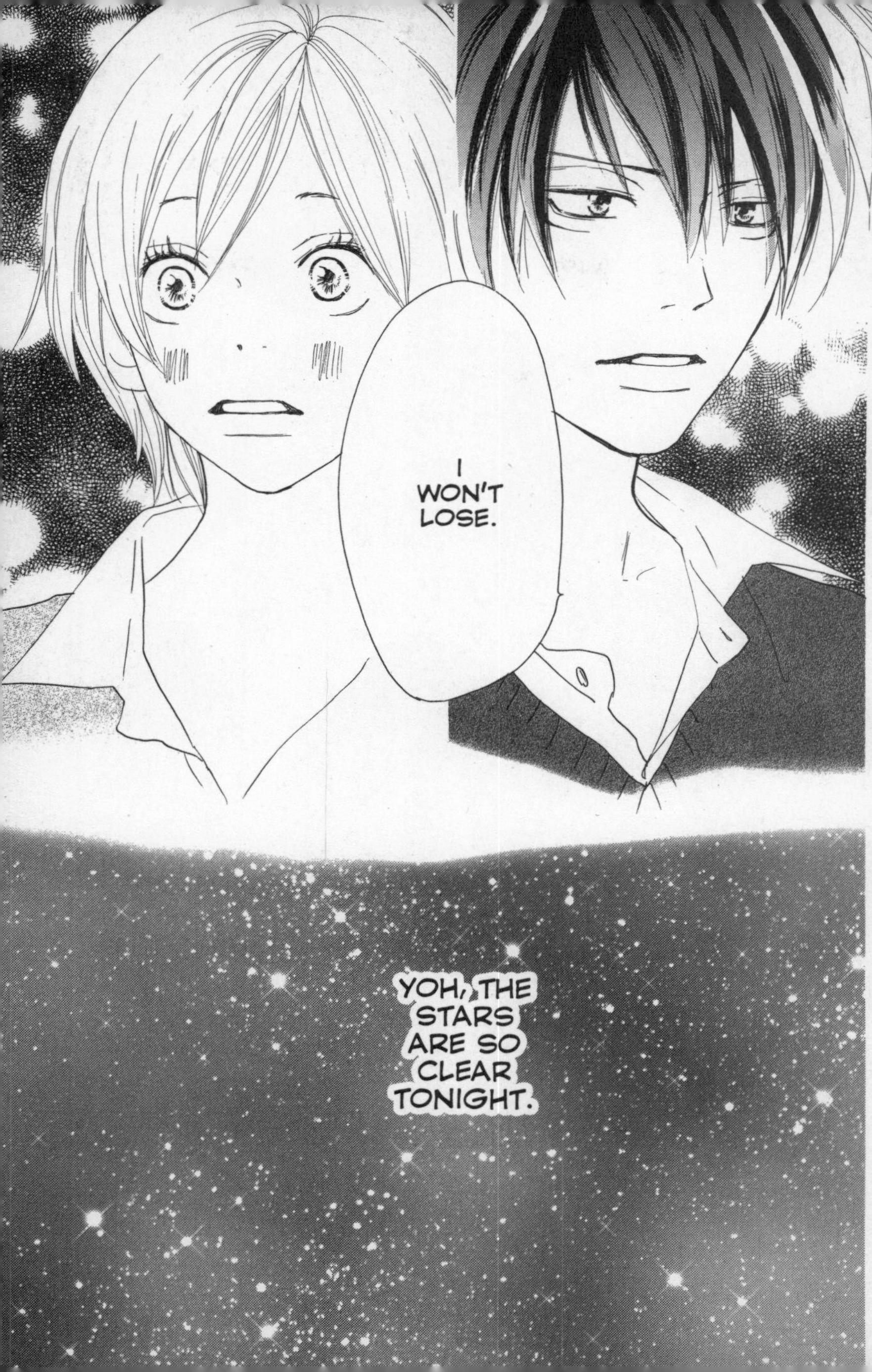
I WON'T LOSE.
YOH, THE STARS ARE SO CLEAR TONIGHT.

IT LOOKS LIKE IT'S GOING TO BE GOOD WEATHER FOR TOMORROW.
TO BE CONTINUED...

Usually when these books are compiled, I get to fill up the spaces where ads originally appeared in the magazine version. This time, though, there were no spaces, so I didn't get to write anything! I'm so upset! In the next volume I want to write loads of boring stuff!

– Kazune Kawahara

Kazune Kawahara is from Hokkaido Prefecture and was born on March 11th (a Pisces!). She made her manga debut at age 18 with *Kare no Ichiban Sukina Hito* (His Most Favorite Person). Her other works include *Sensei!*, serialized in *Bessatsu Margaret* magazine. Her hobby is interior redecorating.

HIGH SCHOOL DEBUT
VOL. 9
The Shojo Beat Manga Edition

STORY & ART BY
KAZUNE KAWAHARA

Translation & Adaptation/Gemma Collinge
Touch-up Art & Lettering/HudsonYards
Cover Design/Izumi Hirayama
Interior Design/Courtney Utt
Editor/Amy Yu

Editor in Chief, Books/Alvin Lu
Editor in Chief, Magazines/Marc Weidenbaum
VP, Publishing Licensing/Rika Inouye
VP, Sales & Product Marketing/Gonzalo Ferreyra
VP, Creative/Linda Espinosa
Publisher/Hyoe Narita

Printed in Canada

Published by VIZ Media, LLC
P.O. Box 77010
San Francisco, CA 94107

Shojo Beat Manga Edition
10 9 8 7 6 5 4 3 2 1
First printing, May 2009

www.viz.com

store.viz.com

RATED T FOR TEEN

PARENTAL ADVISORY
HIGH SCHOOL DEBUT is rated T for Teen and is recommended for ages 13 and up. This volume contains suggestive themes.
ratings.viz.com

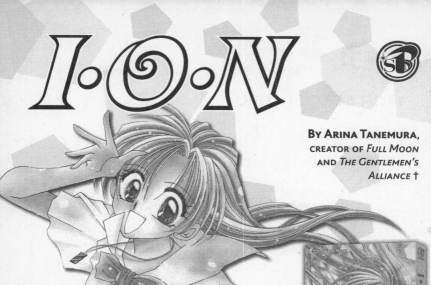

I·O·N

BY ARINA TANEMURA,
CREATOR OF *FULL MOON*
AND *THE GENTLEMEN'S ALLIANCE* †

Ion Tsuburagi is a normal junior high girl with normal junior high problems. But when a mysterious substance grants her telekinetic powers, she finds herself struggling to keep everything together! Are her new abilities a blessing...or a curse?

Find out in *I·O·N*—manga on sale now!

On sale at www.shojobeat.com
Also available at your local bookstore
and comic store.

I·O·N © 1997 by Arina Tanemura/SHUEISHA Inc.

RATED
T
FOR
TEEN
ratings.viz.com

VIZ
MEDIA

www.viz.com

love ★ com

By Aya Nakahara

Class clowns Risa and Ôtani join forces to find love!

Tell us what you think about Shojo Beat Manga!

Our survey is now available online. Go to:

shojobeat.com/mangasurvey

Help us make our product offerings better!

Shojo Beat™
MANGA from the HEART